THE MAKING OF A FISCAL-MILITARY STATE IN POST-REVOLUTIONARY FRANCE

Drawing on a wide range of archival and published documents, this book explains how the French Revolution of 1789 transformed the French state and its fiscal system, and how further reforms in the nineteenth century created a stable, post-revolutionary state. Instead of presenting the nineteenth-century French state as primarily the creation of the Revolutionary and Napoleonic era, as most scholars have done, Jerome Greenfield emphasises the importance of counter-revolution after 1815 in establishing a durable state, capable of surviving revolutions in 1830 and 1848 intact. The years 1815–70 thus marked a crucial period in the development of the French state, not least in stimulating the economic interventionism for which it has become notorious and facilitating the resurgence of France as a great power after Napoleon's defeat at Waterloo.

JEROME GREENFIELD was awarded his PhD from the University of Cambridge and subsequently held a Leverhulme Early Career Fellowship at King's College London (2017–20). His articles have been published in numerous journals, including the *English Historical Review*, the *Historical Journal*, *French Historical Studies*, *French History*, *Histoire, Économie et Société* and the *International History Review*.

T0382457

NEW STUDIES IN EUROPEAN HISTORY

Edited by
PETER BALDWIN, University of California, Los Angeles
HOLLY CASE, Brown University
CHRISTOPHER CLARK, University of Cambridge
JAMES B. COLLINS, Georgetown University
KARIN FRIEDRICH, University of Aberdeen
MIA RODRÍGUEZ-SALGADO, London School of Economics
and Political Science
TIMOTHY SNYDER, Yale University

The aim of this series in early modern and modern European history is to publish outstanding works of research, addressed to important themes across a wide geographical range, from southern and central Europe, to Scandinavia and Russia, from the time of the Renaissance to the present. As it develops the series will comprise focused works of wide contextual range and intellectual ambition.

A full list of titles published in the series can be found at:
www.cambridge.org/newstudiesineuropeanhistory

THE MAKING OF A FISCAL-MILITARY STATE IN POST-REVOLUTIONARY FRANCE

JEROME GREENFIELD

CAMBRIDGE
UNIVERSITY PRESS

Shaftesbury Road, Cambridge CB2 8EA, United Kingdom

One Liberty Plaza, 20th Floor, New York, NY 10006, USA

477 Williamstown Road, Port Melbourne, VIC 3207, Australia

314–321, 3rd Floor, Plot 3, Splendor Forum, Jasola District Centre, New Delhi – 110025, India

103 Penang Road, #05–06/07, Visioncrest Commercial, Singapore 238467

Cambridge University Press is part of Cambridge University Press & Assessment, a department of the University of Cambridge.

We share the University's mission to contribute to society through the pursuit of education, learning and research at the highest international levels of excellence.

www.cambridge.org
Information on this title: www.cambridge.org/9781108813556

DOI: 10.1017/9781108884815

First published 2022
First paperback edition 2024

A catalogue record for this publication is available from the British Library

ISBN   978-1-108-83967-9   Hardback
ISBN   978-1-108-81355-6   Paperback

Contents

Figures and Tables

Figures

Table

Acknowledgements

I have incurred many debts in writing this book. There are three people to whom I am particularly obliged. Robert Tombs supervised my doctoral dissertation with consummate patience and generosity, and his profound knowledge of nineteenth-century France saved me from many errors. To have been so brilliantly supervised was an unforgettable privilege. Martin Daunton has been an invaluable source of support and his comments on my manuscript made it significantly stronger than it would be otherwise, while his books on the political history of taxation in Britain, *Trusting Leviathan* and *Just Taxes*, exercised more influence than any others on my conceptualisation of this project. David Todd not only provided detailed and highly insightful comments on my work, he supported my application for a Leverhulme Early Career Fellowship at King's College London without which this book would not have been completed.

In reviewing the manuscript for Cambridge University Press, James Collins very generously provided detailed comments on multiple drafts, which did much to refine my understanding of the finances of the *ancien régime* and to sharpen the overall book. In examining my doctoral dissertation, David Todd and Brendan Simms offered useful suggestions and pushed me to think more carefully about the extent to which the nineteenth-century French fiscal-military state emulated that of eighteenth-century Britain. Charles Walton and Talitha Ilacqua, too, read chapters, for which I am extremely grateful. I also benefited from conversations with a range of scholars, some of whom drew my attention to important research. In this respect, I would like to thank Jean-François Chanet, Maria-Stella Chiaruttini, Chris Clark, Nicolas Delalande, Quentin Deluermoz, Sean Eddie, Joël Félix, Julian Hoppit, Alejandra Irigoin, Munro Price, Michael Rowe, Stephen Sawyer and Sabine Schneider. I am obliged, too, to the anonymous readers for Cambridge University Press, and to the editor, Liz Friend-Smith, for her patience and encouragement.

For the financial support that enabled me to complete this project, I am particularly grateful to the Leverhulme Trust, the UK Arts and Humanities Research Council and St Catharine's College, Cambridge. The first provided me with my Early Career Fellowship, while the other two funded my doctorate at the University of Cambridge. Grants from the Society for the Study of French History, the Economic History Society and the Faculty of History, Cambridge, allowed me to attend conferences and undertake archival work. For their assistance in housing me during some of my periods of research in France, I am indebted to Yue Wang, Benoît Chandesris and Yvette and Roland Cheux. I am also grateful for having been granted permission to consult documents in the Archives de la maison de France and the Greffulhe papers in the Archives nationales, the Rothschild, Thuret and Neuflize papers in the Archives nationales du monde du travail and the manuscripts of the Bibliothèque Thiers; similarly, the staff of the Baring Archive, the Rothschild Archive, London, the Bank of England Archive and the Archives of the Banque de France allowed me access to their collections.

Finally, I wish to thank my family, particularly my parents, and my friends for their unfailing support throughout my work on this book.

Abbreviations

ABF	Archives de la Banque de France, Paris
AD	Archives départementales
AGR	Archives générales du Royaume, Brussels
AN	Archives nationales, Pierrefitte-sur-Seine
ANMT	Archives nationales du monde du travail, Roubaix
AP	J. Mavidal et al. (eds.), *Archives parlementaires: recueil complet des débats législatifs et politiques des Chambres françaises*, 222 vols. (Paris, 1862–present)
Arsenal	Bibliothèque de l'Arsenal, Paris
BA	Baring Archive, London
BIS	Bibliothèque interuniversitaire de la Sorbonne, Paris
BL	British Library, London
BNF	Bibliothèque nationale de France, Paris
BoE	Bank of England Archive, London
BT	Bibliothèque Thiers, Paris
HL	Hartley Library, University of Southampton
Lois	J.B. Duvergier, *Collection complète des lois, décrets, ordonnances, règlements et avis du Conseil d'État*, 149 vols. (Paris, 1834–1949)
MAE	Archives du Ministère des affaires étrangères, La Courneuve
NAF	Nouvelles acquisitions françaises
RAL	Rothschild Archive, London
SA	Stadsarchief, Amsterdam
SAEF	Service des archives économiques et financières, Savigny-le-Temple
SHD	Service historique de la Défense, Vincennes

CHAPTER I

The Nineteenth-Century French State and Its Rivals

Napoleon's defeat at Waterloo in 1815 presaged a transformation of the French state. The fiscal-military system, geared towards mobilising men and money for potentially large-scale warfare, was downsized and recast. France, though, remained a great power; as the statesmen who reconstructed the international order at the Congress of Vienna in 1814–15 clearly understood, France presented a grave potential threat to European peace for the foreseeable future. Indeed, within a few years, France had developed one of the most effective fiscal-military systems in the world, despite some historians' tendency to see post-Napoleonic France as a waning power. While the Franco-Prussian War of 1870–1 sealed France's decline, the two sides were evenly matched in important ways. In 1869, France's population was 38,890,000 to Germany's 38,914,000 while its gross domestic product (GDP), in 2011 US dollars, was $3,301 million to Germany's $3,758 million.[1] In an unfortunately timed article published the day before Napoleon III surrendered at Sedan, the economist Paul Leroy-Beaulieu argued that, while France and the German states had similar-sized populations and economic resources, France's were better organised; the French military and naval forces were superior, and the French systems of taxation and public credit were even more so.[2] Others such as Adolphe Thiers, who became the Third Republic's first president in 1871, were more pessimistic about France's chances of victory.[3] Still, flawed though Leroy-Beaulieu's analysis now appears, it embodied an element of truth. His argument reflected the nineteenth-century reconstruction of the French fiscal-military system, to which historians have given little systematic attention, but which was among the principal achievements of post-revolutionary France.

Recent scholarship has increased the need to revisit the early and mid-nineteenth century, often seen as a parenthesis falling between the drama of

---

[1] Bolt et al., 'Rebasing "Maddison"'.   [2] Leroy-Beaulieu, 'Ressources de la France et de la Prusse'.
[3] Thiers to Duvergier de Hauranne, 17 July 1870, and to Rémusat, 19 July 1870, Thiers MSS, BNF, NAF 20620, fols. 196–203.

the Revolutionary and Napoleonic era and the creation of a durable republic after 1870. Historians have demonstrated that the abolition of feudalism, among the major achievements of the Revolution of 1789, was a slow process and did not entail a major redistribution of economic means.[4] Indeed, not until the mid-twentieth century was inequality in France noticeably reduced.[5] Still, in overhauling property rights and centralising the power of eminent domain, the Revolution removed many of the legal obstacles that had hindered the exploitation of land under the *ancien régime*, stimulating agricultural improvements in the early to mid-nineteenth century.[6] Influenced by Alexis de Tocqueville, François Furet claimed that the Revolution began before 1789 and ended in the 1870s.[7] In effect, this conceptualisation underplays the significance of attempts in the early and mid-nineteenth century to fashion a post-revolutionary order. While the republican teleology remains highly influential, historians have begun to reassess the intellectual, political and cultural history of the period 1815–70, starting with the rediscovery of Restoration and Orleanist political thought.[8] Rather than simply marking transitional stages between the *ancien régime* and the advent of the Republic, the constitutional monarchies of the early nineteenth century reflected a distinctive attempt to fashion a stable, 'liberal' sociopolitical order.[9]

The reappraisal of the early nineteenth century has clear ramifications for the study of public finance, a subject which historians have largely overlooked. Though the reassessment of the period has extended to economic history, scholars have prioritised economic life.[10] As a result, customs aside, the early and mid-nineteenth-century fiscal system has received little attention since the 1920s. Most of the 'new French fiscal history' has focused on the *ancien régime*. Other recent work on public finance concerns the Revolutionary and Napoleonic periods, reinforcing the existing narrative that the nineteenth-century fiscal system was established between 1789 and 1815.[11] Thereafter, as Jean Bouvier has observed, the fiscal system was characterised by 'immobilism'; change was largely restricted to the almost imperceptible growth of indirect taxes.[12] This narrative, Bouvier suggests, merits greater scrutiny – 'a critical study of immobilism' – to appreciate the subtle shifts in the fiscal system

---

[4] Markoff, *Abolition of Feudalism*; Sutherland, 'Peasants, Lords and Leviathan'.
[5] Piketty, *Le Capital*, 541–7.   [6] Rosenthal, *Fruits of Revolution*.
[7] Furet, *De Turgot à Jules Ferry*; Furet, *Penser la Révolution*, 13–109.   [8] Chabal, *Divided Republic*.
[9] Rosanvallon, *Moment Guizot*; Girard, *Libéraux français*; Jardin, *Histoire du libéralisme*; Jaume, *Individu effacé*; Craiutu, *Liberalism under Siege*.
[10] E.g. Vause, *In the Red and in the Black*.
[11] Branda, *Prix de la gloire*; Bonney, 'Apogee and Fall'; White, 'Politics of Government Finance'.
[12] Bouvier, 'Système fiscal'. For an explanation of 'immobilisme' as resulting from the power of interest groups, see Baccouche, 'Déterminants sociaux et politiques'.

over the course of the century. Moreover, through fiscal history we can qualify the significance of the Revolution and further refute the republican teleology.

Scholarship on nineteenth-century French fiscal history, Bouvier observes, has been dominated by the work of two historians: Marcel Marion and Robert Schnerb. Marion presented 'finances studied from above, defined by the parade of budgetary laws and parliamentary debates'. He began his research before France acquired an income tax in 1916 and defended the nineteenth-century fiscal system as part of the ongoing debate over fiscal reform during the late nineteenth and early twentieth centuries. By contrast, Schnerb, influenced by the *Annales*, sought to integrate 'financial history into a global history.'[13] Historians, Bouvier suggested, should move away from Marion's high politics and towards Schnerb's integration of fiscal and social history, but the difference between Marion and Schnerb is less than Bouvier implies. Both relied heavily on the same sources: parliamentary papers and the writings of the intellectual and policymaking elite. In part, their dependence on these materials reflects the scarcity of documents in central government – as opposed to local – archives following the incineration of the finance ministry archives during the Paris Commune of 1871. Both historians also focused heavily on the Revolution. Of Marion's six volumes covering the period 1715–1914, three are devoted to the years 1789–1817.[14] Likewise, much of Schnerb's *oeuvre* covers Revolutionary and Napoleonic taxation and, though it also ranges across early and mid-nineteenth-century France, does little to challenge Marion's overall interpretation.[15] In the work of both, the post-Napoleonic period appears as one of relatively little change. In this respect, furthering Schnerb's *oeuvre* is unlikely to reshape our understanding of the nineteenth-century fiscal system. More recently, scholars such as Nicolas Delalande and Jean-Claude Caron have written on the social history of taxation, and the former's work in particular also includes extensive analysis of politics.[16] Yet, Delalande's focus is mainly on the Third Republic, as is that of other recent research on nineteenth-century fiscal history.[17] While some scholars have acknowledged the importance of the years after 1815 in entrenching the post-revolutionary fiscal system, they have generally not trawled the archives, and the politics of public finance of the period continue to be

---

[13] Bouvier, 'Système fiscal', 226–7.   [14] Marion, *Histoire financière*.
[15] For a list of Schnerb's publications, see Hérody-Pierre, *Robert Schnerb*, 271–4.
[16] Delalande, *Batailles de l'impôt*; Caron, *Été rouge*.   [17] Sawyer, 'Fiscal Revolution'.

neglected.[18] These politics are essential to understanding how the fiscal system came to be, allowing us to reconsider the narrative established by Marion and others.

Given the loss of the finance ministry archives, reconstructing French fiscal history before 1871 is problematic, especially for the period after 1815. Revolutionary and Napoleonic finance can be gleaned from parliamentary proceedings, the correspondence of the committees that governed France in the 1790s and the archives of the centralised secretariat established under the Directory and Napoleon. After 1815, documentation on finance from the executive is harder to find. Parliamentary papers and proceedings, therefore, assume a greater importance – though many documents sent to parliamentary committees were returned to the finance ministry and thus do not survive. Some finance ministry correspondence exists in the records of other government departments, such as the foreign and justice ministries. Documents from police, prefects and judicial officials – all involved in taxation – offer some indication of the debates shaping policy in official circles. Like parliamentary and private papers, though, these documents are unsystematic in their attention to fiscal issues. Material in local archives, meanwhile, though it generally illuminates how the tax system functioned on a local level, can be less revealing of the national picture. Reconstructing the politics of public finance, therefore, requires a synthesis of material drawn from a range of central and local government archives and private collections.

In recounting the development of the nineteenth-century French state from the Revolution to the Third Republic through the lens of its finances, Louis Fontvieille's *oeuvre* is suggestive, as is that of Pierre Rosanvallon. For Fontvieille, the history of the state is about quantification: the growth of the budget and the relative size of different aspects of government.[19] As Rosanvallon observes, however, analysing the state is more than a matter of checking data. As the state's functions change, there may be growth in one facet and contraction in another. How the state is conceived, what it does and how, are as important as quantification. The state, he suggests, is 'a *form of social representation*'.[20] Gary Gerstle's study of the American state follows a similar logic in stressing the importance of the law and the constitution as the repository for the theory of the state.[21] While the study of the state's 'territorial integrity, financial means and staffing may be the

[18] Kang, 'État constructeur', 170–5.
[19] Fontvieille, *État*; Fontvieille, *Administration départementale*.
[20] Rosanvallon, *État*, 11–16. Emphasis in the original.   [21] Gerstle, *Liberty and Coercion*.

place to start in any investigation of its capacities to realize goals', the history of the state is about more than a rational and benign bureaucracy defined along Weberian lines.[22] Rather, the state reflects political and social developments. Thus, for Michael Mann, the modern nation-state emerged from the interplay of political, economic, military and ideological factors.[23] More recently, scholars have conceived of a 'democratic state', emphasising the porousness of the state and the way in which democratic institutions mediated relations between the state and civil society.[24] Similarly, Pieter Judson demonstrates the ways in which the nineteenth-century Habsburg state permeated public life.[25] As such scholarship suggests, analysis of the state is inseparable from that of the political process – hence the value of studying public finance, which enables us to integrate the analysis of institutions and data with that of politics and society more generally. An appreciation of the state's inextricability from political and social processes allows us to further reconsider the French Revolution's significance. Many institutions and elites of the *ancien régime* re-emerged from the mid-1790s onwards and the new state functioned like the old in fundamental ways; hence, concludes Pierre Bourdieu, the Revolution 'in essence, changed nothing'.[26]

The interactions between states means that, as Charles Maier has put it, 'they often reform themselves as a group ... Renovation ... has come in waves.'[27] Following a similar logic, Gabriel Ardant suggests that the fiscal systems of a particular period tend to be alike and develop along parallel lines.[28] Thus, the eighteenth century was characterised by frequent and lengthy wars which stimulated the growth of the fiscal-military state, as governments strove to mobilise growing quantities of money and men.[29] The scale of government borrowing rose, supported by increasingly extractive tax systems. Demand for commodities such as tea and sugar grew sharply over the course of the century, while fashion and luxury goods became more widely available, the trade and manufacture of which created new, taxable wealth.[30] Consequently, revenue from indirect taxes rose, particularly since – in France, as in other states – tax rates increased and collection became more efficient during the eighteenth century. Between

---

[22] Skocpol, 'Bringing the State Back In', 17.   [23] Mann, *Sources of Social Power*, II.
[24] Novak et al., 'Beyond Stateless Democracy'; Sawyer, *Demos Assembled.*
[25] Judson, *Habsburg Empire.*   [26] Bourdieu, *Sur l'État*, 544–6.   [27] Maier, *Leviathan*, 7–8.
[28] Ardant, *Histoire de l'impôt.*
[29] Storrs, *Fiscal-Military State*; Sánchez, *War, State and Development*; Brewer, *Sinews of Power.*
[30] Sewell, 'Empire of Fashion'. There is a large literature on eighteenth-century consumption: see, most notably, Vries, *Industrious Revolution.*

1726 and 1788, the French government's revenue from indirect taxes rose from 88.6 million livres to 219.3 million, while that from direct taxes grew less substantially from 79.9 million livres to 163 million, the nominal increases being 157.5 per cent and 104 per cent respectively.[31] In Britain, the quintessential fiscal-military state, the creation of a highly effective system of indirect taxes eased the government borrowing that underpinned Britain's ability to finance the wars of the eighteenth century. By contrast, public credit proved to be a fatal weakness for the pre-revolutionary French fiscal-military state. While the War of American Independence cost Britain slightly more than it did France, the British state managed its debts more effectively and proceeded to borrow significantly to finance the Revolutionary and Napoleonic Wars; despite substantial tax increases to fund the latter, most notably the creation of an income tax in 1799, Britain's debt-to-GDP ratio reached 200 per cent by the time peace returned in 1815.[32] France, meanwhile, borrowed at higher rates than Britain during the American war and had difficulty servicing its debts thereafter. In the 1780s, the French government struggled to reorder its finances, raise taxes and control expenditure, which increased borrowing costs.[33] The ensuing financial and political crisis triggered the collapse of the *ancien régime* in 1789, prompting the construction of a new, more sustainable fiscal-military system in the nineteenth century. Moreover, the absolute monarchy's limited success in the wars of the eighteenth century weakened public confidence in the *ancien régime*, spurring the creation of a post-revolutionary fiscal-military system capable of maintaining France as a great power.[34]

The eighteenth-century state was more than a purely fiscal-military operation, since its development also arose from non-military factors. While the growth of the eighteenth-century British state, for example, was driven primarily by war, Steven Pincus and James Robinson have argued that it sought to legitimate its expansion by seeking to ensure the provision of some basic amenities for its citizens.[35] Though local government evolved to accommodate this burden, Pincus and Robinson perhaps overstate their case, given the limitations of civil expenditure. The latter comprised 8.2 per cent of British government spending between 1689 and 1815, while the army and navy together accounted for 56.7 per cent. Even

[31] Morineau, 'Budgets de l'État', 314.
[32] Harris, 'French Finances'; Daunton, *Trusting Leviathan*, 47.
[33] White, 'Financial Dilemma'; Legay, 'Capitalisme, crises de trésorerie et donneurs d'avis'.
[34] Skocpol, *States and Social Revolutions*, 60–4.
[35] Brewer, *Sinews of Power*; Pincus and Robinson, 'Faire la guerre et faire l'État'.

taking only peacetime years in this period when army and navy expenditure was lower, totalling 40.4 per cent of spending, civil expenditure remained relatively small at 12.2 per cent.[36] In *ancien régime* France, meanwhile, peacetime army and navy expenditure seems to have consumed a smaller share of the budget than in Britain: in 1775, for instance, these accounted for 30.1 per cent of French spending, falling to 25.1 per cent in 1788.[37] As in Britain, civil expenditure also increased, particularly from local and regional government; whereas many towns had previously earmarked much of their budgets for military purposes, for instance maintaining defensive walls, in the eighteenth century they increasingly redirected resources towards infrastructure and poor relief. The French army and navy claimed a slightly higher proportion of expenditure in the nineteenth century than they had in the eighteenth, consuming 35.1 per cent of spending from 1815 to 1869, a reflection of the greater capacity of the post-revolutionary fiscal system relative to its *ancien régime* predecessor.[38] Simultaneously, the nineteenth-century state embarked on a considerable expansion directed at public works, spending on which grew by 296.8 per cent between 1815 and 1869, when adjusted for inflation.[39] As such expenditure suggests, in some respects the nineteenth-century French state may have resembled Pincus and Robinson's conception of the eighteenth-century British state more closely than the latter itself did. Certainly, France reflected something of the transition that Mann has observed from the 'fiscal-military' state of the eighteenth century to a 'civil-military' state during the nineteenth.[40]

The nineteenth-century state defies easy classification. Several scholars have recently suggested the century was characterised by a 'liberal state', though without explaining the term, presumably because it evades a succinct, broadly acceptable and yet meaningful definition.[41] Nevertheless, across much of Europe, many aspects of the fiscal-military state survived after 1815. While war in Europe was less frequent in the nineteenth century than in the eighteenth, it remained a central preoccupation for governments and continued to stimulate the growth of the state,

---

[36] Mitchell, *British Historical Statistics*, 578–80. I am grateful to Julian Hoppit for providing me with these data.
[37] Morineau, 'Budgets de l'État', 315.
[38] The figure falls to 33.7 per cent if we discount the years of major war, while excluding more protracted conflicts such as the campaigns to conquer Algeria: 1815, 1823, 1854–6 and 1859–60.
[39] Fontvieille, *État*, 2105–16.   [40] Mann, *Sources of Social Power*, II, 378.
[41] Cardoso and Lains, *Liberal State*.

as it did in the United States.[42] The label of a 'liberal state' may also give
the misleading impression that the nineteenth-century state was committed to a limited role in the economy. Indeed, several scholars have claimed
that the mid-nineteenth-century French state was 'liberal' on the basis that
it limited its involvement in economic life, before the emergence of a more
actively interventionist state at the end of the century.[43] The market,
though, was very much a construction of the state, being shaped by
regulation, which accumulated significantly over the course of the early
and mid-nineteenth century.[44] Moreover, though the Revolution of
1789 produced a reaction against the economic institutions of the *ancien
régime*, the Revolutionary and Napoleonic regimes reaffirmed the state's
economic interventionism, partly to mitigate the threat of revolutionary
activity by facilitating greater prosperity.[45] Whereas the Napoleonic and
Restoration states did not move far beyond the parameters developed by
the *ancien régime*, using the law or limited public works expenditure to
affect economic activity, the state became much more economically interventionist from the 1830s as public works spending increased. By contrast,
the reform of the British state from the 1830s onwards may have reflected
a greater compliance of civil society with the aims of the state, as the
government pursued the creation of a cheaper and more laissez-faire state
or, perhaps more accurately, a 'delegating-market' state in which the state
delegated functions to the private sector while retaining overall responsibility.[46] Still, the difference between the British and French states should
not be overstated; as we shall see, the mid-nineteenth-century French
state combined characteristics of both a 'delegating-market' and a 'fiscal-
military' state. Moreover, despite their supposedly laissez-faire state, the
British were more heavily taxed than the French until the late nineteenth
century.[47] As François Jarrige therefore concludes, France was 'far from the
strong, interventionist, oppressive state conveyed in representations'.[48]
The French state, in other words, was both economically interventionist
and committed to private enterprise. Though perhaps more interventionist
than its British counterpart, the French state was not necessarily an
economic drag; the development of the nineteenth-century French

[42] Mann, *Sources of Social Power*, II, 370–8; Edling, *Hercules in the Cradle*.
[43] Gueslin, *L'État, l'économie et la société*; Daumard, 'État libéral'.   [44] Stanziani, *Rules of Exchange*.
[45] Horn, *Path Not Taken*.
[46] Daunton, *Trusting Leviathan*, 26 and *passim*; Harling and Mandler, '"Fiscal-Military" to Laissez-Faire State'; Mandler, 'State and Society', 2.
[47] Plessis, 'Impôt des français', 24.   [48] Fureix and Jarrige, *Modernité désenchantée*, 296.

economy was not markedly inferior to that of Britain, however much scholars might idealise the latter.[49] Indeed, as Mariana Mazzucato has argued, the state can be an effective agent of economic development, something that may have been true of nineteenth-century France.[50]

The Revolutionary and Napoleonic Wars had global ramifications, and triggered the reform of the state across Europe and the Americas.[51] The process of transformation did not end with the return of peace, since states then had to adapt to the post-war world. Spurred by the need to buttress the counter-revolutionary order, reform continued after 1815, stimulating the growth of government as more state regulation emerged.[52] Under pressure to reduce expenditure and curb the bloated state that arose from the politics of 'old corruption', the British government abolished income tax in 1816.[53] Meanwhile, the end of the 1812 Anglo-American War in 1815 presaged a period of retrenchment for the United States, like that pursued in Europe, as the federal government ended temporary wartime taxes; from 1817 to 1861, the tariff – an import duty – was the only federal tax.[54] In 1816, the Second Bank of the United States was established, and a central bank was founded in Austria, to stabilise public and private credit.[55] Four years later, the Prussian Seehandlung, a state bank created under Frederick the Great, was made independent partly in the hope of enhancing its credit.[56] The change to the Seehandlung dovetailed with a process of fiscal reform in Prussia, stimulated by the costs of Napoleonic extortion from 1806 to 1814 – estimated to have totalled 80 per cent of Prussia's 1805 GNP – and the abolition of serfdom between 1807 and 1816.[57] The post-war settlement gave Prussia large swathes of territory in the Rhineland, which had a different tax system and a more commercial economy than the agrarian Prussian heartland. This problem of fiscal heterogeneity aside, the government also needed revenue, not least to cover its war debts. Following unsuccessful attempts to introduce an income tax in 1808 and 1812, between 1818 and 1822 the government raised direct taxes by establishing a class tax (*Klassensteuer*), which divided

[49] O'Brien and Keyder, *Economic Growth*; Crouzet, 'French Economic Growth'.
[50] Mazzucato, *Entrepreneurial State*.
[51] Armitage and Subrahmanyam, *Age of Revolutions in Global Context*; Desan et al., *Revolution in Global Perspective*.
[52] Bayly, *Birth of the Modern World*, 139–47; Graaf, *Fighting Terror after Napoleon*.
[53] Daunton, *Trusting Leviathan*, 47–57.   [54] Einhorn, *American Taxation*, 117, 157–8, 195–6.
[55] Hammond, *Banks and Politics*, 230–50; Beer, *Die Finanzen Oesterreichs*, 90–97.
[56] Radtke, *Die preussische Seehandlung*, 54–7.   [57] Eddie, *Freedom's Price*, 311–14.

taxpayers into five classes and was levied mainly on land. The government also instituted a new business tax, similar to the *patente* which the Napoleonic regime had imposed on commerce. Meanwhile, the government sought to shift the fiscal burden from eastern Prussia towards the newly acquired or reconquered, wealthier western areas. Though overall indirect tax revenues did not change much, the rates of these taxes rose considerably in the west while falling in the east, redistributing much of the fiscal burden towards the urban poor in the west.[58] The government of the newly constituted Kingdom of the Netherlands likewise pursued a more homogeneous fiscal system, seeking to equalise the fiscal burden between the north and the south. While this entailed raising taxes in the latter, the Dutch government, like others in Europe, sought to reduce taxes. Thus, between 1816 and 1822 a series of measures reduced customs duties while seeking to offset the adverse effects on Dutch industry through subsidies.[59]

Like Prussia and the Netherlands, Spain suffered heavily from Napoleonic plundering and embarked on a similar process of fiscal reform and administrative rationalisation after the French invaded the country in 1808. In 1813, the government introduced a new uniform direct tax, intended to replace the plethora of different *ancien régime* provincial taxes.[60] The reform, however, proved short-lived. The restoration of Ferdinand VII in 1814 presaged the revocation of the 1812 constitution and, reasserting his authority, he repealed the *contribución directa* and revived the *ancien régime* system. In subsequent years, constitutional crisis hampered fiscal reform in Spain, as Ferdinand sought to govern without the Cortes. Raising new taxes was problematic and the public finances remained unstable.[61] The turmoil in Spain that followed Napoleon's invasion fuelled a crisis of empire in Latin America, leading many colonies to establish their independence in a struggle that lasted into the 1820s. The ensuing growth of military expenditure and the loss of colonial resources combined to exacerbate Spain's fiscal problems. Meanwhile, the former colonies overhauled taxation as they established themselves as newly independent states – though this process of state formation lasted longer than the post-war period of reform in Europe and the United States, and frequent conflict in Latin America demonstrated the capacity of war to

[58] Spoerer, *Steuerlast, Steuerinzidenz und Steuerwettbewerb*, 47–55.
[59] Fritschy, 'Staatsvorming en financieel beleid'; Zanden and van Riel, *Nederland*, 117–21.
[60] López Castellano, *Liberalismo económico*.
[61] Fontana Lázaro, *La quiebra*; Fontana Lázaro, *Hacienda y estado*.

hinder state formation and not just to stimulate it.[62] Regarding public finance, therefore, the years after 1815 were seldom a 'restoration'. The global upheaval wrought by the French Revolution and the Napoleonic Wars made this impossible.

In adapting to the post-war geopolitical order, the French faced a different problem to their Continental European counterparts. Rather than having to deal with the incorporation of new territory or the end of the Napoleonic occupation, the French had to learn to survive without exploiting the resources of conquered territories, which were vital to Napoleonic finance. From 1811, imperial budgets exceeded 900 million francs annually, and such a level of expenditure was unsustainable after 1814 given France's reduced means.[63] Thus, the first Restoration government cut the 1814 budget from Napoleon's projected 1.245 billion francs to 827 million, with further reductions planned for 1815.[64] In addition to having to align its expenditure with its income, the government faced serious discontent over taxation from late 1813, which created further pressure for fiscal reform. As Marion, Schnerb and others demonstrated, the Revolutionary and Napoleonic period was crucial in the creation of the nineteenth-century fiscal constitution. By 1806, the principal taxes were all established. Nevertheless, these historians did not fully appreciate the ramifications of constant tax increases to cover the costs of war, which impeded the stabilisation and legitimacy of the fiscal system. In 1815, therefore, public finance had to be placed on a more sustainable footing, and doing this was the achievement of the Restoration. Historians have recently cast the Restoration as a period in which France developed a new political culture through an apprenticeship in relatively stable parliamentary government.[65] Most notably, for our purposes, from 1814 onwards the budget was voted annually by the legislature. With the post-war reconfiguration of the state, the Restoration also marked the entrenchment of the nineteenth-century fiscal system. The latter, as in the eighteenth century, relied heavily on indirect taxes, which rose from around 37 per cent of central government revenue in 1815 to 55 per cent by 1905 – surpassing the *ancien régime*, for which indirect taxes provided 47 per cent of ordinary revenue in 1788.[66]

[62] Centeno, 'Blood and Debt'; Grafe and Irigoin, 'Spanish Empire and Its Legacy'.
[63] Branda, *Prix de la gloire*, 583–5.   [64] Bruguière, *Première Restauration*, 75–80.
[65] Gunn, *When the French Tried to Be British*; Rosanvallon, *Monarchie impossible*.
[66] *Proposition de loi ... 1815, 1816, 1817*; *Projet de loi ... 1905*; Morineau, 'Budgets de l'État', 314.

Like the famous *Code Napoléon*, the French tax system was exported across the conquered territories during the Napoleonic era, with lasting consequences. In states as varied as Bavaria, Baden, Württemberg, Hesse, Piedmont and the Low Countries, direct taxes reflected the French model after 1815. Repartitioned according to external signs of wealth, these states commonly had a tax on land, a tax on buildings and a tax on industry, which replaced a patchwork of eighteenth-century taxes.[67] The indirect tax model also proved influential. German chancellor Otto von Bismarck, for instance, sought to emulate the effectiveness of France's system of indirect taxes when designing the new federal German fiscal constitution following unification in 1871.[68] The rise of indirect taxes in France partly reflected the influence of the model of eighteenth-century Britain. Yet, with the re-establishment of income tax in 1842, which was extended to Ireland in 1853, Britain moved towards greater reliance on direct taxation, leaving France as the standard bearer for indirect taxation. In this respect, France reflected the more typical development of the nineteenth-century European state, which was characterised by growing reliance on indirect taxation as economic development increased consumption.[69] Indeed, in an age of urbanisation, indirect taxes offered the easiest way to tax the rising numbers of urban poor, who tended to have few taxable assets, while direct taxes fell principally on property owners.

The entrenchment of indirect taxation benefited the landowners and many of the industrialists that dominated nineteenth-century French politics; it also suited the small cabal of bankers, industrialists, finance ministry officials and select politicians and journalists – the 'experts' – who dominated public finance. 'The financiers formed ... a small church in the Chamber,' recalled the Orleanist politician Charles de Rémusat, 'a sect with which ministers of finance sometimes liked to consult more often than with their colleagues.'[70] The difficulty of penetrating the sect was apparent in the process of appointments at the finance ministry. An Austrian observer noted in 1855 that the ministry 'recruits itself almost exclusively from its own fold'.[71] Like the rest of the bureaucracy, the finance ministry was an invaluable source of patronage and political influence. A closed shop, it was hardly conducive to new ideas or major change. On the contrary, it comprised a constellation of largely

---

[67] Borscheid, 'Influence du modèle fiscal', 380–4.   [68] Stern, *Gold and Iron*, 202.
[69] Neal, 'Monetary, Fiscal and Political Architecture'.   [70] Rémusat, *Mémoires*, III, 152.
[71] Hock, 'Ministère des finances', 632.

conservative interests, aligned with wider lobby groups. Indeed, beyond the legislature and the finance ministry, pressure groups such as chambers of commerce were highly influential.[72] Despite the instabilities and regime changes that affected nineteenth-century French politics, the fiscal administration and the clique that dominated fiscal policy remained strikingly consistent, in their membership and in the policies they promoted. This is not to say that men of a uniform opinion made policy. Fissures existed and, as we shall see, appeared most clearly in the aftermath of policy failures. Splits emerged in 1824, for example, when the legislature rejected the government's proposal for a debt conversion, and in 1832, when major protests forced the revocation of a reform to direct taxation passed the previous year. Still, given the general coherence of the fiscal policymaking elite, the politics of public finance offer a striking case of continuity in a period notorious for the political, social and economic changes arising from recurrent revolution and industrialisation.

The quest for stability dominated the fiscal policymaking elite. Haunted by the disorders of the 1790s, they sought to maintain consent to taxation, which had been strained by Napoleon's exactions. This desire for consent pushed central governments to cultivate local elites, not least because tax collection relied on their cooperation, as did the wider legitimacy of the state; indeed, the centralisation of nineteenth-century French government should not be exaggerated.[73] While taxpayers rarely pay gladly, states seek what Margaret Levi has termed 'quasi-voluntary compliance' to taxation, in which the threat of compulsion secures consent.[74] Partly to minimise the problems arising from non-compliance, governments rarely introduce major new taxes, given the controversies that these often entail. Instead, they usually opt for a process of 'fringe tuning' or 'churning', according to which existing taxes are adjusted to meet the needs of the budget.[75] Thus, the 1816 budget, which established the principles of Restoration finance, merely amended the rates of several duties, the means of collection and fiscal administration. The peace terms of 1815, imposing the costs of an allied army of occupation alongside reparations, retarded tax reform. Only once these expenses were discharged could the French reconfigure their fiscal and military systems – though, even then, tax reform proceeded gradually.

---

[72] Lemercier, *Un si discret pouvoir*.   [73] Barreyre and Lemercier, 'Unexceptional State', 487–90.
[74] Levi, *Rule and Revenue*.
[75] Daunton, *Trusting Leviathan*, 15–16; Rose and Karran, *Taxation by Political Inertia*; Delalande, 'Économie politique des réformes fiscales'.

The most important fiscal innovation of the Restoration was the ascent of public credit. Though public credit in the early nineteenth century has received some scholarly attention, historians have not fully appreciated its significance for the development of the fiscal system.[76] Unlike Napoleon, who struggled to borrow on a large scale, French governments from the 1820s onwards could borrow easily and cheaply, which enabled them to preserve the tax system by insulating it from spikes in government expenditure. Thus, France emulated eighteenth-century Britain's reliance on public credit, creating a new fiscal-military apparatus that underwrote France's resurgence as a great power in Europe and provided the means for the revival of French overseas imperialism, which was more extensive in the early and mid-nineteenth century than historians have often suggested.[77] Simultaneously, public credit facilitated the growth of state economic interventionism from the late 1830s onwards.

Like France, other European states expanded in the mid-nineteenth century, becoming increasingly concerned with promoting economic development. Belgian customs policy, for example, was designed to protect domestic industry while maximising its potential market abroad. Simultaneously, the Belgian authorities stimulated industrialisation by facilitating railway construction.[78] The Prussian government sought to do likewise, though political impediments to the growth of public expenditure hindered the development of a more interventionist Prussian state in the 1840s.[79] Meanwhile, in the United States, the state proved more interventionist than in Prussia, spending significant sums on 'internal improvements'.[80] Though heavily indebted state governments reduced expenditure after a financial crisis in 1837, that of localities rose in the 1840s to mitigate the ensuing slump, continuing the growth of the state overall.[81] Meanwhile, the federal government, aside from funding limited infrastructure programmes, used the law to regulate economic life on the cheap.[82] The 1848 revolutions, argues Christopher Clark, produced a 'European revolution in government' in the 1850s, as many countries embarked on political, administrative and constitutional reform.[83] Simultaneously, the socio-economic shift wrought by industrialisation intensified – the 1850s were characterised by, in Eric Hobsbawm's phrase,

---

[76] Most work on credit in early and mid-nineteenth-century France concerns private credit and banking; e.g. Gille, *Banque et le crédit*; Stoskopf, *Banquiers et financiers*; Hoffman et al., *Dark Matter Credit*.
[77] Todd, 'Imperial Meridian'.   [78] Schöller, 'Transformation économique de la Belgique'.
[79] Tilly, 'Political Economy of Public Finance', 485–7, 489–90; Brophy, *Capitalism*, 36–49.
[80] Dunlavy, *Politics and Industrialization*, 48–56.   [81] Sylla, 'Experimental Federalism', 520–6.
[82] Novak, *People's Welfare*, 83–113.   [83] Clark, 'After 1848'.

a 'great boom'.[84] Urban populations grew rapidly while railways and telegraphs facilitated territorial integration, increasing the centralised state's claim to legitimacy by rendering it more effective.[85] These were not new phenomena in the 1850s, but the 1848 revolutions threw them into sharper relief. In France and elsewhere, the insecurities of governments and elites pushed them into raising expenditure. In this respect, the pattern inaugurated from the late 1830s onwards continued after 1848, when the July Monarchy of 1830–48 was overthrown and Louis-Napoleon Bonaparte, Napoleon's nephew, became president of the Republic. Indeed, Louis-Napoleon's exploitation of universal male suffrage, established in 1848, reflected the renewed pressure on the state to meet the needs of the wider population. The ensuing transformation of the state, historians such as Adrien Dansette and Alain Plessis have argued, marked the 'birth of modern France'.[86] At least for our purposes, the advent of universal suffrage made public finance more 'modern', not least by reinforcing the sensitivity of tax politics to public opinion. In this respect, the arrival of universal suffrage built on the abolition of *ancien régime* status-based taxation in the 1789 Revolution, and the development of legislative consent to government spending and greater financial transparency particularly after 1814.

The growth of public expenditure in the 1850s pushed governments into fiscal reform which, in reassuring potential creditors, increased their capacity to borrow and thus perpetuated still more spending. In the 1850s, Piedmont, an aspirant to great power status, sought higher revenues by exporting the tax system it had acquired under Napoleon to Sardinia.[87] Reform and economic liberalisation, much of the Piedmontese elite believed, would stimulate prosperity and reduce iniquities in the fiscal system, deflecting discontent and harnessing political economy as a bulwark against socialism.[88] The pressure for fairer taxation was apparent in debates over income tax that emerged in 1848 in Prussia, Austria and France, which partly reflected the influence of Britain's recently introduced income tax. In Prussia, industrialisation spurred the growth of the urban middle class, which had avoided major tax increases in the early 1820s, thus stimulating discontent with the fiscal system. Consequently, in 1851, the government established an income tax throughout the state.[89] Austria, too, acquired an income tax in 1849, despite ministers' concerns

[84] Hobsbawm, *Age of Capital*, 29–47.   [85] Maier, *Leviathan*, 88.
[86] Dansette, *Naissance*; Plessis, *De la fête impériale*.
[87] Dincecco et al., 'Warfare, Taxation and Political Change', 901.
[88] Romani, 'Reluctant Revolutionaries', 51–6.
[89] Spoerer, *Steuerlast, Steuerinzidenz und Steuerwettbewerb*, 56–60.

that the tax risked provoking discontent.[90] Moreover, as in Prussia and Sardinia, the government sought to reduce the heterogeneity of the fiscal system in favour of greater uniformity.[91] In 1850, the tariffs separating the Hungarian lands from the rest of the Habsburg Monarchy were abolished.[92] Other duties were also reformed. As a result, government revenue rose by two-thirds across the Habsburg Monarchy, with a fourfold increase in Hungary.[93] In 1852 and 1854, tariffs regulating external trade were reduced and, in 1853, the Austrians secured an agreement with the Zollverein, the Prussian-dominated customs union of German states.[94]

The reforms to direct taxation in Prussia survived with little change until the 1890s. In Britain, while the income tax was supposedly temporary, it was never abolished – though William Gladstone, the leader of the Liberal Party and one of the architects of the nineteenth-century British fiscal constitution, contemplated the possibility. Ironically, it was Gladstone who entrenched the income tax with his reform of death duties in 1853. Since the rich paid more in death duties than the poor, that those eligible for the income tax paid the same proportional rates became more acceptable: the rich could afford to pay more, and they did, just not through income tax.[95] By contrast, mid-century fiscal reforms in the United States and France were more ephemeral. Not until the civil war of 1861–5 were new federal taxes introduced in America, principally an income tax and duties on alcohol and tobacco. Meanwhile, the government sought to issue 'national' loans by mass public subscription, emulating the system of public credit that, as we shall see, emerged in France to finance the Crimean War of 1853–6.[96] This new method of public borrowing aside, French public finance changed little under the Second Empire, the regime that Louis-Napoleon established in 1852 when he became Napoleon III. France already had a relatively homogeneous tax system and despite various proposals for an income tax, none passed the legislature. Indeed, the difficulties that states such as Prussia and Austria had with their income taxes after 1848 provided an argument against introducing one in France. The continued expansion of the French state in the 1850s and 1860s was financed by exploiting the existing fiscal system, not by overhauling it.

[90] Brandt, *Neoabsolutismus*, I, 454–65.   [91] Pammer, 'Austria-Hungary, 1820–1913', 137–8.
[92] Brandt, *Neoabsolutismus*, I, 508–9.   [93] Evans, *Austria, Hungary and the Habsburgs*, 269.
[94] Brandt, *Neoabsolutismus*, I, 415–17.   [95] Daunton, *Trusting Leviathan*, 153, 230–3.
[96] Edling, *Hercules in the Cradle*, 178–221.

As with the United States, war played a major role in the development of the European state in the 1860s. Not only did the Crimean War precipitate lasting expansion and reform of the state for many of the belligerents, but the wars that unified Italy and Germany created new states. These wars in Europe and America furthered the democratisation of foreign policy and thus of politics more generally, forcing states and fiscal-military systems to accommodate increasingly politicised publics.[97] Moreover, the economic boom ended in the late 1850s. In France, the ensuing economic malaise encouraged the growth of the interventionist state, as the government sought to mitigate rising discontent. Simultaneously, France pursued military actions abroad, imposing further burdens on the fiscal-military system and raising questions about the priorities of government spending, which, as we shall see, shaped the decline and fall of the Second Empire from the mid-1860s onwards.

The expansion of the state in the mid-nineteenth century provided a crucial foundation for developments later in the century. From the 1880s, the welfare state began to emerge as social spending – on education, on welfare – in Europe and the United States surged.[98] Meanwhile, state power was extended over large parts of the extra-European world which previously had not been directly controlled by European-style states, while the state simultaneously extended its power in Europe. The integration of the national space through roads and railways accelerated; in France, this, combined with more effective primary education and a new military system of universal conscription, made 'peasants into Frenchmen'.[99] With the reconfiguration of the state, public spending grew increasingly sharply. The fiscal system, though, was not overhauled. As in the mid-century, it was adapted to the government's needs.[100] In this respect, the significance of the 1870s as a turning point should not be exaggerated. Moreover, the government contemplated military reform throughout the Second Empire, while the teaching of French history to stimulate national sentiment, debated since the July Monarchy, became mandatory in 1867. The Third Republic was sufficiently conservative that the transformation of the state which it oversaw was foreshadowed in the earlier 'wave' of reform that affected the European states in the mid-nineteenth century. Indeed, the rapid expansion of the American state in 1860s offered the French a model for raising revenues in the 1870s as they faced a surge in

[97] Simms, *Struggle for Supremacy*, 221–48.
[98] Lindert, *Growing Public*, I, 171–6; Nord, 'Welfare State'.   [99] Weber, *Peasants into Frenchmen*.
[100] Marion, *Histoire financière*, VI; Sawyer, 'Fiscal Revolution'.

government expenditure, arising principally from the costs of reparations in the aftermath of the Franco-Prussian War.[101]

The study of the French fiscal-military state in the early and mid-nineteenth century, therefore, serves three major purposes. First, it enhances our understanding of the development of the French state, since many of the means for financing it originated in the early nineteenth century. Despite the imposition of income tax in 1916 and subsequent reforms in the interwar period and after 1945, indirect taxation remained crucial to financing the twentieth-century state. Second, the French 'model' exercised a considerable influence over the fiscal development of other states. Under Napoleon, the French exported across Continental Europe their tax system, vestiges of which generally survived after 1815. Meanwhile, for other European governments, the French system, relatively homogeneous and seemingly effective at raising money, presented an attractive prospect. Third, the reconstruction of the fiscal-military system after 1789 allowed France to operate as a great power in the nineteenth century, playing a central role in European and global geopolitics. Therein lies the global significance of the history of the nineteenth-century French fiscal-military state, to whose detailed workings we now turn.

---

[101] Sawyer, *Demos Assembled*, 129–31.

CHAPTER 2

The Revolutionary Quest for Fiscal Stability, 1789–1799

The taxes that comprised the nineteenth-century French fiscal constitution were established in pursuit of a just and stable fiscal system, which the *ancien régime* failed to provide. The pre-revolutionary tax system not only failed to produce sufficient revenue for the government's needs, it was widely regarded as oppressive, inequitable and inefficient. Different regions levied disparate taxes at different rates. Particularly in the *pays d'états*, where the monarchy's authority was more diluted, direct taxation was far from uniform. Indirect taxes, too, varied extensively. Thus, the *aides*, a collection of sales taxes levied mostly on alcohol, were collected in the area of *pays d'aides*, within which the taxes differed considerably. *Provinces réputées étrangères* such as Brittany, meanwhile, paid no *aides*, but still had customs duties – the *traites* – on imported alcohol. Other provinces, such as the Auvergne, paid an *équivalent* in exchange for exemption from the *aides*. A major component of the *aides* was the *octrois*, collected by towns, usually in the form of tolls at town entrances and sales duties within towns – though the taxes varied. These formed the basis of municipal revenues, but the provincial and central governments claimed a sizeable proportion of *l'octroi* by the 1780s.[1] While seemingly arbitrary, the system had a certain logic. Brittany, for example, the largest salt producer in France, paid no salt tax, which would have been difficult to enforce. Instead, the region had to import wine, which faced high customs duties.[2] For its defenders, this system had the advantage of adapting to regional needs; the wine industry in Burgundy, for instance, benefited from low alcohol duties, which facilitated prosperity. Critics, though, typically disliked what were effectively subsidies to special interests, which allocated resources inefficiently. Furthermore, the number of taxes and the complexity of the system provoked extensive criticism, alongside complaints

[1] Bossenga, *Politics of Privilege*, 28–9; Gebhart and Mercadier, *Octroi de Toulouse*, 9–10.
[2] Collins, *State in Early-Modern France*, 26.

about the weight of imposition.[3] The Revolution therefore presaged a simplification of the fiscal system. The abolition of privilege on 4 August 1789 reflected a commitment to legal equality which, among other things, meant that all would be eligible for the same taxes supposedly at the same rates. Thus, the incidence of taxation would become more equitable and, partly as a result, the fiscal system would attain greater legitimacy.

Prominent among critics of *ancien régime* taxation were the physiocrats, a group of early economists who believed that Enlightenment would deliver a new socio-economic order, in which free and rational individuals would serve their own interests. Perhaps because of the physiocrats' prominence in pre-revolutionary and Revolutionary fiscal debates, historians have ascribed to them a considerable influence over the Constituent Assembly, formed in 1789 to design a new constitution.[4] As we shall see, though, the Assembly's fiscal reforms were heavily pragmatic and the result, a tax system based on direct taxes, was largely conditioned by circumstances. Moreover, the physiocrats were far from having a monopoly on eighteenth-century economic thought, and many deputies in the Assembly were not especially sympathetic to their ideas. Thus, despite the at least ostensible interest of physiocrats and others in social rights including education and the welfare of the poor, such concerns were subordinated to servicing the debts of the *ancien régime*.[5] While default had its adherents in 1789, prominent advocates of constitutional reform preferred otherwise, since raising the taxes necessary to service the debt would require the consent of elected representatives, providing leverage to force the overhaul of the political system.[6]

The revolutionaries' new taxes quickly proved inadequate to cover public expenditure, particularly since France was at war from 1792. The ensuing financial disorder discredited the moderate, pragmatic political economy of the early Revolution. The war succoured the ideological extremes, producing the Terror which ended with the coup of Thermidor in July 1794. The Thermidorians reimposed moderation, seeking a middle ground – a *juste milieu* – between Jacobinism and royalism, an outlook which underlay the Directory, the regime that they established in 1795. Indeed, historians have recently reconceived the period 1794–9, often overlooked hitherto, as years of intellectual and political ferment.[7] In their quest for moderation, the Thermidorians

[3] Decroix, *Question fiscale et réforme financière*, 45–8.   [4] Weulerrse, *Physiocratie à l'aube*, 363–423.
[5] Walton, 'Why the Neglect', 512–13.   [6] Sonenscher, 'Nation's Debt'.
[7] E.g. Livesey, *Making Democracy*; Serna, *République des girouettes*; Jainchill, *Reimagining Politics*.

orchestrated the return of a more pragmatic attitude to public finance, playing an important role in the stabilisation of the post-revolutionary fiscal system.

Revolutionary Political Economy

The fiscal reforms of 1789–91 were supposed to produce a new tax system that aligned with the Revolution's ideals. This process began with the abolition of privilege, which ended exemptions to the *taille*, one of the principal direct taxes that, depending on the region, was levied on land and other assets. Enjoyed to varying degrees by nobles, clergymen, the professions and many large towns, the exemptions provoked vehement criticism of the fiscal system. Of the *cahiers de doléances*, lists of grievances compiled by members of the three estates in preparation for the Estates General, 11.4 per cent demanded the equalisation of the tax burden, while 44 per cent wanted it to be more proportional to the means of different social groups.[8] The abolition of privilege undermined what remained of the tax system's legitimacy, encouraging refusals to pay taxes, tithes and seigneurial dues.[9] Meanwhile, for some, for example in *pays d'états* such as Provence, the abolition of privilege portended a loss of regional autonomy.[10] The heterogeneity of the pre-revolutionary tax system therefore complicated the process of simplifying it. Despite the difficulties with tax collection, the Assembly retained the *ancien régime* taxes for 1790 to gain time to redesign the fiscal system. The idealism and expectations that arose with the revolutionary *élan* made this task harder. The ensuing difficulties of reconciling such principles with the treasury's needs contributed to the fiscal instability of the 1790s.

For the fiscal – and political – system, a major long-term consequence of the Revolution was to greatly increase the importance of legislative consent.[11] Thereafter, taxes had to be approved by the elected representatives of the nation, though under Napoleon this requirement became more nominal than real. Not only would taxpayers be protected from arbitrary demands, taxes would have greater legitimacy, which could mitigate resistance. The idea of seeking the consent of representative institutions was not new; they featured prominently in pre-revolutionary attempts to reform the fiscal system.[12] Indeed, consent to taxation was a core principle

---

[8] Shapiro and Markoff, *Revolutionary Demands*, 258.   [9] Hirsch, *Nuit du 4 août*, 315–18.
[10] Blaufarb, *Politics of Fiscal Privilege*, 203–22.   [11] Delalande, *Batailles de l'impôt*, 24–37.
[12] Kwass, *Privilege and the Politics of Taxation*, 257–73; Miller, 'Provincial Assemblies'.

of the *ancien régime*. The convocation of the Estates General in 1789 and
the Third Estate's claim to embody the nation reflected the connection
between taxation and representation. Four days after the Third Estate
seceded from the Estates General to become the National Assembly, it
declared existing taxes invalid, since these were levied without representatives' approval. Partly because of this renewed emphasis on representation,
direct taxes were at the centre of Revolutionary fiscal reform. Unlike
indirect taxes, they were attributable to an individual, and could therefore
define citizenship. As a result, the years 1792–5 aside, suffrage rested on
direct tax qualifications until 1848. In addition to defining citizenship,
direct taxation could potentially strengthen national consciousness. For
some revolutionaries, the nation's claim to sovereignty was to be reinforced
by the creation of Frenchmen. Abbé Grégoire famously promoted the
propagation of the French language to forge national unity, and taxation
could potentially serve a similar purpose. As one deputy in the Constituent
Assembly put it, 'we can therefore regard this sacrifice [taxation] as one of
the primary foundations for all political association.'[13] The nation could
only be united through the act of paying taxes if taxpayers believed them to
be just and were conscious of paying them – something to which direct
taxes were better suited than indirect. Strengthening the sense of nationhood could also potentially generate consent: to pay taxes was to serve the
nation, an imagined community of taxpayers.

The physiocrats were among those who emphasised the connection
between taxation and citizenship. Citizenship, believed François
Quesnay, the founding physiocrat, depended on owning land, which he
saw as the ultimate source of wealth. Not only was a direct tax on land
therefore the optimal form of taxation, but 'the greatest number of
landowners is advantageous to a state' because this maximised the potential
number of citizens invested in the state's well-being.[14] Direct taxation
would allow rational individuals to appreciate better their relationship with
the state, and would facilitate the economic liberalisation the physiocrats
deemed necessary for economic growth and social amelioration. The
physiocrats' commitment to direct taxation reflected their concern for
social justice, since indirect taxes weighed more heavily on the poor.
Thus, those such as Anne-Robert-Jacques Turgot, an economist who
sympathised with aspects of physiocracy though he did not accept the full
credo, supported state intervention in providing poor relief, despite

[13] Delley, 16 September 1790, AP, 1st series, XIX, 5.
[14] Quesnay, *Essai sur l'administration des terres*, iii.

favouring economic liberalisation.[15] His interest in social justice was apparent in his support for progressive taxation, shared by several critics of physiocracy, which would make the rich pay higher rates of tax.[16] In potentially redistributing wealth, direct taxation could ease the creation of the society of landowning citizens that Quesnay and his successors sought.

The physiocrats considered indirect taxes, by contrast, as unsuited to making citizens. As the Marquis de Mirabeau observed, 'without property [there is] no state, no subjects attached to territory, no union of men.'[17] The well-being of the state and society were intrinsically bound through property, particularly land; indirect taxes undermined property by being less transparent and, therefore, less conducive to consent. Thus, Turgot wrote, 'taxes, established *on work or on consumption*, are only paid indirectly by landowners.' Taxes paid by labourers or the poor were '*an advance* that landowners have to reimburse through either wages or charity; but they are an advance from the poor to the rich'.[18] Not only did the difficulties associated with consent to indirect taxes cause them to undermine property and, thus, the well-being of the state; they were also regressive. This injustice, Turgot claimed, provoked resistance, and therefore necessitated a more expensive and intrusive state, which did not suit taxpayers and militated against economic liberalisation. Moreover, the physiocrats criticised indirect taxes for undermining growth by regulating economic activity, for instance by affecting purchasing patterns and inhibiting free trade – a criticism made more acute by the wide variations in indirect taxes across France. Indirect taxes were the greatest of 'the barriers which prevent affluence'.[19]

At least superficially, the physiocrats' views reflected the complaints expressed in the *cahiers*. The most common grievances outlined in the latter concerned taxation, particularly indirect taxes. Gilbert Shapiro and John Markoff, in their quantitative analysis of the *cahiers*, suggest that

> the Farmers General, because of their responsibility for collecting the indirect taxes, [were] the most hated of the financiers ... 13.3 percent of the Nobles, 19.7 percent of the Third Estate, and 9.7 percent of the Parishes express grievances on the Subject. Furthermore, the actions

---

[15] Rothschild, *Economic Sentiments*, 29–34, 72–86.
[16] Gross, 'Progressive Taxation', 96–101. On Turgot's relationship with physiocracy, see Gouette and Klotz, 'Turgot'; Meyssonnier, *Balance et l'horloge*, 325–31.
[17] Mirabeau, *Théorie de l'impôt*, 105.
[18] 'Mémoire pour Franklin', in Turgot, *Œuvres de Turgot*, V, 514. Emphases in the original.
[19] Mirabeau, *Théorie de l'impôt*, 187.

demanded are relatively extreme: of those documents that discuss the Subject, 55 percent of the Nobles, 62 percent of the Third Estate, and 51 percent of the Parishes want to abolish the organization, rather than merely reform or regulate it.[20]

Yet, the physiocrats and authors of the *cahiers* perhaps disliked the *fermes générales* for different reasons. The physiocrats' criticism of indirect taxes as stealth taxes may have resonated, but they paid little attention to the conspicuousness of the *fermes générales* which was a major cause of complaint. The farmers' wealth was highly visible, as were the methods by which they collected taxes – the toll barriers of *l'octroi*, for instance – in addition to the taxes themselves.[21] Moreover, the violence of taxation produced a high degree of antagonism towards the *fermes*. Anti-smuggling actions were commonly framed as 'war', while the *fermes'* commissions imposed notoriously draconian punishments on tax evaders.[22]

The physiocrats' impact on fiscal policy was most apparent with regard to direct taxes. Their influence, coupled with the undesirability of increasing reliance on the unpopular and inefficient *fermes générales*, meant that much pre-revolutionary fiscal reform concerned direct taxation. To maximise revenues, governments sought greater administrative efficiency and eroded privilege in favour of more progressive taxation. In this, they had limited success, given the entrenchment of vested interests, and direct taxes yielded significantly less revenue than indirect taxes until the 1790s. The Constituent Assembly, by contrast, preferred proportional taxation.[23] Still, the difference between pre-revolutionary fiscal reform and that of the revolutionaries should not be overstated. In 1787, Charles-Alexandre de Calonne, controller-general of finances, convened an Assembly of Notables to secure approval for a universal land tax and reductions to the *taille* and gabelles, the latter comprising a series of taxes and monopolies on salt. His proposed land tax was broadly similar to that adopted by the Constituent Assembly in November 1790 and, moreover, mirrored plans prepared under Turgot when he served as controller-general from 1774 to 1776. Indeed, physiocrats such as Pierre-Samuel Dupont de Nemours shaped Calonne's fiscal proposals for the Notables.[24]

While the *contribution foncière*, the land tax, was to form the basis of the new fiscal system, less reflective of physiocracy was the creation of two

---

[20] Shapiro and Markoff, *Revolutionary Demands*, 254, 258, 265, 267–8.
[21] Hincker, *Français devant l'impôt*, 82–7; Durand, *Fermiers généraux*; Nicolas, *Rébellion française*, 91–117.
[22] Kwass, *Contraband*, 217–35.   [23] Touzery, *Invention de l'impôt sur le revenu*, 359.
[24] Hardman, *Overture to Revolution*, 9–10, 20–34, 51–2, 148–60.

more direct taxes. To tax only land, deputies believed, was unjust; they therefore sought to tax other forms of wealth, including returns on capital invested in public securities, industrial enterprises and 'salaries from all kinds of work which . . . entail an apprenticeship, the costs of which can be considered as an investment in oneself'.[25] Consequently, in January 1791, the Assembly established the *contribution personnelle et mobilière*, to be levied on external signs of wealth, including residences, servants and horses. Initially, this tax was also intended to cover the profits of industry but, in March, the Assembly approved the *patente* for this purpose, which was levied at 10 per cent of the rental value of a business's premises. Thus, the physiocratic programme of a single land tax was discarded. The government needed more revenue than such a tax alone could provide. More importantly, landed interests successfully diverted some of the fiscal burden towards commerce, foreshadowing a central dynamic of nineteenth-century tax politics.

The mode of assessing the new direct taxes encapsulated the desire to minimise the state's intrusiveness. Although reflective of the physiocratic vision of a state that avoided infringing freedom, the Assembly was motivated principally by the aim of securing taxpayers' consent. The *contributions foncière* and *personnelle et mobilière* were conceived as proportional taxes, but they were to be assessed by repartition, which would ensure that receipts would not exceed the government's needs. Thus, instead of setting a tax at a particular rate, the government decided how much each tax was to raise in total and allocated each *département* a share to pay; the *conseil général* of each *département* then divided this sum between the communes that comprised the *département*, and finally the *conseil municipal* of each commune assessed the taxes payable by individuals. Any further revenue from direct taxes – not least necessary to fund local government – could then be raised through *centimes additionnels*, surtaxes assessed at a proportion of the initial repartition. Based on external signs of wealth, repartition avoided the imposition of requiring taxpayers to declare their incomes or the value of their assets, which was necessary for proportional taxation. Ultimately, repartition was to be assessed through a cadastre. This was not a new idea. The *taille* had been assessed by repartition since the fourteenth century, while land surveys – *compoix* – had long existed in southern France, and the state had experimented with plans for a cadastre in the 1730s and 1740s. Following the example of other European states, the government decreed a *cadastre général* in

---

[25] Defermon, 7 December 1790, AP, 1st series, XXI, 301.

1763 to repartition direct taxes more evenly while finding ways to boost revenue after the Seven Years War. This had little success given resistance from local elites and the absence of a uniform fiscal system.[26] Lacking a cadastre, therefore, the Assembly decreed its creation in 1791, but undertaking it proved time-consuming and technical, and made little progress in the 1790s.

In the meantime, repartition followed the practices and data of the *ancien régime*. Being consequently far from proportional, it prompted fierce disagreements and did little to legitimise the new taxes.[27] Assessing newly de-privileged land for taxation could be a contentious process, fuelling disputes over ownership and the value of seigneurial rights. Moreover, the boundaries of the administrative units into which Revolutionary France was divided were not all defined, and municipalities generally sought to minimise their own liability for taxes.[28] Indeed, instead of reinforcing a sense of nationhood, particularism pervaded disputes over the repartition of direct taxes. Although the Assembly reduced the imposition on some of the *départements* in an attempt to equalise the weight of taxation, the first repartition of 1791 failed to spread the burden evenly; Paris and the surrounding *départements* paid a higher proportion of their means than some areas in the Midi and the west. The perceived unfairness of repartition was to prove a recurring source of complaint in later years. Since changes to direct taxes became so politically fraught, the ability to increase revenues, necessary to balance the budget, became more difficult. Still, as Schnerb suggests, the repartition of 1791 marked the beginning of an effort to equalise the incidence of taxation that continued through the nineteenth century.[29]

Problems affecting indirect taxation amplified the pressure in 1790 to base the new fiscal system on direct taxes. Most *cahiers* that mentioned the *aides*, *octrois* and the gabelles favoured their abolition.[30] Likewise, the *tabac*, the tobacco monopoly administered by the *fermes générales* with their customary brutality, aroused stringent opposition. After 1789, these indirect taxes elicited so much resistance that they stopped being collected, while the monopolies effectively collapsed.[31] In this respect, their de jure abolition made little difference. Historians have emphasised the physiocrats' influence over the abolition of indirect taxes, but the surge in

---

[26] Touzery, *Invention de l'impôt sur le revenu*, 73–86; Alimento, 'Rêve de l'uniformité'.
[27] Schnerb, *Péréquation fiscale*, 4–5, 7–34.
[28] Marion, *Histoire financière*, II, 184–94; Jones, *Peasantry*, 183–7.
[29] Schnerb, *Péréquation fiscale*, 6, 50–3, appendix 6.   [30] Markoff, *Abolition of Feudalism*, 100.
[31] Marion, 'Recouvrement des impôts', 30–43.

resistance and the collapse of the *fermes* made the retention of most of these taxes and monopolies unfeasible.[32] While direct taxes also faced resistance, there was a wider acceptance of the need to retain them on a reformed basis; the abolition of exemptions was more expensive for the rich, and hence could secure a degree of consent among the wider population. The ensuing reliance on direct taxes meant that the latter were markedly heavier by the mid-1790s than they had been a decade before.[33] The landed classes being well represented in the Constituent Assembly, many deputies initially sought to alleviate taxation on land by preserving indirect taxes, albeit in a modified form. Whereas direct taxes weighted more heavily on land, indirect taxes were more burdensome to commerce. Moreover, many deputies believed that the issue of consent, a problem for *ancien régime* indirect taxes, could be resolved. 'Being nearly always voluntary, [indirect taxes] are never exaggerated,' claimed Charles-Maurice de Talleyrand, *rapporteur* on the *droits d'enregistrement*. 'The poor see, in the consumption of the rich, a supplement to the *contribution personnelle*.'[34] This argument, particularly the notion that the poor would be satisfied to see the rich pay more because they consumed more, clearly disregarded the physiocratic condemnation of indirect taxes as regressive and inefficient. The physiocrats, though, did not have a uniform attitude. Dupont de Nemours, the *rapporteur* on indirect taxes, argued that, while they should not be levied on 'goods of primary necessity', moderate indirect taxes were sensible and should be collected simply and unobtrusively.[35] On this basis, he saw an alcohol duty as acceptable. Physiocracy aside, this idea was inherently unpopular with the alcohol industry and much of the wider public; despite Dupont's claims, the daily consumption of alcohol by most of the population suggests it was difficult to live without. His proposal was, thus, denounced as resurrecting the detested *aides*.[36] While accommodating opposition to the principle of indirect taxes and the practical difficulties in their collection, the Assembly nevertheless retained two sets of indirect taxes: customs and the *droits de contrôle*, *d'insinuation* and *de centième denier*, which were levied on legal and property transactions and were repackaged as the *droits d'enregistrement*. Although many *cahiers* criticised customs, discontent was directed

[32] Schnerb, 'De la Constituante à Napoléon', 20, 22–3.
[33] Sutherland, 'Peasants, Lords and Leviathan', 7–8.
[34] Talleyrand, 22 November 1790, AP, 1st series, XX, 638–9.
[35] Dupont de Nemours, 29 October 1790, AP, 1st series, XX, 98–9.
[36] Gillet de La Jacqueminière and Le Chapelier, 29 October 1790, AP, 1st series, XX, 105.

principally at internal tolls, which were abolished.[37] Meanwhile, free international trade, despite support from the physiocrats, faced mounting unpopularity following the damage caused to French industry by a Franco-British commercial treaty of 1786.[38] Thus, customs were probably reformed in a way that accommodated popular demands; seeking to reduce smuggling and tax evasion, the Assembly created a national market and adopted moderate protectionism. Moreover, in rejecting free trade, the government retained revenue-raising customs duties, intended to compensate for the loss of income from internal tolls.[39]

Across the *cahiers* of all three estates, the taxes which attracted the most complaints were the *droits de contrôle*, *d'insinuation* and *de centième denier*.[40] Still, in contrast to other complaints about indirect taxes, many, particularly rural, *cahiers* sought reform rather than outright abolition.[41] Shapiro and Markoff offer five reasons for the prominence of these taxes in the *cahiers*: first, the taxes had risen significantly over the eighteenth century; second, the impact of the taxes 'was very widespread and directly personal', arbitrarily requiring people to pay substantial sums; third, the taxes limited economic activity by regulating many legal and business transactions; fourth, potentially private matters, such as marriage contracts and the extent of taxpayers' assets, were made public as a result; fifth, the laws governing the taxes were complex and exempted certain privileged groups.[42] Taxpayers' dislike of having to divulge information about their assets was especially intense, since doing so disclosed information that could increase their liability for direct taxes – this was particularly the case with the *centième denier*, which was levied on property transactions and was thus invaluable for facilitating the repartition of taxes given the limitations of land surveys and the cadastre.

All of these grievances remained applicable, in some form, to the *droits d'enregistrement*. The new taxes continued to have a widespread incidence and remained personal. Taxpayers therefore continued to disclose their assets, facilitating tax repartition, though this raised the possibility of a more equitable allocation of direct taxes which could ultimately ease the problem of consent to direct taxes by reducing the number of people able to evade them. Large landowners in particular stood to lose a lot from

---

[37] Shapiro and Markoff, *Revolutionary Demands*, 260–1, 270.   [38] Walton, 'Fall from Eden'.

[39] Whiteman, 'Trade and the Regeneration of France'; Goudard, 27 August 1790, AP, 1st series, XVIII, 303–15.

[40] Shapiro and Markoff, *Revolutionary Demands*, 270–1.

[41] Markoff, *Abolition of Feudalism*, 100–1, 107.

[42] Shapiro and Markoff, *Revolutionary Demands*, 272–4.

more effective direct taxation and, moreover, tended to undertake a greater number of transactions to which the taxes applied than other economic groups. Still, concerns over privilege were probably reduced, since every-body paid *l'enregistrement*, and at uniform rates across the country. Complaints about the weight of the taxes and their effects on economic activity may also have been alleviated; certainly, the duties were simplified and the burden reduced. As had been the case with its predecessors, *l'enregistrement* was also relatively difficult to evade, which enhanced its attractiveness for the treasury while providing another reason for the tax's unpopularity. The same was true of the *droits de timbre*, the stamp duty on legal documents, which the Assembly also retained and reformed, drawing on the example of the tax's successful British counterpart and highly unpopular proposals Calonne had made in 1787 to extend the *droits de timbre* to commercial transactions and newspapers for the sake of increasing revenue.[43] Moreover, in contrast to other indirect taxes, *l'enregistre-ment* and the *timbre* were relatively easily collected: those eligible had to go to the authorities to pay for whatever document they needed. Thus, the state's capacity to tax shaped the Assembly's policy. *L'enregistrement* and the new *timbre* reflected the compromises required of revolutionary fiscal policy, which was driven by the need to secure revenue while removing some of the most vilified aspects of pre-revolutionary taxes.

Difficulties with tax collection, already severe in 1789–90, became more acute as the Assembly reorganised fiscal administration. The receivers general, charged with collecting government money, were abolished in 1790 and replaced by men chosen by the *conseils généraux*. Indirectly elected through the *conseils municipaux*, those charged with lower level fiscal administration, observed Dominique-Vincent Ramel, finance minister from 1796 to 1799, were

> chosen by the administered among which were their parents [i.e. relatives] and their friends; retained by the dual interest of appeasing their electors and preparing themselves for the time when they return to the class of simple citizens; foreign to the Government from which they have nothing to gain and little to fear, they regard themselves, ultimately, less as agents of this same Government, but as defenders of their co-citizens.[44]

Such a system of tax collection ran counter to the higher direct taxes that the Assembly had imposed. While this recourse to local *notables* suited revolutionary ideals of a state run by voluntary consent, it was also a matter

---

[43] Margerison, 'Rœderer', 35–42.
[44] Rapport aux directeurs, by Ramel, 22 nivôse an V [11 January 1797], AN, AF/III/117.

of practical realities; the Assembly had difficulties imposing its will across the country and needed the cooperation of the *notables*. Indeed, for other taxes, the Assembly opted pragmatically to re-employ those involved in *ancien régime* fiscal administration. Thus, the farmers of the pre-revolutionary *droits de contrôle* were hired to collect *l'enregistrement*.[45] Despite claims to the contrary, the overhaul of the tax system in 1789–91 was a largely pragmatic exercise, shaped as much by practicalities and the pressures of different interests as by ideals.

War, Hyperinflation and the Reforms of the Directory

The demands of war after 1792 quickly underscored the shortcomings of the Revolutionary fiscal system. Taxation, alongside the plunder of the territories France conquered, proved insufficient to balance the budget. The government covered the resulting deficits by printing *assignats*.[46] These were initially bonds secured against the *biens nationaux*, that is the assets of the Church 'nationalised' in 1789, to which was gradually added the property of émigrés, as royalists and others left France to escape the Revolution. Despite the mismanagement of government debt in the 1780s, public credit remained attractive as a potential engine of social improvement and nation-building – much like commerce or taxation.[47] Increasing the number of investors in government debt would give more people an interest in maintaining political stability and in supporting a new, post-revolutionary order, particularly since the revolutionary governments were unwilling or unable to cultivate support for the state by other means, such as spending on education or public works; having instead opted to make honouring debt a sacrosanct principle in 1789, they sought to turn this into a political asset. However, the government lacked the credit necessary to cover its deficits, pushing the Assembly to decree in September 1790 that *assignats* not bearing interest would be used to discharge the national debt: they became money. The scale on which these were issued after the outbreak of war coupled with rising grain prices due to poor harvests contributed to runaway inflation by the mid-1790s. The depreciation of the *assignat* was not merely a consequence of how many were printed. Backed by the lands of the Church, they also elicited objections from Catholic counter-revolutionaries, for example, which devalued them further. The inflation was a result of revolutionary politics

[45] Bruguière, *Gestionnaires et profiteurs*, 56–7.   [46] Belhoste, 'Financement de la guerre'.
[47] Sonenscher, *Sans-Culottes*.

in addition to economics.[48] To buttress public credit as inflation rose, the Convention, which ruled France after the removal of Louis XVI in 1792, sought to enhance the administration and transparency of government debt. Already, the National Assembly had begun to distinguish between the *dette flottante*, of short-term debts, and the *dette perpétuelle*, of perpetual bonds. To improve further the administration of public credit, in 1793 the Convention established the *Grand-Livre de la Dette Publique*, denominating the *dette perpétuelle* in 5 per cent *rentes*.[49] Meanwhile, tax collection, already difficult, became more so. Computing *assignats* and quantities of grain, which could be used to pay taxes in kind, became almost impossible without stable prices.[50] A sustainable fiscal system could only emerge with a stable monetary system – which itself required an effective fiscal system. Though the *assignats* may have been partly intended as an instrument of fiscal and political stability, they played a major role in the dislocation of public finance in the 1790s.

The Convention attempted to bring inflation under control, adopting proposals for more progressive taxation as it sought higher revenues to mitigate its reliance on *assignats*. Given the needs of war and the difficulties of collecting existing taxes, even moderate deputies inclined towards seeing the rich as undertaxed; progressive taxes were thus necessary to raise revenue and defuse the risk of unrest over injustices in the fiscal system. In 1793, several Girondins, then the pre-eminent faction in revolutionary politics, proposed to convert the *contribution mobilière* into a *contribution progressive*. Their proposal followed the lead of some communes and *départements* that had introduced progressive taxes for their own finances. Targeted at income rather than land, the shift towards progressive taxation reflected a further move away from physiocracy, even among its more committed adherents. In 1788, the Marquis de Condorcet, a disciple of Turgot, had argued forcefully that 'Indirect taxes must be eradicated and replaced by a single direct tax' on land.[51] By the early 1790s, having become a prominent Girondin, his position was more qualified. In 1793, the weight of the *contribution foncière* induced his reluctant support for 'an *impôt personnel*', though he emphasised the need to find a way 'to reduce the arbitrary aspect of the *impôt personnel*, and to avoid it leading to

---

[48] Spang, *Stuff and Money*, 214–18.   [49] Pinaud, 'Settlement of the Public Debt', 420–1.
[50] Spang, *Stuff and Money*, 213–14.
[51] 'Essai sur la constitution et les fonctions des assemblées provinciales', part 2, in Caritat, *Œuvres complètes de Condorcet*, XIV, 92.

an inquisition contrary to the rights of citizens'.[52] In reforming the *contribution personnelle et mobilière*, deputies hoped to address continuing disputes over its repartition, which were compounded by disagreements arising from the tax's complexity over exactly what it was supposed to tax. Favouring landed interests and the upper bourgeoisie of the provincial cities, the Girondins' proposals for progressive taxation were relatively mild. The Jacobins, though, supplanted the Girondins in June 1793, as unrest in the provinces stimulated by the burdens of wartime taxation and conscription, economic dislocation and a deteriorating military situation raised questions about their patriotism. The Jacobins' power base lay in the sans-culottes – militant patriots touting the interests of the urban poor – and, thus, they hastened the drive towards more progressive taxation through a series of forced loans and extraordinary taxes aimed at the rich.[53]

To mitigate inflation and assist the urban poor, in May 1793 the Convention, despite the economically liberal inclinations of many deputies, introduced price controls – the Maximum. Initially applied only to grain, in September the Jacobins imposed a general Maximum on a range of 'primary necessities' including soap, tobacco and salt. This provoked considerable resistance, spawning an extensive black market. Moreover, the Maximum amounted to stripping rural areas of their assets – grain – in order to subsidise urban areas. Seeking support from landed interests, the Thermidorian Convention ended the Maximum, abandoning the Jacobins' economic *dirigisme*; indeed, many influential Thermidorian politicians and publicists aspired to make the Directory into a democratic republic of citizen farmers.[54] Yet, the abolition of the Maximum, alongside a poor harvest in 1794–5, rising military expenditure and inadequate tax receipts, produced a new surge of inflation. Not only was the government pushed to issue more paper money to cover its deficit, but farmers' unwillingness to sell grain for rapidly depreciating *assignats* exacerbated the subsistence crisis. In 1795, forsaking the *assignat*, the Directory created a new paper currency, the *mandat territorial*. The latter, though, quickly collapsed into hyperinflation. Given the effects of inflation, in 1796 the government sought to stabilise public credit by pledging to pay a quarter of *rentes* in specie in the second semester of an IV. This, though, proved impossible, since specie was scarce following capital flight. Faced with

---

[52] 'Sur l'impôt personnel', in Caritat, *Œuvres complètes de Condorcet*, XX, 186; Pisanelli, *Condorcet et Adam Smith*, 102–8.
[53] Gross, 'Progressive Taxation', 109–21; Herrmann-Mascard, *Emprunt forcé*.
[54] Livesey, *Making Democracy*.

persistent difficulties in managing public credit, the government effectively resorted to default. In 1797, the *banqueroute des deux tiers* reduced the cost of interest payments by reimbursing two-thirds of *rentes* in *bons au porteur*, which were only exchangeable for *biens nationaux*. Rentiers, in other words, found their assets reduced to rapidly depreciating paper.[55] Honouring the debt had been a sacrosanct principle of 1789; with the inflation and then the two-thirds reimbursement, this ideal, like others, was compromised in the name of necessity.

Alongside introducing the *mandat*, the Directory sought to restore tax revenues, which had collapsed during the inflation. In 1795, the government required that half of taxes be paid in specie or in kind and, the following year, prohibited entirely the use of paper money to pay taxes. Meanwhile, the regime sought cuts in public expenditure to facilitate the withdrawal of paper money and reduce the need to print more.[56] To mitigate the ensuing shortages of money and the slump that resulted, in 1796 the Directory established the Caisse des comptes courants, intended to stimulate the economy by facilitating credit and issuing a limited number of short-term banknotes. Paper money was never completely abandoned and, indeed, the government continued to print limited amounts for its expenses, while various bankers also issued their own notes in a system of free banking.[57] Nevertheless, monetary problems continued, not least because of discord over the value of different coins that remained in circulation. Though the franc was introduced in 1795 as part of an attempt to create a more rational, metric measurements system, écus, liards and other *ancien régime* currencies did not simply disappear. Taxes, therefore, were assessed in francs but often paid in older currencies, which provoked disputes about the latter's validity. These problems persisted over several decades.[58]

The Directory sought to reinforce the effects of monetary stabilisation on tax revenues by reforming the fiscal bureaucracy. Historians have emphasised continuity in Revolutionary administrative history, framing it in Tocquevillian terms. The administrative apparatus of the *ancien régime* was revived and remodelled, building on pre-revolutionary reforms, as governments sought to improve fiscal administration, particularly the collection of direct taxes.[59] Thus, the receivers general re-emerged after 1795, as the hope that local *notables* could be entrusted with tax collection

[55] Crouzet, *Grande inflation*, 423, 466–71.
[56] Marion, *Histoire financière*, III, 406–8, 433–5, 480–90.
[57] Crouzet, *Grande inflation*, 475–8, 485–91; Jacoud, *Billet de banque*, 17–31, 93–127.
[58] Spang, *Stuff and Money*, 247–50, 252–70; Thuillier, *Monnaie*.   [59] Bosher, *French Finances*.

yielded to the reality of inefficiency, disorganisation and inadequate receipts. The resurrection of the receivers general presaged greater centralisation to improve tax collection, and dovetailed with the general revamp of the bureaucracy under the Directory, spurred in part by the need to organise the state more effectively for war.[60] The finance ministry itself was reconstituted in 1795, having been abolished in 1794. The new receivers general were appointed to each *département* by the central government and required to provide a deposit, which ensured their commitment to the treasury's business.[61] Likewise, in 1797, Ramel established *agences des contributions directes* in each *département*, to oversee the collection of direct taxes as the central government wished.[62] Still, despite the Directory's reforms, inefficiencies and corruption in fiscal administration remained endemic, and improvements were slow.

The need for higher revenues also pushed the Directory to raise direct taxes substantially.[63] Nevertheless, the regime, in its quest for rural support, did not wish to risk unrest by increasing the heavy burden on the peasantry. Alongside high direct taxes, many landlords had responded to the abolition of feudalism with rent increases that were the equivalent of feudal dues, and rents continued to rise following the inflation and collapse of the *assignats*.[64] Moreover, improvements to tax collection effectively increased taxes on landowners, who were forced to sell produce in order to obtain the specie to pay them.[65] The need for revenue, combined with the pain of hyperinflation and then deflation, hobbled the Directory's appeal to the landed classes. Though the Thermidorians could not entirely spare landed interests from higher direct taxes, their increases targeted mainly commerce and the rich. Encouraged by discontent over taxation, they had abolished the Jacobins' revamped *contribution personnelle et mobilière* for 1794 as too intrusive and unjust, but proponents of moderate progressive taxation revived it as a sumptuary tax in 1795. Thus, the Directory retained something of the Jacobins' programme of taxing the rich but in a restrained form as the Thermidorians sought to broaden their appeal through more centrist politics. Indeed, Ramel, the longest-lasting finance minister of the Directory, had previously been a moderate Jacobin in the Convention. Revenues, however, remained insufficient. In 1797–8, the Directory therefore opted to assess the *contribution mobilière* on the basis

---

[60] Church, *Revolution and Red Tape*, 111–44; Brown, *War, Revolution and the Bureaucratic State*.
[61] Pinaud, *Receveurs généraux*, 40–3.   [62] Marion, *Histoire financière*, IV, 13–16.
[63] Le Goff and Sutherland, 'Révolution française et l'économie', 107.
[64] Sutherland, 'Peasants, Lords and Leviathan'.   [65] Schnerb, 'Dépression économique', 31–3.

of rental values, as had been the case before 1794; simultaneously, the government converted the *contribution personnelle* into a graduated tax, raising the burden on the wealthier, in addition to retaining sumptuary taxes. The *patente*, having been abolished in 1793 due to discontent, was resurrected alongside the sumptuary tax in 1795 to help identify bona fide merchants and so prevent fraudulent business practices. The new *patente* took the form of a *droit fixe*, which varied according to the business or profession. The 10 per cent *droit proportionnel* that had comprised the original *patente* re-emerged in 1796 to be collected alongside the *droit fixe*, and, in 1798, the government reformed the tax to address concerns over its fairness and increase revenue by enlarging the number of people liable to pay it.[66] The Directory also created a new direct tax. Influenced by the example of the British window tax, the Directory in 1798 created the *contribution des portes et fenêtres*, a tax on doors and windows aimed at the wealthy – much like the sumptuary taxes retained in the *contribution personnelle et mobilière*.[67] Probably to avoid inflaming the issue of repartition, the new tax was initially proportional, but from 1802 it was repartitioned alongside the *contributions foncière* and *personnelle et mobilière*.[68] For landed and commercial interests alike, therefore, the Directory coincided with higher taxes; by the time the regime collapsed in 1799, its economic and fiscal policies had done much to alienate these highly influential constituencies.

Given the limitations of direct taxation and the treasury's continuing penury, indirect taxation received more extensive consideration under the Directory than in previous years. The most vehement opponents of indirect taxation, the urban poor, found their influence curbed as the Thermidorians dismantled the network of popular societies and section assemblies that had underwritten Jacobin rule. Still, the legislature rejected various proposals for indirect taxes under the Directory, most notably on salt which would have burdened agriculture, and refused to re-establish the tobacco monopoly. Customs duties, meanwhile, could offer little, given the war's disruptive effect on trade and the Directory's commitment to the prohibition of commerce with France's enemies introduced in 1793. More generally, indirect taxes had limited potential since the economy languished and industry and commerce suffered particularly badly, not least because of the money shortages that followed

[66] Stourm, *Finances de l'ancien régime*, I, 253–63, 282–9; Jarvis, *Politics in the Marketplace*, 214–15. For a detailed discussion of the *patente* in the 1790s, see Jarvis, *Politics in the Marketplace*, 201–29.
[67] Marion, *Histoire financière*, IV, 116–19.   [68] Stourm, *Finances de l'ancien régime*, I, 270–1.

the return to specie. Nevertheless, the government imposed duties on imported tobacco and on tobacco production in France, while raising the *timbre* and *l'enregistrement* and levying new taxes on the use of canals and travel in public coaches. Though limited, these new indirect taxes offered the government some scope to reduce the *contribution foncière* – foreshadowing the fiscal politics entrenched under Napoleon and pursued by subsequent regimes of using indirect taxes to appeal to landowners by easing the burden of direct taxes and mitigating discontent over repartition.[69]

Most importantly, for the future development of the tax system, the Directory reintroduced *l'octroi*. The tax had been abolished alongside other internal tolls in 1791, depriving municipal governments of most of their income and, by the end of the revolutionary decade, many of them faced serious financial problems. Moreover, their obligations had not diminished in line with their revenues; if anything, the chaos of the Revolution had increased them. Public buildings had been damaged or destroyed during the upheaval. French cities needed to be rebuilt. The nationalisation of the Church's property and its withdrawal from public life during the 1790s had greatly reduced a source of charity for the poor and education provision.[70] The pressure on poor relief was especially acute during the subsistence crisis of 1795. Meanwhile, schools and hospices saw their endowments collapse due to hyperinflation and the government's partial repudiation of the *rentes* on which they depended.[71] Consequently, local governments faced greatly increased burdens, which they struggled to finance through inadequate *centimes additionels*. Not only did *l'octroi* ease this problem to an extent; it also allowed propertied taxpayers, who controlled the *conseils municipaux* charged with deciding communal taxation, to reduce their own liabilities by shifting taxation towards consumers, redistributing some of the burden towards the poor. At the same time, *l'octroi* eased demands on direct taxation by the communes and thus increased potential revenue for the central government. Indeed, the constraints on *centimes additionnels* and the limitations of *l'octroi* meant that communal finances remained generally tight, even after the introduction of the new tax.[72]

[69] Balland, 'Dominique Vincent Ramel', II, 242–3, 269–88; Crouy Chanel, 'Définition de l'impôt idéal'.
[70] Jones, *Liberty and Locality*, 204–6, 216–17.
[71] Sutherland, 'Taxation, Representation and Dictatorship', 419.
[72] Woloch, *New Regime*, 145–55.

The Directory re-established *l'octroi* in Paris on 27 vendémiaire an VII (18 October 1798) to finance a reduction of the *contribution mobilière* in the city – which would suit the propertied classes to which the regime sought to appeal. Soon afterwards, on 11 frimaire an VII (1 December 1798), *conseils municipaux* were permitted to levy indirect taxes for local expenses, upon authorisation from the legislature. The reintroduction of *l'octroi* was a gradual process, partly for practical reasons, since the toll barriers at which the tax had been collected under the *ancien régime* were destroyed in the aftermath of 1789. The timing of its reintroduction, however, resulted mainly from concerns over consent. The toll barriers, run by the *fermes générales*, had made *l'octroi* synonymous with *ancien régime* corruption and venality. Hatred of *l'octroi* was so intense that, in the days before the storming of the Bastille in July 1789, the barriers surrounding Paris were burned and pillaged with popular support.[73] Neither ministers nor legislators wished to revive this antipathy and the resistance it produced. *Conseils municipaux*, too, were wary of being responsible for such a potentially unpopular tax. In Lyon, for instance, officials were markedly reluctant to reintroduce *l'octroi*, despite acute budgetary problems.[74] Similarly, authorities in Bordeaux preferred to raise extra funds for the budget of an XI (1802–3) through *centimes additionnels* rather than through an *octroi*.[75] Overcoming this caution was essential to the development of indirect taxation under Napoleon.

Conclusion

The growing idealisation of political, and thus fiscal, stability after the radicalism of the Jacobin Convention and the hyperinflation of the mid-1790s facilitated the rise of Napoleon. In 1800, Pierre-Louis Rœderer, who participated in Napoleon's coup and served him through to Waterloo, delivered a series of lectures at the Lycée républicain. His aim was to see 'if it is possible to save the science of economics from the ridicule to which it is subjected alongside the *économiste* sect and the *financier* sect'.[76] The *économistes*, essentially physiocrats, Rœderer defined as opponents of public borrowing and of all taxes except a land tax; the *financiers*, meanwhile, favoured public credit and condemned direct taxation. Rœderer defended the fiscal *œuvre* of the Constituent Assembly, of which he had been a prominent architect, as a synthesis of the ideas of the *économistes* and the

---

[73] Markovic, 'Révolution aux barrières'.   [74] Cottez, *Un fermier général*, 25–7.
[75] Rapport à l'empereur, n.d., AN, AF/IV/1076.   [76] Rœderer, *Mémoires*, 4–5.

financiers. In doing this, the lectures reflected Rœderer's ambiguous relationship with physiocracy. In 1790, he had criticised the proposed continuation of the *ancien régime* tobacco monopoly along seemingly physiocratic lines, asserting that it would 'violate property and liberty', and he restated his adherence to these rights in the first two lectures.[77] However, he rejected the physiocrats' claim that all taxes ultimately fall on land: 'taxes necessarily hit everyone.'[78] Although he had proposed the abolition of the *fermes générales* in 1790, he had been a prominent sponsor of the *droits de timbre* and, like Dupont de Nemours, did not necessarily oppose indirect taxes.[79] His lectures in 1800 reflected the decline of physiocratic influence; Turgot, he claimed, was the only *économiste* worth reading.[80] Political economy, Rœderer argued, was best redeemed by exorcising the physiocrats.

Rœderer's repudiation of previous economic thought reflected the supposedly destabilising effect of ideology on revolutionary political economy. Indeed, reconciling competing visions of what the new fiscal system should look like – the extent to which it should entail progressive or proportional, direct or indirect taxation – proved very difficult. Problems of collecting taxes and the scale of the government's obligations, not least the cost of war, exacerbated the challenge. Under these cumulative pressures, no regime of the 1790s succeeded in establishing a sustainable fiscal system. In the tumult of the revolutionary decade, political economy was transformed. Whereas physiocrats and their contemporaries regarded it as a broader sociopolitical science, at the turn of the nineteenth century politics and economics were separated.[81] At least ostensibly, therefore, the politics of taxation became less ambitious; instead of potentially re-engineering society, they became even more concerned than before with raising revenue and avoiding political instability.

---

[77] Rœderer, 12 June 1790, AP, 1st series, XVI, 196.   [78] Rœderer, *Mémoires*, 93.
[79] Margerison, 'Rœderer', 34–5, 52.   [80] Rœderer, *Mémoires*, 78.
[81] Stedman Jones, *An End to Poverty*.

CHAPTER 3

Developing a Post-Revolutionary Fiscal Politics, 1799–1814

Seizing power in 1799, Napoleon presented himself as the man of order, capable of surmounting ideological divisions and the volatility of revolutionary politics. He formed a centrist coalition, seeking the loyalty of those whose abilities would enable him to govern France effectively. Capitalising on their talents, he presided over a series of reforms that produced much of the legal and administrative architecture of nineteenth-century France. The most famous of these innovations, the *Code Napoléon*, was mainly the work of Jean-Jacques-Régis de Cambacérès, the Second Consul. Likewise, Napoleon did not determine the details of fiscal reforms; though he maintained a keen interest in them, they were left to his finance and treasury ministers.[1] The most important of these was Michel Gaudin, later Duc de Gaëte, who served as finance minister from 1799 to 1814 and during the Hundred Days, Napoleon's short-lived return to France from exile in 1815. As the man charged with raising money, Gaudin was the principal architect of tax reforms, the most important of which concerned indirect taxation. The treasury minister, initially François Barbé-Marbois and then, from 1806, Nicolas Mollien, was tasked with overseeing government expenditure. As we shall see, these men presided over changes to public credit and fiscal administration, the main purpose of which, like the development of indirect taxation, was to stabilise the public finances.

In branding himself as the saviour of France, Napoleon had an obvious interest in belittling the achievements of the Directory. Largely following his narrative, historians have generally ascribed the Consulate a pivotal role in the creation of the nineteenth-century fiscal system, in line with their tendency to emphasise the significance of the legal and administrative reforms of the Bonapartist regime.[2] As Jean Tulard has observed, most

---

[1] Branda, *Prix de la gloire*, 240–2, 300. [2] Stourm, *Finances du Consulat*; Lentz, *Grand Consulat*.

condemnations of the Directory emphasise 'the penury of the Treasury'.[3] Certainly, fiscal problems massively undercut the Directory, in addition to the continuing political dislocation that followed the end of the Terror. Hyperinflation aside, the ongoing difficulties with tax collection weakened the central government's authority and pushed the army into supporting itself by pillaging the conquered territories. Left in the role of satraps, the generals felt little allegiance to a regime that gave them nothing; nor did the men who served under them. Such disaffection in the army led directly to Napoleon's coup.

More recently, historians have begun to appreciate better the Directory's role in laying the foundation for the Consulate's achievements. Thus, for example, the *loi Jourdan* of 1798 institutionalised near-universal conscription, which the Napoleonic regime maintained and refined. Similarly, the order Napoleon championed benefited from the emergence of the police apparatus of what Howard Brown has termed a 'security state' in the Directory's final years, which eased the enforcement of tax collection.[4] Indeed, not only did the Directory make major progress in establishing the fiscal bureaucracy on which the Napoleonic state relied, it initiated the return to specie, a particularly painful process given the capital flight and hoarding of specie caused by the Revolution. Ramel wrote after Napoleon's seizure of power that, with the financial experiments of the revolutionary decade, 'we have invented nothing, but we have had a great number of experiences. It is time to take advantage of them.'[5] The Consulate did so by developing the *oeuvre* of the Directory. The latter's reintroduction of *l'octroi* in 1798 was particularly significant, though historians have generally overlooked its importance; the most recent study of Napoleonic finance, for example, does not mention it.[6] As we shall see, *l'octroi* played a crucial role in facilitating the extension of indirect taxation. As a result, the principal taxes of the nineteenth-century French fiscal system were all established by 1810.

Alone, however, indirect taxes could not stabilise the public finances, certainly not in wartime. David Bell has characterised the conflict of 1792–1815 as a 'total war', which pushed European societies to unprecedented levels of mobilisation. While only 60,000 troops fought at Marengo in 1800, 500,000 were present at Leipzig in 1813.[7]

---

[3] Tulard, *Thermidoriens*, 227.   [4] Brown, *Ending the Revolution*.
[5] 'Des Finances de la République française au commencement de l'an 8', by Ramel, n.d. [an VIII], AN, AF/IV/1081.
[6] Branda, *Prix de la gloire*.   [7] Bell, *First Total War*, 251.

Consequently, French military spending exploded, doubling between 1806 and 1813.[8] Meeting the need for men and money presented a severe challenge and, as we shall see, undermined the legitimacy of the fiscal-military system, proving fatal to Napoleon's regime.

The Politics of Indirect Taxation

The rise of indirect taxation from the late Directory onwards reflected the revival of elements of the pre-revolutionary fiscal system. Indeed, Gaudin, Barbé-Marbois and Mollien all gained administrative experience under the *ancien régime*. Of the three, Barbé-Marbois was the only one new to finance in 1799, having been a diplomat, official and then a member of the legislature under the Directory. Gaudin and Mollien, who proceeded to form an effective partnership, had become acquainted when they served in the fiscal administration of the *ancien régime*.[9] Mollien held a post in the *fermes générales* from 1775 until their abolition, and oversaw the collection of *l'enregistrement* in the Eure from 1790 to 1792. Meanwhile, Gaudin before 1789 was director of a *bureau* charged with administering taxation, and he held several posts relating to public finance until 1795, when he refused an offer to become finance minister under the Directory. His patron before 1789, Henri Lefèvre d'Ormesson, was among those who unsuccessfully attempted to reform the *ancien régime* fiscal system, which may have influenced Gaudin's attitude to fiscal reform, though his memoirs only mention d'Ormesson briefly. In any case, Gaudin's *oeuvre* amounted to a modified version of the *ancien régime* fiscal system, suiting the tendency of historians to interpret the Revolution's administrative achievements in Tocquevillian terms.

Alongside the legacy of the *ancien régime*, the British example influenced the revival of indirect taxation. Britain's success at raising money through loans and indirect taxes persistently intrigued the French. Indeed, British public finance fascinated Mollien, though he appreciated its limits as a model for France.[10] The influence of the British system over French policymakers grew in the 1790s as revolutionary hubris faltered. Though the *timbre* was partly modelled on the British stamp duty, the Comité de l'imposition, charged by the Constituent Assembly with designing the new fiscal system, dismissed the British model as no better than that of the *ancien régime*: in England, no land of liberty, tax collection 'was defiled by

---

[8] Gabillard, 'Financement des guerres napoléoniennes', 557. [9] Mollien, *Mémoires*, I, 215.
[10] Wolff, *Napoléon et l'économie*, 114–15, 118–22.

a revolting inquisition'.[11] Yet, the success of the British model became all the more striking as war finance in Britain in the 1790s appeared much more effective than in France. In the search for a relatively stable fiscal system, therefore, the British example recovered its force; as we have seen, it provided a model for the *contribution des portes et fenêtres*.

L'octroi was crucial to the rehabilitation of indirect taxes. Ostensibly, it existed to finance local government expenditure but, in reality, it had a national importance. *Conseils municipaux* took responsibility for reintroducing indirect taxes that were notoriously unpopular before 1789, facilitating the adaptation of these taxes to local circumstances to maximise consent. The risk of instability was therefore reduced. *L'octroi* continued to lend the fiscal system flexibility in subsequent decades; during the early and mid-nineteenth century, increasing amounts of the money raised by *l'octroi* seem to have been diverted towards communes' repartitioned share of direct tax.

When Napoleon took power, thirty-four towns were collecting *octrois*. Benefiting from this foundation, the Consulate quickened the process of reviving the tax.[12] The more this was delayed, the more acute the financial problems affecting local government became. While the government was undoubtedly concerned about the possibility of resistance to *l'octroi*, extending the new tax was intended to bolster Napoleon's support among the propertied classes – though perhaps with limited success since many local elites remained circumspect.[13] Moreover, the initial caution receded as *octrois* were being established seemingly without facing much resistance; these taxes weighed the heaviest on urban workers, whose organisation and political influence had not recovered since Thermidor. The *octrois* were, moreover, raising substantial revenue. By 1801, for example, Marseille was raising 800,000 francs of its 1.3 million annual budget through *l'octroi*.[14] Antoine Français de Nantes, the man with overall authority for communal budgets, noted in 1804 that 'there still exist 124 arrondissements of sub-prefectures in which there are no *octrois*. These arrondissements are in poor *départements* in the interior and in *départements* reunited to France since the Revolution.'[15] Indeed, being consumption taxes, *octrois* proved less fruitful in rural communes where commerce was less substantial. Due to this constraint on the tax, several

[11] 'Etat actuel des travaux du comité de l'imposition', 18 August 1790, AP, 1st series, XVIII, 158.
[12] Marion, *Histoire financière*, IV, 135–6, 138, 202–4.
[13] Petiteau, *Les Français et l'Empire*, 133–42.
[14] Miot, journal, 3 ventôse an IX [22 February 1801], Miot de Mélito MSS, MAE, 413PAAP/2.
[15] Français de Nantes to Bonaparte, 20 pluviôse an XII [10 February 1804], AN, AF/IV/1078.

conseils municipaux sought to levy *octrois* on certain professions rather than goods, which the government vetoed.[16] Some local officials also began looking beyond *l'octroi*, seeking to reintroduce taxes that had existed in regional or local traditions.[17] If the Revolution had engendered a wariness of *ancien régime* taxes, this was receding, particularly with regard to local government. Doubts about indirect taxes were certainly disappearing, given central and local governments' need for money and the difficulties that hindered direct taxation in the 1790s.

The arrears affecting direct taxes increased the pressure to extend indirect taxes; on 1 vendémiaire an IX (23 September 1800), for instance, 349 million livres of the direct taxes for an VIII were yet to be remitted. Seeking to eliminate these arrears, Gaudin continued the Directory's drive for more effective tax collection. Thus, tax collectors, for example, were required to provide a deposit similar to, but smaller than, those taken from receivers general to ensure their conduct.[18] Partly to ensure that taxes were paid in coins of acceptable quality, the government enacted monetary reform in 1803, stipulating that a franc would contain 5 grams of silver, 4.5 of which should be fine. For some officials, low-quality coins perpetuated the shortages of specie that followed the capital flight and hoarding prompted by the turmoil of the 1790s, since people were not pushed to disburse their hoardings. The standardisation of the franc would, the government hoped, boost confidence, facilitating lower interest rates, greater economic activity and consequently higher tax revenues; meanwhile, in reducing shortages of specie, standardisation was supposed to ease tax collection.[19] Furthermore, Gaudin had to respond to continuing complaints about the weight of direct taxes and the unfairness of repartition. The situation was so bad, wrote the prefect of the Seine-Inférieure, that in an IX (1800–1) some communes refused to pay their allocations of direct taxes.[20] Similarly, in an X (1801–2), the *conseil général* of the Allier complained that the *département* paid 'over a fifth of its income' in the *contribution foncière* – the tax officially comprising a fifth of the income from all land across France. Other *départements* likewise felt the tax was too high. Complaints also emerged about the other direct taxes. The *conseil général* of the Loire claimed that 'The repartition of the *contribution*

---

[16] Circular to the prefects, by Gaudin, 9 June 1807, Beugnot MSS, AN, 40AP/5, fol. 33.
[17] Français de Nantes to Bonaparte, 4 pluviôse an XII [25 January 1804], AN, AF/IV/1078.
[18] Marion, *Histoire financière*, IV, 178–80, 192–4, 199, 266–9, 310–11.
[19] Thuillier, *Monnaie*, 63–92, 183–7.
[20] Note, 'en ouvrant la session de l'an IX', by Beugnot, n.d. [1800–1], Beugnot MSS, AN, 40AP/3, fols. 91–2.

mobiliaire is more equal from *dép[artemen]t* to *dép[artemen]t* than from one individual to another.' The *patente*, too, faced criticism; the *conseils généraux* of the Moselle and the Nord, major industrial areas with large numbers of *patentés*, demanded its repeal. While the Moselle simply suggested replacing the *patente* with 'other taxes that would be less onerous to the people', its counterpart of the Nord was more explicit, proposing 'an indirect tax on the objects of consumption'. The Dyle, too, proposed 'a tax on consumption' in lieu of 'the *contributions personnelle, mobiliaire* and *somptuaire*'.[21] Industrialists, having faced tax increases with the revival of the *patente* under the Directory, now sought to displace the burden towards the lower classes through indirect taxation. Similarly, Gaudin noted the preference of the prefect and *conseil général* of the Gironde for 'adding to direct and *indirect* taxes'.[22] *Conseils généraux*, moreover, had a clear incentive to encourage indirect taxation and so ease the pressure on direct taxes, since *centimes additionnels* from the latter provided most of their revenues – *l'octroi* was for communes rather than for *départements*. The grievances over direct taxes were not new, and Gaudin could not afford to ignore them; to do so would risk compromising the regime's fragile support among local – often landed – elites, who dominated the *conseils généraux* and stood to gain personally from lower direct taxes. Seeking to mitigate the complaints and the resistance that beset the *contribution personnelle et mobilière*, in 1803 Paris financed its share of the tax with an increase in *l'octroi*. Within two years, Marseille and Lyon had done likewise.[23] In these cities, the sumptuary tax was now paid by regressive means.

The return of peace with the Treaties of Lunéville and Amiens in 1801–2 offered Gaudin an opportunity to pursue a wide-ranging reconfiguration of the fiscal system in favour of indirect taxes. His proposal had two strands. First, direct taxes were to be cut, partly as a peace dividend, but more importantly to facilitate a redistribution of the tax burden and relieve the hardest-pressed *départements*. The reduction was to be offset, however: 'Only a wise combination of indirect taxes can reconcile the means to secure necessary relief for taxpayers with the needs of the treasury.'[24] Indirect taxes were not simply established to finance the Napoleonic Wars. Rather, their creation reflected a reconceptualisation

[21] AN, AF/IV/1054, dossier 3.
[22] Gaudin to Bonaparte, 24 messidor an XI [13 July 1803], AN, AF/IV/1081. Emphasis in the original.
[23] Marion, *Histoire financière*, IV, 252–5.
[24] Rapport aux consuls, by Gaudin, [an IX (1800–1)], AN, AF/IV/1081.

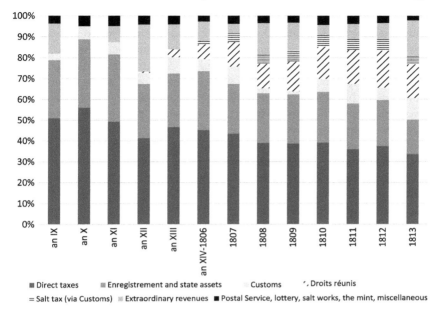

Figure 3.1   Sources of central government revenue, an IX–1813.
(Source: Branda, *Prix de la gloire*, 572–85)

of the fiscal system, in which they provided a counterbalance to excessive direct taxation, and thus improved fiscal and political stability. The Constituent Assembly, Gaudin and others believed, had produced a fiscal system too dependent on direct taxes; in abolishing most indirect taxes, the Assembly 'had, in fact, pronounced *financial ruin*'.[25] Gaudin's conception of the importance of indirect taxation lasted into the Restoration and beyond.

The resumption of war made reducing direct taxes more difficult, but the rise of indirect taxation facilitated some redistribution of the tax burden (Figure 3.1). Responding to complaints about unfair repartition and the weight of taxation, Gaudin enacted a series of reductions to direct taxes beginning in 1801, though their effects were partly offset by rising *centimes additionnels*. Hence, while the aggregate and per capita burdens of direct taxation fell noticeably from 1800–1 to 1801–2, they stabilised thereafter, when war resumed.[26] In particular, Gaudin targeted the

[25] Gaudin, *Mémoires*, I, 127. Emphasis in the original.
[26] Le Goff and Sutherland, 'Révolution française et l'économie', 107.

contribution personnelle et mobilière. In 1806, the sumptuary tax associated with the latter was abolished, because it 'gave rise to wearisome enquiries for taxpayers and aroused many complaints for a mediocre revenue'.[27] The sumptuary tax, in other words, infringed the principle that taxation should be as inconspicuous as possible, particularly among the wealthy landed elites that the regime courted. Reductions to direct taxes raised new questions about the fairness of repartition, which pushed the government towards renewed efforts to establish a cadastre. Decreed in 1802, the *cadastre par masse de culture* divided land according to boundaries defined by what it produced, without accommodating variations in land use within these units and without representing the disparities in the value of what different areas of land produced. Two vineyards of similar size in different locations would be recorded as equal, for instance, despite differences in value of their output. Such a survey had limited utility for equitably repartitioning taxes. Partly as a result, in 1807 the government initiated a more detailed survey of land values, the *cadastre parcellaire*, which became a central part of nineteenth-century taxation.[28]

The government proposed to use *l'octroi* to cover some of the revenue lost by lowering direct taxes. Indeed, the central government's reliance on *l'octroi* had increased steadily since the tax was first reintroduced. Not only was it used to reduce the burden of the *contribution personnelle et mobilière* but, from 1802, the government claimed 5 per cent of *octroi* revenues collected in towns of over 4,000 people, supposedly to finance the town garrison.[29] In 1806, this rose to 10 per cent for towns where *l'octroi* produced over 20,000 francs per year.[30] As these claims on *l'octroi* suggest, the war-induced growth of government expenditure meant that the second facet of Gaudin's proposal – of raising new revenues through indirect taxes – acquired increasing importance. The willingness of Gaudin and, as we have seen, *conseils généraux* to contemplate new indirect taxes partly reflects the success of *l'octroi* in making such taxes politically feasible.

As with the extension of *l'octroi*, the revival of national indirect taxation occurred gradually. In 1804, the government imposed a *droit d'inventaire* on the storage of alcohol, a *droit de fabrication* on the manufacture of beer, and a *droit de licence* on the distillation of spirits – though the the *droit d'inventaire* yielded little immediate revenue given the need to organise its

[27] Gaudin, *Notice historique*, 96–8, 117–18, 120–1, 152–3, 166–7, 178, 185.
[28] Santana-Acuña, 'Making of a National Cadastre', 329–63.
[29] Arrêté of 24 frimaire an XI [15 December 1802], *Lois*, XIII, 343–4.
[30] Law of 14 April 1806, titre 13, *Lois*, XV, 336.

collection.[31] In subsequent years, these were supplemented by new alcohol duties, while the government also created a salt tax in 1806. In 1810, the government awarded the Régie des droits réunis, created in 1804 to administer national indirect taxes, a monopoly on the right to grow, manufacture and sell tobacco.

Historians generally present the revival of indirect taxes as a decision taken reluctantly. Certainly, under the Consulate, Gaudin failed to convince Napoleon to approve their reintroduction. Necessity, argues Pierre Branda, forced Napoleon to gradually abandon his opposition. Indeed, without indirect taxes, the rise of government expenditure outpaced increases in revenue, especially after 1811.[32] No doubt Napoleon was concerned about the possible consequences of reintroducing indirect taxes, but his reluctance should not be exaggerated. In 1803, for example, he showed no qualms about raising *l'enregistrement*.[33] Likewise, Napoleon acquiesced in the rapid extension of *l'octroi*. Moreover, once the *droits réunis* were created, he willingly raised them – and dramatically so – as Branda himself demonstrates. Ultimately, Napoleon shared Gaudin's conception of the fiscal system, in which indirect taxes were a stabilising force; by 1806, he was expressing pride in the creation of indirect taxes that would provide the fiscal system with sufficient flexibility to ensure that the government in the future would have the resources it needed.[34] He was determined that France would never again face the deficits that had contributed to the financial turmoil of the revolutionary decade. Meanwhile, revenues from customs, the lottery and *l'enregistrement* stagnated or declined, which threw into sharper relief the success of the *droits réunis*.[35]

Administrative problems with *l'octroi* probably influenced Napoleon's reluctance to rush the creation of the *droits réunis*. In 1805, he informed Gaudin that 'The *octrois* in general deserve your undivided attention. The costs of collection are too high. Scandalous misappropriations have provoked outrage in several towns. In others, we have taxed not consumption, but primary goods and commerce and established in this way shackles that would push our industry into chaos.'[36] Such concerns did nothing to justify an extension of indirect taxation. Napoleon's observations about

[31] Gaudin, *Mémoires*, I, 215.   [32] Branda, *Prix de la gloire*, 358, 364.
[33] Bonaparte to Gaudin, 18 nivôse an XI [8 January 1803], in Bonaparte, *Correspondance*, IV, no. 7412.
[34] Lentz, *Premier Empire*, III, 402.
[35] Gaudin to Napoleon, 1 November 1806 and 17 January 1807, AN, AF/IV/1081.
[36] Napoleon to Gaudin, 5 ventôse an XIII [24 February 1805], AN, AF/IV/909, dossier 7.

the costs and method of collection and the commodities being taxed suggest that he was worried about possible resistance. But he showed no interest in repealing *l'octroi*; rather, it had to be made to work. These problems affecting *l'octroi* were all the more important because the *droits réunis* were collected through the same infrastructure, reducing the costs of tax collection for the central government. As Français de Nantes, the first *directeur général de la Régie des droits réunis*, wrote in 1805, 'If the Régie des droits réunis had to pay all the collectors of *l'octroi* that it employs, it would have to double its costs.'[37] Indeed, in 1804, when the *droits réunis* were established, there were 2,250 *octrois* in France, employing 10,217 people.[38] The *octrois* not only provided an invaluable means of acclimatising taxpayers to indirect taxes, and thus potentially reducing resistance; they also hired and trained the collectors of the *droits réunis*. Though principally a toll, *l'octroi* was usually also collected within towns – for instance at breweries – which eased the addition of the *droits réunis* to *l'octroi* collectors' task. In postponing the creation of the *droits réunis*, therefore, Napoleon probably sought to pre-empt problems in their collection, and minimise any instability that ensued from the new taxes.

The administrative relationship between *l'octroi* and the *droits réunis* can clearly be seen in Français de Nantes. Charged with overseeing communal accounts, he was intimately involved in the creation, extension and administration of *l'octroi*. From this position, he promoted additions to existing *octrois* and encouraged the creation of the *droits réunis*.[39] As André Cottez suggests, historians, most notably Marion, have underrated his importance.[40] In 1807, Gaudin, marvelling at the effectiveness of the *droits réunis* at raising money, observed that 'I have to praise the industriousness and oversight of M. Français. Funds are remitted with order and efficiency to the *caisse générale* in Paris so that the situation is presented to me every Monday: everything in the *caisse* is transferred, also weekly, to the treasury.'[41] The efficiency of this operation undoubtedly encouraged the government's willingness to increase the *droits réunis* and to embrace the administrative fusion of these taxes with *l'octroi*.

Despite the advantages of merging the collection of *l'octroi* and the *droits réunis*, the relationship between the two taxes caused problems. For most of the Napoleonic period, *conseils municipaux* oversaw the collection of

[37] Rapport au ministre des finances, by Français de Nantes, 29 pluviôse an XIII [18 February 1805], AN, AF/IV/1078.
[38] Francais de Nantes to Bonaparte, 18 pluviôse an XII [8 February 1804], AN, AF/IV/1078.
[39] AN, AF/IV/1078.   [40] Cottez, *Un fermier général*, ii.
[41] Gaudin to Napoleon, 17 January 1807, AN, AF/IV/1081.

l'octroi, and the ensuing lack of uniformity probably created difficulties in the administration of the *droits réunis*. Communes had three options for collecting *l'octroi*. They could collect it themselves (*une régie simple*), it could be farmed, or they could contract collection to a private company while retaining oversight of the accounts (*une régie intéressée*). The latter seems to have been the most popular option, since it offered 'the advantages of the farm and those of the *régie simple*.'[42] The *conseil municipal* was guaranteed an income, while overseeing the accounts and personnel of the *régie* and thus supposedly preventing the abuses for which the *fermes générales* had been notorious. In practice, though, the *régie intéressée* proved problematic. In 1799, the overseer of the Paris *octroi* criticised the corruption of its collectors; the latter, Français complained a few years later, were 'a coalition of parasitical men, long accustomed to enriching themselves at the city's expense'.[43] For similar reasons, the *régie intéressée* in Lyon also elicited criticism from the central government and, after 1807, collection was undertaken by a *régie simple*.[44] 'This mode of collection benefits the town,' the *commissaire général de police* observed in 1808, 'so that revenue has increased.'[45] In 1812, the government responded to the problems with *l'octroi* by moving control over collection from the communes to the Régie des droits réunis, which probably facilitated greater uniformity in the collection of both *l'octroi* and the *droits réunis*.[46]

The relationship between these taxes also raised the risk of resistance to alcohol duties. After 1804, alcohol was generally subjected both to *l'octroi* and the *droits réunis*, which became a cause of recurrent protest and resistance during the nineteenth century, especially because the rates of *l'octroi* varied according to locality and those brewers and vintners who lived outside town limits did not pay the tax. These disparities prompted complaints, which resurfaced in later years. In 1828, for example, Parisian brewers complained that *l'octroi* gave an advantage to their competitors outside the city limits, who only had to pay the *droit du Trésor*.[47] While the brewers disliked paying the latter, *l'octroi* aroused the greatest ire and, thus, drew their protest. In this case, *l'octroi* attracted complaints that would otherwise have been directed at the *droits réunis*. Indeed, the toll

---

[42] Cottez, *Un fermier général*, 35.
[43] Le Comte to Pons (de Verdun), 21 germinal an VII [10 April 1799], AN, AF/III/120; Français de Nantes to Bonaparte, 17 nivôse an XII [8 January 1804], AN, AF/IV/1078.
[44] Cottez, *Un fermier général*, 103–62, 221–57.
[45] *Commissaire général de police*, Lyon, to the '*conseiller d'état*', 29 June 1808, AN, F⁷ 8742.
[46] Decree of 8 February 1812, *Lois*, XVIII, 116–18.
[47] Ayliés and Martin, *Observations pour M. Julliard*.

barriers of *l'octroi* were a popular site of unrest during the nineteenth century, particularly in hard times.[48]

Many taxpayers probably saw the *droits réunis* as an extension of *l'octroi*. Faced with rising resistance to indirect taxes in 1814, the Prefect of the Gard noted that 'if their collection was divided, that of the *octrois* would experience fewer difficulties.'[49] Still, resistance to the two taxes could take different forms, given the disparities in their modes of collection. Unlike the *droits réunis*, *l'octroi* could be resisted easily and legally by keeping commodities on which the tax was levied outside the boundaries of the towns or cities. In 1814, as Strasbourg prepared itself for a siege in the face of the imminent allied invasion, those bringing provisions into the city 'were so surprised to see that we were still demanding the duties of *l'octroi* at the entrance [of the town] on primary necessities, that many turned back and others threw away their goods instead of paying the duties'.[50] Alternatively, toll barriers could be circumvented or bypassed. In Lyon, since *l'octroi* was collected during the day, butchers initially evaded the tax by bringing cattle into the city at night – though this was quickly banned. Thereafter, those butchers that continued to evade *l'octroi* tended to do so by armed smuggling.[51] Despite initial complaints when various *octrois* were introduced, and some resistance thereafter, they seem to have achieved a degree of consent. The *commissaire général de police* in Marseille noted in 1808 that, despite some dissatisfaction, the collection of *l'octroi* 'is undertaken with both rigidity and regularity, it experiences no difficulties'.[52] His counterpart in Lyon was similarly unconcerned about resistance.[53] Still, generalising about levels of resistance to any tax is dangerous, especially *l'octroi*, which differed so much between towns. Historians have emphasised that resistance to conscription varied both geographically and over time; the same is true of resistance to taxation.[54] Nevertheless, *l'octroi*, at least in cities such as Lyon where the tax was significant, achieved a working level of consent by 1810. In this respect, the rebalancing of the fiscal system towards indirect taxes had some success.

[48] Merriman, *Margins of City Life*, 73–6.   [49] Bulletin, 5 May 1814, MAE, 53MD/336, fol. 45.

[50] Prefect of the Bas-Rhin to Rœderer, 9 January 1814, Rœderer MSS, AN, 29AP/70.

[51] Cottez, *Un fermier général*, 58, 91.

[52] *Commissaire général*, Marseille, to the *conseiller d'état du 2ᵉ arrondissement de la police*, 12 July 1808, AN, F⁷ 8742.

[53] *Commissaire général de police*, Lyon, to the '*conseiller d'état*', 29 June 1808, AN, F⁷ 8742.

[54] Crépin, 'Une France plurielle', 18.

While Français was aware that taxing alcohol, a commodity already subject to *l'octroi*, risked provoking resistance, he seems not to have anticipated how much of a problem this would become. 'The need for a new tax being universally felt,' he wrote shortly before the creation of the *droits réunis*, 'alcohol presents itself as the most suitable taxable commodity.' As for possible resistance, 'No problem for beer? It is mass-produced. Most citizens are not concerned. We tax only the brewers; they have long been accustomed to being rigorously taxed in this manner. In towns, the *octrois* are at [town] entrances and in all the breweries ... the difficulty concerns the wine.' He was conscious of the difficulty of taxing the contents of wine cellars, which would be placed in 'a perpetual servitude'.[55] While brewers were familiar with alcohol duties, having paid *l'octroi* since 1798 and the *aides* before 1789, they were as used to resisting as they were to paying indirect taxes. From the government's perspective, though, the risk of discontent over alcohol duties was worth taking. As Français noted, alcohol was mass-produced, which allowed taxes on it to raise significant sums. Despite being so widely consumed, the government denied that alcohol was a 'primary necessity'. The regime deflected criticism of indirect taxes using the argument articulated in the 1790s by Dupont de Nemours, Talleyrand and others that, in taxing inessential commodities and not 'goods of primary necessity', indirect taxes became 'voluntary'.[56] Likewise, tobacco, also subjected to indirect taxes, was not a luxury for most people.[57] Most consumers probably did not see these taxes as 'voluntary'. Attitudes to these commodities, as with bread, were affected by the belief that they had to be accessible – a rise in prices risked infringing the 'moral economy' by which brewers and vintners justified resisting alcohol duties. The government, for its part, probably hoped that the higher prices caused by duties would reduce alcohol consumption, which was seen to fuel unrest.[58] Taxing alcohol, if done carefully, could potentially do more to facilitate political stability than merely raising revenue.

The variations in alcohol duties created divergent interest groups based on locality and occupation – the brewers in Paris versus those outside it, for example. Nevertheless, the Napoleonic administration aspired to create a homogeneous national fiscal system, which would supplant the plethora of different traditions that had existed under the *ancien régime*. This aim

[55] Français de Nantes to Bonaparte, 17 nivôse an XII [8 January 1804], AN, AF/IV/1078.
[56] Cretet, 24 pluviôse an XII [14 February 1804], AP, 2nd series, V, 488.
[57] Jones and Spang, 'Sans Culottes, *Sans Café, Sans Tabac*', 40, 49–56.
[58] Plack, 'Drinking and Rebelling', 616–17; Cobb, *Police and the People*, 18–20.

was particularly problematic with indirect taxes on a commodity such as alcohol, given their widely divergent customs of collection: it could be taxed at the point of manufacture, at the point of entry to a settlement, at the point of storage and at the point of sale. The requests from local government for the resurrection of taxes which had been specific to particular regions reflected, in part, a desire to raise revenue through means with which taxpayers were familiar and which suited the local economy. Such proposals were intended to minimise resistance, but they were not conducive to creating a relatively homogeneous national tax system, efficiently centralised and with its burden spread evenly across France, which had been one of the aims of 1789. Thus, Provence and Languedoc, for example, had never been subjected to 'the very innocent *droit d'inventaire*'.[59] This duty raised so much discontent that it was abolished in 1808 and replaced with the *droit d'entrée*, on the movement of alcohol.[60] Still, as Français put it optimistically, 'Opinion, even when false, as long as it is universal, should be respected or at least redressed.'[61] Despite the caution that influenced the initial reintroduction of indirect taxes, the government was prepared to countenance some resistance in order to impose its vision of effective indirect taxation. The French people would have to become accustomed to uniformity for the sake of administrative efficiency.

Historians have tended to emphasise the resistance to the *droits réunis*, but they have not yet analysed the temporal or geographical distribution of unrest. It seems likely that resistance was most acute around 1804–6, when the taxes were introduced, necessitating 'very active enforcement'.[62] This is unsurprising: new taxes are seldom popular. Resistance rose again from late 1813, encouraged by both royalist agents and the growing burden Napoleon imposed on society. In the intervening period, however, the taxes seem to have gained a greater degree of consent; while there was intermittent disorder, this was often limited and probably arose in response to frequent tax increases. Similarly, in making discontent more difficult to express legally, press censorship and the ineffectiveness of the legislature may have encouraged unrest. Still, Gaudin, Français and others sought to

---

[59] Français de Nantes to Bonaparte, 17 nivôse an XII [8 January 1804], AN, AF/IV/1078.
[60] Ultimately, the *droits réunis* on alcohol, which were retained into the Restoration, comprised six duties: the *droit de circulation* on the sale of alcohol by the producers; the *droit de détail* on retail; the *droit d'entrée*, collected in addition to *l'octroi* at town entrances; the *droit de licence* paid to permit the sale or trading of alcohol; the *droit de consommation* on the sale of spirits to consumers; and the *droit de fabrication* on the production of beer and cider.
[61] Français de Nantes to Bonaparte, 17 nivôse an XII [8 January 1804], AN, AF/IV/1078.
[62] Gaudin to Napoleon, 4 fructidor an XIII [22 August 1805], AN, AF/IV/1081.

make tax collection as efficient as possible, and this meant minimising resistance. Revenues were not consumed by the need to counter non-compliance or the administrative problems inherent in a new tax. Whatever resistance there was, it deterred neither Napoleon nor Gaudin from further increasing the *droits réunis*, despite their desire to retain taxpayers' consent.

The salt tax aroused less resistance than alcohol duties, though it was more difficult to justify politically, since salt was unquestionably a 'primary necessity'. Partly as a result, alcohol bore the heaviest indirect taxes; as Marion has observed, 'the great and most profitable innovation' of the law of 24 April 1806 was the creation of the *droit de détail* on the sale of alcohol, rather than the re-establishment of the salt tax.[63] The salt duty also elicited less discontent than the *ancien régime* gabelles. The latter were notoriously unpopular, in part because they did not apply evenly across the country, which was divided into six major regions for the management of the salt trade. The *pays francs des gabelles* paid no salt taxes, while the *pays rédimés des gabelles* were exempt from all but import duties on salt – in contrast to other regions that were subject to monopolies and import and excise taxes on salt. These iniquities produced an endless epidemic of salt smuggling, to which the *fermes générales* responded with their customary brutality. The form of the gabelle, moreover, was often antagonistic; for instance, in the area of the *sel d'impôt* in the *pays des grandes gabelles*, that is the region around Paris and Orléans, the gabelle was a monopoly which required households to purchase a set quantity of salt irrespective of their actual needs. The Napoleonic salt tax, by contrast, was collected as unobtrusively as possible at the sources of salt production by customs officials and agents of the *droits réunis*. Still, the salt tax provoked discontent, in part because of the particularist traditions that also aroused unrest over various alcohol duties. In the Vendée, for instance, the introduction of the salt duty prompted a surge of smuggling, with those involved claiming ignorance of the new tax, the area having been exempt from the pre-revolutionary gabelles.[64] Some communes, such as Salies-de-Béarn in the Basses-Pyrénées, successfully petitioned the government for relief from the tax. Having been exempt from the gabelles, the new tax threatened the town's economy, which depended heavily on a saltwater spring. Though the government refused to grant complete exemptions, the

---

[63] Marion, *Histoire financière*, IV, 301.
[64] Rapport, by the police, 17 July 1806, AD, Vendée, La Roche-sur-Yon, 4M/436; Prefect of the Vendée to Saint-Cricq, 22 February 1815, AD, Vendée, 5P/20.

commune was granted a lower salt duty which was only abolished in 1835.[65] In this respect, the government perpetuated some of the logic – and the attention to special interests – that had shaped the *ancien régime* fiscal system, albeit on a smaller scale than before 1789. Like their direct counterparts, the new indirect taxes were meant to intrude on taxpayers' lives as little as possible, since the authorities sought to minimise resistance. They had limited success with regard to alcohol duties, which were collected in ways reminiscent of the *ancien régime*, but the intention was nevertheless apparent. The use of *l'octroi* to acclimatise taxpayers to indirect taxation and the recourse to the same infrastructure to collect *droits réunis* on alcohol reflected an attempt to make the introduction of the new duties as seamless as possible. The indirect taxes that Gaudin deemed necessary to stabilise the fiscal system were to be established with minimal disruption.

The Mechanics of War Finance

Napoleon relied heavily on the occupied territories to finance his wars, perfecting the practices of the Directory, which had done more than its predecessors to systematise the exploitation of France's conquests. Whereas the eighteenth-century fiscal-military state had aimed to fund extraordinary spending by borrowing and so avoid overburdening the tax system in a process of tax smoothing, the Napoleonic state opted to pursue this process through plunder instead of debt. Historians have often asserted Napoleon's opposition to public credit, attributing it to the experience of the financial disasters of the *ancien régime* and the revolutionary decade. The reality was more nuanced. While Napoleon remained sensitive to the fragility of public credit in the aftermath of the 1790s and regarded borrowing unenthusiastically, he was not averse to it.[66] Debts, like taxes, were a necessary evil – though such a view was far from universal, and the advantages and disadvantages of government borrowing remained hotly contested.[67] To proponents of public credit, the effectiveness of British war finance demonstrated its potential. As Vital Roux, the celebrated jurist and regent of the Banque de France, wrote in 1811:

> it is by the magical power of public credit that England had obtained this political preponderance of which it has made such cruel use ... If the English government had not had the resources of loans, it would have been

[65] Hissung-Convert, 'Impôt sur le sel', 374–6.   [66] Branda, *Prix de la gloire*, 373–89.
[67] Leuchter, 'Illimitable Right', 17–19.

reduced to asking for peace, or to devouring its revenue for the following year through advances which would only have delayed by a few years the inevitable bankruptcy or perhaps a revolution in the state.

An effective system of public credit, therefore, insured against revolution in addition to lubricating the sinews of power. As 1789 had shown, however, debt could also be a polity's undoing. Under the *ancien régime*, Roux wrote, 'loans were made without planning; we only saw the disadvantages and regarded them as disastrous.'[68] At least partly influenced by such logic, the Napoleonic regime sought to preserve political stability by careful management of public credit and by borrowing cautiously, not by avoiding debt altogether.

The government created a raft of new institutions to improve public credit. The Caisse d'amortissement was established in 1799, under Mollien's direction, to expedite the redemption of government debt. Though designed to stimulate confidence in public debt, it was often raided for other purposes. The following year, the government permitted a group of bankers to create the Banque de France, which merged with the Caisse des comptes courants to realise proposals formed under the Directory to improve the availability of credit and the circulation of money. Though founded primarily for commercial purposes, the Banque quickly became crucial to the management of government debt. Not only did it provide the state with credit; within months of its foundation, it was tasked with paying *rentes* and pensions. Benefiting from steady tax remittances and the deposits of receivers general, Gaudin believed, the Banque would allow interest on government debt to be paid in specie, boosting investors' confidence.[69] Consequently, the government developed a strong interest in the survival of the Banque, which became increasingly precarious in the wake of its foundation, as its commitments depleted its reserves. By early 1803, the pressure was such that the government accorded the Banque a monopoly on the issue of paper money, increasing its capital and effectively ending the free banking system of the Directory.[70] Despite these early difficulties, the Banque eased the government's ability to fulfil its obligations to investors. Indeed, the price of *rentes* rose under Napoleon: from a low of 7 in 1799, it eventually peaked at 94.40 in 1807 before oscillating between the mid-70s and mid-80s until

---

[68] 'Mémoire sur l'état des finances et du crédit public de l'Angleterre', by V. Roux, 1 June 1811, MAE, 7MD/11, fols. 62–3.
[69] Rapport aux consuls, by Gaudin, thermidor an VIII [July–August 1800], ABF, 1069199609/5.
[70] Jacoud, *Billet de banque*, 32–55, 227–76.

1813.[71] The stability of the tax system facilitated the rise of the *rente*, allowing interest payments to be made punctually and encouraging investors to believe that the public finances were managed prudently. As Mollien noted in 1807, the price of *rentes* benefited from 'the precision in the payment of direct taxes, which meets only a few local difficulties, and the growing revenue of indirect taxes'.[72]

While the regime diligently honoured obligations to its creditors, it struggled to issue long-term debt. In part, this may have reflected the doubts about the long-term viability of the Napoleonic Empire, which were widespread among French elites. Perhaps a more serious problem was the limitation of the capital market. The violence of the 1790s had in part been directed at financiers, resulting in capital flight and the execution of several bankers and farmers general. Though Napoleon induced some émigrés to return, bankers' capital resources remained shallow, and their growth was hindered by war and the mismanagement of the public finances, both of which contributed to a series of financial crises.

The first of these resulted from a poor harvest, producing a relatively limited subsistence crisis in 1803, which was compounded by commercial difficulties arising partly from the resumption of war after the brief peace provided by the treaties of Lunéville and Amiens.[73] More severe was the crisis of 1805–6, which resulted partly from difficulties of government borrowing. With the resurrection of the receivers general, the state acquired a source of short-term credit; in an arrangement reminiscent of the *ancien régime*, tax collectors lent to the state.[74] Invariably rich, given the deposit they had to pay the government to guarantee their conduct, the receivers general were an invaluable source of capital. They often invested the tax revenues they collected and compensated for the inadequacy or absence of local banking services by taking deposits from people in the towns in which they were stationed. Given this array of funds at their disposal, many enriched themselves considerably. One, for example, was appointed receiver general in Colmar under Napoleon with a personal fortune of 50,000 francs; when he died thirty years later as receiver general in Rouen, his fortune exceeded 6 million and had previously been even greater.[75] In providing public credit, however, the receivers general faced competition from bankers. Thus, seeking to impove the availability of

[71] Latour, *Grand argentier*, 111–21.
[72] Rapport à l'empereur, by Mollien, 4 March 1807, AN, AF/IV/1083/A.
[73] Bergeron, 'Problèmes économiques', 478, 482.   [74] Thérét, 'Système fiscal'.
[75] [Barthélemy,] *Souvenirs*, 27.

short-term credit, the government facilitated the creation of a group of financiers called the *Négociants réunis*, which entirely supplanted the receivers general as government creditors in 1804. Unfortunately for the French government, the outbreak of war between Britain and Spain at the end of that year proved disastrous for the *Négociants réunis*. Only a few days before hostilities began, one of their number, the financier and speculator Gabriel-Julien Ouvrard, had been contracted by the Spanish government to transport Mexican piastres to Europe. The war delayed the fulfilment of this contract, bankrupting the *Négociants réunis* and leaving them unable to honour their obligations to the French government. Meanwhile, rising tensions between France and Austria, which culminated in war in September 1805, left financiers cautious just as the government's need for specie to finance military preparations increased. The Banque de France, under mounting pressure, lacked the reserves to provide sufficient liquidity; a series of bankruptcies ensued, while the *rente* plunged, falling to 53.70 upon the outbreak of war with Austria. The British victory over the French and Spanish fleets at Trafalgar in October added to the unease on the Bourse.[76] The government responded to the crisis by creating the Caisse de service, which held public money until disbursement and provided a reservoir of funds on which the state could draw to support the *rente*. The Caisse de service, recalled a *directeur général* of its successor in 1814, the Mouvement général des fonds, effectively made the receivers general – again – into the 'banker of the treasury'.[77]

Despite the regime's efforts to improve its financial infrastructure, problems of liquidity lasted the duration of the Empire, and contributed to another financial crisis in 1810–11. When, in 1810, the government responded to the ongoing circulation of substandard coins by attempting to demonetise them, it raisied fears in some quarters of a return to unstable paper currency, provoking a scarcity of money.[78] Indeed, some officials suggested that the scarcity would make paper money essential because of, as the prefect of the Côtes-du-Nord put it, 'the impossibility of constantly gathering a sufficient mass of specie for public service'.[79] The regime's commitment to 'hard' money constrained economic activity, reducing the tax base and making taxation more burdensome.[80] These monetary problems aggravated the economic strains imposed by the Continental

[76] Branda, *Prix de la gloire*, 259–80; Marichal, *Bankruptcy of Empire*, 154–83; Zylberberg, *Une si douce domination*, 417–43.
[77] Jourdan, 'Receveurs généraux', 571–2.   [78] Thuillier, *Monnaie*, 107–52.
[79] Prefect of the Côtes-du-Nord to Montalivet, 30 November 1810, AN, F^{Icl} 25.
[80] Thuillier, 'En Nivernais', 444–9.

Blockade, through which Napoleon used tariffs to control access to the European market, imposing heavy duties on colonial goods. The costs of these pushed several vendors into bankruptcy in late 1810, initiating this last financial crisis which was compounded by a poor harvest in 1811.[81] These persistent crises encouraged the state's economic interventionism, which the Napoleonic regime pursued while maintaining a pragmatic commitment to free enterprise. The state introduced new regulation, sought to develop the technical skills of French entrepreneurs, provided limited financial support for firms to mitigate the impact of economic turbulence and undertook public works.[82] Nevertheless, the frequent crises hindered bankers' attempts to build their resources and did little to boost confidence in the public finances, both of which constrained the government's ability to borrow. Given the fragility of the financial system reflected in these crises, maintaining the price of *rentes* required careful institutional support. The ensuing caution over loans lasted almost the entirety of the Napoleonic period.

Problems securing credit aside, Napoleon's belief that 'war must pay for war' encouraged him to finance his campaigns through plunder.[83] Hence, between 1802 and 1814, conquered territories provided 41 per cent of the French budget, easing Gaudin's programme of reducing direct taxation in France, where tax rates were generally higher than in the satellite states.[84] Following the logic of 'total war', defeated states such as Austria or Prussia paid heavy indemnities and lost large tracts of land. Thus, Napoleon reordered Europe; some territories were incorporated into France as *départements réunis*, while others were converted to satellite states. From these, the French extracted increasing amounts of money and men – perhaps a million non-Frenchmen in all.

As in the 1790s, conquered territories remained subordinate to the military, but Napoleon placed them under civilian administrations, which ultimately aimed to civilise subject peoples by importing French institutions.[85] Finance played an important role in this process. 'These countries can become French only through the efforts of the finance minister,' Napoleon wrote in 1804; meanwhile, to inculcate these territories with French customs, he wanted local notables involved in their

[81] Bergeron, *Banquiers, négociants et manufacturiers*, 288–97.
[82] Horn, *Path Not Taken*, 194–210.   [83] Branda, *Prix de la gloire*, 315.
[84] Branda, 'Guerre a-t-elle payé', 270–1; Connelly, *Satellite Kingdoms*, 341–2.
[85] Woolf, *Napoleon's Integration of Europe*, 69–74; Broers, *Napoleonic Empire in Italy*, 94–121.

administration.[86] As this suggests, the French sought to appease local sensibilities to some extent. Nevertheless, many non-French appointees, such as Giuseppe Prina and Isaac Gogel, finance ministers of the kingdoms of Italy and of the Netherlands respectively, shared French preferences for centralising and rationalising fiscal administration.[87] In eroding regional traditions, centralisation was both to civilise and to secure control of the resources Napoleon needed, much as in France itself, where he developed the centralising tendencies of the *ancien régime*.

The desire for uniformity was most clearly reflected in direct taxation. The *contribution foncière* became ubiquitous in the *départements réunis* and many satellite states, but this did not always have good results. In 1811, a year after Illyria was incorporated into France, Gaudin noted that the collection of direct taxes there was 'very behind'.[88] Still, such problems were not universal. Rœderer, prefect of the Trasimène in Italy, noted at the beginning of 1812 that the *contribution foncière* – the *département* had no *contributions personnelle et mobilière, des portes et fenêtres*, or *patente* – was being paid fully and on time.[89] Moreover, there remained scope for flexibility in the manner of collection. In April 1811, Gaudin noted that in the Netherlands 'Direct taxes, according to the customs of the country, are not yet being collected: they will be collected only in the final months of the year, and their collection seems to present no doubts.'[90] Thus, the French made some efforts to accommodate regional sensibilities, subordinating administrative uniformity to the need for resources.

Flexibility was more apparent with indirect taxes, which utilised local customs in a way that Gaudin was unwilling to do in France proper, as the French sought a balance between new taxes and existing customs that would allow them to maximise revenue. In 1804, Gaudin observed that the Piedmontese were accustomed to a government tobacco monopoly, and that this was a potential revenue source that the French could exploit.[91] Similarly, while some local indirect taxes were abolished when the *département* of the Trasimène was created in 1810, others were retained. A complete overhaul of the tax system, wrote Rœderer, 'if it

---

[86] Bonaparte to Gaudin, 22 fructidor an XII [9 September 1804], in Bonaparte, *Correspondance*, IV, no. 9196.
[87] Grab, 'Politics of Finance', 138–9; Pfeil, '*Tot redding van het vaderland*', 202–8, 249–57.
[88] Rapport à l'empereur, by Gaëte, September 1811, AN, AF/IV/1076.
[89] 'Exposé de la situation du Département du Trasimène au premier janvier 1812', by Rœderer, Rœderer MSS, AN, 29AP/16.
[90] Rapport à l'empereur, by Gaudin, April 1811, AN, AF/IV/1069, dossier 3.
[91] Gaudin to Napoleon, 8 frimaire an XIII [29 November 1804], AN, AF/IV/1069, dossier 1.

had not succeeded, would have compromised the administration of the communes, in other words of the government'. Although conscious of the need for revenue, the French were cautious in pursuing fiscal reform. As in France, the regime sought to use *l'octroi*, based on taxes that preceded the French conquest, to facilitate the growth of indirect taxation. In central Italy, however, the model did not work perfectly. The 'Roman states', Rœderer noted, lacked an effective infrastructure to collect indirect taxes.[92] In his view, the immediate establishment of *l'octroi* in every commune of the *département* was impossible; a more gradual approach was necessary. Not only was introducing indirect taxes difficult, there were also abuses in their collection.[93] Ultimately, flexibility was only a matter of convenience, and did not necessarily reduce the unpopularity of the taxes imposed. Despite limited attempts to adapt taxation to regional customs, French rule remained highly intrusive and the absence of effective representative institutions left unrest as one of the only ways to express discontent over taxation, which could force concessions from the regime.[94] In July 1809, for example, an attempt in the Kingdom of Italy to rebalance the tax burden towards rural areas with the introduction of a milling tax provoked a major revolt. Troops soon restored order and the tax was suspended, reflecting the flexibility the government was prepared to show to retain the modicum of consent required for effective taxation.[95]

The regime's willingness to adapt was most apparent in the areas outside the Empire's heartland of northern France, the Low Countries and western Germany.[96] In Corsica, regarded as essentially foreign since its incorporation into France in 1769, the government proved particularly versatile. In 1800, following protracted unrest, Napoleon sent André-François Miot to the island as *administrateur général*, where he remained until 1802. Miot's mission was to quell disorder and create an effective administration, a large part of which concerned finance; he was to review all taxes, especially indirect ones, which in 1800 meant principally *l'enregistrement*. 'Almost all the revenue from indirect taxes is absorbed by the costs of collection', Napoleon informed him. 'You will reduce these by treating Corsica as a

[92] 'Exposé . . . au premier janvier 1812', Rœderer MSS, AN, 29AP/16.
[93] 'Exposé de la situation du Département du Trasimène au 1er octobre 1812', by Rœderer, Rœderer MSS, AN, 29AP/16.
[94] Pagano, *Enti locali e stato*, 205.
[95] Grab, 'State Power, Brigandage and Rural Resistance', 55–62.
[96] On this conception of an 'inner' and 'outer' Empire, see Broers, 'Napoleon, Charlemagne and Lotharingia'.

single *département* and by reducing the number of employees.'[97] While Miot made several alterations to direct taxes, abolishing the *contribution des portes et fenêtres*, his main act was to reduce *l'enregistrement* by granting exemptions, for instance for marriage licences.[98] He also sought to reduce smuggling – to which Corsica's coastline was well suited – by lowering customs duties on trade with France. The introduction of the *droits réunis* in 1804 provoked fresh resistance to indirect taxation. As a result, in 1811, the *droits réunis* were abolished in Corsica, and replaced with a 30,000-franc augmentation to the *contribution personnelle et mobilière*.[99] Customs, *l'enregistrement* and the *timbre* aside, *l'octroi* was thereafter the only indirect tax collected on the island. In Corsica, the Napoleonic state adapted to what would work; the resistance aroused by high indirect taxes risked compromising the consent essential to effective taxation. The outcome was a distinct Corsican fiscal system that lasted into the twentieth century.

Over customs duties, too, the regime adapted to circumstances. The Continental Blockade, at least ostensibly designed to undermine the British economy by excluding British trade from Europe, was most stringently applied in 1808–9; thereafter, partly owing to difficulties of enforcement, licences to trade were granted in increasing numbers as the government succumbed to the need for revenue. While relaxing the blockade increased customs revenue, whether European commerce benefited is less clear.[100] Like their penchant for centralisation in the conquered territories, the blockade reflected the French desire for control over Europe.[101] It was, in other words, part of a process of European integration, one aim of which was to sustain the French Empire by providing revenue.

Despite the willingness to adapt the fiscal system for the sake of greater stability or higher revenues, the French saw no need to modify their system of indirect taxes in many *départements réunis*. Along the Hanseatic coast, for instance, the *droits réunis* were established apparently without significant problems. Their collection, wrote two officials sent to inspect the region in 1811, was effective and reflected French 'moderation [and]

---

[97] Bonaparte to Miot, 24 frimaire an IX [15 December 1800], in Bonaparte, *Correspondance*, III, no. 5837.
[98] Gaudin, *Régime fiscal de la Corse*, 13–19.
[99] Napoleon to Gaëte, 13 March 1811, AN, AF/IV/909, dossier 7; Orsini, *Arrêtés Miot*, 150–4, 158.
[100] Clinquart, *Administration... sous le Consulat et l'Empire*, 142–3; Marzagalli, *Boulevards de la fraude*, 207–20.
[101] Schroeder, *Transformation of European Politics*, 385. Historians have distinguished between the 'Continental Blockade', designed to strangle British trade, and the 'Continental System', intended to facilitate French economic domination of Europe.

benevolence; every day we improve revenue and win the trust of the population'. Direct taxes, meanwhile, were 'collected without difficulty'.[102] The seeming absence of major problems does not mean that there were neither complaints nor resistance, particularly since the economy slumped after 1811 while taxes, conscription and requisitions remained heavy.[103] Encouraged by the Belgian and Dutch reputation for riches, the French also imposed a heavy burden on the Low Countries, which was a recurrent cause of discontent throughout the period of French rule.[104] Between 1806 and 1810, the Dutch public debt rose from 1,163 million florins to 1,475 million, largely because of military expenditure.[105] In the Rhineland, too, the French imposed high direct and indirect taxes, though they allowed older administrative practices to survive in an attempt to conciliate local elites.[106] Such concessions were criticised for facilitating corruption but, as with modifications to the fiscal system, they were designed to extract as much as possible without incurring unnecessary resistance.[107] Despite the discourse of 'reunification' surrounding *départements réunis* such as these, the tax system did little to make them 'French' not least because it diverged, often quite considerably, from practices in France.

Whatever care French administrators took to impose taxation that might attain consent from conquered peoples was often negated by the needs of the military. Extraordinary taxes and requisitions were widespread, particularly in regions most affected by conflict, which required a large military presence. The billeting of troops was inherently intrusive and did much to arouse discontent, as did conscription. The Napoleonic regime further exacerbated its unpopularity with its growing demands as the costs of war escalated. Even before the invasion of Russia in 1812, the burden on many occupied territories verged on unsustainable; in April that year, for example, the viceroy of Italy asked Napoleon to reduce the kingdom's obligations.[108] Defeat in Russia overstretched the Napoleonic fiscal-military system, both by stimulating unrest – the Empire no longer appeared invulnerable – and by increasing Napoleon's need for men and money. New classes of conscripts were mobilised, taxes were raised and, in 1813, *biens communaux* were nationalised.[109] With these impositions,

---

[102] Rapport à l'empereur, by Chaban and Faure, 23 November 1811, AN, AF/IV/1069, dossier 3.
[103] Aaslestad, 'Paying for War', 654–60.
[104] Oliveira, *Routes de l'argent*, 335–94; Schama, *Patriots and Liberators*.
[105] Woolf, *Napoleon's Integration of Europe*, 173.   [106] Rowe, *Reich to State*, 99–105.
[107] Graumann, *Französische Verwaltung am Niederrhein*, 110–25.
[108] Grab, 'Politics of Finance', 140.   [109] Marion, *Histoire financière*, IV, 365–6.

resistance in the conquered territories reached new heights, and presaged the disintegration of the Napoleonic order.

The Implosion of the Napoleonic State

The overstretch of the Napoleonic fiscal-military system intensified with the allied invasion of Germany in 1813, which hindered exploitation of its resources. In the Hanseatic *départements*, which had become a theatre of war, Gaudin noted in May 1813 that revenue from the *droits réunis* was falling, though collection was making satisfactory progress in the rest of the Empire.[110] On 1 October, Mollien wrote that the budget 'was clearly more upset this year than in any other, because there had been, relative to previous years, a greater rise in spending and more delays in revenues'.[111] The conquered territories, in other words, were no longer providing the means to balance the budget. To cover the shortfall, either taxes would have to rise sharply or the government would have to borrow.

Given the pressure on taxation, in October Ouvrard, whose ambitions were undimmed by the debacle of the *Négociants réunis* and his subsequently turbulent relations with Napoleon, submitted the first of two memoranda proposing to use the *biens nationaux* as collateral to persuade taxpayers to subscribe to government *rentes* in proportion to their *contribution foncière*.[112] Napoleon, Mollien and Gaudin were presumably unconvinced. Aside from difficulties in the scheme's practicability, they also probably found it too reminiscent of the *assignats*. Moreover, they had already rejected the possibility of a loan, Mollien having written at the beginning of October that 'A loan constituted in *rentes* would not succeed.' The *rente*, indeed, was falling (Figure 3.2). After rejecting other options, such as further sales of *biens communaux*, as unfeasible, he had concluded that 'the only remaining resource is taxation.'[113] Mollien did not make this recommendation lightly – he was aware that taxes could not be raised much higher.

By late 1813, perhaps because of growing war-weariness, French taxpayers were becoming increasingly disillusioned with the fiscal system. In October, the mayor of Maubeuge, in the Nord, noted the widespread 'tendency to oppose the establishment of taxes, although collection has

[110] Gaëte to Napoleon, 17 May 1813, AN, AF/IV/1081.
[111] Rapport à l'empereur, by Mollien, 1 October 1813, AN, AF/IV/1083/B.
[112] Ouvrard to Rovigo, 16 October and 11 November 1813, AN, AF/IV/1081.
[113] Rapport à l'empereur, by Mollien, 1 October 1813, AN, AF/IV/1083/B.

Figure 3.2   Weekly closing prices of 5 per cent *rentes*, as quoted in Paris,
January 1812–April 1814.
(Source: *Le Moniteur universel*)

never faced difficulties'.[114] Mollien, conscious that the government was
reaching the limits of consent, informed Napoleon that the only indirect
tax which could be raised was that on salt.[115] Nearly three weeks later, in
mid-October, Napoleon was defeated at Leipzig, which destroyed the
French Empire in Germany and exacerbated his need for money.
Judging that direct taxes had previously been 'greatly reduced', he therefore rejected Mollien's caution.[116] In November, he raised both direct and
indirect taxes in France, with further increases in January 1814.[117]
Resistance to taxation proliferated, encouraged by Bourbon agents promising lower taxes. As the prefect of the Manche observed following the
Restoration in 1814, taxation 'suffers from the imprudence, which a few
zealous friends of the new order of things showed, in circulating emphat-
ically that indirect taxes would be abolished and the *contribution foncière*
would be sharply reduced'.[118] Indeed, resistance was not limited to

---

[114] Bulletin, 12 October 1813, in Gotteri, *Police secrète*, VII, 299.
[115] Rapport à l'empereur, by Mollien, 1 October 1813, AN, AF/IV/1083/B.
[116] Napoleon to Cambacérès, 25 October 1813, in Bonaparte, *Correspondance*, XIV, no. 36853.
[117] Branda, *Prix de la gloire*, 367–72.
[118] Prefect of the Manche to Beugnot, 2 May 1814, AN, F⁷ 7029.

indirect taxes, despite the attention that historians have given them. Napoleon's increase of direct taxes provoked discontent, as did requisitions. The prefect of the Gers, for instance, noted the 'general discontent' caused by 'the system of prolonged requisitions' for the army in Spain. Unrest over taxation was not universal, however. In the Tarn, for example, both requisitions and surtaxes were met with 'the same submission. All the inhabitants recognise that these sacrifices are necessary.'[119] Such comments perhaps exaggerate the degree of acquiescence, not least given the pressure on officials to ensure that the state appeared effective. Still, nationalism and the needs of war offered the means of retaining some taxpayers' consent. Furthermore, not wishing to provoke unrest and anticipating the imminent end of the regime, several officials in 1813–14 proved noticeably lethargic in implementing Napoleon's tax increases.[120] Consequently, resistance to taxation and the pressure for reducing or abolishing taxes peaked after the return of peace in 1814, particularly given the Bourbons' alleged promises of tax cuts.

The growing demands of conscription and the ensuing rise in desertion further stimulated resistance to taxation. Since the 1790s, conscription had provoked fierce opposition, particularly in the far north and parts of the Midi.[121] As the demand for soldiers increased after 1812, resistance became more intense.[122] Many deserters turned to banditry, and proceeded to undermine the fiscal system, for instance by smuggling.[123] In November 1813, troops mutinied in Hazebrouck, deserting and spurring others to do likewise. These bands of deserters roamed northern France, inciting refusals to pay taxes.[124] In the west, too, around Nantes, groups of armed men committed themselves to resisting taxation.[125] Most of the unrest over taxation in 1813–14 surfaced in areas resistant to conscription – the latter, indeed, was more pronounced than discontent over taxation, not least because of widespread war-weariness. The effects of the slump of 1810–11 probably further intensified resistance to taxation and conscription. Unemployment and destitution increased and food prices rose, contributing to mounting unrest.[126] The economy, therefore, was in no condition to meet Napoleon's rising demands after 1812, and the failure to alleviate this malaise contributed to the erosion of the

---

[119] Bulletins, 13 November and 2 December 1813, in Gotteri, *Police secrète*, VII, 384, 449, 509.
[120] Lentz, *Premier Empire*, II, 501.   [121] Lignereux, *France rébellionnaire*, 24–31.
[122] Crépin, 'Une France plurielle', 16–19.   [123] Broers, *Napoleon's Other War*, 57.
[124] Boudon, *Ordre et désordre*, 248.
[125] Bulletin, 30 and 31 January 1814, in Gotteri, *Police secrète*, VII, 655.
[126] Boudon, *Ordre et désordre*, 207–18.

state's legitimacy. The regime was ready to collapse when the allies invaded France in January 1814.

Conclusion

The Napoleonic fiscal-military state proved no more sustainable than its predecessors of the revolutionary decade or the *ancien régime*. The ever-growing demands of 'total war' forced the fiscal-military system to become increasingly extractive, weakening its legitimacy and destabilising the political order. Still, the Napoleonic administration made significant progress in laying the foundations for a durable fiscal system, developing the *oeuvre* of the Directory to extend indirect taxation, continue the professionalisation of the fiscal bureaucracy and entrench monetary institutions such as the Banque de France. In some respects, the new fiscal system effectively revived that of the *ancien régime*, for instance in the use of receivers general and in the reliance on alcohol duties, but there were also important differences. The post-revolutionary state was considerably more centralised, certainly with respect to finance. This greater centralisation had clear limits; the centre relied heavily on cooperation from *notables* and local and regional officials, who retained the power to repartition taxes alongside an ability to influence the degree of consent to taxation.[127] Still, the patchwork of *ancien régime* taxes and financial institutions was replaced by a national fiscal system in which the same rules and institutions applied across the whole country. Both in France and elsewhere in Napoleonic Europe, such centralisation facilitated higher per capita taxation during the nineteenth century than before.[128] One of the major advantages of the eighteenth-century British fiscal-military state was the British government's ability to levy indirect taxes on the rest of the country in London, which served as the main port of entry for goods into Britain.[129] Lacking a comparable concentration of economic activity in one place, obtaining a similar level of taxation in France required deeper extraction across a wider geographical area, a process made easier for the central government if it could more effectively impose its will over the entire country. Likewise, greater centralisation allowed for more extensive conscription, as central authorities could more easily overcome obstruction from local officials influenced by their constituents' aversion to the draft.

[127] On the political influence of local *notables* see, for example, Thoral, *L'Émergence du pouvoir local*.
[128] Dincecco, 'Fiscal Centralization'.   [129] Hoppit, *Britain's Political Economies*, 277–305.

Thus, Napoleon could raise troops and taxes on a greater scale than had been necessary for the wars of the eighteenth century.

Despite these achievements, the Napoleonic fiscal-military state made only limited progress in developing public credit. Indeed, the inability to embark on sustainable, large-scale borrowing undermined the French fiscal-military states of the *ancien régime*, the revolutionary decade and Napoleon. The *ancien régime*'s mismanagement of its debt led to the Revolution of 1789, while the absence of effective public credit thereafter pushed the governments of the 1790s to monetise their deficits, a practice undermined by hyperinflation. Though excessive debt did not cause the financial problems of the Empire, its failure to undertake large-scale borrowing culminated in ever-heavier taxation and requisitioning, eroding the state's legitimacy. Only during the Hundred Days in 1815 did Napoleon attempt large-scale borrowing in *rentes*. In a manner reminiscent of Ouvrard's 1813 proposal, he sought to float 150 million francs of *rentes* and to acquire 200 million francs in a forced loan from taxpayers.[130] Napoleon was driven to these last resorts by desperation, all other means having been exhausted. The Bourse was falling, but Napoleon badly needed money and tax receipts were almost non-existent, given the political chaos that his return to France produced. In these circumstances, the loans had little success. Instead, the development of public credit was principally an achievement of the Restoration, which established the means for the state to borrow large amounts relatively cheaply, and sustain the interest payments without needing to default or provoke a political crisis. Certainly, this achievement benefited considerably from institutions of Napoleonic vintage such as the Banque de France. Still, despite historians' emphasis on Napoleon's accomplishments in state-building, only after 1815 did France acquire a sustainable fiscal-military system.

---

[130] Branda, *Prix de la gloire*, 494; rapport à la commission du Gouvernement, by Mollien, 28 June 1815, MAE, 53MD/346, fols. 182–4.

CHAPTER 4

Recasting the Fiscal-Military System, 1814–1821

The Napoleonic state's legitimacy relied heavily on its claim to effectiveness and its ability to guarantee public order. By 1814, though, it was politically bankrupt, as resistance to taxation and conscription grew. Napoleon's failure to provide stability undermined his support among French elites, and facilitated the Bourbon Restoration. The conditions on which the Bourbons resumed the throne were designed to minimise upheaval. There was to be no redistribution of *biens nationaux*, and the public debt contracted under previous regimes was to be respected. Still, Louis XVIII wanted to ascend the throne on his own terms. The new constitutional Charter was therefore presented as a gift from the king, making it part of a wider attempt to 'renew the chain of time' and thus legitimise the Bourbon regime. For the liberals who engineered the Restoration, these were concessions of form, not of substance, and Louis's acquiescence reflected his own commitment to stability.

Historians have recently given the Restoration renewed attention, emphasising the innovativeness of the regime's political culture.[1] In doing so, they have largely overlooked finance, though the reshaping of the fiscal-military state was central to the development of post-Napoleonic politics.[2] With the Charter, representative government re-emerged, justified principally by the need for legislative consent to taxation. As François Guizot, a prominent intellectual and doctrinaire, put it, 'the Chambers are charged only with providing in the name of the nation the means to undertake its affairs and to ensure that these resources are used in its interest.'[3] Among the leading theorists of constitutional monarchy, the doctrinaires were a political group that sought to reconcile a strong monarchical executive

---

[1] Scholz, *Die imaginierte Restauration*; Kroen, *Politics and Theater*.
[2] Not all recent work on the Restoration has disregarded finance: e.g. Haynes, *Our Friends the Enemies*.
[3] 'Faut-il payer les députés des départemens au corps législatif?', by Guizot, 25 May 1814, Guizot MSS, AN, 42AP/28.

with liberty. The need to ensure that government spending reflected the public interest was used to extend the Chambers' authority over other matters of government policy, such as public works and military service. Liberals justified the Chambers' power over the latter by postulating an equivalence between taxation and conscription, famously labelled 'the tax of blood'. Deputies were elected by those who paid, annually, 300 francs of direct tax, which enfranchised around 110,000 of a population of 30 million. The Chambers were, therefore, dominated by a small elite, drawn principally from the landed classes – precisely the group that had the most to gain from continuing the shift towards indirect taxation instigated from the Directory onwards. Indeed, as Mounir Baccouche has observed, the Restoration proved decisive in this respect.[4] Accounting for inflation, revenue from indirect taxation rose by 91.9 per cent between 1815 and 1829. In 1816, the finance minister, Comte Louis-Emmanuel Corvetto, described direct taxes as 'the principal resource of the State'.[5] In 1830, by contrast, Baron Joseph-Dominique Louis, a serial finance minister who held the post during the First Restoration in 1814, at the beginning of the Second in 1815 and again in 1830, argued that 'all states have two elements of revenue: direct taxes and indirect taxes. One is a resource for wartime, the other is a resource for peacetime. Landed property must respond in wartime to all the repeated appeals of government; but, to respond, it must be managed during peacetime, with the greater part of the public expenses weighing on indirect taxes.'[6] Thus, discourse about public finance reflected the shift towards indirect taxation, in line with the ascendancy of the landed classes.

Despite dominating politics, these elites had to accommodate something of the broader currents of public opinion. Public opinion was a major concern for the government, particularly given the political upheavals of the previous quarter-century. The *ancien régime*, though similarly concerned with shaping public opinion, had struggled to manage the development of the public sphere in the eighteenth century; the proliferation of subversive discourses played a central role in weakening the monarchy before 1789. After 1814, the Restoration parliamentary system stimulated the dissemination of information, producing a public that could make more informed judgements. Consequently, the new

---

[4] Baccouche, 'Déterminants sociaux et politique', 340.
[5] 'Extrait du compte du produit brut des impôts pour l'année 1816', by Corvetto, in Audiffret, *Système financier*, 1st ed., II, 3.
[6] Louis, 6 October 1830, AP, 2nd series, LXIV, 81.

regime pursued the more detailed and systematic study of public opinion.[7] Government became more 'scientific', as opinion was to be managed and accommodated in order to unify society and preserve stability. This concern for public opinion played a central role in the politics of government finance, given the importance of maintaining consent to taxation and the increasing public availability of information about state finances. The ensuing effectiveness of tax collection had direct ramifications for public credit, tax revenues being necessary to honour government debt. Moreover, with reforms to financial institutions such as the Caisse d'amortissement, the government sought in part to convince financiers and the public of its commitment to fiscal prudence, reassuring investors; in this respect, too, cultivating public opinion could benefit public credit. The latter was to prove pivotal to Restoration government finance.

In conjunction with the quest for stability and the biases of the Restoration political system, the peace settlement of 1814–15 and the new international order did much to shape the overhaul of the fiscal-military system. The peace treaty that followed Napoleon's first abdication in 1814 had been relatively lenient. France was reduced to its borders of 1792 and required to compensate private interests in allied lands for damages, for a sum finally set at 320.8 million francs in 1818. By contrast, after Napoleon's Hundred Days in 1815, which ended in defeat at Waterloo and a second allied invasion of France, the allies imposed harsher terms. In addition to compensating private interests, France had to pay 700 million francs of reparations over five years – around 10 per cent of GDP in 1815 – and finance an allied army of occupation of 150,000 troops, expected to cost around 150 million francs annually, for an equal period. In the meantime, France had to give the allies 7 million francs of *rentes*, worth a nominal 140 million francs, which could be sold to cover non-payment.[8] Besides ensuring the payment of reparations, the army of occupation was supposed to guarantee a modicum of political stability in France and, hence, security for Europe. Given the humiliating presence of allied troops, a major aim of French diplomacy after 1815 was to secure their early departure from France by convincing the allies that the army had the destabilising effect of reinforcing the regime's image as one imposed by foreigners.

The payment of reparations was essential to securing the evacuation of the allied troops, creating pressure on the French government to find the

---

[7] Karila-Cohen, *État des esprits*.
[8] Nicoll, *Comment la France*, 13–14, 129–34, 189; Toutain, 'Produit intérieur brut'.

necessary funds quickly. While the government pursued cuts to public expenditure, these were on too small a scale to meet the obligations that arose from the treaty of 1815. Still, reducing the state held appeal across the political spectrum. Liberals disliked the authoritarian, overbearing Napoleonic state, while ultra-royalists favoured decentralisation to restore the power of great landowners.[9] Although the bureaucracy underwent some reductions – such as when the finance and treasury ministries were merged in 1814 – ministers had no desire to dismantle the Napoleonic state. A large bureaucracy provided an invaluable source of patronage, while centralisation permitted the government greater influence over local politics, both of which were useful for managing elections. Reducing the costs of servicing the public debt by converting it to securities bearing a lower rate of interest was also a non-starter. In 1815, the debt-to-GDP ratio was slightly under 20 per cent, and the *rente* was well below par, fluctuating between the high 50s and low 60s following Louis XVIII's return to France in 1815.[10] Instead, to resolve the reparations problem, the government developed a system of large-scale long-term public borrowing. Public credit thus became a means of easing political stability in France, developing into a central pillar for both the post-Napoleonic fiscal-military system and the nineteenth-century French state more generally.

The Fiscal Crisis of the Early Restoration

The re-establishment of effective tax collection was a priority during the early Restoration, given the growth of resistance from 1813 onwards. The *girouettes*, men who transferred their allegiance from one regime to the next, ensured that this stabilisation of the tax system occured in accordance with the fiscal politics developed from the Directory onwards. Indeed, many former Napoleonic officials held a wide range of government positions during the Restoration, and they exercised a pronounced influence over finance.[11] Budget commissions in the Chamber of Deputies were often dominated by *girouettes* who tended to be better orators than returning émigrés and, unlike many of the latter, sufficiently understood how the fiscal system worked. The banker Jacques Laffitte, custodian of Napoleon's fortune from 1815, was provisional governor of the Banque de France from 1814 until 1820 and was a highly influential deputy in the

---

[9] Tort, *Droite*, 302–6; Thadden, *Restauration und Napoleonisches Erbe*; Craiutu, *Liberalism under Siege*, 162–72.
[10] Greenfield, 'Financing a New Order', 377.   [11] Kieswetter, 'Imperial Restoration'.

Chamber. As the financier James de Rothschild observed, 'owing to his gifts and fine oratory, Laffitte is here regarded as a god.'[12] *Girouettes* also dominated the finance ministry. Jean Berenger, who succeeded Français de Nantes in 1814 as *directeur général des contributions indirectes*, had served the Napoleonic administration, as had Comte Pierre de Saint-Cricq, who became *directeur général des douanes*.[13] Baron Louis had entered politics in the 1780s as a protégé of Talleyrand, who served as Napoleon's foreign minister until 1807 and was one of the chief architects of the Restoration. In 1787, Louis had assisted Calonne in drafting his tax programme for the Assembly of Notables, before later entering the Napoleonic bureaucracy, ultimately becoming an agent of the treasury.[14] His successor as finance minister in 1815, Corvetto, was a Genoese lawyer who had been director of the Bank of St George from 1804 to 1805, when he had entered Napoleon's service, joining the Conseil d'état in 1806 and serving as a senator from 1809. Comte Antoine Roy, first appointed finance minister in 1818, was a lawyer turned landowner and industrialist who began his political career with election to the Chambre des représentants, the legislative chamber Napoleon established during the Hundred Days. Roy's misstep was excused as political naivety and thus he survived the White Terror, the purge of Bonapartists and republicans during the Second Restoration, to become a regular member of the budget commission in the Chamber of Deputies.[15] All these men knew each other well; Louis recommended Corvetto and later Roy to the king for the post of finance minister.[16] Moreover, Gaëte and Mollien were well placed to defend their fiscal legacy during the Restoration. Although neither held ministerial office again, Mollien was twice offered the post of finance minister.[17] He refused these offers, but oversaw the Caisse d'amortissement from 1819 to 1825. Gaëte, meanwhile, served as a deputy until 1820, when he became governor of the Banque de France. The *girouettes*, therefore, were well placed to ensure continuity in the fiscal system between the Empire and Restoration.

The continuity was evident in the finance ministry's commitment to indirect taxation. As one official put it in 1814, 'Indirect taxes are

[12] James de Rothschild to Nathan Rothschild, 21 July 1817, RAL, T27/291.
[13] Bruguière, *Première Restauration*, 44; Clinquart, *Administration ... sous le Consulat et l'Empire*, 235–9.
[14] Guéna, *Baron Louis*.   [15] Bernot, *Comte Roy*.   [16] Pinaud, 'Ministres des Finances', 315.
[17] Mollien, *Mémoires*, IV, 217; Molé to Richelieu, 2 November 1818, Richelieu MSS, BIS, MSRIC 78, fol. 11; Villèle, *Mémoires*, V, 290–1.

unquestionably the most just.'[18] The ministry, therefore, was disinclined to yield to the pressures for abolition that arose alongside the growth in resistance to taxation. Many officials saw resistance to the *droits réunis* as arising from false promises and rumours of abolition, given the Bourbons returned to France in 1814 associated with the mantra 'no more conscription, no more *droits réunis*'.[19] Invading allied troops exacerbated the problem, interrupting collection and sometimes even unilaterally proclaiming abolition; the Austrians, for instance, scrapped the *droits réunis* in the Côte d'Or.[20] Such actions undermined the French authorities and fuelled rumours of abolition. The government's first response to the unrest, on 17 April 1814, was to reduce direct taxes by a third, pending the approval of a new budget. Although the *droits réunis* faced more intense resistance than direct taxes, not until 27 April did the government authorise their continued collection, while amending 'all the most infuriating aspects' of these taxes. The increase of 1813 was repealed and some of the alcohol duties were reduced.[21] Nevertheless, these changes were limited. The mode of collection was unaffected, though this was where, according to one observer, 'all the difficulties' with these taxes lay.[22] Indeed, many taxpayers found tax collectors' visits to establishments holding or producing alcohol to be particularly intrusive, confrontational and humiliating.[23]

The limited concessions of 27 April attracted criticism from those officials who saw the abolition of the *droits réunis* as the best way to restore order. One official in the Vosges and the Meurthe wrote that the 'single obstacle' preventing the 're-establishment of complete confidence' in the king's government was 'fear of the return of the *droits réunis* . . . The decree of 27 April has done a great harm.'[24] The finance ministry, however, saw little alternative. It had attempted to mitigate resistance by reducing the duty, but the abolition of indirect taxes was unthinkable. A finance ministry commission concluded that 'we could not completely destroy a part of the tax system without risking the overthrow of the whole and expunging resources which are indispensable.'[25] Since indirect taxes were necessary for fiscal equilibrium, abolishing the *droits réunis* risked a return

---

[18] 'Mémoire sur les droits réunis ou contributions indirectes', 17 April 1814, AN AF/V/4.
[19] Ploux, 'Rumeurs et expériences collectives'.
[20] Prefect of the Côte d'Or to Montesquiou, 24 May 1814, AN, F⁷ 7030.
[21] Decree of 27 April 1814, *Lois*, XIX, 21–2.
[22] 'Mémoire sur les droits réunis ou contributions indirectes', 17 April 1814, AN, AF/V/4.
[23] Bogani, 'À bas les rats! À bas les contributions!', 136–8.
[24] *Commissaire extraordinaire du roi, 4ᵉ division militaire*, to Montesquiou, 10 May 1814, AN, F⁷ 7027.
[25] Rapport à Monsieur, by Louis, 27 April 1814, AN, AF/V/1.

to the chaos of the 1790s, which the ministry was determined to avoid. Moreover, given the connection between the *droits réunis* and *l'octroi*, the latter also faced resistance in 1814. The prefect of the Haute-Vienne, for example, noted that people refused to pay *l'octroi* and the *droits réunis* in Limoges. Here was another reason for the government to retain the *droits réunis*, since abolition could create further problems with *l'octroi*; as the prefect observed, the resistance 'deprived' communal government of 'its principal means'.[26]

Baron Louis persuaded the Chambers to retain the *droits réunis*, although, in the hope of assuaging unrest, the duties were further reduced.[27] Meanwhile, wrote the justice minister, the *droits réunis* were 'abolished down to their name', since the Régie des droits réunis was subsumed by the new Direction générale des contributions indirectes.[28] Undertaken as part of the administrative rationalisation that accompanied the Restoration, this rebranding, like other changes to the *droits réunis*, did little to alleviate the causes of unrest. Furthermore, despite the modifications of 1814, indirect taxes were projected to increase in 1815 and were raised sharply in 1818 and 1819.[29] Given the reparations and the army of occupation imposed after the Hundred Days, indirect taxes were essential. As Prosper de Barante, Berenger's successor and another *girouette*, stated in 1815, 'far from reducing the rate of indirect taxes, we have had to find all taxable material.'[30]

Given the importance of indirect taxes, the finance ministry pushed a hard line in dealing with resistance. Adherence, Louis wrote in July 1814, 'is indispensable. Only when it is obtained can the severity cease.'[31] This policy seems to have been effective. The justice minister was 'certain' that the arrest of offenders 'has strongly contributed to the re-establishment of order and taxation'.[32] Repression remained the policy of choice in later years. In May 1816, for example, a cartload of tobacco was seized in Thiennes, a village in the Nord, by men who 'opposed taxation with blatant force'. The sub-prefect responded by ordering that the perpetrators be arrested and that the expense of doing so 'will be at the cost of the

---

[26] Bulletin, 5 May 1814, referring to correspondence of 30 April 1814, MAE, 53MD/336, fol. 44.
[27] Bruguière, *Première Restauration*, 75–6; Berenger and projet de loi, 24 September 1814, AP, 2nd series, XII, 709–18.
[28] Rapport au roi, by Dambray, 13 January 1815, AN, BB[18] 946.
[29] Bruguière, *Première Restauration*, 76–8.
[30] Barante, 23 December 1815, AP, 2nd series, XV, 558.
[31] Louis to Graverend, 27 July 1814, AN, BB[18] 945.
[32] Dambray to Berenger, 24 December 1814, AN, BB[18] 946.

inhabitants of the commune and repartitioned exactly in accordance with their direct taxes'.[33] The whole village was effectively punished, particularly the wealthier inhabitants who paid a higher share of direct tax – indeed, this was probably done to induce local *notables* to enforce the law. A few days later, Barante wrote to the prefect asking him to 'apply all the force of your authority [in dealing with the rebellion]. The circumstances seem to me to merit decisively giving greater force to tax collectors in your *département*.'[34] For Barante, leniency risked stimulating unrest by condoning infringements of the law.[35]

The government adopted a similarly hard line in dealing with resistance to customs after 1814. Napoleon's Continental Blockade was dismantled, but the customs service remained heavy-handed in its anti-smuggling efforts, enforcing a new protectionist system established by the 1816 budget. Like indirect taxation, protectionism was justified by the need to preserve the social order and, thus, stability. Moreover, as with other indirect taxes, the pressure of the fiscal situation pushed the government to seek higher revenue from tariffs. In 1816, therefore, the government proposed duties on imports of raw cotton and colonial goods. These were projected to raise customs revenue by a third, but the Chambers reduced the cotton duty, given agitation from manufacturing interests.[36] Still, customs revenue, like that of other indirect taxes, grew steadily during the Restoration, more than doubling in value between 1815 and 1830 (Figure 4.1).

The new regime, in its commitment to indirect taxation, also reaffirmed the importance of *l'octroi*. The centralisation of *l'octroi* under the Régie des droits réunis in 1812 had acquired the appearance of an arbitrary measure, because several communes had been allowed to retain control over their own *octrois*.[37] The Restoration government, attempting to reduce its responsibility for the weight of indirect taxation while accommodating pressure for decentralisation, sought to return control of *l'octroi* to local government. Proposed in 1814, the measure was enacted in 1816.[38] Despite this decentralisation, the finance ministry maintained close interest

[33] 'Extrait des actes de la sous-prefecture de l'arrondissement d'Hazebrouck', 24 May 1816, AD, Nord, Lille, 135M/19. The arrest took place on the night of 3–4 August 1816.
[34] Barante to the Prefect of the Nord, 31 May 1816, AD, Nord, 135M/19.
[35] Rapport au ministre, by Barante, 20 April 1819, Barante MSS, BT, MsT 1345.
[36] Todd, *Free Trade*, 20–54; Clinquart, *Administration. . . sous la Restauration et la Monarchie de Juillet*, 47–8.
[37] Rapport au roi, by Corvetto, presented to the Chamber of Deputies, 14 November 1816, AP, 2nd series, XVII, 520.
[38] Projet de loi, 17 November 1814, titre 7, AP, 2nd series, XIII, 560; law of 28 April 1816, chapitre 7, titre 2, art. 147, *Lois*, XX, 331.

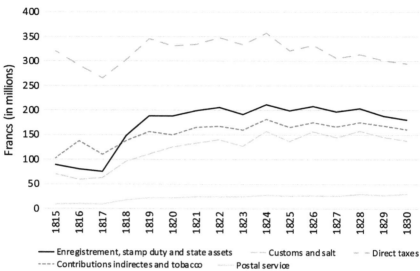

Figure 4.1   Sources of central government revenue, 1815–30 (in 1815 prices). (Sources: *Proposition de loi ... 1815, 1816, 1817; Présentation des comptes ... [1818–1821]; Présentation des comptes ... [1822–1827]. . .; Proposition de loi ... [18281830].* Nominal prices were adjusted to those of 1815 using the index of agricultural and industrial prices provided in Toutain, 'Imbroglio des indices de prix', 175–6.)

in the collection of *l'octroi*, for instance reminding prefects that '[tax] farming presents real advantages amidst problems and abuses that are no less certain.'[39] This attention to collection was all the more important, since, extending the practice developed under Napoleon, the finance ministry took 10 per cent of the proceeds of all *octrois* and encouraged communes to use the tax to finance the sums repartitioned to them for the *contribution personnelle et mobilière*.[40] *L'octroi* was not the only means used to alleviate the burden of direct taxes. In the 1820s, Paris, for instance, used credit to cover *non-valeurs*, that is to say shortfalls, in its *contribution personnelle*.[41] The issue of *non-valeurs* arose, in part, from the continuing inadequacies of repartition, which thus pushed the state towards greater reliance on indirect taxes.

The problems surrounding repartition also reinforced the finance ministry's inclination to reform direct taxes – as we have seen, the latter were

[39] Circular to the prefects, by Corvetto, 6 November 1816, AD, Mayenne, Laval, P/55.
[40] Law of 28 April 1816, chapitre 7, titre 2, art. 153, *Lois,* XX, 331.
[41] Corbière to the Prefect of the Seine, 3 May 1825 and 6 April 1827, AN, F³(II)/SEINE/26, dossier 4.

more readily reduced in 1814 than the *droits réunis*. The willingness to lower land taxes endured, in part because the problems affecting direct taxes lasted longer than the resistance to the *droits réunis* in 1814. In 1816, Corvetto noted 'The gradual and easy process of remittances obtained on indirect taxes' that year. Direct taxes, meanwhile, were in arrears, which arose more from the effects of economic malaise and requisitions than from the unpopularity that affected the *droits réunis* in 1814.[42] Thus, in the Morbihan, as in other *départements*, a 'lack of specie' hindered the payment of direct taxes.[43] Indeed, the turbulence of the late Napoleonic and early Restoration eras seems to have prompted renewed hoarding of specie. In the Seine-et-Marne, 'The collection of direct taxes is almost non-existent. Grain, cattle, property, objects of commerce, all that generate money and facilitate the payment of taxes seems to have been pillaged, taken, used. Still, indirect taxes and *octrois* are being re-established and paid without too many problems'.[44] For a *département* such as the Seine-et-Marne, with a relatively heavy burden of direct taxes, the looting that accompanied two allied invasions and the requisitions imposed by Napoleon and the allies were crippling. Officials fled in the face of the invasion, exacerbating administrative disorder. The allies, moreover, having themselves been subjected to the harshness of Napoleon's depredations, showed little sympathy for the French plight. Their brutal invasions in 1814 and 1815 were associated with the dynasty, which relied on allied forces for its restoration, and contributed to dissatisfaction with the regime.[45] Consequently, when France was occupied following the 1815 treaty, the government did whatever it could to satisfy the allies while seeking to minimise their influence over civil administration.[46]

The difficulties affecting direct taxes in 1814–15 reinforced the belief that they were too high. Like Gaudin, however, Restoration finance ministers found themselves unable to cut direct taxes as they wished; instead, direct taxes temporarily increased after the Hundred Days. Napoleon's return, and the resistance it elicited in France, threw administration into chaos and exacerbated difficulties with tax collection.[47] In

---

[42] 'Extrait du compte du produit brut des impôts pour l'année 1816', by Corvetto, in Audiffret, *Système financier*, 1st ed., II, 1–5; Audiffret, *Souvenirs*, 164.
[43] Rapport, from Vannes, to Montesquiou, 20 August 1814, AN, F⁷ 4338, dossier 7.
[44] *Commissaire extraordinaire du Roi, 1ère division militaire*, to Montesquiou, 31 May 1814, AN, F⁷ 7027.
[45] Hantraye, *Cosaques aux Champs Élysées*.   [46] Guerrin, *France après Napoléon*, 140–1.
[47] AN, C 719, especially rapport au roi, by Corvetto, 20 December 1815 (reprinted in AP, 2nd series, XV, 517–25); Marion, *Histoire financière*, IV, 392–5.

August 1815, after Napoleon's final abdication, the government resorted to a 'contribution extraordinaire' of 100 million francs, which was repartitioned in a manner that showed leniency towards areas ravaged by war.[48] Given the desire to avoid provoking resistance, and probably influenced by the belief that direct taxes were too heavy, the finance ministry seems to have shown more caution in collecting this tax than the *droits réunis* in 1814. When the prefect of the Loire-Inférieure sought to take action against an individual who had not paid the tax, Corvetto refused: 'if the taxpayer does not possess or own any security which can alleviate his burden, the total of his tax will fall under *non valeurs*.'[49] Despite the latitude afforded some taxpayers, the pressure on the public finances meant that the tax was nevertheless collected doggedly.[50] Consequently, it yielded 92,662,000 francs.[51] Still, ever-concerned about the weight of direct taxation, in 1816 the government began to reimburse these extraordinary taxes, effectively turning them into forced loans. This measure may have eased the problems of legitimacy facing the Restoration government, particularly among the landed classes who were the principal beneficiaries of the reimbursement, but it aggravated the burden on the treasury.[52]

The pressure on the public finances redoubled in 1816 following the climatic effects of an Indonesian volcano, which caused harvest failure across Europe. While the Duc de Richelieu, the leader of the government, could claim in January that 'taxes are paid with exactitude', by the summer tax collection faced mounting problems.[53] The prefect of the Cantal, for example, observed that 'The collection of taxes slowed in August. The only reason for this is the late harvest.'[54] Although reducing taxes could have perhaps alleviated some of the problems caused by harvest failure, the dearth itself made this more difficult. The rise in food prices increased the maintenance costs of the occupying allied army from 138,100,000 francs in 1816 to 173 million in 1817, 23 million more than projected in 1815.[55] Already a financial and logistical problem, the upkeep of the allied troops became more difficult, amplifying the pressure to secure their

---

[48] Marion, *Histoire financière*, IV, 397.
[49] Corvetto to the Prefect of the Loire-Inférieure, 28 November 1815, AD, Loire-Atlantique, Nantes, 1P/56.
[50] La Bouillerie to the Prefect of the Loire-Inférieure, 28 January 1817, AD, Loire-Atlantique, 1P/56.
[51] *Proposition de loi . . . 1815, 1816, 1817*, 44.   [52] Haynes, *Our Friends the Enemies*, 215–19.
[53] Richelieu to Alexander I, January 1816, Richelieu MSS, BIS, MSRIC 71, fol. 31.
[54] Bulletin, 18 September 1816, Lainé MSS, AN, 232AP/1.
[55] *Proposition de loi . . . 1815, 1816, 1817*, 68–9.

withdrawal from France.[56] The subsidising of bread prices in an attempt to maintain public order further strained the public finances. These subsidies were made all the more necessary by the presence of the allied troops, which were used to quell unrest over food prices, reinforcing the perception that the regime was imposed by foreigners.[57] The use of the troops in this way also weakened the case for an allied withdrawal, while the troops' upkeep diverted money from poor relief, hindering the government's attempts to pre-empt unrest.

The dearth, in short, stretched the government's already limited means. Moreover, private charity, still suffering from the effects of the Revolution and the turmoil of the previous years, was inadequate, as were local government resources. Despite the regime's best efforts, between October 1816 and August 1817, central and local government combined provided only 26,816,572 francs of relief funds – 76.8 per cent of the extra money required for the upkeep of the allied army.[58] This limited assistance ensured that hardship and discontent remained acute. A typical police report from Paris in spring 1817 noted 'rumours and complaints' about the 'poor quality and light weight' of available bread.[59] The situation was sufficiently combustible that, if the dearth continued, Richelieu concluded, 'The foundations of the social order would be compromised.'[60]

The Financing of Reparations

Reparations imposed another, more serious burden on the treasury. In August 1815, the Russian ambassador in Paris estimated that, with reparations of only 600 million francs, fulfilling the terms of the treaty would require close to 1.5 billion francs.[61] The actual cost proved to be 1.8635 billion, around 25 per cent of GDP.[62] Discharging the peace terms was the principal focus of Richelieu's government, which was formed in September 1815 when its predecessor refused to take responsibility for signing the peace treaty.[63] Having served as governor of Odessa from 1803 to 1814, Richelieu had the confidence of the tsar – giving him credibility with the allies – and government experience without being tainted by association with Napoleon. Thus, he seemed an ideal candidate to reintegrate

[56] Haynes, *Our Friends the Enemies*, 51–73.   [57] Bourguinat, *Grains du désordre*, 155–6.
[58] Lainé, *Rapport au roi*, 3.   [59] Rapport, by the police, Paris, 25 May 1817, SHD, 3D 132.
[60] Richelieu to Osmond, 8 May 1817, in Charléty, *Lettres*, 111.
[61] 'Rapport sur le projet de traité présenté à Sa Majesté l'Empereur de Russie par le général Pozzo di Borgo', 15/27 August 1815, in Pozzo di Borgo, *Correspondance diplomatique*, I, 206.
[62] White, 'Making the French Pay', 341.   [63] Waresquiel, *Richelieu*, 245–6, 255, 257.

Bourbon France into the European order. In October 1815, Castlereagh, the British foreign secretary, suggested that a 25 per cent 'extraordinary contribution' could be levied, drastically reducing the money the French government would have to raise through loans or the sale of assets.[64] It is unlikely that such a proposal was ever realistic; the difficulties with tax collection after the chaos of the Hundred Days were too great for further tax increases, and harvest failure exacerbated these problems. As Richelieu observed, 'only confidence and credit will suffice to meet our needs.'[65]

Borrowing, though, was not easy, particularly since the political turmoil of the early Restoration did not reassure investors. Just before Richelieu took office, James de Rothschild noted that 'I doubt things will stay as they are. Yesterday the whole Ministry resigned ... how can we give credit under such conditions?'[66] The *Chambre Introuvable*, the Chamber of Deputies elected in August 1815 with an ultra-royalist majority, also worried investors. The ultras had been instrumental in instigating the White Terror after the Hundred Days, and the election of the *Chambre Introuvable* ensured the continuation of this process, inhibiting the stabilisation of politics that was necessary to reassure financiers. Even more troubling was the new Chamber's attitude to the budget, and particularly the *biens nationaux*. During the First Restoration, the Chambers had approved a plan to refinance the Napoleonic regime's unfunded debts (*l'arriéré*) by issuing three-year bills secured against the *biens nationaux*. As far as investors were concerned, the use of these assets offered an invaluable means of alleviating France's financial woes without impairing public credit.[67] The use of the *biens nationaux* allowed the government to pay an interest rate of 8 per cent, around the same as the real rate on *rentes*, which traded in the low to mid-60s in June 1814.[68] The bills would provide time for the *rente* to recover from the depredations of war and, once they matured, they could be converted to *rentes* at a lower rate. At the same time, the government avoided using the *biens nationaux* to underwrite the *dette perpétuelle*; disposing of these assets for such a purpose for much longer than three years would have been very difficult if not impossible politically, something made abundantly clear by the opposition to using them to support the *rente* during the Second Restoration. Given the sharp deterioration of the public finances during the Hundred Days,

---

[64] Memorandum by Castlereagh, 10 October 1815, in Wellington, *Supplementary Despatches*, XI, 192.
[65] Richelieu to Alexander I, 22 June/4 July 1816, Richelieu MSS, BIS, MSRIC 72, fol. 46.
[66] James de Rothschild to Nathan Rothschild, 22 September 1815, RAL, T30, XI/109/2/3/99/2.
[67] 'French finances in August 1816', Hope & Co. MSS, SA, 735/1935.
[68] Bruguière, *Première Restauration*, 80–2.

Corvetto proposed to continue and extend the 1814 scheme by issuing more bills to cover the needs of *l'arriéré* for 1815.[69] This plan was vetoed by the ultra-royalists in the *Chambre Introuvable*, since the mortgaging of land to bourgeois financiers defied their conception of land as the buttress of the socio-economic order.[70] Others among the ultras refused to sanction the use of land appropriated from the clergy to pay for the usurper's wars.[71] Instead, the government was allocated 6 million francs of *rentes* to balance the 1816 budget, which sold sluggishly, at an average price of 58.135.[72] These bonds proved insufficient, leaving a shortfall that forced Richelieu to obtain from the allies a deferral of reparations payments.[73] The ultras' impact on public credit was likewise apparent when their attitude deterred the City financier Alexander Baring from entering into negotiations for loans to finance reparations, the French banker Charles Baguenault having invited Baring to Paris in early 1816 for this purpose.[74] Notwithstanding the problems it caused, the *Chambre Introuvable* facilitated some improvement to French public credit through the reform of the Caisse d'amortissement. In 1816, the deputies approved the creation of a Caisse des dépôts et consignations to hold most of the assets consigned to the Napoleonic Caisse d'amortissement, while the government reasserted its commitment to debt amortisation through a revamped Caisse d'amortissement.

Despite the deputies' obstructiveness, Richelieu was initially reluctant to dissolve the *Chambre Introuvable*. Nevertheless, under pressure from his colleagues and allied diplomats, he eventually relented and Louis XVIII ordered fresh elections in September 1816. The government gained seats and reinforced its position with a new electoral law, passed in February 1817. Thereafter, voters had to be present in the administrative centre – the *chef-lieu* – of their *département* for elections, which was easier for more liberal urban voters than for the landowners that favoured the ultras. Though financiers remained cautious, the new Chamber's attitude to credit soon assuaged their concerns, not least because the deputies allowed the government to use the *biens nationaux* to underwrite the new Caisse d'amortissement. Joseph de Villèle, a leading ultra who served as *rapporteur*

[69] Corvetto, 23 December 1815, AP, 2nd series, XV, 511–12, 520–2, 526.
[70] Tort, *Droite*, 276–7.   [71] Waresquiel and Yvert, *Histoire de la Restauration*, 184.
[72] 'Rapport à Son Excellence le Ministre Secrétaire d'État des Finances', by Jourdan, 1 May 1817, AN, C 722.
[73] 'Rapport à Son Excellence le Ministre Secrétaire d'État des Finances, concernant les besoins du trésor, du 25 9ᵇʳᵉ au 31 décembre 1816', by Jourdan, 25 November 1816, MAE, 53MD/346, fols. 243–5.
[74] Pasquier, *Mémoires*, IV, 148.

for the budget commission in the *Chambre Introuvable*, had criticised this use of the *biens nationaux* as a 'disastrous financial system' the previous year; nevertheless, he admitted that using them 'raises public funds'.[75] The reinforcement of the Caisse d'amortissement, noted James de Rothschild, boosted investors' confidence, and so eased the improvement of public credit in 1817.[76]

The government began preparing for the loan it needed in 1817 following the dissolution of the *Chambre Introuvable*. Within days of the election of the new Chamber, Ouvrard presented a proposal similar to that which he had offered in late 1813.[77] He proposed a massive issue of *rentes* to cover the unfunded debt, France's obligations to the allies and the government's budget deficit. These *rentes* would be floated directly to taxpayers, who would be encouraged to invest by a system of *bons supplémentaires*. These would pay bondholders in *rentes* the difference between the price in *rentes* at par and their price at a designated time – in October 1816, Ouvrard suggested that these should be redeemable between 1825 and 1830. He also advocated the creation of a Caisse de réserve, backed by the sale of *biens nationaux*, to support the price of *rentes* and thus minimise the potential cost of *bons supplémentaires*.[78] Ouvrard, in effect, proposed to stimulate demand for *rentes*, and thus lower interest rates, by broadening the investing public.

How earnestly the government considered this proposal is unclear. It was not particularly novel. Even before the attempt to create a democratic monarchy after 1789 and the experiment of the *assignats*, between 1716 and 1720 John Law had sought to resuscitate the state's finances after Louis XIV's wars by using government credit to widen the number of investors with a stake in the political order. Ouvrard's scheme was much less sophisticated and ambitious than Law's, which had entailed overhauling the monetary system.[79] Still, while the government saw the appeal of a 'nationalised' public debt, it was not certain that taxpayers would subscribe in sufficient numbers.[80] Shortages of specie were widespread, as was economic hardship. Moreover, many of the *girouettes* who dominated fiscal politics were either admirers of the British system, which relied on

[75] Villèle to his father, 24 March 1816, and to Mme de Villèle, 10 January 1817, in Villèle, *Mémoires*, II, 13, 164.
[76] James Rothschild to Nathan Rothschild, 11 January 1817, RAL, T5/138, XI/85/1; Bruguière, 'Techniques d'intervention', 102–3.
[77] Greenfield, 'More Precious Than Gold', 205–6.   [78] Greenfield, 'Financing a New Order', 385.
[79] For a development of this argument, see Greenfield, 'More Precious Than Gold'.
[80] Note [by the finance ministry], 29 October 1816, Hope & Co. MSS, SA, 735/1936.

bankers to provide credit, or had little interest in a 'nationalised' public debt. Laffitte, for instance, clearly preferred to see government debt contracted to a consortium of bankers – preferably under his aegis. In October, he wrote to Baring, inviting him to join a syndicate of Paris firms to issue a loan of 200 million francs. Baring did not respond, and so other Paris bankers approached him and his brother-in-law Pierre César Labouchère, a senior partner of Hope & Co. in Amsterdam. Ouvrard also courted Baring, keeping his options open, given the opposition to his initial proposal. These overtures, emphasising his indispensability to a loan, made clear to Baring that he could negotiate his own terms with the French government and the Paris banks from a position of strength, without having to subordinate himself to an existing syndicate; he therefore disregarded many of the solicitations from Paris. Indeed, the government's consideration of Ouvrard's plan for a mass subscription may have been intended to push the Paris bankers out of the impasse into which they sank following Baring's unresponsiveness.[81]

The Paris bankers, though, had little immediate pressure to engage with Baring after his indifference to their proposed syndicate became clear. The *haute banque*, that is the elite Paris banking houses, would be essential to floating *rentes* in Paris for any loan that the French government contracted with Baring. The Paris firms could therefore afford to wait for Baring to reach a deal with the French government. The banker Jean-Conrad Hottinguer, since he could expect to partake in the loan regardless, even encouraged Ouvrard to pursue Baring. By contrast, Ouvrard, falling outside this elite group, would have to earn his share of a loan: he thus had a continuing interest in courting Baring. Consequently, by December 1816, Ouvrard was essentially the French government's agent, and he succeeded in bringing Baring and Labouchère to Paris for loan negotiations in January.[82]

A loan from Barings and Hopes had clear attractions for the French government. It would facilitate the sale of *rentes* in London and Amsterdam, and so reduce pressure on the Paris market, probably more effectively than Ouvrard's earlier proposal to supplement the Paris bourse with capital from provincial France. Indeed, the shallowness of the Paris capital market was a major constraint on the French government during

---

[81] Hottinguer appealed to Baring and Labouchère in October 1816; Greffulhe, too, approached Baring in late 1816, though the details are unclear; other bankers may have done likewise (Greenfield, 'Financing a New Order', 385–6; L. Greffulhe to J. Greffulhe, 22 January 1817, Greffulhe MSS, AN, 61AQ/291, fol. 232).

[82] Greenfield, 'Financing a New Order', 387–9.

the early Restoration. Besides the resources he could mobilise, Baring was politically well-connected and benefited from good relations with allied diplomats and the Duke of Wellington, commander of the army of occupation. All these men, particularly Wellington, were essential to Richelieu's hopes of securing the early withdrawal of allied troops from France.

In January, as the French government pursued its loan with Baring, Wellington agreed to reduce the allied army by 30,000, concluding the arrangement with Richelieu on 10 February, the same day that the first loan contract of 1817 was signed. In easing the pressure on the French treasury and raising the possibility of further reductions to the allied army, the agreement encouraged the rise of the *rente*. The loan itself, meanwhile, comprised 9,090,909 francs of *rentes* issued at 55 by Barings and Hopes in conjunction with the French firms of Baguenault, Greffulhe, Hottinguer and Perregaux-Laffitte. A further tranche of 8,620,689 francs of *rentes* was floated at 58 by the same firms in April and, in July, Laffitte joined Baring and Labouchère in signing the contract for a third loan of 9 million francs of *rentes* at 64, of which the firms of Baguenault, Delessert, Greffulhe, Hottinguer and Laffitte each took a tenth and Barings and Hopes took half.[83] Altogether, these three loans raised a total of 315,199,991.40 francs. The rising *rente* reflected not only the improved political situation and the reinforcement of the Caisse d'amortissement, but also 'the excessive abundance of money'.[84] The end of Napoleon's exactions and British wartime borrowing liberated capital which was then invested in *rentes*. Moreover, the influx of foreign capital risked creating diplomatic repercussions should France default, reassuring investors of the French government's commitment to honouring its debts and thus pushing *rente* prices up.[85] As the *rente* rose, so did Paris bankers' appetites to invest. They proved essential to the loans' success, with the Paris Bourse probably providing around half the total capital.[86]

This demonstration of the Bourse's capacity raised the possibility of a challenge to the supremacy of Barings and Hopes, particularly from those Paris firms that resented their exclusion from the 1817 loans. Already in January 1817, before the first loan was even contracted, the banker and opposition deputy Casimir Perier had criticised the recourse to foreign bankers, supporting instead spending cuts and the transfer of *biens*

---

[83] Greenfield, 'Financing a New Order', 390–3; contract of 11 March 1817, AN, C 722.
[84] J. Greffulhe to Sartoris, 8 October 1817, Greffulhe MSS, AN 61AQ/292, fol. 118.
[85] Oosterlinck et al., 'Baring', 1092.   [86] Greenfield, 'Financing a New Order', 391–2.

nationaux to the Caisse d'amortissement to boost the confidence of French financiers in government debt.[87] In May 1818, Perier and the banker Isaac Thuret proposed to issue the loan the French government needed that year through a consortium of Paris firms. Though they asserted their willingness to cooperate with 'all foreign companies', the essence of their proposal lay in reducing Baring's pre-eminence. Richelieu rejected their offer; not only was Baring better able to assure public credit with his ability to issue *rentes* in London, Paris and Amsterdam, he also had Wellington's support. The latter was no small concern to Richelieu, who wanted to use an upcoming congress of allied leaders at Aix-la-Chapelle to secure an end to the occupation of France. Should the indemnity be paid, Wellington noted, the allied troops would probably be withdrawn at the end of 1818. In May, therefore, the government contracted a loan with Barings and Hopes for 24 million francs of *rentes* at 67, raising a capital of 321,600,000 francs, covering most of the outstanding reparations. At Aix-la-Chapelle in October, the allies agreed to accept 100 million francs in *rentes*, alongside the 165 million francs that remained of the loan from Barings and Hopes, to cover the rest of the indemnity, which was reduced by by 15 million francs. Thus, the reparations were paid and the allied troops left France.[88]

The French government had little choice but to accept Baring's supremacy. Besides his good relations with Wellington and other allied diplomats, and his capacity to issue *rentes* in London and Amsterdam, he retained support among the *haute banque*. Still, the latter, like Perier, Thuret and, moreover, the French government, sought to reduce Baring's dominance. While Laffitte complained to Baring about having been excluded from the 1818 loan contract, he, like the government, clearly wanted Barings' and Hopes' involvement; indeed, he sought a share of the loan and, therefore, ultimately accepted Baring's ascendancy.[89]

In addition to needing credit to pay reparations, the government had to cover its budget deficit in 1818. Thus, Corvetto issued a further 14.6 million francs of *rentes* by public subscription at 66.5 to raise a capital of 189,800,000 francs. The recourse to public subscription was partly a response to Baring's doubts about whether he could finance all the French government's needs. Despite his initial wariness of the idea, the subscription suited him, since it meant that the issue would not be contracted to a rival firm and therefore it enabled him to retain his hold

---

[87] Perier, *Réflexions sur le projet d'emprunt*.
[88] Greenfield, 'Financing a New Order', 393–9; Nicoll, *Comment la France*, 164–7.
[89] Greenfield, 'Financing a New Order', 386–7.

on French public credit. Crucially, the subscription was of a much smaller scale than that which Ouvrard had proposed in 1816, while it allowed ministers to 'attend to their own popularity by satisfying the desire of the public to participate in the loan'. Indeed, the total value of subscriptions exceeded 168 million francs of *rentes*, over eleven times the sum required.[90]

The subscription was well received among the government's opponents. Perier, for example, conceded that 'we cannot but applaud this decision'.[91] The subscription succeeded because, in part, it followed Barings' and Hopes' flotations of 1817, but its success provoked suggestions that the larger loan should have been issued in the same way, and thus criticism of the government's arrangement with Baring intensified. The issuing rate was condemned as too low, an indication that the government was beholden to foreign interests.[92] The system of issuing *rentes*, noted one critic, followed the British model and did not account for 'some differences, in the state of affairs and in the disposition of minds' between the two countries. The low price of *rentes*, essential to attract foreign investors, diverted capital from industry and commerce; this was less of a problem in England, where bond prices were higher. Moreover, since French capital was not concentrated in Paris to the same degree that English wealth was in London, he argued that financing the public debt should be a national project, utilising the infrastructure that collected the *contribution foncière*.[93] Others among the government's opponents also advocated something similar to Ouvrard's original scheme, but this notion of a more democratic public credit was not implemented effectively until the 1850s.

Still, the success of the subscription made a lasting impression. In 1821, when the government contemplated a new loan, Sartoris's bank noted that 'Some allege that it will be done *à la Corvetto*, that is to say by general subscription like the loan of 14 million, while others claim that the English custom of sealed bids will be adopted.'[94] While the government opted for the latter in the 1820s, issuing loans '*à la Corvetto*' remained an option; as we shall see, the question re-emerged in the 1830s. In the meantime, the notion of broadening the investing public continued to gain support among liberals. In 1826, Adolphe Thiers, a journalist who emerged as a major political player following the 1830 Revolution, published a pamphlet that labelled Law as an 'unfortunate genius' whose 'very well-designed' system

---

[90] Greenfield, 'Financing a New Order', 394.   [91] Perier, *Réflexions sur l'emprunt de 16 millions*, 6.

[92] [Anon.], *Réflexions sur les 280 millions de francs*, 2–3, 5.

[93] Mr M. J. B. B., *Observations contre le système d'emprunter*, 10, 19–24, 32–6, 38–42.

[94] Sartoris, d'Echerny et Cie to U. Sartoris, 20 June 1821, Greffulhe MSS, AN, 61AQ/218, fol. 71.

aimed to revitalise public and private credit and so facilitate a post-war economic recovery.[95] Growing interest in these ideas of broadening the investing public gave them increased influence after the 1830 Revolution.

Meanwhile, the *caisses d'épargne*, created to encourage saving by the lower classes, played a role in democratising further the financial system. Inspired by the development of similar institutions in Britain and several German states, the first *caisse* was established in Paris in 1818 by the banker Benjamin Delessert and the Duc de La Rochefoucauld-Liancourt, backed by eminent financiers such as Laffitte and Hottinguer. It is perhaps no coincidence that many major sponsors of the *caisse d'épargne* – Laffitte, for example – were associated with the liberal opposition. Though historians have often emphasised the philanthropic purposes of the *caisses d'épargne*, from their inception they were intended to facilitate the development of public credit, since deposits were to be channelled into *rentes* purchased in the account-holder's name.[96] Like the *assignats*, therefore, the *caisses* were to make public debt an engine of social improvement, alleviating the pressure on poor relief and broadening the investing public, while simultaneously keeping government borrowing in the hands of the banking elite. In 1819, the government furthered this agenda by requiring receivers general to open a 'small *grand-livre*' in their respective *départements* to allow provincial small investors to purchase *rentes* more easily; likewise, the minimum investment in *rentes* was reduced in 1822 from 50 francs of *rente* to 10, the latter representing a nominal capital of 200 francs.[97] Meanwhile, a *syndicat des receveurs généraux*, created briefly in 1818, disseminated *rentes* in provincial France, foreshadowing the role played by the *caisses d'épargne*.[98] Extended to other cities from the 1820s onwards, the *caisses*, like the Banque de France, the Caisse d'amortissement and the Caisse des dépôts et consignations, became increasingly important in supporting public credit.

Despite their later significance, these aspirations to broaden the capital base had little impact on the ascent of public credit in 1817–18. Still, the *rente* rose as speculation surged: from 69 at the end of May 1818, the *rente* reached 80 by the end of August.[99] Corvetto stimulated the rise, investing idle funds into the market.[100] The boom, however, was unsustainable, and

---

[95] Thiers, 'Law', 55–65, 127.
[96] Rapport au roi, by Lainé, 14 July 1818, SAEF, B/14935; Gueslin, 'Invention des Caisses d'épargne'; Christen-Lécuyer, *Caisses d'épargne*.
[97] Laws of 14 April 1819 and 17 August 1822 (titre IV, §V, art. 24), *Lois*, XXII, 127–8, XXIV, 57.
[98] Michelat, *Placements des épargnants*, 32.   [99] Nicoll, *Comment la France*, 171–3.
[100] Marion, *Histoire financière*, IV, 429.

produced a financial crisis in late 1818. Already in August, consols began to fall in London, perhaps because, as *The Times* suggested, investors preferred the higher-yielding *rente* and other continental European bonds.[101] Indeed, Prussia, Austria and Russia floated major loans in 1818, which increased demand for capital just as governments were beginning to return to specie after the wartime monetary expansion. From September, *rente* prices gradually declined, for which Comte Élie Decazes, the minister of police, offered three reasons:

> 1. the treasury's 25 million that are invested in the market, the withdrawal of which is expected anytime, and which will need to happen sooner or later. 2. the rumour in the streets that Baring has an interest in a fall [in prices] given our first contract [of May 1818]. 3. that there will be considerable payments to the allies in October; therefore, the funds will need to be withdrawn from the market or elsewhere which will result in a severe downturn.[102]

The stimulation provided by government money receded as the latter was withdrawn from the market. The Congress of Aix-la-Chapelle, though it produced some speculation on a rise, established a tight schedule for the payment of the remaining reparations which caused the *rente* to continue falling.[103] Moreover, in approving the withdrawal of the allied troops from France, the Congress unnerved some investors, who worried that the end of the occupation removed a guarantor of stability in France.[104]

The commotion on the Bourse reached a climax in early November. Baring attributed the crisis to the Banque de France which, its reserves dwindling, tightened short-term credit.[105] Seeking to reassure the markets, the government began buying *rentes*, as did several Paris bankers.[106] Simultaneously Richelieu, still at Aix-la-Chapelle, contemplated renegotiating the timetable for indemnity payments to relieve the pressure on the market. Given his exposure, Baring supported this idea, as did several of Richelieu's colleagues.[107] On 11 November, the allies accepted an extension: reparations were to be paid over eighteen months instead of nine. Nevertheless, the downturn continued, accelerating in December,

---

[101] *The Times*, 31 August 1818.
[102] Decazes to Richelieu, 22 September 1818, Richelieu MSS, BIS, MSRIC 77, fol. 47.
[103] Nicoll, *Comment la France*, 170–1; Gontard, *Bourse*, 152–3.
[104] Oosterlinck et al., 'Baring', 1084–5.
[105] Baring to Corvetto, 28 October 1818, MAE, 53MD/694, fols. 163–6.
[106] *Le Moniteur universel*, 5 and 7 November 1818; Decazes to Richelieu, 6 November 1818, Richelieu MSS, BIS, MSRIC 78, fol. 27.
[107] Corvetto to Richelieu, 6 November 1818, Richelieu MSS, BIS, MSRIC 78, fol. 38.

probably because of the escalating political turmoil that, as we shall see, culminated in the collapse of Richelieu's ministry. Consequently, the allies were pushed towards further leniency and a final arrangement was concluded in February 1819.

The financial crisis of 1818 was the burst of a bubble; it did not reflect long-term doubts about the French public debt. The loans of 1817–18 demonstrated the potential of the Paris Bourse and facilitated the emergence of an infrastructure through which France could borrow. The newness of this system of public credit, suggested the *Journal des débats*, had made the crisis more likely: 'It is mainly in the new states that irregular variations are most frequent. Our financial system is still only two years old.'[108] Indeed, as Charles Kindleberger has observed, a shock to the markets 'might consist of an unexpected financial success' such as the loans of 1817–18.[109]

Direct Taxation and Political Stability

The payment of reparations and the consequent allied evacuation of France eased the pressure on the French treasury. Cutting direct taxes was now feasible, and the question arose even before Richelieu left Aix-la-Chapelle. In early November, Corvetto presented the cabinet with a proposal to reduce the *contribution foncière*.[110] With the allied evacuation and the tax cut, wrote the navy minister Comte Mathieu Molé, 'we will have too much support to fear anything from the next session [of the Chambers].'[111] High taxes were associated with war and allied occupation. To reduce direct taxes would provide a peace dividend and strengthen the legitimacy of the regime that the allied occupation had in some ways weakened. Moreover, cutting the *contribution foncière* could help satisfy the government's aim of surmounting revolutionary antagonisms. In 1820, the Russian ambassador observed that 'Many royalists refuse to pay extraordinary taxes on the pretext that they should be paid only by men of the Revolution.'[112] To reduce the *contribution foncière* would mark a break with the revolutionary and Napoleonic past without overhauling the fiscal system – the kind of change characteristic of the Restoration.

---

[108] *Le Journal des débats*, 6 November 1818.   [109] Kindleberger, *Financial History*, 266.
[110] Corvetto to Richelieu, 1 November 1818, in Nervo, *Comte Corvetto*, 415–20.
[111] Molé to Richelieu, 6 October 1818, Richelieu MSS, BIS, MSRIC 77, fol. 119.
[112] 'Rapport sur l'état actuel de la France', by Pozzo di Borgo, 1820, Richelieu MSS, BIS, MSRIC 95, fol. 18.

Reducing the *contribution foncière* held great appeal on the right. Indeed, in 1816, the ultras had rejected Corvetto's proposal for a supplement to the tax.[113] Land was important ideologically on the right both as a sign of social status and as the basis of the economy. Only the major landowners should form the electorate, since only they were truly independent and thus able to exercise their vote for the benefit of society.[114] Cutting the *contribution foncière* entailed curbing the size of the electorate, which furthered this objective and, moreover, benefited the great landowners who tended to support the right. Despite his wariness of the ultras, Richelieu preferred them to the liberals. Thus, he supported Corvetto's proposal to cut the *contribution foncière*.

Despite the attractions of reducing the *contribution foncière*, the war minister, Laurent Gouvion-Saint-Cyr, and Decazes opposed Corvetto's proposal. Though the minister of police, Decazes's real power extended far beyond law enforcement. He had established himself as Louis XVIII's favourite, and had used his relationship with the king to manoeuvre himself into a dominant political position. As head of the government, Richelieu provided a respectable front and had the credibility with the allies necessary to secure their cooperation in discharging the terms of 1815. Yet, while Richelieu was occupied with foreign policy, Decazes reigned supreme in domestic politics.

Notwithstanding the end of the occupation, Decazes claimed, the government's financial situation did 'not present much scope for savings'.[115] This attitude, Molé suggested, was driven by ulterior motives: 'His principal objective was, I think, to be agreeable to the Marshal [Saint-Cyr] who insisted... that we give him thirty-four million [francs] more [for the army budget] than last year.'[116] Discerning Decazes's intentions is difficult. The political inclinations of Richelieu and Decazes diverged at the end of 1818, and it is in this context that we must consider his refusal to accept a tax cut. With the allied evacuation of France, Richelieu's ministry fulfilled its main purpose. The incentive for Richelieu and Decazes to overcome their political differences thus receded.

The liberals made gains in the October 1818 elections, accentuating the disagreements between Richelieu and Decazes. For the latter, the election results meant that the ministry should move towards the centre-left, a

---

[113] Marion, *Histoire financière*, IV, 400–13.   [114] Tort, *Droite*, 275–9.
[115] Decazes to Richelieu, 5 November 1818, Richelieu MSS, BIS, MSRIC 78, fol. 26.
[116] Molé to Richelieu, 7 November 1818, in Noailles, *Comte Molé*, IV, 84–5.

policy he believed that most ministers, including Molé, supported.[117] Decazes sought to navigate a 'juste milieu' between the liberals and ultras and, while Richelieu accepted this policy, he preferred to achieve it by moving towards the centre-right.[118] To this end, Richelieu planned to replace Saint-Cyr, a former Napoleonic marshal, who was unpopular among the ultras and with whom he had an uneasy relationship.[119] Decazes, meanwhile, was no doubt sensitive to the electoral repercussions of cutting direct taxes, which risked reducing the left's electorate to a greater extent than the right's. Supporting Saint-Cyr in his quest to prevent reductions in the army's budget, therefore, perfectly suited Decazes's policy of a coalition with the liberals. Simultaneously, he retained Saint-Cyr's support and avoided a tax cut that could compromise his move to the left.

Richelieu resigned in December 1818, and Decazes became minister of the interior in a new centre-left government. Out of office in 1819, Richelieu regretted his failure to reduce the *contribution foncière*. For him, the cut would weaken the liberals electorally in favour of moderate royalists.[120] The presumed electoral consequences of reducing the *contribution foncière* were as attractive to Richelieu as they were unpalatable to Decazes. Yet, the latter's victory proved pyrrhic. Without Richelieu, the ministry was weak, with almost no support on the right. Perhaps in a bid to court the right, therefore, Decazes accepted a modest cut to the *contribution foncière* in the 1819 budget.[121] Still, the government proved short-lived, given its weakness in the Chambers. In 1820, Richelieu formed a new ministry, orientated towards the centre-right and, the following year, the government presented the Chambers with a new, larger cut to the *contribution foncière*.[122]

The budget of 1821, which encompassed this reduction to the *contribution foncière*, faced sustained liberal opposition. Given these 'party politics', Richelieu later complained, the deputies' budget commission took five months to complete its work.[123] The principal objection to the budget arose over the scale of government spending. As one member of the commission observed, 'In the six years that we have been seeking economies, the ministry has done nothing. Our central administrative system is

[117] Daudet, *Louis XVIII et le duc Decazes*, 255–6, 262–3, 268.   [118] Yvert, *Restauration*, 55–79.
[119] Waresquiel, *Richelieu*, 355–6.
[120] Richelieu to unknown, 2 June 1819, Richelieu MSS, BIS, MSRIC 79, fol. 98.
[121] Louis, 20 March 1819, AP, 2nd series, XXIII, 290, 293.
[122] Roy, 16 January 1821, AP, 2nd series, XXIX, 594, 605–6, 608.
[123] Note by Richelieu, 2 January 1822, Richelieu MSS, BIS, MSRIC 96, fol. 184.

almost as complex as it was when Europe obeyed our laws. If the ministers could be excused in 1815, given the state of affairs, how can we not accuse them of negligence today?'[124] Although the budget presented economies, the commission spent most of its time seeking more. Meanwhile, the principle of cutting the *contribution foncière* was uncontroversial because, as the main direct tax, it weighed heavily on all voters. Since the tax was levied on all real estate, reducing it appealed to multiple interest groups, not just the landed royalist elites who paid the bulk of the tax in many *départements*. Thus, in Paris, one of the most heavily taxed areas in France, the commercial elite paid the highest *contribution foncière*.[125] Moreover, groups such as bankers tended to own a wide range of assets, encompassing industrial concerns, *rentes* and real estate. The hereditary Chamber of Peers, a fusion of Napoleonic and *ancien régime* elites, also supported reducing the tax. Many peers were drawn from Paris and its environs and, like bankers, had fortunes based on a mixture of real estate and other assets, and so stood to gain substantially from the cut.[126] More contentious was the issue of repartition; that of the proposed cut drew fierce criticism as 'incomplete, inexact and tainted with partiality and injustice'.[127] Still, the principle of cutting the *contribution foncière* was widely accepted, and the commission eventually endorsed it.

In the ensuing debate in the Chamber, 'party politics' were also apparent. Several deputies criticised the budget on grounds of foreign policy. In 1820–1, Spain and several Italian states succumbed to revolution, which Richelieu sought to overcome through cooperation with the other great powers. His policy was vilified by those on the left for whom France had a mission to uphold the values of the Revolution. This did not necessarily reflect a desire for war; rather France needed maintain the armed forces that would give it 'the moral and political strength' to influence events.[128] Conveniently for some opposition deputies, more military spending would entail higher taxes, and thus could impede the reductions to direct taxes that risked disenfranchising their voters. Conversely, many ultras regarded the army with suspicion, seeing it as a bastion of Bonapartists. In this respect, reducing the *contribution foncière* suited them perfectly, helping to justify reducing the army's budget, and hence its size. Much of the opposition, meanwhile, was caught between a desire to reduce spending,

---

[124] Procès verbaux, commission du budget, 13 February 1821, AN, C 728.
[125] Bergeron, *Banquiers, négociants et manufacturiers*, 19–22.
[126] Waresquiel, *Un groupe d'hommes*, 240–1, 248–52, 257.
[127] Procès verbaux, commission du budget, 24 March 1821, AN, C 728.
[128] Sébastiani, 8 June 1821, AP, 2nd series, XXXII, 61.

an awareness that lowering the *contribution foncière* appealed to voters and a dislike of the electoral implications of the proposed tax cuts. As one 'voter of Seine-et-Marne' put it, ministers had 'a sacred duty . . . to alleviate the burden that weighs on the people . . . Another duty, no less important for them in a representative government, is to respect citizens' political rights.' In Seine-et-Marne, the author calculated, the 1819 and 1821 cuts would decrease the *contribution foncière* by a fifth from its 1814 level. Thus, he proposed, the tax qualifications for voting and eligibility in national elections should be reduced.[129] In the Chamber, several deputies sponsored an amendment to this effect, but without success.[130] Much of the opposition focused on the electoral system, and the way in which the voting qualification was calculated, rather than the tax cut. The proposed reform also encouraged opposition deputies and petitioners outside the Chambers to air grievances against indirect taxes, prompting proposals for the abolition or reduction of duties on salt, colonial sugar, alcohol and *l'enregistrement*.[131] Given the now 'brilliant' and 'flourishing' state of the public finances, claimed merchants and distillers from Béziers, the government should honour the promise of 1814 and abolish alcohol duties.[132] As Perier observed, though, the Chamber represented 'property' and was thus more attentive to the interests of larger landowners than the needs of industry and the poor.[133] Despite such rhetoric, Perier quickly endorsed cutting the *contribution foncière* and withdrew a proposal he had made to reduce *l'enregistrement*, which would have benefited landowners in any case since much of the revenue from *l'enregistrement* arose from land. Still, more radical opposition deputies continued to criticise the government's proposed reduction of the *contribution foncière* as a misplaced priority while endorsing the principle of lower taxation. For them, cutting the *contribution foncière* equitably required corresponding reductions to indirect taxes.

The cuts to the *contribution foncière* after 1819 reflected the problems that affected the collection of direct taxes during the early Restoration, the broad appeal of reducing a tax with such a wide incidence and, perhaps to a lesser extent, the ultras' conception of land. Those strands of liberal and

---

[129] Un électeur de Seine-et-Marne, *Ministère peut-il, sans violer la charte, réduire les listes électorales*, 1, 25–8.
[130] Calmon, *Restauration*, I, 383–5.
[131] Saint-Géry, 12 July 1821, AP 2nd series, XXXII, 749–54.
[132] Petition, *négociants et distillateurs de la ville de Béziers* to the Chamber of Deputies, n.d. [1821–2], AN, C 2065.
[133] Perier, 12 July 1821, AP, 2nd series, XXXII, 759.

republican political economy that favoured a smaller state had little influence. The republican Jean-Baptiste Say, for instance, saw direct taxes as preferable to indirect; he even supported progressive taxation.[134] Such a view was not averse to cutting the *contribution foncière*, particularly on the poor. All taxes, Say argued, hindered economic development: 'The financial regime established by Bonaparte,' he complained in 1829, 'and sadly maintained since then in all its inadequacies, has been praised too much.'[135] Partly as a result, he echoed physiocratic objections to indirect taxes, arguing that it was difficult for taxpayers to know precisely how much they paid in such taxes.[136] This view did not dovetail easily with the growing reliance on indirect taxes that resulted from the cuts to the *contribution foncière*. Still, both inside and outside the Chambers, the principle of reducing the *contribution foncière* seems to have attracted little criticism.

As was the case during the discussions of the proposed reduction, more contentious was the issue of how the latter should be repartitioned. Some were displeased that their taxes rose following the cuts, as the government and *conseils généraux* continued to pursue a fairer repartition of direct taxes. The mayor and tax assessors (*répartiteurs*) of Pleubian in the Côtes d'Armor complained about a higher *contribution foncière*, for example.[137] As this discontent indicates, fairness was highly subjective. Moreover, displeasure with the repartition increased pressure on the government to cut direct taxes further. The question of how the reductions to the *contribution foncière* should be repartitioned renewed interest in the cadastre. Though around a third complete by 1814, the cadastre suffered from budget cuts during the early Restoration.[138] In 1820, those charged with undertaking it in the Manche complained that they 'receive no fixed salary ... Since 1814, they have been reduced to an almost continuous inactivity.'[139] More seriously, the cadastre's credibility was under threat – it was not possible, claimed one deputy, 'to doubt the flaws in its execution'.[140] An official in the Maine-et-Loire noted the expectation that the cadastre 'will re-establish equality between communes for the repartition without affecting the comparative burden from *Dép[artemen]t* to

[134] Say, *Traité*, II, 309.   [135] Say, *Cours complet*, VI, 87.   [136] Say, *Traité*, II, 325–44.
[137] Petition, *maire adjoint et répartiteurs de la commune de Pleubian* to the Chamber of Deputies, 1 March 1822, AN, C 2067.
[138] Bruguière, *Première Restauration*, 14.
[139] *Les Géometres du cadastre du département de la Manche* to the deputies of the same *département*, 3 April 1820, AN, C 727, dossier 9.
[140] Morisset, 11 June 1819, AP, 2nd series, XXV, 86.

Département.'[141] These criticisms presented potentially serious problems; the cadastre could only work if it was perceived as fair and impartial. Finance Minister Roy's solution was twofold. Firstly, he proposed relying on 'The work of special commissioners' to form the 'principal basis of the reduction' of the *contribution foncière*, though he was content for the cadastre to remain the basis of repartition within *départements*. Secondly, he proposed to shift the onus for funding the cadastre onto *conseils généraux*.[142] Thus, its completion would be 'simpler, less costly and quicker', with the added benefit of appeasing the continuing pressure for decentralisation.[143]

Within *départements*, the cadastre had to be undertaken carefully. Persuading people that repartition according to the cadastre might increase their taxes was difficult; those most supportive of completing it were those who felt their taxes were too high.[144] Like taxes themselves, the cadastre was susceptible to resistance. Both the payment of taxes and the process of valuing land for the cadastre were processes of negotiation between the state's agents and taxpayers. Cadastral surveyors, for instance, could be manipulated or deceived and their integrity questioned or undermined. Thus, the cadastre could cease to be seen as fair or impartial. Such doubts about the cadastre could potentially stimulate resistance to taxation. In addition to reducing the finance ministry's costs, Roy hoped that leaving the cadastre to *conseils généraux* would allow it to accommodate local sensibilities more effectively, mitigating the threat to its legitimacy. These problems with the cadastre generated difficulties not only in reducing direct taxes but also in raising them, reinforcing the government's inclination to seek any revenue increases it might need from indirect taxes.

The reduction of the *contribution foncière* and the attendant reform of the cadastre reflected a desire to create a stable, post-revolutionary fiscal system. Nevertheless, these changes had limited results. While the reductions of the *contribution foncière* affected both the principal and the *centimes additionnels*, the product of direct taxes only fell slightly, before gradually rising again (Figures 4.1 and 4.2). The decline of revenue in the late 1820s was due to an economic slump, which affected all taxes, in addition to the government's attempts to ease the burden on land. Still, some redistribution of the tax burden was achieved.[145] By the time

---

[141] Rapport, to Montesquiou, n.d. [August 1814], AN, F⁷ 4338, dossier 4.
[142] Rapport au roi, by Roy, January 1821, AP, 2nd series, XXIX, 605–6.
[143] Roy, 29 January 1820, AP, 2nd series, XXVI, 115.
[144] Schnerb, 'Quelques observations sur l'impôt', 72–3.
[145] Marion, *Histoire financière*, V, 8, 13–14.

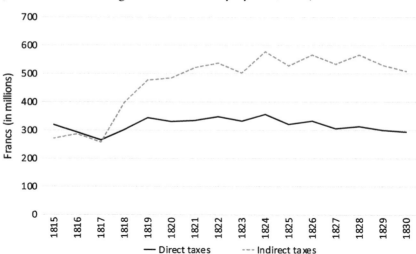

Figure 4.2   Central government revenue from direct and indirect taxes, 1815–30
(in 1815 francs).*

* *Data for the* droits d'enregistrement *and the* droits de timbre *for the years 1815–26 are unavailable separate from those for the revenues of the* domaines. *The latter, however, were generally negligible; between 1827 and 1836, these amounted to between 1.1 per cent and 4.2 per cent of the revenue collected under the remit of* l'enregistrement. *A linear regression shows almost no relationship between revenue from the* domaines *and overall revenue from the* enregistrement, timbre *and* domaines *for the ten years 1827–36, and the annual percentage changes vary as wildly as +142 per cent and −73 per cent. With no real trend discernible, to very crudely estimate total revenues from indirect taxes between 1815 and 1826, the average revenue from the* domaines *over the period 1827–36 (5,108,428 francs) has simply been deducted from each of the years 1815–26. The revenues from the* domaines *for 1815–26 may have been slightly higher than these estimates suggest, since the numbers for 1827–8 are higher than the data for the subsequent years, but it is difficult to know with certainty.*

(Sources: *Proposition de loi ... 1815, 1816, 1817; Présentation des comptes ... [1818–1821]; Présentation des comptes ... [1822–1827] ...; Proposition de loi ... [1828–1830].* Nominal prices were adjusted to those of 1815 using the index of agricultural and industrial prices provided in Toutain, 'Imbroglio des indices de prix', 175–6.)

Restoration tax revenues peaked in 1824, those from customs and the salt tax had risen by 151.4 per cent since the low point of 1817 and those from indirect taxes and the tobacco monopoly had grown by 179.9 per cent (Figure 4.1), when corrected for inflation. These revenues benefited from the revival of the French economy and the resurgence of trade during the early Restoration. By contrast, direct tax revenues grew by only 34.5 per cent from 1817 to 1824, a reflection both of the reductions and of the structure of these taxes which rendered them slightly less sensitive to economic fluctuations than their indirect counterparts. The result was that the ratio of revenue from direct and indirect taxes came to emulate that which had prevailed under the *ancien régime*. In 1788, if we exclude non-tax revenues, indirect taxes provided 57.4 per cent of revenue while direct taxes accounted for 42.6 per cent; during the Restoration, direct taxes fell from 53.7 per cent of tax revenue in 1815 to 36.7 per cent by 1830, with indirect taxes rising from 46.3 per cent to 63.3 per cent over this period.[146] Changes to the cadastre had a less immediate impact. As Roy observed, 'the cadastre promises results only in the future.'[147] Perhaps the principal effect of these reforms and the debates over taxation that produced them was to reinforce the belief that land taxes were too high, which made raising them in future potentially more difficult. The fiscal system became increasingly regressive, which suited the landed elites on which the regime depended.

The Restoration Military System

The desire to cut taxes and the demands on the treasury arising from reparations and dearth increased the need to reduce military and naval expenditure from wartime levels. Furthermore, allied pressure aside, the government wanted peace, which did not require large armed forces. The wars of 1792–1815 made war synonymous with revolution and disorder, much as the 1789 Revolution had allegedly shown untrammelled democracy to be tyrannical and chaotic.[148] As the debate over the reduction of the *contribution foncière* indicates, many Restoration politicians saw no need for a large army. In fulfilling the terms imposed in 1815, Richelieu sought to integrate France into the international order created after 1813. France needed peace to recover from the wars of 1792–1815, and, more-over, to impose excessive burdens of conscription and taxation was to risk emulating Napoleon's fate. Lightening the burden of the state as much as possible, therefore, could facilitate the political stability that Restoration elites regarded as a *sine qua non*. By their logic, instead of spending on war, which would risk weakening the regime, the government should devote itself to rebuilding the sociopolitical order. At the same time, an army was indispensable, and thus the government ultimately opted for a system of limited conscription, which provided sufficient troops to meet the needs of national defence and public order.

---

[146] Morineau, 'Budgets de l'État', 314.   [147] Roy, 29 January 1820, AP, 2nd series, XXVI, 116.
[148] Engberg-Pedersen, *Empire of Chance*.

The cuts to the armed services began in 1814, as the army's budget fell by 34 per cent from 673 to 446 million francs, a third of units were disbanded and the size of the army reduced by half. The government also sought to 'royalise' the army, instituting the white flag instead of the tricolour, for example. Both the reductions and 'royalisation' generated disaffection that induced the army to rally to Napoleon when he returned to France in 1815. The navy faced deeper cuts. In 1814, Louis reduced the navy's budget by 58 per cent, from 167 to 70 million francs. While the army's share of total government expenditure was projected to fall from 54 per cent to 53.5 per cent, the navy's was to go from 13.4 per cent to 8.4 per cent, a greater loss than any other ministry.[149] This, though, was only the beginning; the costs of demobilisation inflated expenses during the first year of peace.

Further reductions followed the Hundred Days, affecting both the army and navy. The army's defection to Napoleon in 1815 reinforced the allies' and royalists' suspicions of its loyalties. Consequently, the army suffered heavily during the White Terror. Instead of rebuilding the army, the Duc de Feltre, the royalist war minister from 1815 to 1817, zealously purged it and the war ministry – being a *girouette*, Feltre had to prove his loyalty to the Bourbons.[150] Moreover, during the early Restoration, the ultras generally supported a pacific foreign policy. Thus, the *Chambre Introuvable* sought to cut military spending and dismantle the Napoleonic leviathan. In early 1816, Richelieu lamented that Feltre 'and the navy minister want to defend doggedly against economies that the [deputies' budget] commission proposes', when the government should instead 'concede honourably'.[151] They resisted successfully; the commission accepted Corvetto's original cuts to the army and navy budgets, without recommending any more.[152] Still, the army remained small, while the navy lacked the means the rebuild its fleet.

Despite the commitment to peace, the regime was under pressure to reassert France's great power status following the defeat of Napoleon and the humiliation of the reparations and allied occupation. The post-war international system was designed to contain French power in Europe and to counter revolutionary outbreaks. Like the domestic politics of the Restoration, it was supposed to preserve stability. In part, fiscal pressures

[149] Bruguière, *Première Restauration*, 73–4, 76–7.
[150] Waresquiel and Yvert, *Histoire de la Restauration*, 172.
[151] Richelieu to Decazes, 1816, Richelieu MSS, BNF, NAF 20280, fol. 47.
[152] Corbière, 9 March 1816, AP, 2nd series, XVI, 442. Army expenditure was set at 180 million francs and the navy at 48 million.

induced the French to accept the new European order; they did not wish to repeat the costs of the Revolutionary and Napoleonic Wars. Simultaneously, some French policymakers sought to compensate for a less aggressive policy in Europe by developing a more global grand strategy, which required a navy – itself a considerable expense. Indeed, the cost of such a strategy made implementing it difficult. In January 1817, France possessed fifty-four ships of the line and thirty-two frigates.[153] Instructed to reduce expenditure, Molé, as navy minister, overhauled naval strategy, seeking to align it with France's resources. His predecessor had proposed a fleet of fifty ships of the line and fifty frigates. Rejecting this plan, Molé argued that France could not compete with the Royal Navy; even in the Mediterranean, which was essential to French security, France 'will only have a defensive attitude'. Instead, France should capitalise on the far-flung nature of the British Empire by constructing a fleet designed to threaten British commerce and communication in the event of war. Since ships of the line were very expensive, Molé proposed to reduce their number gradually to thirty-eight, while boosting the number of frigates to sixty.[154] In this respect, Molé's strategy reflected the need to defend scattered possessions in Guyana, Guadeloupe, Martinique, St-Pierre-et-Miquelon, St-Louis-du-Sénégal, l'île Bourbon and France's Indian outposts, all lost during the Revolutionary and Napoleonic Wars and regained after 1814. Baron Pierre-Barthélémy Portal, Molé's successor in December 1818, has generally been credited with the reform of France's navy during the Restoration.[155] In reality, however, Portal's contribution was limited. He largely accepted Molé's strategy; indeed, as *directeur des colonies* under Molé, he probably influenced its development.[156] His principal change was to reduce the number of frigates to fifty because of budgetary constraints.[157] The pressure for economies probably contributed to Portal's willingness to renounce the reconquest of Haiti, a French colony before 1789 which had declared independence in 1804, after more than a decade of revolutionary upheaval.[158] In 1814 and again in 1816, French emissaries seeking the reintegration of Haiti into the French colonial empire were rebuffed. Regaining the colony would therefore require force – with

---

[153] Rapport au ministre, 28 January 1817, SHD, BB¹ 53, fols. 48–51.
[154] Rapport au roi, by Molé, 1817, SHD, BB¹ 53, fols. 3–11; note, March 1819, SHD, BB¹ 55, fol. 26.
[155] Battesti, *Marine*, I, 16–20.
[156] Albarèdes, *Mémoires*, 17; Noailles, *Comte Molé*, III, 99–100, 104.
[157] Note, March 1819, SHD, BB¹ 55, fol. 42.
[158] On the Haitian Revolution, see Dubois, *Avengers of the New World*.

estimates of the cost reaching 50 million francs in 1815 – and reimposing slavery there could require a substantial long-term military presence.[159] Molé believed that to maintain itself the navy needed 63 million francs annually; as one of his subordinates observed, 'it is desirable that we do not allow the impression to form that 44,000,000 [francs] will suffice.'[160] Nevertheless, only seven times from 1815 to 1830 (six if adjusted for inflation) did the ministry's budget exceed 60 million francs.[161] While Portal attempted to secure increases, his principal achievement as a minister was adapting to economy.[162]

The army, too, was reformed in a manner that reduced expenditure, while suiting the potential extension of French power abroad. The abolition of conscription in 1814 had been a response to its mounting unpopularity under Napoleon. Indeed, since the regime did so little to appease the tax demand in the slogan 'no more conscription, no more *droits réunis*', it perhaps felt greater pressure to abolish conscription. Voluntary service, though, proved inadequate. In 1817, Saint-Cyr succeeded Feltre as war minister and, the following year, reintroduced conscription. Liberals and ultras both attacked the notion of a large standing army as a threat to liberty, while ultras also lambasted conscription as a democratising, and thus revolutionary, force. Still, the Chambers approved the annual conscription of a maximum of 40,000 men for six-year terms to produce a total force of up to 240,000, after which soldiers would pass into a reserve that could be mobilised in the event of war. This smaller army, in addition to reducing costs, indicated that the government did not aspire to recreate Napoleon's *Grande Armée*. The government sought to minimise potential resistance by alleviating the burden of conscription for most of those eligible, since those enlisted were chosen by lot and, even then, budgetary constraints meant that most saw no active service. Moreover, around a quarter of the army consisted of replacements, paid for by those wishing to avoid military service.[163] As with reductions to the *contribution foncière*, the system of replacements appealed to the wealthy, on whose support the government relied.

[159] Brière, *Haïti et la France*, 77–85; procès-verbaux, 'Conseil tenu à Paris le 30 janvier 1815', AN, AF/V/4.

[160] Rapport au roi, by Molé, 1817, SHD, BB¹ 53, fol. 3; rapport au ministre, by Jurien, 9 March 1818, SHD, BB¹ 54, fol. 83.

[161] *Proposition de loi ... 1815, 1816, 1817*; *Présentation des comptes ... [1818–1821]*; *Présentation des comptes ... [1822–7]...*; *Proposition de loi ... [1828–1830]*.

[162] Albarèdes, *Mémoires*, 223–65.   [163] Crépin, *Conscription en débat*, 35–49, 177–88.

Conclusion

The Napoleonic fiscal-military system was recast after 1814 in a manner that sought to reinforce the Bourbon regime's standing among the elites, particularly the landed classes. The government accelerated the trend apparent under Napoleon towards greater reliance on indirect taxes, created a new system of public credit and replaced mass conscription with limited military service. In establishing the contours of the post-Napoleonic fiscal-military state, which lasted with relatively little change until the Third Republic, the Restored Bourbons also established the parameters of French power abroad. Moreover, the system of public credit created after 1817 exercised a decisive influence over the subsequent development of the French state, facilitating greater economic interventionism from the 1830s onwards. In these respects, the Restoration played a crucial role in laying the foundations of the post-revolutionary French state, an achievement historians have typically credited to Napoleon.

The embryonic Restoration fiscal-military system was entrenched from the 1820s onwards, and came to command a degree of consensus across the political spectrum. Despite the intransigence of the *Chambre Introuvable*, the ultras ultimately accepted the Napoleonic heritage. Though they despised the 'Corsican ogre', few of them wished to revive the disorder of the 1790s. Instead, they accepted Napoleon's fiscal legacy, with its reconstruction of many aspects of *ancien régime* taxation. In the *Chambre Introuvable*, though they attacked the government's proposals to use the *biens nationaux* to refinance the public debt as we have seen, this was not an attempt to overhaul or reconfigure the fiscal system. As Villèle noted, 'We attack the liquidation of the *arriéré*, the sale of the forests, the supplementary land tax.'[164] Underlying principles of public finance, such as the reliance on indirect taxation, the need to honour government debt, or the desire for administrative efficiency remained uncontroversial.

As finance minister from 1821 and leader of the government from 1822 to 1828, Villèle engineered the ultras' political supremacy in the early and mid-1820s by pushing them towards the centre-right. Though his memoirs and correspondence are littered with scathing remarks about his predecessors, he maintained the programme of incremental fiscal reform initiated after 1814. Thus, he continued the reorientation of the fiscal system towards indirect taxes and rationalised the bureaucracy of the finance ministry, reducing its expenses, while accepting legislative

---

[164] Villèle to his father, 12 January 1816, in Villèle, *Mémoires*, I, 451.

scrutiny.[165] Simultaneously, he sought the continued development of public credit. The legacy of the early Restoration likewise survived the overthrow of the restored Bourbons in the 1830 Revolution, which brought several architects of the post-1815 reform of the state, such as Baron Louis, back into office; as in 1814–15, the servants of previous regimes played a decisive role in ensuring continuity. As a result, the Restoration established a durable post-revolutionary fiscal-military state.

[165] Surleau, *Réformes financières*, 25–6, 93–123, 136–42; Marion, *Histoire financière*, V, 23–9, 92–3.

CHAPTER 5

The Resurgence of French Power, 1821–1830

The entrenchment of the post-Napoleonic fiscal-military system depended heavily on its successful exploitation. It had to deliver for French power and prestige, and thus for the legitimacy of the regime – and that of the state as a whole – while not destabilising the political order. Consequently, the politics of the fiscal-military system in the 1820s were dominated by three major, interrelated considerations: the ongoing desire to ensure sociopolitical stability; the objective of reasserting the prestige of France and of the Bourbon dynasty particularly in the light of the Hundred Days and Waterloo, which weakened the standing of both; and the question of managing the new system of public credit. Though historians have given all three of these issues considerable attention, they have not always illuminated the connections between them. Recent work has emphasised the aggressiveness and innovativeness of Restoration foreign policy, but historians have largely overlooked the fiscal-military system that underlay it.[1] Some have even downplayed the relationship between the growth of the public debt and military spending, disregarding the scale of the latter.[2] Nevertheless, military action abroad relied heavily on credit, and was a major cause of French government borrowing in the 1820s, the success of which raised the prospect of a debt conversion by the middle of the decade. At the same time, the need to manage public debt shaped foreign policy, particularly since Villèle, as finance minister, dominated the government for most of the 1820s. As we shall see, the Bourse became more than a

---

[1] E.g. Price, 'French Forward Policy'.
[2] Leuchter, 'Finance beyond the Bounds'. Leuchter argues that the increase in public debt during the Restoration owed little to military spending. However, he does not explain why the government borrowed so much in the 1820s, and massively understates the scale of borrowing for military purposes. He claims, for instance, that the 1823 Spanish expedition required a loan of just over 23 million francs. This, though, was only the value of the 5 per cent coupon: the principal exceeded 460 million francs, while the real amount raised was almost 414 million francs, more than that of any other loan issued between the creation of the franc and the Crimean War loans of 1855.

means to finance armed intervention abroad; it played a central role in Villèle's thinking about foreign affairs.

The ultras generally appreciated the advantages of the new fiscal-military system. Comte Pierre-Louis-Auguste de La Ferronays, the ultra-royalist ambassador to Russia and later foreign minister, observed in 1822 that the institutions of the constitutional monarchy had 'introduced order in our finances'; should war come in Europe, France 'appears in fact to have the liberty to choose the role that would best suit its interests and its policy [given] the state of its finances, the ease with which it could raise promptly a great army, formed in part of battle-hardened soldiers, [that it could] entrust to experienced generals'.[3] Public credit gave France the capacity to assert itself as a great power without resorting to Napoleonic-style tax increases and requisitions, but, as La Ferronays suggests, waging war depended on more than sound finances. Leadership and effective armed forces, which France acquired after 1818, were essential. The new fiscal-military system could support an active foreign policy: the question was whether the ultras could turn this to their advantage politically.

The Quest for Stability

Like many on the right, Villèle saw bolstering landed elites, which dominated ultra-royalist politics, as a means of reinforcing political stability. Consequently, he continued the policy of reducing direct taxes, so that the combined burden of the *contributions foncière, personnelle et mobilière* and *des portes et fenêtres* was nominally reduced by 91,865,347 francs between 1818 and 1827.[4] Adjusted for inflation, direct tax revenues fell by 12.8 per cent between 1819 and 1829.[5] Meanwhile, in 1825, the government modified *l'enregistrement* to the benefit of landowners.[6] The commitment to land was also reflected in customs duties, which became more protective of agriculture. Influenced by the British Corn Laws, in 1819 the government linked tariffs to the price of grain: the higher the latter became, the lower the import duties. Agricultural profits were protected, while bread was supposedly kept affordable, thereby reducing the risk of food riots. In 1821, following a bumper harvest and electoral gains by the ultras, the Chambers approved a prohibition on the import of foreign grain.[7]

---

[3] 'Refléxions sur la situation actuelle de la France dans le système politique de l'Europe', by La Ferronays, April 1822, MAE, 53MD/699, fols. 156, 165.
[4] *Présentation des comptes . . . 1824 . . .*, 129–31.
[5] *Présentation des comptes . . . 1819*; *Proposition de loi . . . 1829.*
[6] Chabrol, 5 April 1824, AP, 2nd series, XXXIX, 715–18.   [7] Todd, *Free Trade*, 46–7.

Benefiting from the commercial expansion of the early 1820s as the economy recovered from the subsistence crisis of 1817, the incidence of taxation shifted towards commerce and the poor as revenue from indirect taxes rose by 8.3 per cent from 1820 to 1829, when corrected for inflation.[8] Indeed, the increases in economic activity, with GDP rising by 19.4 per cent during these years, eased the reduction of rates for duties such as *l'enregistrement*, while expediting the continued growth of indirect taxes.[9]

The desire for stability induced the government to pursue public works. Though the Napoleonic regime spent 799,599,055 francs on public works between 1804 and 1813, French infrastructure suffered from underinvestment as the government prioritised trunk roads between Paris and the frontiers to meet the needs of war.[10] By 1814, local and regional roads and canals were falling into disrepair. Following the fulfilment of the 1815 peace terms, and the consequent easing of pressure on the public finances, the government turned towards improving infrastructure. In 1820, Louis Becquey, *directeur général des Ponts et Chaussées et des Mines*, proposed a radical extension of France's canal network. For Becquey and others, developing infrastructure would further the integration of the French nation through the creation of a national market and the extension of commerce.[11] Moreover, better transport links would facilitate the movement of grain, not least by the private sector, which would alleviate the problems caused by harvest failures like that of 1816–17. Such an approach – free enterprise assisted by state interventionism – was generally characteristic of Restoration economic policy.

As in the eighteenth century, local government was essential to undertaking and financing public works; in many parts of *ancien régime* France, provincial estates spent significantly more on infrastructure than the royal government. By the 1820s, local governments' resources were little greater than they had been during the 1790s and under Napoleon, not least because the *notables* who dominated local politics preferred not to impose *centimes additionnels* on themselves to finance projects such as road-building.[12] The central government therefore assumed a major role in funding public works. Still, following the British example, it sought to minimise its own expenses in canal construction by relying on private finance. Indeed,

[8] *Présentation des comptes . . . 1821*; *Proposition de loi . . . 1829*.
[9] Toutain, 'Produit intérieur brut'.   [10] Lentz, *Premier Empire*, III, 423.
[11] Démier, *France de la Restauration*, 348–50, 400–5, 414, 432.
[12] Woloch, *New Regime*, 169–70.

the rise of the Bourse after 1815 eased the undertaking of public works on a greater scale than ever before, benefiting from the growth of international financial markets that underwrote the stability of the post-Napoleonic political order across Europe.[13] Moreover, Becquey estimated that the annual cost of maintaining roads would fall by 6 million francs once France acquired 'a good system of navigation', since the greater use of canals would reduce road traffic.[14] The process that emerged to undertake canal, and later railway, construction operated like government borrowing. Companies of bankers bid for the canal concession in question and, instead of receiving interest on *rentes*, they profited from the revenues of the canal, often in partnership with the state.[15] The system worked admirably. In 1821–2, a swathe of canal concessions were adjudicated, as eminent members of the *haute banque*, including Laffitte, Sartoris and Rothschild, presented bids. City firms such as Barings also invested.[16] To hasten construction, in 1821 Laffitte proposed to create a large joint-stock company capitalised at 240 million francs, an unprecedented sum. While ministers rejected the idea, he revived it with equally little success in 1825, advocating a government loan of 100 million francs to finance canal construction and industrial development.[17] Not only did the government seek to maintain competition between bankers, but it was wary of large-scale canal construction and, despite Becquey's grand design, was committed 'to not deploy instantly a great apparatus of works'.[18] While historians have billed the Restoration as a major period of canal-building, ministers worried that allowing rapid canal construction would encourage speculation and raise the costs of the necessary labour and raw materials.[19] Much of these costs would have to be met by the state, which had to cover any expenses that exceeded the sums originally agreed with the concessionaires. Indeed, the adjudications of 1821–2 ultimately cost the government 322 million francs.[20] Given the government's caution, the extension of the canal network in the 1820s was more limited than the mid-nineteenth-century railway boom.

---

[13] On the intersection of finance and security, see Sluga, 'Economic Insecurity'; Sluga, 'Who Hold the Balance of the World?'.

[14] Becquey, *Rapport au roi*, 3, 6, 8, 14–17.

[15] Nieradzik, 'Construction du réseau de canaux', 464–5.

[16] Baring Brothers to U. Sartoris et Cie, 17 April 1827, 29 June 1827, 13 July 1827, Greffulhe MSS, AN 61AQ/215.

[17] Gille, *Banque et le crédit*, 109–13.   [18] Corbière, *Rapport au roi*, 6.

[19] Reverdy, *Travaux publics*, 10–7.   [20] Nieradzik, 'Construction du réseau de canaux', 469.

As with ongoing reductions to the *contribution foncière*, budget surpluses eased government spending on public works. Except for 1823, when the budget was in deficit, ordinary revenues averaged 109.34 per cent of expenditures between 1819 and 1825, after which an economic slowdown pushed the budget back into deficit.[21] Surpluses also allowed a gradual increase in military and naval spending during the 1820s, as the need for improvements to the armed forces became apparent in the wake of French military action abroad. Indeed, in 1824, the navy minister emphasised the growth of indirect tax revenues as he sought to overcome Villèle's aversion to increasing his department's budget.[22] Beyond facilitating higher military, naval and public works spending, surpluses probably reinforced investors' confidence in the management of French government finances, improving public credit and thus facilitating a more active foreign policy in the 1820s.

The Ascent of Public Credit

Prima facie, Restoration France may appear to support the North–Weingast thesis, derived from the study of seventeenth-century England, that the rise of public credit rested on the entrenchment of property rights through an elected legislature that allowed the state to make a 'credible commitment' to honouring its debts.[23] Certainly, parliamentary government could be reassuring. Negotiating a Prussian loan in 1818, Nathan Rothschild insisted that it be secured against royal domains on the basis that, unlike France and Britain, Prussia lacked a constitutional regime.[24] Following a similar logic, for the French government, one attraction of financing the reparations of 1815 through credit was that the ability to borrow on the scale required would demonstrate the effectiveness of the Restoration parliamentary system.[25] Still, much depended on the nature of the parliamentary regime. As David Stasavage has observed of eighteenth-century Britain, a parliamentary system alone did not necessarily guarantee creditors' interests.[26] Indeed, property rights in Britain became less secure, since Parliament asserted its power to appropriate and regulate property.[27]

---

[21] Fontvieille, *État*, 1937.
[22] Rapport au Conseil, by Clermont-Tonnerre, 23 March 1824, Clermont-Tonnerre MSS, AN 359AP/75.
[23] North and Weingast, 'Constitutions and Commitment'.
[24] Ferguson, *World's Banker*, 132, 143.   [25] Rabault-Mazières, 'Discours et imaginaire', 53.
[26] Stasavage, *Public Debt and the Birth of the Democratic State*.
[27] Hoppit, 'Compulsion, Compensation and Property Rights'.

The case of the United States provides a further indication that parliamentary government did not necessarily favour creditors. Though the country's relative prosperity made American securities attractive to foreign – mainly British – investors in the early nineteenth century, a financial crisis in 1837 brought several states to default in 1841–2, with the acquiescence of their elected legislatures.[28] Conversely, creditors' interests could be upheld independently of a meaningful parliamentary system, as the authoritarian Napoleonic regime suggests: it accepted the property rights of rentiers.[29]

For a parliamentary system to provide long-term reassurance to creditors, they had to believe it would survive and, in this sense, they were uncertain about the Restoration. France, Baring wrote in 1821, was 'like a child's card house'; 'you must not blow or shake the table, and unfortunately the requisite stillness cannot in the nature of things be preserved.'[30] Still, investors did not necessarily expect the collapse of the regime to imperil public credit: the Restoration of 1814–15, for instance, had not changed the state's commitment to honouring its debts. In this respect, the *girouettes* were no doubt reassuring. As we have seen, they offered continuity in finance ministry personnel and thus in policy, assisted by their disproportionate influence over financial debates in the Chambers. Their prominence gave them a clear interest in maintaining the price of *rentes*: should markets fall as a result of the policies they endorsed, their influence might recede. The same was true of the financiers both inside and outside the Chambers. Perhaps more importantly, much French government debt – in contrast to that of the American states – was was held by Frenchmen, not least because of the number of *rentes* absorbed by the domestic market in 1817–18. Larger rentiers were men wealthy enough to have a high social status, and thus political influence. Such men were too important for any government to risk default, irrespective of whether a parliamentary system existed. Still, their influence in the Chambers allowed them to promote policies favourable to rentiers, not least the pursuit of a balanced budget. Able to scrutinise the government's accounts, deputies could see clearly that France had the fiscal capacity to sustain interest payments on the public debt. In 1816, debt service required only 9.1 per cent of government spending, which grew to 13.54 per cent in 1818 and rose to 18.66 per cent in 1819 before oscillating around 20 per

---

[28] Roberts, *America's First Great Depression*, 50–66, 73–83.   [29] Leuchter, 'Illimitable Right'.
[30] Baring to L. Greffulhe, 20 March 1821, Greffulhe MSS, AN, 61AQ/276.

cent in the following years.[31] These figures represented a marked improvement over the *ancien régime*, which devoted over 40 per cent of government expenditure to interest payments by 1788.[32] Confidence in the
state's financial transparency also benefited from institutions such as the
Caisse d'amortissement, while during the Restoration the bureaucracy was
streamlined and the standardisation of public accounting procedures pursued under Napoleon continued.[33]

While prominent bankers such as Baring and the Rothschilds did not sit
in the Chambers, the presence of many of their colleagues from other firms
reinforced bankers' influence over the policymaking process. The need to
cater to financial and rentier interests in the Chambers compelled ministers
to maintain good relations with eminent bankers, allowing the latter
privileged access to political and financial news. As Marc Flandreau and
Juan Flores have argued, in the early nineteenth century firms' financial
power and prestige served to overcome information asymmetries; the most
eminent bankers were better informed than the average investor, and thus
could signal a good loan. Should they deem a prospective borrower to not
be particularly creditworthy, they could restrict that government's ability
to borrow.[34] In this respect, the bankers' prominence among the French
fiscal policymaking elite probably benefited the *rente*. Moreover, the
Parquet, the official market which regulated the Bourse, provided a centralised, public quotation process through the Compagnie des agents de
change.[35] The relative transparency of pricing, alongside the endorsements
of bankers and the reassurance provided by institutions such as the Caisse
d'amortissement, eased the entry of small investors into the market for
rentes. Many of these were individuals with a relatively small capital for
whom information was crucial, since they needed to be certain of their
coupons, as did institutions reliant on endowments such as schools and
hospices. Bankers and financial institutions, in other words, acted to shape
public opinion in a manner favourable to public credit.

The state of the money markets further assisted the rise of the *rente*
(Figure 5.1). The liquidity shortage that provoked the crisis of 1818 was
only temporary. By the early 1820s, markets were awash with capital,
which provided for a rising *rente* amid falling interest rates across Europe.
The *rente*, noted Sartoris in 1820, was sustained by a 'great abundance of

[31] Oosterlinck et al., 'Baring', 1077.   [32] Morineau, 'Budgets de l'État', 315.
[33] Kott, 'Restaurer la monarchie', 217–35.   [34] Flandreau and Flores, 'Bonds and Brands'.
[35] Hautcoeur and Riva, 'Paris Financial Market', 1330–1, 1334.

money'.[36] The availability of capital to provide this abundance partly reflected the structure of the French economy. French industrialisation did not depend on capital investments of the same scale as in, say, Britain; most French industry was relatively small, and was financed with agricultural surpluses, which grew substantially during the Restoration.[37] While bankers were essential in mobilising the capital necessary for more sizeable industrial projects, they sought to diversify their portfolios, allowing *rentes* and canal shares to assume important roles as large-scale investments in the 1820s.[38] As Sartoris put it, 'monied men' saw *rentes* as 'the only means of obtaining any tolerable interest for their capital', while remaining sensitive to the risk of political instability.[39]

It is important not to exaggerate the doubts about the Restoration's longevity, particularly after 1821. The survival of the regime following the outbreak of revolution in Spain and Italy that year was reassuring. The fear that revolution in France risked general upheaval across Europe may have pushed some bankers to sustain the *rente* and so preserve the 'card house', since its collapse would threaten their existing investments in France and elsewhere. Nevertheless, France looked stable compared to Spain or the Italian states. Responding to a circular from Thuret in 1821 who sought to form a consortium to bid for an issue of 12 million francs of *rentes*, the Amsterdam firm of Luden observed that 'this operation can offer very good opportunities, because we believe like you that the peace of Europe will not be troubled soon and so your stocks must improve in the long run . . . On the other hand, all the public securities have reached such high prices, that they have more to lose than to gain.'[40] Luden was willing to invest, and reached the decision quickly; he replied to Thuret's circular of 30 June on 5 July. By contrast, when Thuret sent him details of a prospective Neapolitan loan in December, he was much more cautious – unsurprisingly so, given the revolution that year in the Two Sicilies.[41] The *rente*, in other words, benefited from the relative unattractiveness of other governments' bonds. Sartoris's firm noted in 1821 that Neapolitan bonds were 'not much sought', while they had 'a strongly negative opinion' of Spanish

[36] Sartoris, d'Echerny et Cie to Ewart Taylor & Co., 25 August 1820, Greffulhe MSS, AN, 61AQ/219, fol. 128.
[37] Démier, *France de la Restauration*, 364–79.   [38] Barker, 'Perier Bank'.
[39] Sartoris, d'Echerny et Cie to Heywood Brothers & Co., 20 November 1820, Greffulhe MSS, AN, 61AQ/219, fol. 208.
[40] Luden et fils to Thuret et Cie, 5 July 1821, Thuret MSS, ANMT, 68AQ/35.
[41] Luden et fils to Thuret et C[ie], 4 December 1821, Thuret MSS, ANMT, 68AQ/35.

bonds.[42] On the day these observations were made, French 5 per cent *rentes* closed at 84.10, while Neapolitan and Spanish 5 per cents were at 68 and 69 respectively, though the *Journal du commerce* noted that the real value of Spanish bonds was closer to 55.[43] French *rentes* were a safer investment, particularly since the British were not borrowing.

The wars of 1792–1815 facilitated the Bourse's ascent, not least in destroying the financial centres of eighteenth-century Europe, with the exception of London. Though Paris bankers also suffered during the 1790s, several prominent eighteenth-century firms survived the turmoil and re-emerged as major players in nineteenth-century finance. Meanwhile, other foreign bankers such as Thuret and Rothschild arrived in Paris, perhaps prompted in part by the the considerable influence that the French exercised over government borrowing and international finance in Napoleonic Europe. In 1810, Count Klemens von Metternich, the Austrian foreign minister, informed Emperor Franz I that an Austrian loan depended on two conditions: '1. On the active approval of the French Emperor; 2. on our greater or lesser credit.'[44] Public credit in Napoleonic Europe relied heavily on the Bourse and, in this situation, Paris suffered less as a financial centre than its rivals. The loans of 1817–18 demonstrated the potential of the Paris capital market and, consequently, foreign government bonds quickly came to be traded there.

Neapolitan bonds were particularly common. The Austrians having quelled the 1820 Revolution in Naples, the Rothschilds floated four major loans for the Two Sicilies between 1821 and 1824. In addition to having branches in Naples and Vienna, they maintained close relations with Metternich and the Austrian finance minister. The Viennese market, however, was too weak to absorb Neapolitan bonds, which therefore drew heavily on British and French, in addition to Neapolitan, investors. For the Neapolitans, recourse to British and French markets provided a welcome counterbalance to Austrian power.[45] On some level, the French shared this point of view, having tried and failed to prevent Austrian intervention; moreover, the loans eased the stabilisation of Italian politics. Inconveniently, Neapolitan bonds could not be listed legally by the Parquet, which was only permitted to quote French *rentes*, and

---

[42] Sartoris, d'Echerny et Cie to U. Sartoris, 19 May 1821, Greffulhe MSS, AN, 61AQ/218, fol. 61.

[43] *Le Journal du commerce*, 20 and 22 May 1821.

[44] Metternich to Franz I, 23 August 1810, in Metternich, *Aus Metternich's nachgelassenen Papieren*, II, 389.

[45] Ferguson, *World's Banker*, 137–9, 168–70; Schisani, 'How to Make a Defaulting Country Credible'.

consequently they were traded through the coulisse, the free market formed of those brokers outside the Compagnie des agents de change. The government was both reluctant to enforce the full letter of the Parquet's monopoly, which risked constraining investment and so exerting a downward pressure on the markets, and averse to encouraging French investors to put their money into foreign securities.[46] In 1821, the banker Martin d'André noted the 'apprehensions that the great elevation of our *rente* and the multitude of loans of various states have given to ordinary buyers of securities'.[47] For small investors, as for the French government, the risk in allowing so many foreign securities to be placed in Paris was that these diverted funds away from *rentes*, depressing the price. Given the competing needs of domestic and foreign policy, therefore, the government was content to overlook the trade in foreign bonds on the Paris market, while not encouraging it.

Just as foreign governments attracted French investors, French public credit after 1818 continued to rely on foreign, especially British, capital. In 1821, Sartoris wrote to London that 'Our market has depended entirely on yours for some time.'[48] As we have seen, the loans of 1817–18 depended heavily on capital from London and Amsterdam, in addition to French investors, and many of the *rentes* floated abroad were probably not repatriated to France quickly.[49] In this respect, as in others, the loans of 1817–18 marked a departure. Thereafter, foreign investors were crucial holders of *rentes*.[50] What changed after 1818 were the bankers. While the loans of 1817–18 were dominated by Barings and Hopes, their importance receded in the 1820s, though their interest in French public credit did not evaporate. Barings invested readily in the loan of 1821, which was contracted to Hottinguer, Delessert and Baguenault, and continued to place *rentes* in London.[51] Indeed, the influx of British capital was crucial to sustaining the rise of the *rente*. Thus, the loan of 1821, of 9,585,220 francs of 5 per cent *rentes*, was issued at 85.55, raising 164 million francs. Thereafter, the Rothschilds emerged as the dominant force in French government borrowing.

---

[46] Hautcoeur and Riva, 'Paris Financial Market', 1331.

[47] Martin d'André et fils to Thuret et Cie, 11 January 1821, Thuret MSS, ANMT, 68AQ/146.

[48] Sartoris, d'Echerny et Cie to U. Sartoris, 19 May 1821, Greffulhe MSS, AN, 61AQ/218, fol. 61.

[49] White, 'Making the French Pay', 348.

[50] For lists of investors in French *rentes* from 1818 onwards, see Rothschild MSS, ANMT, 132AQ/7094–6. Foreign investors came from all over Europe, though most seem to have been British.

[51] Sartoris, d'Echerny et C[ie] to Baring Brothers, 9 August 1821, Greffulhe MSS, AN, 61AQ/219, fol. 335; Hottinguer et C[ie] to Baring Brothers, 13 August 1821, BA, HC 7.1.3.

Exploiting the New Fiscal-Military System

Underwritten by the ascent of public credit, the ultras pursued an aggressive foreign policy in the 1820s, but without repudiating the early Restoration's commitment to the post–Napoleonic international order. Certainly, some, such as Vicomte François-René de Chateaubriand, an ultra-royalist and poet who served as foreign minister in 1822–4 and as ambassador to Berlin, London and Rome during the Restoration, wished to extend France's borders to the Rhine – the country's 'natural frontiers'. They seldom proposed to do so by frontal assault, instead seeking cooperation with other powers, chiefly Russia, to reassert French power and prestige abroad and thus bolster the regime's popular legitimacy in France.[52]

The ultras' acceptance of the constraints of the international order was evident in their attitude to the post-Napoleonic military system, with its quasi-professional army that was ill-adapted to the *guerre à outrance* of 1792–1815. Such an army suited the ultras' commitment to domestic political stability. Ever wary of the democratising effects of conscription, the ultras abolished the reserve in 1824, compensating for this by increasing the size of the army to 400,000 and extending military service to eight years. The consequently greater separation between the military and society facilitated the army's role as the guarantor of domestic order, tasked with suppressing revolutionary activity.[53] Seeking to buttress the army's loyalty to the regime, the ultras' move towards greater professionalisation was driven principally by domestic political concerns and set a major parameter for the conduct of military action abroad.

The success of military intervention in Spain in 1823 increased the ultras' willingness to entrust political stability to the army.[54] In 1820, a group of liberals and army officers had successfully forced the Spanish king Ferdinand VII to accept a constitution. Despite Villèle's wariness, with Russian backing the French launched an expedition of 56,000 French and 35,000 Spanish troops in April 1823, under the command of the Duc d'Angoulême. While the French presented themselves as restoring Ferdinand's power in the interests of European stability and the status quo, other European governments were concerned. Metternich sought to restrain and control French action as much as possible, while the British, worried about the growth of French influence in Spain and the

---

[52] Price, 'French Forward Policy'.   [53] Griffith, *Military Thought*, 43–50.
[54] Porch, *Army and Revolution*, 9–13.

Mediterranean, opposed the intervention altogether; both feared the consequences of greater French power through the creation of a pro-French Spanish government.[55] In France itself, opponents of military action cited the Revolutionary and Napoleonic Wars as evidence that intervention would radicalise the Spanish revolution by uniting the Spanish nation behind it. Others expressed fears that the costs of a potentially drawn-out intervention would be so high as to bankrupt the French government and thus destabilise the regime. For such critics, the fall in the *rente* in January 1823, when the government announced its decision for war, was an ominous sign.[56]

Once the campaign began, investors were unsettled by rumours that the army – untested since Saint-Cyr's reform – was disorderly and ineffective.[57] Despite plentiful supplies near the Spanish border, the war ministry had not considered their transportation or the problems of supplying the army in Spain. In early April, therefore, Ouvrard stepped in, presenting himself to Angoulême and securing contracts to supply the French army in Spain – at high prices. Ouvrard's machinations landed him in prison in 1824, as the costs of the Spanish expedition – totalling 207 million francs – produced public outrage when Villèle presented them to the Chamber.[58] While the government no doubt made him a scapegoat, Ouvrard had not helped himself by selling *rentes* in early 1823, speculating on a fall in anticipation of a government loan to cover the costs of military action.[59] Still, the *rente* was sustained (Figure 5.1), albeit with a few fluctuations, allowing the government to borrow easily to fund the intervention. Moreover, by August, operations in Spain were essentially over, and the Bourse gradually recovered as investors' anxieties disappeared. The speed of the campaign came as a welcome surprise to many doubters, and boosted confidence in the army's abilities, though French troops also benefited from the ineffectiveness of Spanish resistance. The regime publicly celebrated victory in Spain as reflecting the dynasty's past glories.[60] Doing so, however, drew attention to the Bourbons' more recent failures, most notably during the Hundred Days, which were commemorated in

[55] Bertier de Sauvigny, *Metternich et la France*, II; Yamada, 'George Canning and the Spanish Question'.
[56] Larroche, *Expédition d'Espagne*, 35, 39, 47–9.
[57] Sartoris, d'Echerny et Cie to U. Sartoris, 9 April 1823, Greffulhe MSS, AN, 61AQ/218, fols. 332–3.
[58] Marion, *Histoire financière*, V, 33.
[59] Sartoris, d'Echerny et Cie to U. Sartoris, 31 January and 5 February 1823, Greffulhe MSS, AN, 61AQ/218, fols. 301, 304; Villèle to Angoulême, 30 August 1823, in Villèle, *Mémoires*, IV, 341–2.
[60] Larroche, *Expédition d'Espagne*, 183–221.

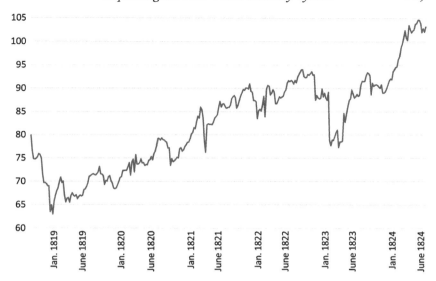

Figure 5.1   Weekly closing prices of French 5 per cent *rentes*, as quoted in Paris,
September 1818–June 1824.
(Source: *Le Moniteur universel*)

popular culture.[61] Though popular in some circles, the Spanish expedition
stimulated disturbances, producing rumours of Napoleon's return, despite
his death in 1821.[62] Nevertheless, victory in Spain aroused sufficient
patriotism to allow the government, with assiduous preparation, to secure
a large ultra majority in the elections of February 1824. The navy,
meanwhile, offered the regime fewer grounds for congratulation.
Chateaubriand, a rather jaundiced observer, complained that 'our navy is
our veritable wound.'[63] Such criticisms pushed the navy minister to defend
his department by claiming that the fleet, given its limited resources, had
done 'all that we could expect of it'.[64] Indeed, cost-cutting rendered the
navy less effective than the army as an instrument of French power and
prestige. Nevertheless, despite the logistical flaws highlighted by the
Ouvrard debacle, the new fiscal-military system had succeeded.

The borrowing required to fund the Spanish expedition facilitated the
Rothschilds' ascent on the Bourse by providing their first major coup in

---

[61] Darriulat, *Muse du peuple*, 23–6.   [62] Ploux, *De bouche à oreille*, 54–6, 178–82.
[63] Chateaubriand to Polignac, 31 July 1823, in Thomas, *Correspondance générale de Chateaubriand*,
IV, 349.
[64] Clermont-Tonnerre to Bonald, 8 September 1823, Clermont-Tonnerre MSS, AN, 359AP/81.

France. Though the Rothschilds were already gaining a fearsome reputation by 1823, they owed their standing to their role as creditors for other states. Facing stiff competition in Britain and France after 1815, they had turned to the other great powers.[65] In addition to the Prussian loan of 1818, in 1820 the Rothschilds agreed to issue Austrian bonds alongside the Hamburg banker David Parish. Two years later, they floated further Austrian and Russian loans. In France, meanwhile, James de Rothschild had joined Laffitte to bid unsuccessfully for the 1821 loan. By contrast, two years later, with Villèle averse to borrowing through liberal bankers, the Rothschilds issued the treasury bills with which the government initially financed the Spanish campaign. Their role in providing the French army with money in Spain once the expedition was launched probably reinforced the impression of their ascendancy. In May, Angoulême noted that 'it would be very useful to profit from the means that M. Rothschild can procure to have funds in Madrid.'[66] Shortly afterwards, in July, the Rothschilds secured the contract to float a loan of 23,114,516 francs of 5 per cent *rentes* at 89.55, raising 413,980,981.56 francs to redeem the treasury bills, reduce the *dette flottante* and cover the remaining expenses of the intervention.[67] The City acquired a prominent role. Shortly before the loan was adjudicated, James de Rothschild informed his brother in London that 'we shall be happy to give you an interest' in addition to 'such of your friends as may be desirous of taking a share'.[68] Indeed, the Rothschilds' triumph reflected the continuing importance of foreign investors to French public credit: with branches in Paris, London, Frankfurt, Vienna and Naples, the Rothschilds embodied international finance. As Villèle noted a few days after the adjudication, 'we have here Rothschild of London, Rothschild of Vienna, Rothschild of Frankfurt and Rothschild of Paris: it is that which contributed in no small way to my confidence in setting my minimum at 89 fr.'[69] Although Villèle preferred the Rothschilds to their opposition-affiliated rivals, he had no particular desire to award them the 1823 loan; he did so because they presented the highest bid. Entrenching their financial supremacy, the Rothschilds rapidly amassed resources that dwarfed those of their rivals. André et Cottier, a reputable Paris firm, had a capital of 4.8 million francs in 1826; a year later, Laffitte's capital

[65] Ferguson, *World's Banker*, 124, 131.
[66] Angoulême to Villèle, 16 May 1823, in Villèle, *Mémoires*, III, 454.
[67] *Le Moniteur universel*, 11 July 1823.
[68] [De Rothschild frères to N.M. Rothschild and Sons], n.d. [June 1823], RAL, XI/85/7A.
[69] Villèle to Angoulême, 14 July 1823, in Villèle, *Mémoires*, IV, 228.

stood at 15 million.[70] Other eminent firms were much smaller. The five Rothschild houses, meanwhile, had a combined capital of 109 million francs in 1828, nearly twice that of the Banque de France; already, in 1825, their capital was ten times greater than that of Barings, with whom they had been roughly equal in 1815.[71] Such resources allowed them to establish a lasting ascendancy over French public credit.

Villèle sought to ensure that 'the effects' of the 1823 campaign were 'as durable as possible'.[72] Thus, the French retained troops in Spain until 1828. Nevertheless, their demands for reimbursement of 31 million francs in costs of both the expedition and maintaining their troops in Spain thereafter, though they had some success, met Spanish resistance.[73] Part of the problem arose from Spain's financial difficulties, which had exacerbated the volatility of Spanish politics after 1814. Raising taxes was difficult, and the government's inability to pay its troops produced discontent in the army – one of the causes of the 1820 Revolution. Following the 1823 Spanish expedition, Ferdinand refused to honour loans contracted in London by his liberal opponents in the Cortes. Consequently, the City regarded him warily.[74] Britain's hope of furthering its commercial interests by supporting the independence of Spain's recently lost Latin American colonies created further friction.[75] Thus, the Spanish government turned to Paris. Given Spain's poor creditworthiness, the French initially supported schemes to reconquer former Spanish colonies, which would restore colonial revenues while mitigating British influence in Latin America and so potentially allow greater French commercial penetration of the region.[76] Supporting reconquest was also useful as a means of retaining influence over the Spanish government. As early as the autumn of 1823, though, French influence over Ferdinand and his entourage was receding, and this trend continued as the French dropped their support for reconquering the colonies as unfeasible; French commerce could prosper under the aegis of independent American states, over which the French hoped to develop their influence by establishing dynastic ties.[77]

Instead, Villèle moved to support a Spanish loan. While many French bankers were as reluctant as their British counterparts, the Spanish

[70] Gille, *Banque et le crédit*, 56.　　　[71] Gille, *Rothschild*, I, 165–6; Ferguson, *World's Banker*, 172.
[72] Villèle to Angoulême, 5 July 1823, in Villèle, *Mémoires*, IV, 198.
[73] Butrón Prida, *Ocupación francesa*, 64–108.　　　[74] Simal, 'National Credit'.
[75] Yamada, 'George Canning and the Concert of Europe', 113–90.
[76] Villèle to Angoulême, 18 July 1823, in Villèle, *Mémoires*, IV, 236–42; Blaufarb, 'Western Question', 748–50.
[77] Larroche, *Expédition d'Espagne*, 303–8; Robertson, *France and Latin American Independence*.

nevertheless contracted two loans with the second-rank firms of Guebhard and Pictet, the first of 200 million reals in July 1823 and the second of 334 million reals in September – altogether worth around 144 million francs.[78] Yet, Pictet withdrew, and Guebhard proved unable to honour his obligations. Alejandro Aguado, a Paris banker of Spanish origin, took over the issue. Over subsequent years, he became Spain's principal financier and, in 1826, the Spanish court's official banker.[79] The French government accepted the Guebhard loans' placement in Paris, since they could strengthen its position in Madrid, further harnessing the Bourse for the needs of foreign policy. An ordonnance of 12 November stated that the 'public securities of foreign governments will be quoted' on the Bourse, allowing the official placement of the Guebhard loans, despite Villèle's reservations about their terms.[80] On one level, Villèle's ordonnance merely endorsed foreign securities' ongoing penetration of the Bourse, seeking to bring the process more within the ambit of state regulation. In formalising the trade of foreign government securities, the 1823 ordonnance marked something of a milestone in the French state's relationship with the Bourse. Still, despite encouraging an influx of Spanish government bonds on the Bourse, the ordonnance could not compensate for a general lack of confidence in Spain's creditworthiness. The day after the ordonnance, Sartoris described the Guebhard loans as 'very bad', reflecting opinion on the Bourse: then oscillating around the mid-20s, the price of Spanish 5 per cent bonds sank into the high teens in 1824.[81] While Villèle regarded credit as necessary to stabilise the country, he was only prepared to go so far. After Guebhard's failure, he refused to guarantee a loan offered by the Rothschilds, Barings and Reid-Irving. Nevertheless, Villèle hoped that the Bourse and the City could provide the necessary funds.[82] By February, he saw issuing in both London and Paris as increasingly attractive, given his growing desire to convert French 5 per cent *rentes* into bonds bearing a lower rate of interest – too much demand on the Bourse risked depressing the price of *rentes* and so rendering a conversion more difficult.[83] A Franco-British loan to Spain also raised the possibility of defusing the tensions that arose with Britain over the 1823 expedition.

[78] Gille, *Rothschild*, I, 115.   [79] Luis, *Ivresse de la fortune*, 149–51, 153–6, 167–80.
[80] Gontard, *Bourse*, 185–6; Luis, *Ivresse de la fortune*, 149.
[81] Sartoris, d'Echerny et Cie to H.A. Koymans, 13 November 1823, Greffulhe MSS, AN, 61AQ/217, fol. 7.
[82] Gille, *Rothschild*, I, 121–4, 130.
[83] The influx of Spanish government securities caused the *rente* to fall in November 1823, though it recovered the following month (Gontard, *Bourse*, 186).

Indeed, Villèle's move towards Britain's policy of supporting Spanish American independence in 1824, suggested the Austrian ambassador in Paris, arose from his awareness of the City's importance for his planned debt conversion.[84]

The difficulties of using credit to secure influence and stability in Spain became more apparent during the 1830s. Continuing discontent over the default on the Cortes's loans in 1823, alongside the difficulties of extracting the reimbursements for the 1823 expedition from Spain, prompted recurrent criticism in France, particularly among the liberal opposition. When members of the latter took power in Paris after the 1830 Revolution, they faced renewed pressure to uphold the interests of the bondholders; simultaneously, they sought to assure the repayment of Spain's debt to France for the 1823 expedition.[85] While negotiations made progress, Ferdinand's death in 1833 eased the way for Spain's agreement to honour the Cortes's loans a year later, contributing to a decline in Aguado's role in Spanish government loans.[86] Following the appointment of a relatively pro-French government in Madrid in 1834, the French foreign minister suggested that the French might be able to assist the Spanish in securing credit.[87] This proposal came to nothing, and though the Rothschilds stepped in nevertheless, they soon found themselves facing default due to the government's weakness and instability and a civil war.[88] Whatever the effect of finance in the 1820s, in the 1830s it failed to provide political stability and the French position – and that of the financiers – became more dependent on intrigues and court politics. In 1836, Thiers, then head of the French government, proposed to assert French influence through military intervention, but this was vetoed by the king; instead the French position in Spain deteriorated until the government sought to restore it in the 1840s.

Following the Spanish expedition, Villèle sought to settle the issue of relations with Haiti, still officially deemed a colony by the French government despite its declared independence. The possibility of Spain seeking to reconquer Latin America caused a delay, by raising the prospect of the French doing likewise in Haiti. Presented in 1823 with Haitian 'proposals for very great commercial advantages' on the condition that France abandon claims to the colony, Villèle stalled, awaiting the 'decision that Spain

[84] Bertier de Sauvigny, *Metternich et la France*, II, 898.   [85] Simal, 'National Credit', 389–95.
[86] Luis, *Ivresse de la fortune*, 179–80, 366–9.
[87] Broglie to Rayneval, 10 February 1834, MAE, 27ADP/18.
[88] López-Morell, *Casa Rothschild*, 61–103.

wants to make for its own colonies'.[89] In 1825, Spanish hopes of reconquest having receded, the French recognised Haiti's independence, in
exchange for favourable trading arrangements and 150 million francs of
compensation for the former planters, many of whom were influential
members of the French elite.[90] This arrangement would suit Villèle's desire
to extend French commerce, and thus influence, in Latin America,
increase investment in the French economy and use the Bourse to address
one of the more difficult colonial legacies of the Revolution.

As with Spain in 1823, Villèle encouraged the Haitian government to
tap the Paris market and facilitated negotiations for a loan of 30 million
francs to cover the first tranche of the indemnity. The loan was contracted
in November 1825 to Laffitte, the Rothschilds, a reconstituted *syndicat des
receveurs généraux* and the firms of Paravey, Hagerman and Blanc-Colin.[91]
The *syndicat*'s re-emergence in 1825 reflected Villèle's desire to reduce the
Rothschilds' supremacy, while providing another source of support for the
rente that could buttress his plan for a debt conversion that year. Though
the *syndicat* may have failed to end the government's dependence on the
Rothschilds, its support proved invaluable for the *rente*, not least during a
financial crisis that struck in late 1825.[92] On 11 November, just days after
the Haitian loan was agreed, the turmoil began in London. Triggered in
part by declining confidence in Latin American bonds, which City banks
had issued in large numbers during the early 1820s, the crisis depressed the
value of Haitian bonds. Consequently, the Haitian government defaulted
on its obligations; moreover, the 150 million indemnity was based on
French estimates derived from the figures of the *ancien régime* colonial
trade and greatly exceeded Haiti's capacity to pay, the value of its exports
having fallen substantially since the eighteenth century. The French government refused to guarantee the indemnity, notwithstanding pressure
from former planters and bondholders. Instead, the French and Haitian
governments agreed to reduce outstanding compensation to 60 million
francs in 1838, producing a total indemnity of 90 million francs, which the
Haitians finally discharged in 1883.[93] Despite Villèle's hopes in 1825, the
indemnity ultimately proved insufficient to stimulate the French economy,
with the sums awarded to 99 per cent of individual claimants being less
than 252 francs apiece.[94] Though the Haitian settlement produced

[89] Villèle to Angoulême, 24 August 1823, in Villèle, *Mémoires*, IV, 326–7.
[90] Joachim, 'Indemnité coloniale' , 370–2.   [91] *Le Journal du commerce*, 11 November 1825.
[92] Gille, *Rothschild*, I, 150–2.
[93] Brière, *Haïti et la France*; Blancpain, *Un siècle de relations financières*.
[94] Beauvais, 'Monnayer l'incalculable', 633–4.

discontent among those bondholders and planters who incurred losses and did little to extend French influence abroad, it nevertheless illustrated one way in which Villèle sought to harness the ascent of the Bourse for the sake of domestic and foreign policy.[95]

Despite Villèle's involvement in its negotiation, the Haitian loan was an arrangement between the financiers and the Haitian government to discharge the latter's obligation to the former planters; as with the Spanish loan of 1823, the transaction was ostensibly independent of the French state. The Greek War of Independence against the Ottomans, which began in 1821, ultimately required more direct commitments from the French government as the price for another opportunity to project French strength and prestige abroad. While the great powers initially refrained from intervention, growing Russian government sympathy for the Greeks raised concerns in London and Paris about the possibility of Russia using the war to extend its influence in the Balkans and at Constantinople. France, Villèle wrote, sought to 'pacify' Greece 'without compromising the existence' of the Ottoman Empire.[96] The latter's decline raised the prospect of greater Russian power in the Mediterranean, threatening British and French ambitions there. France and Britain, therefore, sought to restrain the tsar by joining him in action to support the Greeks, which would also assuage something of the philhellenism that the Greek Revolution engendered among sections of the French and British elites. Thus, in 1827, an Anglo-Franco-Russian fleet defeated the Ottomans at Navarino, catalysing the outbreak of the Russo-Turkish War of 1828–9. This new conflict prompted the French, ever concerned about growing Russian influence in the Mediterranean, to send troops to the Peloponnese in 1828.

As with the intervention in Spain and the Haitian loan, the French government used money as a potential vehicle for influence. Lacking an effective fiscal system, the Greeks solicited funds to assist in their struggle for independence. In addition to raising loans and private donations, chiefly in London and Paris, they petitioned European governments for contributions. Most of the latter came from Britain, but France also erratically provided meagre subsidies in 1828–9, as did Russia.[97] The Greek War of Independence essentially ended in 1829, but it was not until 1832 that Greece acquired its first king. As part of the terms of his accession, France, Britain and Russia each guaranteed a third of a

[95] On the planters' discontent, see Lewis, 'Legacies of French Slave-Ownership'.
[96] Villèle to Polignac, 2 April 1827, in Villèle, *Mémoires*, V, 254.
[97] Schönhärl, *Banken in Griechenland*, 37–110; Dakin, *Greek Struggle for Independence*, 244–7.

60 million franc loan, which was contracted to the Rothschilds in 1833. In 1836, the Greek government defaulted on interest payments, forcing the international guarantees into effect. For French officials, seeking to minimise their liability, this reinforced their contempt for the Greek administration.[98] By the mid-1840s, while Émile Desages, *directeur politique* at the French foreign ministry, sought to maintain French influence in Greece, he complained repeatedly about 'this wretched financial question'.[99] The loan, he wrote, 'holds, at least morally, Greece in a state of dependence from which, if I were Greek, I would want to liberate myself at all costs'.[100] Desages felt that the loan had become a hindrance to French influence through its potential to cause Franco-Greek friction. As with Spain and Haiti in the 1820s, Greece during the 1830s and 1840s reflected the limits of foreign borrowing on the Bourse as a vehicle for French influence.

Evident in the interventions in Spain and Greece, French ambitions in the Mediterranean were similarly apparent in the conquest of Algiers in 1830. Following an altercation between the dey and the French consul in 1827, the French blockaded Algiers. However, would-be gunboat diplomacy failed. The blockade, described by one minister as 'almost illusory', was difficult to maintain and the navy was unable to prevent Algerian attacks on French shipping.[101] Moreover, the Chambers disliked the expense of maintaining a blockade. Commercial interests and deputies therefore demanded decisive military action, particularly given the malaise that beset the economy in the late 1820s. Not only could the conquest of Algiers alleviate the threat to French shipping, but it could allow the realisation of aspirations that arose from the mid-1820s to colonise the regency for France's economic benefit, partly to compensate for the loss of Haiti.[102]

Wanting Algiers off the agenda, Villèle demurred. Still, his days in office were numbered and, as political pressure mounted on the ultras towards the end of the decade, action over Algiers looked increasingly attractive as a means of recovering their political position. Wounded by election defeats

[98] 'Résumé des affaires de Grèce, 1er juin 1835–décembre 1842', March 1843, MAE, 22MD/6, fols. 53–80.
[99] Desages to Piscatory, 31 December 1845 and 10 February 1846, Desages MSS, MAE, 60PAAP/25, fols. 35–7, 41.
[100] Desages to Piscatory, 20 March 1846, Desages MSS, MAE, 60PAAP/25, fol. 51.
[101] 19 December 1829, in Guernon-Ranville, *Journal*, 10; rapports au roi, by Chabrol, 27 June, 16 October, 6 December and 16 December 1827, SHD, BB¹ 67, fols. 17, 30, 32–4.
[102] Todd, 'Imperial Meridian', 169–70; Todd, 'Retour sur l'expédition d'Alger', 210–15.

in 1821 and 1824, the liberals reorganised for the election of 1827. They sought to counter the government's efforts to disenfranchise opposition voters – which were, for example, evident in the reductions to direct taxes.[103] In 1828, Villèle, forced from office after the election defeat, was replaced by Viscount Jean-Baptiste de Martignac, whose centrist ministry was a compromise that satisfied nobody. Composed largely of nondescript technocrats, the ministry was disliked by Charles X as a government imposed on him and was unpopular with the liberals who saw in it too much continuity with Villèle. Having supported the ultras throughout the Restoration, Charles orchestrated the creation of a new ultra ministry under Prince Jules de Polignac in August 1829. Lacking support in the Chamber of Deputies, Polignac sought intervention in Algiers to bolster the government's position in preparation for an election, while seeing an opportunity to enhance French influence in the Mediterranean – which aroused British opposition to the Algiers expedition. Thus, with Russian support, Polignac sent troops to Algiers. Prior to departing France, the soldiers undertook a series of parades for the public, to maximise political capital from the expedition.[104] Still, like the interventions in Spain and Greece, victory in Algiers did little to strengthen the regime. While the expedition stimulated less unrest than the Spanish campaign, it seems to have had little impact either on the 1830 elections or on the revolution that overthrew of the regime in July, a little under a month after the French declared victory. The ensuing conquest of Algeria was the constitutional monarchies' most expensive military enterprise. Paradoxically, it arose partly from the navy's inadequacy, itself largely a consequence of fiscal stringency.

As with the Spanish campaign, initially bankrolled through treasury bills, the interventions in Greece and Algiers were financed through the *dette flottante*. Thus, in 1830, the government issued a new loan of 80 million francs to redeem bills issued principally to fund the action in Greece and the blockade of Algiers, increasing the capacity of the *dette flottante* to finance the conquest of Algiers.[105] The cost of the latter was then reimbursed using the dey's plundered treasury, valued at 48,684,527.94 francs.[106] For all three of these interventions abroad, therefore, the government used the *dette flottante* to finance military and

[103] Kent, *Election of 1827*.   [104] Sessions, *By Sword and Plow*, 35–47.
[105] Rapport au roi, by Chabrol, 6 December 1829, *Le Moniteur universel*, 7 December 1829. The loan was originally approved in the law of 19 June 1828.
[106] 'Inventaire du trésor de la Régence d'Alger', procès-verbaux, 10 August 1830, SHD, 1H 225.

naval action and then reduced these liabilities, either by converting them into *rentes* – as in the cases of Spain and Greece – or by obtaining reimbursement from those it conquered or assisted – as it did in Algiers and to a lesser extent in Spain. The Rothschilds floated the 1830 loan in 4 per cent *rentes* at 102.075, the first issued above par during the Restoration, a success which, one minister remarked, 'surpassed our expectations'.[107] The issuing rate reflected new competition for the Rothschilds from the *syndicat des receveurs généraux*, but the Rothschilds retained the advantage of their unparalleled international connections, not least in the City. Indeed, to facilitate the issue of the 1830 loan, a clerk of the London Rothschilds was designated as an agent of the French treasury and empowered to certify scrip.[108]

In exploiting the fiscal-military system, governments sought to make its apparatus as unobtrusive as possible, while publicising its triumphs. Striking the balance between the inconspicuous and the publicised facets of the fiscal-military system was essential to preserving its legitimacy. For this purpose, debt and a quasi-professional army were preferable to the unrest which arose from the surtaxes and mass conscription utilised during the Revolutionary and Napoleonic Wars. While the rise of public credit in the 1820s allowed the ultras to pursue an aggressive foreign policy, this was shelved after 1830 when the July Revolution replaced Charles X with his cousin Louis-Philippe, of the Orleanist cadet branch of the Bourbon dynasty. The July Monarchy, incurring the suspicion of the Continental powers as a regime born of revolution, lacked the relationship with Russia that had enabled the ultras to send troops to Spain in 1823 and Algiers in 1830. Military action abroad therefore became more difficult after 1830. The Orleanists also proved more reluctant than their Restoration predecessors to finance foreign loans, perhaps in part because the difficulties that arose with the Greek and Haitian loans underscored the shortcomings of credit as a vehicle for influence abroad. Not until the 1850s did the Bourse re-emerge as a major issuing market for foreign loans.

The Politics of Debt Conversion

The success of public credit in the 1820s was apparent in Villèle's proposals for a debt conversion, as the *rente* recovered from the Spanish

---

[107] 12 January 1830, in Guernon-Ranville, *Journal*, 22.
[108] De Rothschild frères to N.M. Rothschild and Sons, 6 February 1830, RAL, XI/85/14A. I am grateful to David Todd for this reference.

expedition. By mid-January 1824, Sartoris was noting 'the upward trend [of the *rente*]. If we have the pleasure of preserving the peace & the appearance of peace for some time, this trend will only grow.'[109] In February, the *rente* reached par (Figure 5.1), providing ideal conditions for conversion, since the state could redeem *rentes* without paying above their market value. To finance the redemption, the government would issue new bonds bearing a lower rate of interest, and hence the conversion would lower the costs of servicing government debt. Several governments contemplated conversions in the 1820s, including those of Britain, Austria and Prussia. Initially, Villèle was reluctant, but the idea became more politically attractive from late February, with the ultras' gains in the 1824 elections. Villèle hoped to exploit this victory by using the money that the conversion saved to compensate émigrés for losses of their property after 1789. In so doing, he sought to reinforce the regime by settling one of the more contentious bequests of the Revolution, much as the agreement with Haiti the following year sought to use the Bourse to resolve the major outstanding colonial question of the Revolution. Like Villèle's fiscal policy, therefore, the conversion was intended to promote stability and meet the aspirations of the ultras, on whose support the government rested. In the longer term, the conversion was to make the public debt more sustainable, and thus improve the government's access to credit.

By February 1824, Villèle was discussing the possibility of a conversion with James de Rothschild, Baring, Laffitte, Mollien, Roy and others. They were generally supportive. Bankers such as Greffulhe and Sartoris favoured the conversion since the exchange of securities it entailed would present an opportunity to offload canal shares.[110] In March, James de Rothschild wrote optimistically that he and Baring were in agreement 'as far as concerns the success of the operation'. As this suggests, Barings retained considerable importance. They were closely involved in preparing the conversion which, as with previous loans, was to be undertaken internationally. Villèle, wrote James de Rothschild, 'confesses that no French House is capable of conducting such an operation'. Still, Villèle wanted half of the conversion to be undertaken by 'the Banking Houses of Paris, [so] that they may not oppose the operation and to prevent clamour'.[111] Laffitte, though associated generally with the liberal opposition, therefore

[109] Sartoris, d'Echerny et Cie to H.A. Koymans, 19 January 1824, Greffulhe MSS, AN, 61AQ/217, fol. 26.
[110] Gille, *Rothschild*, I, 135–40.
[111] James de Rothschild to Baring and Nathan Rothschild, 13 March 1824, BA, HC 7.7.1.

reprised his role of July 1817 and joined James de Rothschild and Baring as the French banker on the committee formed to oversee the conversion.[112] Villèle's effort to ensure that business went to French banks probably neutralised some opposition to the conversion. Laffitte put his name to a pamphlet supporting it forcefully as a means of stimulating the economy by lowering interest rates, while reducing the cost of the public debt.[113] Yet, other Paris bankers, such as Perier and Sanlot-Baguenault, were excluded. This perhaps encouraged their hostility to the conversion, though Perier, for instance, presented himself as opposing Villèle's political machinations and subservience to foreign bankers.[114] In this respect, he recycled arguments levelled against the loans of 1817–18.

In addition to cultivating financiers, Villèle sought to assuage public opinion. On 26 March, the *Moniteur* published an article that addressed concerns about the legality of requiring investors to relinquish their *rentes*.[115] Soon after, Villèle or one of his acolytes approached Thiers, then a journalist at the *Constitutionnel* and probably the ghostwriter of Laffitte's pamphlet, seeking his 'opinion' on the latter – in effect, his support.[116] While lauding the idea of conversion, Thiers evaded the request. He was, observed his correspondent, 'alone among your friends' in favouring the idea; indeed, opposition was widespread among the liberals.[117] Thiers's potential value as an ally was enhanced by his connection to the opposition-affiliated *Constitutionnel*, which had a larger print run than the pro-government Parisian daily newspapers combined.[118]

On 5 April, Villèle presented the Chamber of Deputies with a proposal to replace 5 per cent *rentes* with 3 per cent *rentes* to be issued at 75. Despite his preparations, the plan faced fierce opposition. The liberals aside, 130 royalist deputies voted against the bill, though it passed nevertheless. Ultras such as La Bourdonnaye and Crignon d'Auzouer questioned its legality, and denounced the conversion as harmful to rentiers and thus

---

[112] Contract of 22 March 1824, Rothschild MSS, ANMT, 132AQ/32; procès-verbaux of the committee, Rothschild MSS, ANMT, 132AQ/32.
[113] Laffitte, *Réflexions*.
[114] Perier, 5 April and 28 April 1824, AP, 2nd series, XXXIX, 712, XL, especially 157–8.
[115] 'Du remboursement des rentes 5 pour cent ou de la réduction des intérêts', *Le Moniteur universel*, 26 March 1824.
[116] Unknown to Thiers, 4 April [1824], Thiers MSS, BNF, NAF 20601, fol. 25; Gille, *Rothschild*, I, 143–4.
[117] Thiers to unknown, n.d. [April 1824], and unknown to Thiers, 10 April [1824], Thiers MSS, BNF, NAF 20601, fols. 27–9.
[118] Franke-Postberg, *Milliard des émigrés*, 132.

detrimental to public credit.[119] Even before Villèle presented his proposal, Sartoris observed that 'the true Rentiers are shouting like madmen against this decrease in their revenues. Many are selling.'[120] Beyond complaining about a decrease in their income, which was particularly threatening to small rentiers, these investors and their supporters in the Chambers pilloried the proposal as an assault on property. Owning *rentes*, as with other property, gave these investors a stake in society and helped to define them as citizens; compromising their property rights thus risked destabilising the sociopolitical order.[121] The number of small rentiers was relatively trivial: around 10,000 held between 10 and 50 francs of *rentes*, which comprised only 310,000 francs of the 140 million of 5 per cent *rentes* in circulation in 1824.[122] Nevertheless, they, alongside bankers opposed to the conversion, presented a formidable obstacle. Though other bankers – who sought to profit from the commissions attached to the conversion – sustained the price of *rentes*, Mollien, for instance, opposed the bill on the basis that inadequate 'preparation of opinion' would hinder its implementation.[123] Others such as Sanlot-Baguenault, one of Villèle's associates, criticised the conversion as increasing the public debt: 'The main problem with the proposal is that it increases the capital of the public debt by around a thousand million, under the pretext of an annual economy of 28 million, and it slows, by an inevitable consequence, the effect of amortisation.'[124] Roy, whatever he may have said to Villèle in February or March, made a similar argument.[125] The conversion was both attacked and defended by invoking the same principles of political economy, those of minimising debt and maintaining public credit. The connection between the conversion and the compensation of the émigrés stimulated further opposition. Since the beginning of the Restoration, some had agitated for the return of property they had lost after 1789, encouraging the perception of the émigrés as arch-reactionaries. Still, this does not explain the bill's rejection by the Chamber of Peers; personal grudges against Villèle and the proposal's cost to rentiers proved decisive.[126]

---

[119] La Bourdonnaye, 24 April 1824, and Crignon d'Auzouer, 28 April 1824, AP, 2nd series, XL, 53–63, 163–6.
[120] Sartoris, d'Echerny et Cⁱᵉ to H.A. Koymans, 27 March 1824, Greffulhe MSS, AN, 61AQ/217, fol. 64.
[121] Gain, *Biens des émigrés*, I, 520–36.   [122] Coq, 'De la conversion', 64.
[123] Mollien, 26 May 1824, AP, 2nd series, XL, 737–40.
[124] Sanlot-Baguenault, 26 April 1824, AP, 2nd series, XL, 82.
[125] Roy, 24 May 1824, AP, 2nd series, XL, 692–706.
[126] Waresquiel, *Un groupe d'hommes*, 172–5.

The rejection of Villèle's scheme did not dampen major bankers' willingness for a conversion. 'Despite the heat of the controversy,' the bankers on the conversion committee had written over a month before, 'our opinion is less doubtful than ever on the great results of this vast operation.'[127] Others, however, were relieved by Villèle's failure. David Parish, for instance, complained that the conversion would have 'unhinged the money market throughout Europe'; it had been, he wrote, based on 'a bullying principle brought forward under the sanction of the money aristocracy'.[128] Despite the proposal's rejection, the *rente* remained strong. Louis XVIII's death in September, the possibility of which had aroused fears of political instability during the early Restoration, did not weaken it. As James de Rothschild observed, 'our stocks, far from feeling any disagreeable influence, have received the contrary impulse and have experienced a considerable rise. Things could not go otherwise after the sensible and reassuring manner in which the current King signalled his entry into Government.'[129] Villèle continued in office, and Charles X reaffirmed the government's commitment to conversion. Thus, the 'money aristocracy' remained onside when Villèle presented the Chambers with a fresh proposal in January 1825.

The new plan comprised two bills: one to compensate émigrés through an issue of 3 per cent *rentes* and another for a debt conversion. The new conversion proposal was more cautious. Not only was it optional, but the 3 per cent *rentes* at 75 were now supplemented with an alternative of 4½ per cent *rentes* at par, with a guarantee against the reimbursement of 5 per cent *rentes* until 1835. Of course, these proposals remained open to the charge, made the previous year, that they increased the public debt. Still, those wanting to retain 5 per cent *rentes* were sufficiently mollified, and the bills passed in April. Given Villèle's partiality towards them, landowners were the main beneficiaries, much as they were under Restoration tax policy.[130] Indeed, the 1825 conversion proposal probably benefited from stipulating that any savings it produced would go, from 1826, into reducing 'a number of *centimes additionnels* corresponding to the *contributions foncière, personnelle, mobilière*, and *des portes et fenêtres*'.[131] The appeal to interest groups surrounding land and finance both eased the

[127] Laffitte, James de Rothschild and Baring to Villèle, 22 April 1824, Rothschild MSS, ANMT, 132AQ/32.
[128] Parish to L. Greffulhe, 23 June 1824, Greffulhe MSS, AN, 61AQ/186.
[129] James de Rothschild to Baring, 20 September 1824, BA, HC 7.7.2.
[130] Vidalenc, *Émigrés*, 443–4.
[131] Projet de loi, 3 January 1825 (article 5), AP, 2nd series, XLII, 607.

approval of the proposals and contributed to the controversy surrounding them. The list of deputies and peers who voted in favour of the bills correlates with those who benefited, while no plan would have been feasible without the bankers' cooperation.[132] Nevertheless, the government economised 6,230,157 francs as, of the 140 million francs of 5 per cent *rentes*, 1,149,738 francs were converted into 1,034,764 francs of 4.5 per cent *rentes* and 30,573,794 francs became 24,459,035 francs of 3 per cent *rentes*. Even this modest success was tainted by the crash of November 1825, provoking complaints of losses among those who had converted.[133] Moreover, though rentiers had not been forced to fund the compensation of the émigrés, the cost of doing so now fell to the taxpayer, which provoked renewed opposition; the proposal therefore increased the size and servicing costs of the public debt, as those such as Perier complained.[134] Thus, the liberals that took power after the 1830 Revolution raised the prospect of reclaiming émigré indemnities to mitigate pressures on the treasury. Instead, they merely abolished the *fonds commun* that distributed part of the indemnity, and the idea of reclamations resurfaced in 1848 and 1851 – both years in which the public finances were under strain.[135] The émigrés, therefore, remained an issue of contention in French politics, while the indemnity ultimately added 867 million francs to the public debt.[136]

The failure of Villèle's initial proposal also had a lasting influence. In December 1829, when finance minister Comte Christophe de Chabrol de Crousol presented the cabinet with a proposal to convert 5 per cent *rentes*, he was asked about the rate of conversion. 'Too low,' he replied, 'at 3 per cent, for example, as in the proposal of M. de Villèle, the loss would be enormous for the small rentier and would push him away from the conversion; too high, [at] 4½ or 4¾, the benefit to the State would be feeble, the reduction of the interest rate would have little effect on private transactions.' Chabrol therefore proposed to avoid emulating Villèle's error by converting to 4 per cent *rentes* at par. In effect, his plan differed little from that of Villèle, which had entailed converting to 3 per cent *rentes* at 75; Villèle, in other words, proposed to convert from 5 per cent to 4 per cent, just not with 4 per cent *rentes*. While converting to 4 per cent *rentes* at par avoided increasing the debt, which had been a prominent criticism

---

[132] Vidalenc, *Émigrés*, 441.   [133] Rietsch, 'Milliard des Émigrés', 226.
[134] Perier, 7 March 1825, AP, 2nd series, XLIII, 615–19.
[135] Gain, *Biens des émigrés*, II, 355–84; Franke-Postberg, *Milliard des émigrés*, 287–9.
[136] Rietsch, 'Milliard des Émigrés', 255.

of Villèle's plan, Chabrol's proposal emulated Villèle's real political mistake of seeking to make the reimbursement of 5 per cent *rentes* compulsory.[137] Chabrol, though, never realised his error. Instead, the success of the loan of 80 million francs contracted above par in 4 per cent *rentes* in January undermined his plan. In this situation, to issue 4 per cent *rentes* at par, as Chabrol's conversion entailed, would be to increase the profits of the bankers selling these bonds – not something likely to find favour in the Chambers. Thus, the 1830 loan adjudication left Chabrol, one of his colleagues observed, 'very annoyed at such a beautiful outcome ... [W]ith the 4 per cent exceeding par like this, he finds himself needing to take a lower rate for the conversion and, with the losses on rentiers' revenues then becoming greater, the success of the proposal in the chambers could be compromised.' Although the government remained committed to a conversion, James de Rothschild, whose support was essential, was circumspect.[138] Ill-conceived and ill-prepared, the plan disintegrated.

As P.G.M. Dickson observed of eighteenth-century Britain, a debt conversion needed careful preparation, the lack of which caused many proposed conversions to be stillborn.[139] The cooperation of the financiers was essential, as was a favourable political situation. While Villèle prepared his 1824 proposal carefully, it was scuppered mainly by the rentiers whose capital had aided the *rente*'s rise in the first place. The existence of this highly influential interest group presented a severe problem for Villèle in 1824, and contributed to the failure of proposals for debt conversions until the 1850s.

Conclusion

The 1820s offered a clear demonstration of the potential of the post-Napoleonic fiscal-military system, combining successful management of public credit and victories in Spain, Greece and Algiers with less fruitful attempts to convert the 5 per cent *rente* and exploit the Bourse as an instrument of French influence abroad. Thus, the late Restoration became a golden age of the traditional fiscal-military state, contrary to claims that the latter disappeared after 1815.[140] This fiscal-military state looked broadly similar to that of eighteenth-century Britain and proved more

---

[137] 16 December 1829, in Guernon-Ranville, *Journal*, 4–5.
[138] 12 and 13 January 1830, in Guernon-Ranville, *Journal*, 22–3; Ferguson, *World's Banker*, 229.
[139] Dickson, *Financial Revolution*, 83, 212–14, 229–39.
[140] Leuchter, 'Finance beyond the Bounds'.

sustainable than those of the *ancien régime*, the revolutionary decade and Napoleon, surviving the 1830 Revolution. Thereafter, though, with the growing importance of public works spending from the late 1830s onwards, the French state diverged increasingly from the eighteenth-century model.

The French were conscious of the British example, invoking it frequently, as they had in past debates over public credit and taxation: in 1818, for instance, the government's critics had condemned the 'English' methods used to contract the loan with Barings. The debate over debt conversion was littered with references to the British model. In 1824, Laffitte endorsed conversion as 'real progress for French civilisation, a step in the direction in which the English have outstripped the world'.[141] Thus, debt conversion would mark progression towards 'English'-style finance. By contrast, opponents of the conversion presented it as deviating from the 'English' model. Roy, for instance, invoked 'English' principles to justify his opposition in 1824. The English, he claimed, had never increased the public debt in peacetime on the scale that Villèle's 1824 proposal required.[142] On both sides of the conversion debate, the association between a high *rente* and the progress of civilisation in France was widespread. For the political elite, 'English' finance had two principal advantages. Firstly, in mitigating potential fiscal shocks, an effective system of public credit provided a bulwark against chaos. Secondly, borrowing allowed military action and public works, both of which were intended to ensure the stability and legitimacy of the regime. In facilitating French intervention abroad, 'English' finance reinforced France's status as a great power.

Beyond providing a model for the post-revolutionary fiscal-military state, Britain also provided much of the money that made it possible; as we have seen, British investors were essential buyers of *rentes* after 1817, playing a much larger role in French public credit than before. Though many French nationalists regarded Britain as the 'anti-France', developing Anglophobic discourses of the eighteenth century, in practice conflict with Britain became more difficult.[143] No French government wanted to risk losing access to the London financial market. Indeed, as we have seen, Villèle's sensitivity to the City contributed to his decision to abandon support for a Spanish reconquest in Latin America. The importance of British capital to the French economy grew during the mid-century;

---

[141] Laffitte, *Réflexions*, 8.   [142] Roy, 24 May 1824, AP, 2nd series, XL, 698.
[143] Tombs and Tombs, *That Sweet Enemy*, 310–38.

simultaneously, French financiers and industrialists pursued opportunities in Britain.[144] While the restored Bourbons' foreign policy was generally more hostile to Britain than that of the July Monarchy and the Second Empire, the Restoration's recourse to British investment laid some of the foundations for the Franco-British rapprochement of the mid-nineteenth century. The result, as we shall see, was the *entente cordiale* of the 1840s, a Franco-British alliance in the Crimean War and varying degrees of cooperation in the pursuit of extra-European interests.

[144] Cottrell, 'Anglo-French Financial Cooperation'.

CHAPTER 6

The 1830 Revolution and the Limits of Fiscal Reform

The 1830 Revolution, like that of 1848, underscored the durability of the post-Napoleonic fiscal-military system. This is not to suggest that the revolution changed nothing; historians have conceived of the early July Monarchy as years of reform.[1] The Orleanists being more liberal than their ultra predecessors, they revised the Charter and abolished the censorship of the press that ultra ministers had pursued in the late 1820s. Meanwhile, they lowered the voting qualification for national elections from 300 to 200 francs of direct tax, raising the electorate from 94,000 in 1830 to 166,000 in 1831. The regime deflected pressure for further enfranchisement through the reform of municipal elections, where suffrage was extended to 30 per cent of men aged over twenty-one.[2] This was justified as acclimatising Frenchmen to the political process, forming them into *citoyens capacitaires* capable of exercising reason, and thus as a prelude to a wider franchise for national elections. These invocations of meritocracy reflected a broader shift in political culture arising from the revolution that dovetailed uneasily with the survival of a hereditary monarchy, particularly since the hereditary Chamber of Peers was replaced with an appointed one.[3] The Orleanists also ended the ecclesiastical control over education established by the ultras in the 1820s. In 1833, a new law reduced the restrictions on the private provision of primary education. Simultaneously, Guizot, an eminent Orleanist and the law's architect, sought to improve the quality of state-provided education. For him, education policy was part of a broader agenda, in which the government's role was to foster social cohesion and, thus, stability.[4] In pursuit of this aim, the Orleanists continued the trend evident under the Napoleonic regime and the early Restoration towards more 'scientific' government. In 1833, Thiers, as

[1] Harismendy, *France des années 1830.*   [2] Guionnet, *Apprentissage de la politique,* 10.
[3] Margadant, 'Gender, Vice and the Political Imaginary'.
[4] Rosanvallon, *Moment Guizot,* 231–40.

minister of the interior, established the Statistique générale de la France, tasked with producing data to illuminate the condition of the country and thus improve the effectiveness of government.

The fiscal-military system was not insulated from these reforming ambitions. The army, staffed with many aristocratic, pro-Bourbon officers, was reorganised to assure its loyalty to the new regime. Many of these officers resigned after 1830, to be replaced with men drawn from the lower middle class, committed to long-term service. In 1832, the Chambers reduced the length of service from eight to five years and raised the army's nominal strength to 500,000, while rejecting the war ministry's plans for a reserve. Initiated during the Restoration, the professionalisation of the army continued. The regime had less success in reforming the tax system. Why? Just as a fiscal crisis stimulated the 1789 Revolution and a surge in resistance to taxation and conscription presaged the collapse of the Empire in 1814–15, discontent over taxation rose in the late 1820s. In each case, economic problems provoked unrest over taxation, which weakened the legitimacy of the fiscal system. Partly responding to this discontent, several members of the liberal opposition in the 1820s, some of whom took power after 1830, developed a critique of Restoration political economy. There was, in other words, no lack of pressure for fiscal reform. In response, the new regime proposed changes to direct taxation that were more ambitious than anything devised by Restoration governments. Though largely unsuccessful, this reform reflected a shift away from the Napoleonic and Restoration focus on cutting direct taxes. The Orleanists also implemented limited reforms of other taxes. Still, in considering the fiscal consequences of the 1830 Revolution, we can see both why the tax system survived and the strength of the conservative interests that sought to preserve it as it had developed since the 1790s.

The Slump and the Rise of Liberal Political Economy

The rising pressure for fiscal reform in the 1820s coincided with the growing traction of liberal political economy, though the latter's importance should not be overstated. As with the impact of physiocracy on the 1789 Revolution, the influence of liberal political economy depended on the extent of its alignment with the interests that shaped tax policy. As we have seen, it exercised little influence over the cuts to direct taxes after 1819. The damage that the Revolution inflicted on political economy lasted into the nineteenth century. The field was regarded as conducive to extremes, which fitted uneasily with the moderation championed by many *girouettes*, the doctrinaires and other liberals. When the philosopher and economist Henri de Saint-Simon sent a manuscript to Laffitte seeking his opinion, the latter responded that 'I find the principles too absolute, the outcomes poorly specified, [and] the method … is veritably ridiculous.' Not only did Laffitte disagree with Saint-Simon's notion of an overarching vision of the ideal socio-economic order, he thought it unnecessary: 'You understand that to render all my thought would require me to commit myself to a work almost as comprehensive as your own, for which I do not have the time and still less the pretension.'[5] Practice and experience provided supposedly much better guidance for action than abstract theorising. As Laffitte's attitude suggests, moreover, many members of the opposition had no desire to overhaul the fiscal-military system, instead preferring Restoration political economy, albeit often in a modified form.

Economists sought to reduce such contempt and, in the process, attracted the attention of prominent opposition politicians. Say, for example, published a *Catéchisme d'économie politique* in 1815, which he reissued in 1821. Saint-Simon, likewise, sought to capture public attention with a *Catéchisme des industriels*, while lamenting that 'the principal bankers, businessmen and manufacturers of Paris should have subscribed to the lectures of Mr Say.'[6] Such efforts to disseminate ideas of political economy had some impact. In 1829, Tanneguy Duchâtel, an opposition deputy, doctrinaire and later a minister under Louis-Philippe, favourably reviewed Say's *Cours complet d'économie politique pratique* in the *Globe*.[7] Founded by a group of young intellectuals in 1824, the *Globe* became a prominent opposition newspaper in the late 1820s and frequently printed articles lauding liberal political economy, many of which were written by Duchâtel.[8]

The spread of liberal political economy benefited from the slump of the late 1820s, which stimulated dissatisfaction with the regime and the fiscal system. The failure of the potato crop in 1826 and a bad harvest the following year sharply increased food prices; by 1828, the average price of wheat was 40 per cent higher than in 1825. The wine industry, which had been sluggish throughout the Restoration, was especially badly affected by the ensuing slump.[9] Villèle had attempted to appease the wine lobby's

---

[5] Laffitte to Saint-Simon, n.d., Saint-Simonian MSS, BNF, NAF 24605, fol. 48.
[6] Saint-Simon to unknown, n.d. Saint-Simonian MSS, BNF, NAF 24605, fol. 33.
[7] *Le Globe*, 4 March 1829. Say disliked the review, which he felt contained several misunderstandings.
[8] Goblot, *Jeune France libérale*, 310–22.
[9] Pilbeam, *1830 Revolution*, 40–5; Pinkney, *Revolution of 1830*, 60.

complaints about taxation and to stimulate the industry by reducing the *droit de circulation*, a sales duty imposed on alcohol producers, in the 1825 budget.[10] This did little to deflect discontent; likewise, grain shortages, often blamed on the government, stimulated both food riots and unrest over taxation as a way of channelling grievances against the authorities or the relatively wealthy. Crowds gathered at *octroi* barriers, while others refused to pay taxes.[11] The tobacco monopoly, too, faced criticism both for the abuses it engendered and for inhibiting free enterprise. As the *Globe* proclaimed, 'We dare to submit to examination the justice and the appropriateness of all taxes.'[12] The customs regime, with its prohibitive tariffs, found few adherents beyond large landowners and those dedicated to the development of commerce with France's remaining colonies. Even some committed protectionists saw a need for reform. In winegrowing regions that were more confident of their prospects against foreign competition, journalists such as Henri Fonfrède in Bordeaux promoted a smaller, more decentralised state and trade liberalisation as solutions to the malaise; meanwhile, the reduction of oppressive state apparatus would spur social regeneration.[13] The fiscal system was lambasted as an economic drag. Not only was taxation economically detrimental, it was also inherently antagonistic. 'The position of agents of the fiscal administration, from the minister of finance to the last employee,' Say argued, 'renders them perpetually hostile to citizens.'[14] Though liberal political economy did not always align with Say's republicanism, his critique of the state naturally found favour among many of the government's liberal critics.

Under such pressure to reduce taxes and spending, the government found few resources to spare to mitigate the effects of the slump, not that it necessarily saw a need to intervene. As in 1816–18, poor relief was largely left to private charity and local government.[15] Mayors, local officials and *notables* organised charitable subscriptions to establish and reinforce *bureaux de bienfaisance*, *ateliers de charité* and *dépôts de mendicité* – organisations providing assistance to the destitute – which found their resources stretched under the pressure of the slump.[16] Meanwhile, the central government did little. In 1827, the interior minister argued that economic malaise should be solved through protectionism, which would

[10] Villèle, 21 June 1824, AP, 2nd series, XLI, 530–1.
[11] Gonnet, 'Esquisse de la crise économique', 250–2, 274–80.   [12] *Le Globe*, 18 March 1829.
[13] Todd, *Free Trade*, 66–75; Rosanvallon, *Modèle politique français*, 169–72.
[14] Say, *Cours complet*, VI, 94.   [15] Pinkney, *Revolution of 1830*, 63–72.
[16] E.g. *Le Journal du commerce*, 25 September 1828; *Le Journal du commerce de la ville de Lyon et du département du Rhône*, 14 January 1829, 15 April 1829.

prevent import penetration and stimulate prosperity.[17] Martignac's government took a similar line, doing little to reform customs. Still, aiming for conciliation, Martignac's ministry was not totally passive in the face of unrest over taxation, the liberals' criticism and the petitions for tax relief that deluged the Chambers. In April 1829, the *directeur général des contributions indirectes* presented the Chamber of Deputies with minor amendments to the *droits réunis* on alcohol and proposed to limit the rate of *l'octroi*.[18] However, the power to limit *l'octroi* had already been established by the 1816 budget. Thus, the *rapporteur* remarked, 'the most important improvement' proposed for vintners, 'that resulting from a lower *octroi* duty[,] . . . must be effected by ordonnance'.[19] The commission suggested rejecting the bill; instead, the Chamber deferred voting on it, conscious that rejection risked unwelcome publicity.[20] This feeble gesture aside, the government did little to reduce taxation. For Roy, who returned as finance minister under Martignac, 'we cannot run the risk of destroying [a source of revenue] without the means of an immediate replacement.'[21]

Equally ineffective were the government's attempts to refute accusations of inefficiency and to justify existing taxes as necessary to balance the budget. In March 1830, the finance ministry published a *Rapport au roi sur l'administration des finances*, which emphasised recent improvements in fiscal administration and, its author claimed, 'showed in its true form an administration too often disfigured by ignorance and political passions'.[22] Few seem to have read this lengthy disquisition, and fewer accepted its arguments. Much of the opposition regarded Martignac's ministry, appointed by the king with little regard for the liberal majority in the Chamber, as embodying excesses of bureaucracy and royal power. Condemning the existence of sinecures, the *Globe* claimed that the bureaucracy was as voluminous as it had been under Napoleon and that 'The administration of the empire is a new *ancien régime* which must, in turn, fall.'[23] The appointment of Polignac's hard-line ultra ministry in August 1829 reinforced the notion that the state combined the worst traits of the Empire (disproportionate bureaucracy) and the *ancien régime* (royal

[17] Corbière, 19 May 1827, AP, 2nd series, LII, 175–7.
[18] Projet de loi, 13 April 1829, AP, 2nd series, LVIII, 354–5.
[19] Pavée de Vandeuvre, 27 May 1829, AP, 2nd series, LIX, 506.
[20] Lapeyrade, 27 May 1829, AP, 2nd series, LIX, 509.
[21] Roy, 11 March 1829, AP, 2nd series, LVII, 327.
[22] Chabrol de Crousol, *Rapport au roi*. The document's real author was the Marquis d'Audiffret.
[23] *Le Globe*, 15 July 1829.

absolutism). The Restoration was decried as having achieved nothing. Indeed, both liberals and ultras, when out of office, proclaimed the virtues of a small state, in contrast to the Napoleonic Leviathan maintained by Restoration governments. The arguments the ultras made in the *Chambre Introuvable* or against Decazes in 1819, for instance, foreshadowed those that the liberals directed against the governments of the 1820s. For the ultras, a minimal state would facilitate the transfer of power to the aristocratic elites and local *notables* while, for the liberals, it would reduce the state's capacity to infringe liberty.

Despite popular unrest over taxation and food riots, the idea of an overweening state, buttressed by notions of liberal political economy, was often too heavily focused on elite constitutionalism to garner much popular interest – even if the liberal opposition gained broader public support on other issues, such as anticlericalism.[24] Opposition newspapers and politicians emphasised the deputies' power to reject the budget as a means of restraining the state's excesses.[25] The disconnect between this rhetoric and popular concerns was reflected in the associations established in late 1829 to refuse the payment of taxes, following the appointment of the Polignac ministry. The first of these was the Association bretonne, conceived by a former Breton deputy and announced in the Parisian *Journal du commerce* in September 1829.[26] Officials quickly declared themselves unaware of its existence prior to its appearance in the press.[27] In October, the prefect of the Ille-et-Vilaine, one of the Breton *départements*, observed that 'No resistance shows itself in the recovery of taxes, despite the provocation of liberal newspapers.'[28] In the Finistère, however, around a thousand artisans and small businessmen gave the Association bretonne an existence in Brest, where an opposition deputy, 'after having hesitated', joined in November.[29] The prefect, though, was adamant that the organisation had not existed before September's press announcement and that it did not extend beyond Brest.

The announcement of the Association bretonne stimulated the proclamation of similar organisations elsewhere, but these proved largely elusive. The prefect of the Côte-d'Or, for example, noted that 'The opening of the subscription [for the Association bourguignonne] has produced no

---

[24] Newman, 'The Blouse and the Frock Coat'.   [25] E.g. *Le National*, 6 January 1830.
[26] *Le Journal du commerce*, 11 September 1829.   [27] AN, F⁷ 6776.
[28] Prefect of the Ille-et-Vilaine to La Bourdonnaye, October 1829, AN, F⁷ 6776.
[29] Prefect of the Finistère to Montbel, 20 November 1829, AN, F⁷ 6776; Alexander, *French Revolutionary Tradition*, 265.

result'.[30] Other prefects made similar remarks about associations in their respective *départements*. The creation of the associations coincided with a decline in popular unrest, which had been most intense in the spring of 1829. Aside from a minor resurgence in the autumn and a series of mysterious fires in Normandy for which the government and opposition blamed each other, France under Polignac was generally tranquil. Between January and late June 1830, James Rule and Charles Tilly count only seven 'violent events' across the country.[31] The limited traction of the associations and the fall in disorder does not suggest a sudden acceptance of the tax system. Rather, for many *notables* and other socially influential taxpayers, endorsing the idea of refusing taxes was too drastic, potentially placing them on the wrong side of the law. Instead, many of them channelled their discontent into a more moderate campaign to mobilise opposition to Polignac's ministry, which was conducted through a series of banquets in 1829–30. Despite the decline in violent unrest, the banquets continued to grow in the spring of 1830, promoting moderate liberal politics and gaining public traction across large parts of provincial France.[32]

The liberals' moderation, evident in the hollowness of the associations, probably encouraged Polignac's government to pursue its course of confrontation with the Chamber. 'The question of refusing taxes has become the last refuge of the liberal illusions,' declared the royalist *Gazette de France*; 'the refusal of the budget' was 'impossible', since it amounted to forcing ministers on the king.[33] Charles X and his ministers were nearly vindicated in their assessment of the opposition's weakness. Following the government's defeat in the 1830 elections, Charles approved the four ordinances, which dissolved the Chamber, scheduled fresh elections under a reduced franchise and imposed stringent press censorship. In the face of this *coup d'état*, many opposition deputies vacillated. Instead, the 1830 Revolution was instigated by the journalists and printers, whose livelihood was endangered by the ordinance on press censorship, and who mobilised the Parisian crowd.[34] Even when their interests were directly threatened, the liberals lacked the nerve for bold action, which was essential to overhaul the state. Their caution accompanied them into office and, coupled with the divisions among them and the limited traction

---

[30]　Prefect of the Côte-d'Or to La Bourdonnaye, 9 November 1829, AN, F[7] 6776.
[31]　Rule and Tilly, 'Political Process', 68–9.　　[32]　Robert, *Temps des banquets*, 133–47.
[33]　*La Gazette de France*, 2 January 1830.　　[34]　Pinkney, *Revolution of 1830*, 87–90, 96–9.

of more radical proposals for change, precluded the possibility of fundamental reform after 1830.

The 1830 Revolution and the Tax System

Despite the decline of popular unrest after late 1829, discontent over
taxation quickly became a major problem for the new July Monarchy.
Still, being drawn from the same landed and commercial elites that had
engineered the rise of indirect taxation during the Restoration, relatively
few Orleanists wanted major changes to taxation. Rather, the question was
how to make the existing tax system more acceptable. The nature of the
Orleanist elites, in other words, determined the shape of reform.
Moreover, the liberals who took power in 1830 were not a uniform group,
bound by some shared vision of reform. Two main groups quickly
appeared, the more liberal, reforming *mouvement* and the more conservative *résistance*; between them in the Chamber lay the deputies of the *tiers
parti*. These fissures would prove decisive in determining the extent of
fiscal reform.

Given the liberals' stance in the late 1820s, the revolution was expected
to deliver cheap government, 'un gouvernement à bon marché'. This
would alleviate the suffering of the poor by reducing their taxes while
simultaneously stimulating the economy. Rising unrest over indirect taxes,
the *Globe* argued in October 1830, arose from 'poverty'; 'It is absolutely
necessary to pursue, and promptly, the disappearance of the causes of
malaise that exist in many places in France . . . The government, today, can
only come to the rescue of the population by taking little; a cheap
government, that is what we need.'[35] In demanding such far-reaching
reforms, some of the liberals in the late 1820s to an extent emulated the
Bourbons in 1814, raising expectations that they would not, or could
not, meet.

Hopes of reform after the revolution stimulated unrest, and not least
over the fiscal system. In the Pas-de-Calais, several planters assumed that
the tobacco monopoly was now void because 'All the laws of the government of Charles X fell with him and at present we need the laws of the
government of Louis-Philippe 1er'.[36] Protests, particularly against indirect

---

[35] *Le Globe*, 28 October 1830.
[36] *Directeur des contributions indirectes* to the Prefect of the Pas-de-Calais, 27 August 1830, AN,
F7 6776.

taxes, proliferated and recurred intermittently in the early 1830s.[37] Resistance to alcohol duties intensified. The Prefect of the Haute-Vienne wrote that 'a rebellion took place at Meilhac ... against the employees of the *droits réunis* ... In general, collectors of these taxes face difficulties in this land. The most sensible [taxpayers] endure the assessment; but they do not present themselves for payment of the duties.'[38] In other words, those eligible for the *droits réunis* declined to pay the taxes for which tax collectors had deemed them liable. Given the unrest over alcohol duties, *l'octroi*, too, faced resistance. In the Jura, people in Dole 'seized the posts of *l'octroi*', having toured the streets shouting 'Down with the rats!', a reference to the 'cellar rats', a popular term of abuse for collectors of alcohol duties.[39] Unwilling to exacerbate or provoke unrest and anticipating fiscal reform, some prefects allowed the suspension of alcohol duties.[40] Dissatisfaction with customs, meanwhile, was apparent in a surge of smuggling, particularly along the Rhenish frontier.[41]

The government anticipated the increase in resistance to taxation. Before Louis-Philippe had even been proclaimed king, the *Moniteur* published a 'notice for citizens' requiring authorities 'to protect the collection of legally established taxes' and appealing to citizens to pay them.[42] Nevertheless, the government was aware that 'The collection of certain taxes imposes a heavy burden on the country.'[43] Baron Louis, who returned as finance minister in August, presented the Chamber in October with reforms to indirect taxes, 'the most vilified but the most precious of our taxes'.[44] He aimed less to reduce the duties than to make them more acceptable. Hence Louis's main concern was with the means of collection, though he also planned to reduce some alcohol duties, for instance by seeking to abolish the *droit de circulation*.[45] His proposal was withdrawn following the government's collapse in November 1830. Louis's successor, Laffitte, introduced instead a simpler measure, directed more at reducing the duties than reforming the means of collection – though he proposed to modify, not to abolish, the *droit de circulation*.[46] Nevertheless, the difference between the two proposals should not be

---

[37] Price, 'Popular Disturbances', 326–7, 334–8.
[38] Prefect of the Haute-Vienne to Montalivet, 9 November 1830, AN, F⁷ 6776.
[39] *Sécretaire général délégué du Jura* to Guizot, 14 September 1830, AN, F⁷ 6776.
[40] Pilbeam, *1830 Revolution*, 175.   [41] Todd, *Identité économique*, 171.
[42] *Le Moniteur universel*, 2 August 1830.
[43] 'Proclamation du roi', 15 August 1830, *Le Moniteur universel*, 16 August 1830.
[44] Louis, 6 October 1830, AP, 2nd series, LXIV, 80.
[45] Projet de loi, 6 October 1830, AP, 2nd series, LXIV, 83–7.
[46] Projet de loi, 4 December 1830, AP, 2nd series, LXV, 320.

exaggerated.[47] Both involved abolishing the *droit d'entrée*, a duty collected at town entrances for settlements of less than 4,000 people. Louis expected his reduction to cost 50 million francs, 10 million more than the fall in indirect tax revenue in 1831, though he perhaps more than Laffitte sought to offset the expense through other adjustments to alcohol duties.[48] Both men remained committed to indirect taxation, in line with the politics of taxation developed over the course of the Restoration. 'In good finance,' Laffitte declared, 'indirect taxes are the best.'[49]

Of the *mouvement*, Laffitte was among those who sought to make the July Monarchy into, as the Marquis de Lafayette put it, 'the best of republics', which would promote democratisation at home and the emancipation of other nations abroad. After his resignation on 13 March 1831, Laffitte was affiliated until his death with the dynastic opposition, which opposed the government within the constitutional framework of the Charter, in contrast to those who sought revolution. His was not a politics that appealed to Louis-Philippe. Laffitte had, however, played a central role in the 1830 Revolution and thereafter emerged as one of the principal contenders to form a government. In appointing him as leader of the government and finance minister, Louis-Philippe essentially hoped that Laffitte would self-destruct politically.[50] In this context, Laffitte's failure to restore political and social order is unsurprising.

The fiscal problem was among the greatest that Laffitte's government faced. Total government spending in 1831 was 119,468,860 francs higher than in 1830, a nominal increase of 9.8 per cent but which becomes 19.8 per cent when corrected for inflation. Most notably, army expenditure rose from 233,613,402 to 386,624,854 francs.[51] This was foreseeable. On 4 October 1830, two days before Louis unveiled his reform of indirect taxes, the Belgians declared independence from the Netherlands, following a revolution in Brussels that began in August. That this affair might entail French military involvement was obvious. Likewise, the revolution in France catalysed revolution in Italy. In this situation, military expenditure was likely to rise, particularly given the frosty reception of Louis-Philippe's ascent to the throne in the other European courts. Moreover, partly to facilitate the preservation of public order, *ateliers de secours* were established

---

[47] Marion, for instance, presents Louis as the apostle of fiscal probity in contrast to Laffitte's irresponsibility (Marion, *Histoire financière*, V, 115, 121–2).

[48] Louis, 6 October 1830, AP, 2nd series, LXIV, 82; *Proposition de loi . . . 1830*; *Proposition de loi . . . 1831*.

[49] Laffitte, 4 December 1830, AP, 2nd series, LXV, 325.　　　[50] Antonetti, *Louis-Philippe*, 635.

[51] *Proposition de loi . . . 1830*; *Proposition de loi . . . 1831*.

in Paris in the aftermath of the revolution to assist the destitute.[52] While the costs of these were shared with the municipality, the finance ministry also opened a credit for 60 million francs for advances to industry to mitigate the disruptive effects of the revolution and the ongoing economic malaise. This measure, one Orleanist politician recalled, had to be 'very much necessary' for Louis to 'resign' himself to it.[53] Though the July Monarchy later embarked on substantial economic interventionism, its actions in 1830–1 were limited, even if they amounted to more than those of its Restoration predecessor.

These new military and civil expenditures did not provide an ideal context for tax cuts. Rather, in proposing to reduce indirect taxes, Louis and Laffitte were responding to immediate domestic pressures, rather than considering the longer-term needs of the treasury and the international situation. True, Louis-Philippe had done his best to reassure the powers of his peaceful intentions, and Laffitte had largely adhered to this policy. While he emphasised that 'France wants peace' when he presented the budget, greater military preparedness remained necessary.[54] Indeed, the possibility of armed intervention in Italy to protect French interests was one of the causes of Laffitte's fall; Louis-Philippe had no intention of risking war over Italy. Still, reconciling increased spending with lower indirect taxes made balancing the 1831 budget an unenviable task.

Though intended to deflect pressure for fiscal reform, it was far from clear that modifying the *droit de circulation* would appease discontent over alcohol duties. The *Globe*, for example, criticised Louis's proposed reform as a response to agitation from winegrowers that did not address the underlying causes of unrest: 'the vexations and the obstructions to commerce would be in this way more displaced than abolished.'[55] Discontent might simply shift towards other taxes. Uncertainties over the exact incidence of alcohol duties presented a further problem in assessing the potential consequences of reform. In 1829, the finance ministry had admitted that it had 'no document which shows precisely how much alcohol pays both the *droit de circulation* and the *droit d'entrée*'.[56] Since these duties provoked agitation, Louis and Laffitte proposed to abolish or change them, but how effectively such measures would mitigate unrest was unclear. Indeed, the reform of 1830 proved so inadequate that, in 1832, the government authorised *conseils municipaux* in communes of over 4,000

---

[52] Pinkney, 'Ateliers de secours'.   [53] Broglie, *Souvenirs*, IV, 68.
[54] Laffitte, 11 February 1831, AP, 2nd series, LXVI, 650.   [55] *Le Globe*, 7 October 1830.
[56] Note [1829], AN, C 744, dossier 26.

people to merge duties collected for the central government on wine and cider and the *droit de licence* paid by vendors of alcohol into a single *droit d'entrée*.[57] Despite its shortcomings, the 1830 reform had to be funded. 'Certain direct taxes, differently arranged,' Louis asserted, 'will fill this void, but in part only.' The rest would come from indirect taxes, not least because of the need 'to manage the great resource that is the *contribution foncière*'.[58] In proposing to raise some taxes to finance an unsatisfactory reform of others, Louis, and later Laffitte, risked satisfying nobody.

Louis had proposed to finance cutting alcohol duties partly through 'differently arranged' direct taxes. Although he did not explain this ambiguous phrase, it is almost certain that whatever changes Louis might have proposed to direct taxes would aggravate the ongoing disputes over repartition, while propertied interests would not look kindly on higher taxes. Undoubtedly aware of this, he seems to have inclined towards minimal change, as suggested by his remark that direct taxes could not finance the whole cut to indirect taxes. He was evidently sensitive to the burden on land; as during the Restoration, this was to be alleviated through indirect taxes, which limited the scope for reform. Laffitte was probably more ambitious, proposing 'to convert the *contribution personnelle et mobilière* and the *contribution des portes et fenêtres* from taxes of *repartition* to *proportional* taxes'. Thus, in future, these taxes would be assessed at a uniform, fixed rate relative to each taxpayer's assets, instead of being apportioned between *départements*, then communes and finally individuals according to assumptions about respective wealth. Repartition was uneven, Laffitte noted; in some *départements*, the repartitioned tax was so low that the sums raised for the *contribution personnelle*, supposedly the equivalent of three days' wages, also paid the *département*'s allocation for the *contribution mobilière*, based on the rental value of one's residence. In the most extreme cases, so little was repartitioned to a *département* that only a few individuals were required to pay the *contribution personnelle* to discharge the *département*'s full quota for the *contribution personnelle et mobilière*. Moreover, as we have seen, the burden of the *contribution personnelle et mobilière* could be further reduced by using *l'octroi* to cover some of the tax. Meanwhile, the *contribution des portes et fenêtes* became 'more unequal by the day', as new buildings were erected that had not featured in the original repartition. As Laffitte observed, repartition could follow 'shifts in

---

[57] Ponteil, 'Humann et les émeutes', 317. The taxes that were amalgamated by this reform were the *droit de circulation*, the *droit de détail* and the *droit de licence*.
[58] Louis, 6 October 1830, AP, 2nd series, LXIV, 82.

the taxable material ... only from afar, because a change in the repartition can only be implemented after a long interval, that is to say every 15 or 20 years.'[59] Pressure to address these problems was not new. In 1829, for example, Roy, finance minister under Martignac, had told the Chamber that 'we occupy ourselves ceaselessly with the need to obtain a better repartition of the *contribution personnelle et mobilière*.'[60] The solution to such iniquities adopted by the Napoleonic and Restoration regimes, of reducing direct taxes where possible, did not sufficiently mitigate discontent.

Laffitte's financial programme proved highly contentious. As he acknowledged, imposing a proportional system would create 'difficulties of execution, and it is for this reason that many well-enlightened administrators prefer the tax of repartition.'[61] Rather than assessing the taxes from external signs of wealth as before, the new *contribution personnelle et mobilière* would require taxpayers to declare their wages and the rental value of their residence. Thus, tax collection would become more intrusive. Local authorities, moreover, disliked losing the power to repartition taxes. Uneasy about such difficulties, the Chamber of Deputies diluted Laffitte's proposal.[62] Instead of a wholly proportional system, the *contribution personnelle et mobilière* was split into a proportional *impôt personnel* and a larger, repartitioned *contribution mobilière*. Whereas the former was levied on income, the latter was 'a tax on presumed means according to the rental value of residences' and was therefore suited to repartition.[63] Still, the Chambers endorsed the principle of proportionality. Meanwhile, Laffitte's proposals for the *contribution des portes et fenêtres* were largely accepted, not least because assessing the tax in proportion to the number of doors and windows in a residence was not seen as more intrusive than the process of repartition – the tax would still be assessed according to external signs of wealth.

Laffitte's reform attempted to fulfil some of the hopes that the 1830 Revolution raised for a fairer tax system, which included making direct taxes more equitable. Proportionality, though, could facilitate higher taxes, since raising the tax rate would be easier than adjusting the repartition. This prospect did not fit well with 'un gouvernement à bon marché'. Meanwhile, for some on the left, greater proportionality was

---

[59] Laffitte, 15 November 1830, AP, 2nd series, LXIV, 394–6. Emphases in the original.
[60] Roy, 11 March 1829, AP, 2nd series, LVII, 327.
[61] Laffitte, 15 November 1830, AP, 2nd series, LXIV, 396.   [62] Carrier, 'Répartition ou quotité'.
[63] Rambuteau, 21 January 1831, AP, 2nd series, LXVI, 288.

insufficient. 'Many newspapers in Paris and in the *départements*, and political societies,' observed Francisque de Corcelle in 1833, 'have formed to reclaim a great number of radical reforms pertaining to taxation. Progressive taxes are usually among these.'[64] The Saint-Simonians, who attained greater public prominence after 1830, also sought to reduce indirect taxes or to replace them completely with a progressive income tax. Ultimately, their aim was the abolition of taxation through the development of government credit by public subscription; instead of paying taxes, citizens would voluntarily finance a reformed, benevolent state.[65] Like other opponents of the government, they favoured streamlining the state. Such views found little favour among those in power. Corcelle, a friend of Tocqueville and a deputy of the dynastic opposition from 1839 to 1848, was not alone in believing that progressive taxation would be self-defeating: 'the war of the poor against the rich is at root only a war of the poor or the rich against the poor.'[66]

As a concession to demands for reform, therefore, Laffitte's proposal was relatively mild, even if the introduction of a de facto income tax in the form of the *impôt personnel* was a substantial change. Indeed, anything more radical would probably have been rejected by the Chambers, where Laffitte's position was weak. Facing enemies on both the left and the right of the Chambers, he had little room for manoeuvre and could not afford to displease those groups that disliked higher direct taxes. Laffitte's mismanagement of the public finances, Marion asserts, aroused concern among the financial establishment.[67] Such doubts should not be exaggerated; Laffitte's tax reform seems to have been accepted by many prominent members of the financial elite. Roy, for instance, endorsed the Chamber of Deputies' diluted version only three days before Laffitte's resignation.[68] Similarly, Thiers, a prominent participant in the 1830 Revolution and a future finance minister, served under both Louis and Laffitte as undersecretary at the finance ministry. Though he exercised more power under the latter than under the former, he joined the *résistance* as Laffitte's political position deteriorated.[69] Laffitte, in short, became a scapegoat for a policy that he had promoted, but for which he was by no means solely responsible.

[64] Corcelle, 'De l'impôt progressif', 73.   [65] Coste, 'Penser l'impôt'.
[66] Corcelle, 'De l'impôt progressif', 86.   [67] Marion, *Histoire financière*, V, 121.
[68] Roy, 10 March 1831, AP, 2nd series, LXVII, 523–6.
[69] Thureau-Dangin, *Monarchie de Juillet*, II, 33–9.

The principal opposition to Laffitte's financial programme was directed against his *budget extraordinaire*, rather than his tax reform. Since the latter was inadequate to meet the treasury's needs, Laffitte produced a *budget extraordinaire* that proposed the sale of state-owned forests and treasury bills.[70] The deputies lambasted the sale of state assets, both because the forests produced revenue which would then be lost and because they would be sold too cheaply.[71] Laffitte, claims Marion, followed 'crazy policy', which helped undermine the healthy finances depicted in the *Rapport au roi* of March 1830 and contributed to the collapse of his government.[72] Such a harsh verdict echoes the criticism levelled against Laffitte after his ministry collapsed. Given the deficit, there were no easy options. As Guizot, then among the government's opponents, acknowledged, 'The budget succeeds well enough. No new taxes and no loan, which is what we call for. As for the rest, the sale of the woods likewise seems to me the best expedient.'[73] Laffitte's government was finally destroyed by its response to the sacking of the Saint-Germain-l'Auxerrois church on 14 February, where legitimists were demonstrating their allegiance to the Bourbons by commemorating the anniversary of the Duc de Berry's assassination in 1820. The son of Charles X and an ultra, the duke's murder by a Bonapartist had eased the rightward shift that allowed the ultras to dominate politics under Villèle. The legitimists' action enraged some of those who had participated in the 1830 Revolution, and who therefore proceeded to desecrate the church, initiating a wave of unrest that Laffitte did little to prevent. A policy of *mouvement* became more difficult to pursue and the schism between left and right widened. Laffitte's successor as leader of the government was Casimir Perier who, like Laffitte, had played a prominent role in the July Revolution. A principal figure of the *résistance*, Perier reacted firmly against unrest.

In the ensuing political atmosphere, Laffitte's reform suffered. Opposition developed over the course of 1831, particularly after his resignation. Louis, resuming the finance ministry, found a mounting deficit, partly the result of his earlier policy of reducing indirect taxes. Laffitte's *budget extraordinaire* was scrapped in favour of borrowing and *centimes extraordinaires*, surtaxes which were added to the *contributions foncière* and *mobilière*.[74] For Georges Humann, *rapporteur* in the Chamber

[70] Laffitte and projet de loi, 11 February 1830, AP, 2nd series, LXVI, 646–8.
[71] Calmon, *Monarchie de Juillet*, I, 76–7.   [72] Marion, *Histoire financière*, V, 120.
[73] Guizot to Barante, 13 February 1831, Guizot MSS, AN, 42AP/200.
[74] Projet de loi, 18 March 1831, AP, 2nd series, LXVII, 687; Humann, 28 March 1831, AP, 2nd series, LXVIII, 154–8.

of Deputies, the tax increases were an 'irresistible necessity; it is essential that the request the state is obliged to make to the capitalists be supported by an effort from the country itself, sufficient to show its resources but not so great as to exhaust them'.[75] Higher taxes, in other words, would facilitate a loan on more favourable terms by reducing the amount the government would have to borrow while indicating the state's willingness to repay its debts. Thus, adjusting for inflation, revenue from the *contribution foncière* rose by 8.1 per cent in 1831. The *impôt personnel* and *contribution mobilière* combined were 57.3 per cent greater than the pre-reform *contribution personnelle et mobilière*, and the *contribution des portes et fenêtres* produced an increase of 121.5 per cent.[76]

Given the tax increases due to the *centimes extraordinaires* and proportionality, discontent with direct taxes rose; abolishing repartition raised the burden on some taxpayers and reduced it on others. The new *contribution des portes et fenêtres*, Humann observed, was 'attacked so sharply only because it rectified intolerable inequalities but settled some at the expense of others'.[77] Meanwhile, in the Var, the sub-prefect of Brignoles noted that the proportional *impôt personnel* raised the burden on the poor, provoking complaints.[78] Discontent with the tax increases arose 'in many *départements*', wrote Perier, and needed to be addressed irrespective of whether 'the taxes are collected without difficulty'.[79] Though there was some disorder – in Calvignac in the Lot taxpayers hung the tax collector in effigy and refused to accept the new *impôt personnel* – the resistance of local government officials to the new taxes may have mitigated larger-scale unrest.[80] Their desire to avoid provoking violence and their resentment over losing the power to repartition two taxes perhaps left them disinclined to ensure the rigorous enforcement of proportionality. The *conseil municipal* of Fougères in the Ille-et-Vilaine, for example, vilified 'proportional taxation as an act of the worst centralisation', stigmatising proportionality with the standard opposition critique of an overbearing state.[81] The repartition of the new *contribution mobilière* also elicited criticism. Taxpayers from Armentières in the Nord, for instance, petitioned the

[75] Humann, 28 March 1831, AP, 2nd series, LXVIII, 156.
[76] *Proposition de loi ... 1830*; *Proposition de loi ... 1831*.
[77] Humann, 3 February 1832, AP, 2nd series, LXXIV, 710.
[78] Agulhon, *République au village*, 111.
[79] Perier to Siméon, 12 January 1832, Siméon MSS, AN, 558AP/3.
[80] *Procureur général*, Agen, to Barthe, 29 October 1831, AN, BB[18] 1325.
[81] Petition, *conseil municipal de Fougères* to the Chamber of Deputies, 12 November 1831, AN, C 2112.

Chamber for a more equitable repartition.[82] The government, needing money and concerned about impairing consent to taxation, responded to the discontent by abandoning proportionality, which became easier once its chief architect was out of office. Sacrificing Laffitte's reform was preferable to incurring the discontent.

The return to repartition came in the 1832 budget, for which Humann also served as *rapporteur*. An Alsatian of the *résistance*, he had made his fortune as a businessman and had been elected to the Chamber in 1820, where he acquired a reputation for competence with financial affairs.[83] For him, the revolutionary exuberance had to be tamed. Although Humann accepted that, in principle, proportionality was more equitable than repartition, 'it was necessary to defer this change to calmer times, and to return to repartition, while rectifying the inequalities of the old assessments.' Laffitte's only victory lay in a general acknowledgement that repartition was 'of another era'.[84] As Guizot, now minister of public instruction, observed, 'Our adversaries placed great hopes on the budget discussion; they have almost lost these already, and discouragement is overcoming them.'[85] Still, the repeal of Laffitte's reform did not mean a complete return to the status quo ante. Partly in response to the unrest, the government sought to lower *contribution des portes et fenêtres* for the poor, on whom the tax could impose a heavy burden, by amending the way it was assessed.[86] The pressure to accommodate some discontent about the tax was particularly acute because, though proportionality was abandoned, the revenue increases it generated were largely retained in the new repartition. In 1832, revenue from the *contributions personnelle et mobilière* and *des portes et fenetres* fell by only 7.8 per cent and 10.9 per cent respectively, accounting for inflation, while that from the *contribution foncière* rose a further 5.3 per cent.[87] Though repudiated, Laffitte's reform had lasting consequences.

The return to repartition had ramifications for local taxation, proportionality having reduced the pressure to use *octrois* to ease the weight of taxes repartitioned to communes. With the revocation of Laffitte's reform, *l'octroi* was again to be used to mask inequalities in the repartition and thus to facilitate consent. Nevertheless, while the measure was quickly implemented in municipalities such as Paris, other *conseils municipaux* were

[82] Petition, *contribuables d'Armentières* to the Chamber of Deputies, 4 December 1831, AN, C 2111.
[83] Ponteil, *Georges Humann*.   [84] Humann, 3 February 1832, AP, 2nd series, LXXIV, 709.
[85] Guizot to Barante, 16 February 1832, Guizot MSS, AN, 42AP/200.
[86] Law of 21 April 1832 (titre II, arts. 24–7), *Lois*, XXXII, 235–6.
[87] *Proposition de loi ... 1831*; *Proposition de loi ... 1832*.

more cautious.[88] In July 1832, for example, the *directeur des contributions directes* asked the prefect of the Mayenne to respond 'in the shortest delay' to a circular of two months before, which enquired about 'the decision of the *conseil municipal* of Laval' on whether to use *l'octroi* to cover part of the town's allotted *contribution personnelle et mobilière*.[89] The finance ministry's desire to know whether the authorities in Laval intended to use *l'octroi* for this purpose was perhaps a reason for the dilatory response; the *conseil municipal* may have felt that in indicating how much money it was willing to raise through *l'octroi* the town risked facing a larger *contribution personnelle et mobilière*. The old issues over the fairness of repartition returned.

The revocation of proportionality reflected the regime's caution in pursuing fiscal reform. Committed to stability and to the fundamentals of the fiscal system, the government instead implemented limited reforms designed to buttress public order by easing the effects of economic malaise. Thus, Perier continued a policy initiated by Laffitte of assisting local authorities in the provision of poor relief, which followed the aid that Louis had approved in the wake of the 1830 Revolution. The regime also implemented some customs reforms, reducing the tariffs on many commodities and loosening the prohibition on grain imports in spring 1832, though this proved insufficient to forestall a new wave of unrest over food prices over the summer.[90] Much like the proposals of Louis and Laffitte in 1830 to reduce the alcohol duties, the changes to tariffs were intended to mollify complaints about the customs regime that had emerged in the 1820s; they were not intended to overhaul the system. The government became more ambitious in pursuing customs reform as the political situation stabilised. Indeed, the post-revolutionary violence reached its peak, in the numbers both of disturbances and of participants, in spring 1832.[91] A year earlier, John Bowring, a British government agent, had informally encouraged Louis to seek commercial negotiations with Britain as a means of reforming customs. The French, though, had been unwilling to contemplate significant tariff reductions. Seeking to push the government in this direction, Bowring toured France between 1832 and 1834, promoting free trade. He had some success, encouraging certain commercial interests and much of the press into agitation for trade liberalisation which reached its height in 1834.[92] In 1835–6, Duchâtel, then minister of

[88] Argout to the Prefect of the Seine, 29 August 1832, AN, F³(II)/SEINE/26, dossier 4.
[89] Jourdan to the Prefect of the Mayenne, 27 July 1832, and Louis to the Prefect of the Mayenne, 13 May 1831, AD, Mayenne, P/59.
[90] Pilbeam, 'Popular Violence', 284–5, 292.   [91] Rule and Tilly, 'Political Process', 69.
[92] Todd, *Free Trade*, 97–122; see also Ratcliffe, 'Tariff Reform Campaign'.

commerce, responded by presenting the Chambers with minor tariff reductions, which were enacted under his successor.[93] However, political liberalism did not necessarily equate to economic liberalism, and the rise of the latter produced a protectionist reaction from several liberal politicians and intellectuals, backed by industrial interests.[94] Under pressure, the government deferred further customs reform, satisfied that it had provided a gesture to economic liberalism without compromising either revenue or political stability. The triumph of fiscal *résistance* was reflected in Humann's appointment as finance minister in a new government under Marshal Soult, Perier having perished in the cholera epidemic of 1832. In office, Humann preserved the fiscal system and opposed Duchâtel's customs reform.[95] By the time he resigned in 1836, the revolutionary challenge to the fiscal system had been vanquished.

Continuities in finance ministry personnel underscored the limited change wrought by the 1830 Revolution. In August 1831, the justice minister sent Louis a report by the *procureur général* in Rennes, 'in which this magistrate indicates afresh the danger of leaving the tasks of finance, notably that of customs, in the hands of individuals loyal to the fallen [Bourbon] government'.[96] Personnel changes were limited and largely restricted to those at the top, as ministers manoeuvred clients and political allies into influential positions. A series of ordonnances in January 1831 'abolished the posts of *directeur général* and administrators in various financial administrations for the sake of economy'. Instead, each division of the finance ministry would be 'directed by a director assisted by a deputy director... This organisation has the advantage of being much simpler than its predecessor.'[97] Indeed, in 1832 finance ministry personnel costs were nominally over 25 per cent lower than in 1828, providing a gesture in response to the agitation for cheap government and the financial pressures arising from the budget deficit.[98] Louis, though, was not interested in more comprehensive personnel changes: 'very far from attracting employees by holding them in a state of perpetual worry about their future, it would be wholly fair and healthy to encourage them with a show of confidence that they deserve, as indicated by the results of their work.'[99] Those who were dismissed were often replaced by men who had lost their

[93] Anceau, 'Réforme du régime douanier', 146–7.   [94] Todd, *Free Trade*, 123–54.
[95] Anceau, 'Réforme du régime douanier', 146.
[96] Louis to Barthe, 2 September 1831, AN, BB[18] 1199.
[97] Note, January 1831, SAEF, B/67458/1.
[98] Informal note, n.d. [1832], Duchâtel MSS, AN, 2AP/27, dossier 2.
[99] Louis to Barthe, 2 September 1831, AN, BB[18] 1199.

positions following the Restoration in 1814–15.[100] Still, as in 1814–15, many survived the change of regime in 1830, facilitating the continuities in fiscal policy.

The Maintenance of Public Credit

The survival of public credit facilitated the preservation of the tax system in the aftermath of the 1830 Revolution, as the government floated loans in 1831 and 1832. Conversely, public credit benefited from the stability provided by the limitations of tax reform. Sartoris, who despite having retired from banking in 1826 remained active in managing his own portfolio, suggested to James de Rothschild in 1831 that a larger loan was better than a smaller one.[101] Rejecting Humann's rationale for the *centimes extraordinaires*, Sartoris argued that borrowing more would offer Louis 'the possibility to withdraw his request for an increase in the *contribution foncière*, which, aside from its excessive surcharge, has the inconvenience of complicating in an unfortunate manner the question of the electoral list'.[102] The *centimes extraordinaires* which Louis introduced after Laffitte's departure not only risked provoking unrest; they also potentially threatened political stability by increasing the number of taxpayers qualified to vote, particularly since Laffitte's reform also added voters to the rolls. Indeed, soon afterwards, in July 1831, the first election of the July Monarchy was held with the enlarged electorate created by the lower tax qualification. To maximise the government's resources without resorting to tax increases, Sartoris suggested converting privately owned canal shares into 5 per cent *rentes*. This would suit his desire to clear his portfolio of these shares, which he suggested the government could then resell to cover its deficit.[103] Such a scheme, however, appeared unnecessarily elaborate and both Louis and then Humann disregarded it. Sartoris, though, expressed doubts about how easily a conventional issue of *rentes* could work, the Bourse having been shaken by the effects of the 1830 Revolution. Though his proposal was rejected, it reflected commercial elites' preference for lowering direct taxes even at the cost of higher indirect taxes, which tended to affect industry and commerce more than land.

[100] Bihan, 'Réintégration des percepteurs'.
[101] Circular, by Sartoris, 1 May 1826, Thuret MSS, ANMT, 68AQ/150.
[102] Sartoris to James de Rothschild, 26 March 1831, Greffulhe MSS, AN, 61AQ/222, fol. 51.
[103] Gille, *Banque et le crédit*, 205; Greffulhe MSS, AN, 61AQ/222, fols. 46–9, 51–6, 58–9, 141, 182–4. As we have seen, Sartoris supported Villèle's proposed conversion in 1824, in part, from a desire to divest himself of canal shares.

Higher direct taxes, besides the greater burden they imposed on wealthy commercial elites, risked destabilising the political system and provoking unrest, potentially undermining the *rente* and thus bankers' profits. Indeed, after Laffitte's fall, Sartoris congratulated Louis on his 'return to the ministry of finance, because we were threatened with the greatest disasters, if it had continued to be directed by the same people'.[104] Despite Sartoris's concerns, much of the political elite was relatively open to broadening the franchise, as the voting reform of 1831 suggests; likewise, electoral considerations do not seem to have had a major impact on changes to direct taxes. Rather, Laffitte's reform, before its repudation, was part of a programme to create a fairer fiscal and political system, of which the lower voting qualification was the political component. Moreover, as the recourse to borrowing indicates, the government needed money, which the higher direct taxes provided. While Louis therefore disappointed Sartoris – and others wary of the electoral consequences of raising direct taxes – he embodied a conservative attitude to public finance, which helped to reassure investors.

Though public credit survived intact, the 1830 Revolution produced a financial crisis, but this was delayed by the surprisingly smooth transition from one regime to another. In early August 1830, André et Cottier informed a Brest firm seeking *rentes* at fire-sale prices that 'our stocks are far from falling.'[105] Shortly afterwards they observed that 'politically, all is fine and confidence is reviving with the calm.'[106] By contrast, the conflict between Polignac's ministry and the Chambers had threatened the peace and stability that were so important to the Bourse. The day Polignac's government took office, Hottinguer had predicted that, as a result, 'we will have a further fall and it could be considerable.'[107] Although the loan of January 1830 was contracted above par, the Bourse became increasingly uneasy as the pre-revolutionary crisis matured. 'Stocks fall,' wrote André et Cottier in May; 'here we are a bit worried about the political situation and our affairs in the interior.'[108] In appearing to resolve the political crisis without impairing stability, the 1830 Revolution produced a short-lived rise in the *rente*.

---

[104] Sartoris to Louis, 18 March 1831, Greffulhe MSS, AN, 61AQ/222, fol. 46.
[105] André et Cottier to Paillias et Berard, 10/11 August 1830, Neuflize MSS, ANMT, 44AQ/256, fol. 459.
[106] André et Cottier to Balguerie et fils, 12 August 1830, Neuflize MSS, ANMT, 44AQ/257, fol. 463.
[107] Hottinguer et Cie to Baring Brothers, 8 August 1829, BA, HC 7.1.20.
[108] André et Cottier to B.A. Goldschmidt, 22 May 1830, Neuflize MSS, ANMT, 44AQ/259, fol. 34.

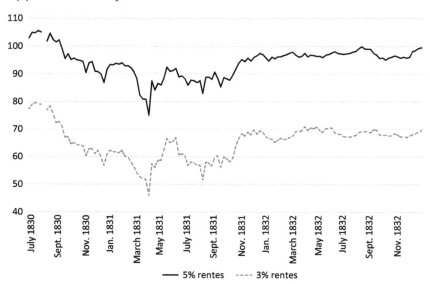

Figure 6.1   Weekly closing prices of *rentes*, as quoted in Paris, July 1830–December 1832.
(Source: *Le Moniteur universel*)

As the consequences of the revolution became apparent, the downturn began. On 1 October, Hottinguer noted that international tensions arising from the Belgian Revolution were driving the markets down. He continued: 'we fear a war; this morning, however, we appeared more reassured, seeing that none of the powers are so inclined.'[109] Still, the government's talk of peace failed to reassure the Bourse, where a climate of uncertainty prevailed; André et Cottier observed in late November that 'the level of the stocks is affected by the fear of war.'[110] Likewise, the rise in unrest that followed the revolution did nothing to reassure investors of the survival of the regime, and the cholera epidemic of 1832 perpetuated this sense of insecurity, creating further anxieties for investors in the risks it posed to stability.[111]

The fall in *rentes* produced a financial crisis (Figure 6.1). Unable to liquidate its large real-estate holdings to meet investors' growing withdrawals, Laffitte's bank became insolvent in January 1831, the highest-

---

[109] Hottinguer et Cie to Baring Brothers, 1 October 1830, BA, HC 7.1.26.
[110] André et Cottier to Baring Brothers, 29 November 1830, Neuflize MSS, ANMT, 44AQ/258, fol. 427.
[111] Lionel Rothschild to his parents, 17 April 1832, RAL, XI/82/6/1/58.

profile casualty.[112] The Rothschilds, too, suffered heavily. Many of the *rentes* they had purchased, as the issuing house of the 1830 loan, were still unsold when the Bourbon regime was overthrown. The principal reason James de Rothschild survived the volatility which affected *rentes* until 1832 was that his brother Nathan, in London, pumped money into de Rothschild frères.[113] The crash was not confined to France; revolution elsewhere in Europe hit the prices of other governments' bonds. In February 1831, André et Cottier advised a client considering investment in French, Neapolitan and Spanish bonds that 'regarding the solidity of these placements, we accord little but to the French stocks.'[114] Despite the fall in French *rentes*, they remained more attractive than other potential investments; while the weekly closing prices of French 5 per cent *rentes* averaged over 92 in February, Neapolitan and Spanish 5 per cents were just over 62 and 44 respectively.[115] Moreover, the specie and bullion from the dey of Algiers's treasury captured in the 1830 expedition was all remitted to the Banque de France by late March 1831, offering the government greater means to support the *rente* if necessary.[116] Still, these were not ideal circumstances for the government to contract a new loan in April.

In abandoning Laffitte's plan to exploit state forests and treasury bills, Louis, as we have seen, proposed to cover the deficit with *centimes extraordinaires* and *rentes*. What remained to be established was whether the government would arrange the loan 'by sealed bids' or 'by general subscriptions . . . as for the loan of M. Corvetto' in 1818.[117] On 28 March, the *Moniteur* announced a loan of 120 million francs in 5 per cent *rentes* for adjudication. On 6 April, a letter in the *Globe* proposed to finance it by appealing to 'The patriotic sentiments of Frenchmen'. 30,000 investors would take 5 per cent *rentes* at par, a reflection of the Saint-Simonian view that the government bonds should be held by the people.[118] This scheme received an enthusiastic response, and banks began receiving subscriptions immediately.[119] Still, issuing *rentes* in this way would take time, and

[112] Laffitte to Gaëte, 30 November 1830, ABF, 1069200401/288; circular by Ferrère-Laffitte, 19 January 1831, Thuret MSS, ANMT, 68AQ/141.
[113] Ferguson, *World's Banker*, 240.
[114] André et Cottier to Bazin, 5 February 1831, Neuflize MSS, ANMT, 44AQ/261, fol. 426.
[115] *Le Journal du commerce*, February 1831.   [116] ABF, 1069200401/290.
[117] Sartoris to Louis, 18 March 1831, Greffulhe MSS, AN, 61AQ/222, fol. 47.
[118] *Le Globe*, 6 April 1831; Coste, 'Penser l'impôt', 52–4.
[119] E.g. *Le Journal du commerce*, 8–10 April 1831. A similar proposal for a public subscription at par (dated 4 April) appeared in the *Journal des débats*, 7 April 1831.

several financiers therefore suggested postponing the adjudication.[120] The government refused, instead establishing an *emprunt national* of 80 million for public subscription and retaining the 120 million for adjudication.[121] Most of the capital raised for the *emprunt national* seems to have come from Paris, but receivers general were instructed to give the loan 'the greatest publicity' and *départements* such as the Rhône and the Haute-Saône produced admirable lists of subscribers.[122] Nevertheless, given the fall in the *rente* and ongoing economic malaise, the public subscription proved limited, reaching only 20.5 million francs.[123]

Meanwhile, the Rothschilds bid successfully for the adjudication, a reflection of Nathan's continuing support for James. Although until at least 1833 the Rothschilds had doubts that the July Monarchy would survive, the loan offered them an opportunity to reassert their predominance in French finance.[124] As a result, Louis was able to push the Rothschilds and their associates from their original offer of 82.10 to 84.[125] The loan bolstered Perier's government, which James saw as a bulwark against chaos. Perier, he believed, was committed to a policy of peace.[126] Moreover, the revolution destroyed the ultra-royalists, to the Rothschilds' benefit; in contrast to the survival rate of finance ministry personnel, 97 per cent of deputies on the right during the Restoration found their political careers terminated.[127] The ultras' dislike of relying on liberal bankers would no longer hinder the Rothschilds. Although the latter had associated themselves with Charles X's regime, they preferred the committed constitutionalism of the July Monarchy and continued to favour Orleanism after 1848.

Despite the financial damage it caused them, the 1830 Revolution offered the Rothschilds the opportunity to enhance their supremacy over French public credit. Rivals such as Laffitte receded or disappeared. Others such as Hottinguer, who sensed the Rothschilds' financial difficulties after 1830, failed to capitalise.[128] Though Hottinguer joined Delessert in contemplating a bid for the 1831 loan in an arrangement that would have relegated Barings to junior partner, an indication of the latter's relative

[120] *Le Globe*, 6, 8 and 14 April 1831.
[121] *Le Moniteur universel*, 14 April 1831. The adjudication and the *souscription nationale* together would thus cover the 200 million franc credit the government announced in March (*Le Moniteur universel*, 27 March 1831).
[122] *Le Journal du commerce*, 9 April 1831; *Le Moniteur universel*, 6 and 9 May 1831; circular to the receivers general, by Louis, 15 April 1831, AD, Mayenne, P/59.
[123] Marion, *Histoire financière*, V, 123–4.   [124] Ferguson, *World's Banker*, 233.
[125] *Le Moniteur universel*, 21 April 1831.   [126] Ferguson, *World's Banker*, 235, 255–7.
[127] Tort, *Droite*, 128.   [128] Ferguson, *World's Banker*, 239.

decline since 1817–18, they ultimately declined to make an offer and withdrew before the adjudication.[129] The Rothschilds cemented their position in 1832, when they joined Hottinguer and Davillier to issue a further 150 million franc loan in 5 per cent *rentes* at 98.50. Reflecting the recovery of French public credit after 1830, the loan sold easily.[130] Thereafter, the Rothschilds remained unrivalled in France until the 1850s.

Conclusion

The fiscal-military system's effectiveness during the 1820s eased its survival after the 1830 Revolution with little change. Hence, Laffitte's invocation of proportional taxation was packaged as refining the existing system, while he remained committed to indirect taxation. Nevertheless, his reform marked a modest departure from the Restoration predeliction for cutting direct taxes. Not only was most of the increase from his reform retained, but economic growth bolstered direct taxes during the Orleanist period. Thus, inflation-adjusted, direct tax revenues rose by 29.9 per cent from 1830 to 1847, in contrast to the 7.7 per cent decrease they underwent between 1815 and 1830.[131] The extent of this shift in tax policy should not be overstated. Like the Restoration, the July Monarchy rested heavily on the *notables*, a propertied elite in which aristocratic families of the *ancien régime* held a prominent place. They remained wedded to political and social stability – it was this that induced them to transfer their allegiance from the Bourbons to Louis-Philippe. Charles X had appeared willing to risk political stability, as he pursued his confrontation with the Chambers in 1830. For this reason, many ultra-royalists, as committed to the Charter as they were to the king, were less than enthusiastic about the four ordinances.[132] Louis-Philippe, by contrast, appeared to guarantee the constitutional settlement of 1814, and with it the primacy of the landed and commercial elites that had promoted the ascent of indirect taxation and public credit under the Restoration. Despite a limited rebalancing of the fiscal burden towards direct taxation, therefore, the July Monarchy secured its support through its credentials as a bulwark against revolution and disorder. In this respect, the regime's fiscal reforms, partly intended to mitigate pressure for more far-reaching changes, became admissible.

---

[129] Hottinguer et Cie to Baring Brothers, 28 March 1831, BA, HC 7.1.33.
[130] Lionel Rothschild to his parents, 6 August 1832, RAL, XI/82/6/1/93.
[131] *Proposition de loi ... 1815, 1816, 1817; Proposition de loi ... 1830; Projet de loi... 1847.*
[132] Tort, *Droite*, 183–5, 305–6.

The 1830 Revolution's limited impact on economic and fiscal policy offered few portents, prima facie, of the transformation of France that occurred with the emergence of a more economically interventionist state from the late 1830s onwards. Indeed, the significance of the 1830 Revolution lay in the limits of subsequent reform. The disappointment of the aspirations for a more far-reaching overhaul of the Restoration state prompted the growth of subversive revolutionary activity, producing a series of uprisings in the early 1830s, most notably in Lyon in 1831 and 1834 and in Paris in 1832 and 1834. The unrest increased pressure on the regime to pursue reform within the constraints of the existing fiscal system, while the survival of the latter gave the government the means to act. The conservative outcome of the 1830 Revolution not only eased the subsequent transformation of the state, it also foreshadowed something of the Orleanist state's later development in reflecting the regime's preference for pragmatism and incremental change. Debates over Laffitte's tax reform showed little concern for the grand economic ideas he had previously disparaged Saint-Simon for propagating; while economic liberalism influenced the arguments favouring trade liberalisation in 1833–4, it had little effect on fiscal policy overall. The limited role of ideology in shaping a conception of political economy and the state may be one reason that historians have generally overlooked the ambitiousness of the Orleanists' economic policies, particularly from the late 1830s. Pierre Rosanvallon, for example, suggests that their underlying rationale was reminiscent of the economic interventionism of the *ancien régime*.[133] As we shall see, though, neither pragmatic conservatism nor the absence of an overarching grand design prevented the Orleanists from presiding over the transformation of the state.

[133] Rosanvallon, *État*, 220.

CHAPTER 7

The Ascent of the Interventionist Orleanist State, 1830–1848

Under Louis-Philippe, the French state was transformed, with an innovativeness that scholars have generally overlooked. Instead, they have emphasised the regime's conservatism, especially in the 1840s, citing its refusal to undertake electoral reform. Moreover, economic historians have presented the Orleanists as partial to laissez-faire, reinforcing the narrative of a conservative regime wedded to an increasingly untenable political and economic order that facilitated the monarchy's collapse in the 1848 Revolution.[1] Historians have begun to revise these interpretations of the Orleanist state. In the 1980s, David Pinkney suggested a need to re-examine social and economic history of the 1840s, years which he labelled as 'decisive' for nineteenth-century France. The economy boomed with the onset of industrialisation, and the state sought to capitalise on the innovations of railways and telegraphs to pursue greater administrative centralisation. With industrialisation came socio-economic transformation, which pushed the professions towards establishing the criteria by which they would be defined. Simultaneously, growing urbanisation encouraged the growth of socialism among Paris's radical luminaries and stimulated fears among elites of a large, potentially subversive urban underclass – the 'social question'. The latter attained growing prominence in public discourse, and the press thrived as circulation increased. Meanwhile, in the arts, realism began to eclipse the romanticism of previous years. Finally, in the 1840s, Pinkney contended, France's place in the world changed with the development of a Franco-British *entente cordiale* and an increasingly global foreign policy – the financial foundations of which, as we have seen, emerged with the investment of British

---

[1] Kemp, *Economic Forces*, 106–34.

capital in France that began with the payment of reparations in 1817–18 and continued thereafter.[2]

More recent research has continued to reappraise the July Monarchy, for instance emphasising the dynamism of its political culture.[3] With regard to political economy, the development of a more economically interventionist state corroborates this scholarship, while refuting the misconception that the Orleanist state was committed to laissez-faire. Though the Revolutionary, Napoleonic and Restoration regimes all contributed to the construction of the post-Revolutionary interventionist state, its greatest expansion hitherto occurred during the July Monarchy, particularly in the 1840s. Adjusted for inflation, total government expenditure rose by 51.01 per cent between 1830 and 1847, notably less than the 21.9 per cent by which it increased from 1815 and 1830, though it remained around 10 per cent of GDP because of economic growth.[4] Indeed, GDP grew an average of 2.17 per cent per year from 1830 to 1847, accounting for inflation, slightly above the annual average of 2.03 per cent for the period 1815–30. The state's rising economic interventionism was most evident in public works. Having previously been shuffled between the ministries of the interior and agriculture and commerce, these became the responsibility of a ministry of public works in 1838. From an initial 79,552,235.63 francs, the new ministry's budget reached 203,590,281.73 in 1847; public works spending, inflation-adjusted, rose 374.07 per cent between 1815 and 1848, with the greatest increase coming from the late 1830s onwards (Figure 7.1).[5] Public works were not the only cause of rising expenditure. An international crisis in 1840 and an escalation of military action in Algeria stimulated the growth of the army and navy budgets. As we shall see, the regime met the challenges of higher expenditure admirably, presiding over the transformation of the French state and demonstrating the potential of the post-Napoleonic fiscal system.

The Rise of Military and Naval Expenditure

The conquest of Algeria was one of the main drivers of rising military expenditure under the July Monarchy, costing more than all the

---

[2] Pinkney, *Decisive Years in France*. On the 'social question', see Chevalier, *Classes laborieuses et classes dangereuses*; Procacci, *Gouverner la misère*; Sage, *A Dubious Science*.

[3] Antonetti, *Louis-Philippe*; Guionnet, *Apprentissage de la politique*; Price, *The Perilous Crown*; Larrère, *L'Urne et le fusil*.

[4] Greenfield, 'Interventionist State'; *Proposition de loi … 1815, 1816, 1817*; *Proposition de loi … 1830*; *Projet de loi … 1847*; Toutain, 'Produit intérieur brut'.

[5] *Proposition de loi … 1838*; *Projet de loi … 1847*.

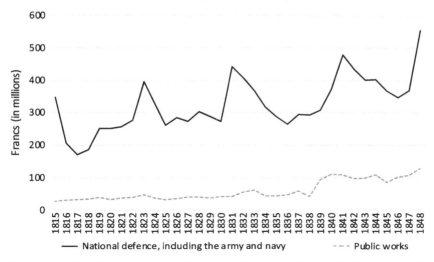

Figure 7.1   Central government spending on public works and national defence, 1815–48 (in 1815 francs).

(Source: Fontvieille, *État*, 2108–16. Nominal prices were adjusted to those of 1815 using the index of agricultural and industrial prices provided in Toutain, 'Imbroglio des indices de prix', 175–6.)

campaigns of the Restoration combined. Whereas other military actions abroad in the 1820s and 1830s were largely intended to preserve or extend French influence within existing political frameworks, operations in Algeria were more about the control of territory and the construction of a colonial state. The much greater expense that Algeria entailed, particularly in the minds of those who opposed the conquest, threatened the stability of the French social and political order. Martin Daunton and Miles Taylor have demonstrated that Britain's ability to export the costs of empire and so retain the loyalty of domestic taxpayers defused social tensions, contributing to the avoidance of revolution in 1848.[6] The French failed to do likewise.[7] Despite their best efforts, revenues from Algeria never exceeded 14 per cent of expenditure there under the July Monarchy, and the colony cost 907,739,133 francs in deficits between 1831 and 1848. The fiscal system covered these expenditures without much difficulty, but resources were nevertheless diverted from domestic spending priorities and many deputies disliked the expense of conquest. While some 'liberal imperialists' saw colonisation as a means of mitigating

[6] Daunton, 'Tax Transfers'; Taylor, '1848 Revolutions'.
[7] The rest of this paragraph draws on Greenfield, 'Price of Violence'.

the 'social question' by offering the French poor the means to become prosperous farmers in Algeria, opponents of the conquest criticised it as drawing resources away from more effective means of addressing the 'social question' within France, such as public works. Partly to ease these pressures, the government sought to stimulate the Algerian economy for the sake of maximising tax revenues, for instance in 1847 compelling the Banque de France to establish a branch in Algiers to ease the supply of credit there. Such efforts had limited success and revenues from Algeria only increased slowly.

Despite the costs of Algeria, there was never any serious consideration of withdrawal. As with the 1823 Spanish expedition, successes in Algeria were exploited to glorify the dynasty and thus legitimise the regime. Louis-Philippe's sons fought in the campaigns and featured prominently in commemorative paintings that were displayed in the Musée de Versailles, which opened in 1837.[8] The Duc d'Orléans, the heir to the throne, wrote in 1835 that the government was determined to give France's African possessions 'all the stability and support which their future requires'; the following year, Thiers, then leader of a short-lived government, declared that one of his central missions was to 'complete the conquest of Africa', in other words Algeria.[9] Notwithstanding such pronouncements, governments generally sought to limit the French presence there in the 1830s, adopting a policy of 'restrained occupation'. Only the outbreak of renewed warfare with the Algerian amir Abd al-Qadir in November 1839, compounded by humiliation during an international crisis in 1840, pushed the French towards conquering Algeria more completely.

The Eastern crisis of 1840 was the nearest France came to facing a general European war between 1815 and 1870 and reflected the central foreign policy problem confronting the Orleanists. The 1830 Revolution undermined the Russian relationship that had facilitated the restored Bourbons' aggression abroad. Under pressure to assert French prestige internationally, Louis-Philippe was therefore more reliant on Britain and Austria, both of which were wary of French ambitions. Restoration governments had competed for influence with Austria in Italy and with Britain in the Mediterranean, particularly in Spain, and these competitions continued under Louis-Philippe; from 1832 to 1838, for instance, French troops occupied Ancona in an attempt to check Austrian domination in Italy. Moreover, the need for Louis-Philippe to demonstrate his

[8] Sessions, *By Sword and Plow*, 83–124.
[9] Orléans to Clauzel, 17 October 1835, Clauzel MSS, AN, 226AP/1; Thiers to Louis-Philippe, 16 August 1836, Thiers MSS, BNF, NAF 20607, fol. 278.

conservative credentials reduced his scope for action abroad. He could not emulate his predecessors' use of their counter-revolutionary reputation to ease an aggressive foreign policy. Consequently, war in Algeria became more important to glorify and legitimise the dynasty. Meanwhile, the French emphasised their commitment to the existing European international system, taking the opportunity presented by the Belgian Revolution in 1830 to renounce their interest in France's 'natural frontiers'. Instead, they sought British goodwill by advocating a neutral, independent Belgium, only acting militarily to expel the Dutch, who had refused to accept Belgium's secession from the Netherlands. Like the 1823 Spanish expedition, the intervention allowed the French to demonstrate – to the Russians in the former case and to the British in the latter – their fidelity to the international order.

For the British, the value of good Franco-British relations lay in the possibility of restraining French activity in Italy and Spain and in facilitating the preservation of the Ottoman Empire. While the French were firmly committed to Ottoman survival, they differed with the British over how to achieve it. Britain opposed the extension of French influence in Egypt, which had grown since the 1820s. In reforming his state, the Egyptian ruler, Muhammad Ali, sought to increase his autonomy vis-à-vis the Ottoman sultan, his nominal suzerain. The French, sensing an opportunity to enhance their position in the Mediterranean, generally supported him. Concurrently, they sought the preservation of the Ottoman Empire as a bulwark against the extension of Russian power into the Mediterranean through the Straits. To an extent, Egyptian independence could facilitate this policy by diverting Ottoman resources from the Levant towards their mission at the Straits. Egypt, wrote Thiers, was 'the most solid rearguard of the Turkish Empire.'[10] Of course, this logic assumed the sultan's acceptance of Egyptian independence.

The outbreak of war in April 1839 between Muhammad Ali and the sultan over the Levant, and the Ottomans' subsequent defeat, precipitated a major international crisis. The powers, partly at French instigation, sought to mediate a settlement of the conflict. The French government, under Marshal Soult, saw collective action as a way of exacerbating divisions between the powers, restraining them and extracting concessions for Muhammad Ali while buying him time to strengthen his position. Thus, the French, in response to British pressure to resolve the crisis, temporised. Thiers, who formed a new government in March 1840, largely

[10] Thiers to Guizot, 21 March 1840, Thiers MSS, BNF, NAF 20613–14, fol. 18.

continued this policy. Wearying of the French attitude, Viscount Palmerston, the British foreign secretary, persuaded the other great powers to join him in signing the Convention of London on 15 July. They demanded that the Egyptians withdraw from Syria, which Thiers had hoped to retain for Muhammad Ali. Humiliatingly, France was merely invited to accede to the convention, producing outrage among politicians and the press. Compromise was difficult and, consequently, tensions escalated over the summer, raising the risk of a general European war.

The Orleanist elites found themselves in a horrible dilemma. 'I want peace with ardour, with passion . . .', wrote Thiers, but if 'France allows itself to be insulted, pushed aside, treated as Louis XV once was, it falls in the ranking of nations; our new dynasty is compromised, public order with it, and the most frightful confusion is the outcome of all this'.[11] Thiers, an historian of the 1789 Revolution, knew well that foreign policy failures had contributed to the collapse of the *ancien régime*.[12] War, though, also risked destroying the July Monarchy; hence, in part, the government's wish to avoid it and some republicans' desire for it. Thiers, therefore, prepared for war because he felt he had no choice. He hoped that the powers would compromise to secure peace; French elites knew that other European governments shared their aim of avoiding war.[13] If no concessions were possible, Thiers may even have felt that war, where France might win, was less threatening to the Orleanist regime than the consequences of accepting defeat without war.

Louis-Philippe was even more desperate to avoid war than Thiers, though it is important not to exaggerate the differences between the two men. Louis-Philippe had been instrumental in shaping foreign policy under Soult.[14] Others of the Orleanist elite, such as Guizot who became ambassador to Britain in January 1840, also largely accepted Thiers's policy.[15] After 15 July, however, Guizot, Louis-Philippe and much of the rest of the elite became more cautious, with many openly opposing war. While they appreciated Thiers's dilemma, self-preservation and a desire for peace precluded their endorsements of his high-risk policy.[16]

[11] Thiers to Sainte-Aulaire, 16 August 1840, Thiers MSS, BNF, NAF 20613–14, fol. 208.
[12] Thiers, *Histoire de la Révolution*, I, 35.
[13] Sainte-Aulaire to Thiers, 22 August 1840, Thiers MSS, BNF, NAF 20612, fol. 248; Thiers to Guizot, 20 August 1840, Guizot MSS, AN, 42AP/246.
[14] Thureau-Dangin, *Monarchie de Juillet*, IV, 15.
[15] Guizot to Thiers, 8 May 1840, Thiers MSS, BNF, NAF 20610, fol. 83; Guizot to Duchâtel, 9 June 1840, Duchâtel MSS, AN, 2AP/8, dossier 1, fol. 17.
[16] Tudesq, *Grands notables*, I, 494–510, II, 781–91.

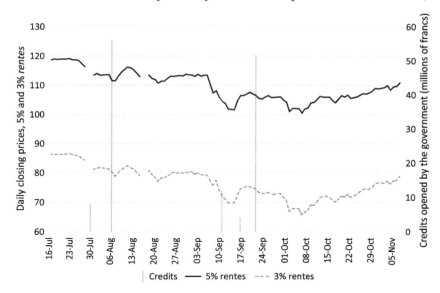

Figure 7.2 Daily closing prices of *rentes*, as quoted in Paris, during the crisis of 1840.
(Source: *Le Moniteur universel*)

Like the conquest of Algeria, the crisis of 1840 presented a challenge to the fiscal-military system that had emerged after 1815. The government authorised credits to finance the expansion of the army and navy, proposing to raise the former to 639,000 men. Throughout the crisis, the government had little difficulty borrowing. While 3 per cent *rentes* fell to a nadir of 66 in October, the Caisse d'amortissement kept 5 per cents above par (Figure 7.2).[17] The downward pressure was mitigated by doubts that war would break out. Investors, like the French government, initially seem to have supposed that the powers would not maintain the 15 July treaty without French inclusion. In early August, Jean-Henri Hottinguer, who had taken control of the family firm in 1833, deemed the idea of a general war 'so extravagant ... that few thinking persons can yet be brought to entertain it'.[18] James de Rothschild expressed a similar view.[19] Still, as the crisis matured, investors' agitation increased. 'The bourse is the centre

[17] Marion, *Histoire financière*, V, 189–90.
[18] Hottinguer et Cie to Baring Brothers, 1 August 1840, BA, HC 7.1.144.
[19] James de Rothschild to his nephews, 4 August 1840, RAL, T35/174.

of many intrigues,' noted the interior minister in late August.[20] Indeed, financiers such as the Rothschilds did what they could to ensure peace.[21]

The fiscal system proved adequate to the needs of the crisis, perhaps because it was only a crisis and not a war. The military presented a greater problem, particularly since the abolition of the reserve in 1824 had reduced France's capacity to fight a general war of the kind threatened in 1840. Moreover, shortly after the passage of his army law, Saint-Cyr had formed a commission to consider frontier defences. Constraints on military spending, however, prevented the construction of many of the fortifications it proposed. A new defence commission, established in 1836 to re-evaluate France's defensive needs following the neutralisation of Belgium and the growth of the federal German army, found that its list of recommended fortifications met the same fate as that of its 1818 predecessor. Drawing heavily on the documents produced by the defence commissions, Gary Cox has emphasised the defensiveness of French military planning from 1815 to 1870. France, he argues, could not fight an offensive war in 1840.[22] He perhaps exaggerates the importance of military planning in a pre-railway age. Napoleon's campaigns, for example, were not planned years in advance, and little about warfare had changed by 1840. For those military leaders who opposed war, the lack of military preparation was probably a convenient excuse to avoid a potentially cataclysmic war they were uncertain of winning. If war came, General Bugeaud wrote, France faced a 'tough and difficult struggle' in Europe.[23] The limits of France's frontier defences increased the appeal of an offensive. Thus, Bugeaud suggested that 'The offensive suits our geographical, political and moral situation. We will only silence the critics with success; we will only make propaganda with early victories; but above all there must be victories.'[24] In military planning, as in other matters, domestic political concerns were paramount.

The crisis ended with Thiers's resignation, forced by Louis-Philippe in October. Soult formed a new ministry, which Guizot dominated as foreign

[20] Rémusat to Louis-Philippe, 21 August 1840, Maison de France MSS, AN, 300AP(III)/42, dossier 4, fol. 96.
[21] Corti, *Das Haus Rothschild*, 205–26.
[22] Cox, *Halt in the Mud*, 52–71, 129–38, 142. There is some circularity to Cox's logic; focusing on the defence commissions is highly likely to produce the conclusion that military planning was defensive. However, a defensive war in the early nineteenth century required more preparation than an offensive one – for example in necessitating the construction of fortifications. Thus, the focus of military planning was naturally defensive.
[23] Bugeaud to Martimprey, 4 September 1840, Martimprey MSS, SHD, 1K 598/1.
[24] Bugeaud to Thiers, 4 September 1840, Thiers MSS, BNF, NAF 20608, fol. 345.

minister. Though over, the crisis had enduring ramifications for the fiscal-military system. As part of his preparations for war, Thiers sought to improve France's defensive capabilities. He hoped that the fortification of Paris, which had made little progress since it was initiated in November 1830, could be completed within a year.[25] Guizot, too, supported the fortification of Paris. For Louis-Philippe, the fortifications were '*the hair of Samson*'.[26] Though he did not want war, he exploited the opportunity offered by the crisis to overcome the Chambers' reluctance to fund higher military expenditure, producing what Marion has labelled a 'real budgetary revolution'.[27] One of the achievements of the Soult–Guizot ministry, which lasted until 1847, was to increase public spending in the face of conservative opposition and the fiscal orthodoxy that had emerged since the 1790s. The expansion of the state from the late 1830s produced a fierce debate over public finance, in which rising military expenditure acquired a prominent place. Humann, who returned to the finance ministry in October 1840, was 'much opposed to any form of fortification for Paris'. Fortification, he complained, was prohibitively expensive, and would have to be financed by borrowing.[28] Indeed, completed in 1844, the fortifications cost around 145 million francs. Many deputies, not least conservatives, disliked the expense inherent in fortifying Paris, while some on the left attacked the fortifications as a means of facilitating military control of the capital.[29] Consequently, the government relied on the centre-left to pass the fortifications bill, for which Thiers served as *rapporteur*. The decision risked alienating conservatives and, if the government collapsed as a result, the Rothschilds observed fearfully, the most probable outcome was a new Thiers ministry. Thus, once the bill passed, Guizot reassured James de Rothschild, the government 'would seek the opportunity to break with the left and M. Thiers' over the upcoming issue of electoral reform.[30]

Despite moving towards the right after the fortifications bill passed, the government maintained heightened military spending, which was 54.9 per cent greater in 1841 than it had been in 1839, corrected for inflation.[31]

---

[25] Thiers to Broglie, 19 September 1840, Thiers MSS, BNF, NAF 20613–14, fol. 285; Thiers to Guizot, 15 September 1840, Guizot MSS, AN, 42AP/246.

[26] Louis-Philippe to Thiers, 21 August 1840, Thiers MSS, BNF, NAF 20611, fol. 195. Emphasis in the original.

[27] Marion, *Histoire financière*, V, 190.

[28] [James de Rothschild to N.M. Rothschild and Sons], 3 and 6 January 1841, RAL, XI/101/4.

[29] O'Brien, 'Embastillement de Paris', 63, 68–9, 71–7.

[30] [James de Rothschild to N.M. Rothschild and Sons], 18 February and 2 April 1841, RAL, XI/101/4.

[31] *Proposition de loi . . . 1839*; *Proposition de loi . . . 1841*.

The increased deployments in Algeria to obtain military success there depleted the forces available to secure France itself, while the consequences of the 1840 crisis in Germany heightened fears for French security. The possibility of war on the Rhine stimulated German nationalism and induced the Prussians to seek a more effective federal German army, though Metternich, fearful of increasing Prussian influence among the German states, diluted their proposals. Given these pressures, the government sought to defer reductions to military expenditure. However, the 1841 budget commission was as reluctant as its predecessors – and successors – to condone higher government spending. Shortly before the 1840 crisis, one deputy on the Chamber's budget commission had condemned military spending as 'enormous', and this attitude did not disappear.[32] In late 1841, therefore, Soult informed army officials that it was 'indispensable to return spending to a figure that was aligned with the habitual resources of the Treasury, and thus to satisfy the wishes expressed by the Chambers'.[33] While the government preserved something of the means to expand the army quickly, it was unable to maintain the level of military spending reached in 1840–2 (Figure 7.1).

The 1840 crisis also stimulated the expansion of the navy, necessary to protect the route to Algiers, defend the French coast and extend French influence in the Mediterranean and across the world. The navy's strength had gradually increased since the Restoration, but continuing pressure from the Chambers for economies had limited its capacity to project French influence globally.[34] The humiliation of 1840 intensified the desire for greater global power to recoup French prestige, while the advent of steam power stimulated navalism by seeming to offer a solution to the problem of British naval supremacy that had confronted Molé in 1817. The prince de Joinville, one of Louis-Philippe's sons, attracted considerable public and diplomatic attention in 1844 when he published an essay emphasising the potential advantages to France of utilising steam power in a war against Britain.[35] Capitalising on the public interest, Admiral Mackau, navy minister from 1843 to 1847, sought to revitalise the navy, securing a *crédit extraordinaire* of 93 million francs to finance shipbuilding. Ultimately, he envisioned a fleet of 326 vessels, 100 of which would be steam-powered.[36]

---

[32] Procès-verbaux, commission du budget, 27 February 1840, AN, C 803.
[33] Circular to the *lieutenant généraux commandant les divisions* etc., by Soult, 13 December 1841, SHD, 1M 2008.
[34] Rapport au roi, by Rosamel, 12 October 1836, Molé MSS, AN, 726Mi/14.
[35] Hamilton, 'Diplomatic and Naval Effects'.   [36] Battesti, *Marine*, I, 46–7.

The navy ministry's budget increased in the final years of the July Monarchy, rising by 43.5 per cent from 1839 to 1847 when adjusted for inflation, but the Chambers continued to restrain naval spending.[37] In 1842, a deputy on the budget commission observed that 'France cannot be simultaneously a first rank continental power and a first rank maritime power. To want to push [France] to attain this double pretension is to impose on its finances a charge which they are unable to support. This would be to weaken France and to weaken its financial resources.'[38] While the navy was essential to the extension of French power abroad, it remained less important than the army, both as a foundation of French security and as a source of prestige. With the ongoing conquest of Algeria, the army seemed to hold greater promise, in addition to being harder to defund. Moreover, naval expansion risked eliciting a response from the British, sparking a naval arms race which, aside from the potential damage it could cause to Franco-British relations, French fiscal policymakers felt they could ill afford.

The Rise of the Interventionist Orleanist State

The surge of public works expenditure in the 1840s reinforced the Chambers' reluctance to condone higher military spending. The ascent of the interventionist state reflected mounting political and socio-economic pressures. Alongside growing urbanisation, the revolutionary unrest of the early 1830s appeared to substantiate the fears contained in the 'social question', particularly since ministers and other members of the elite tended to exaggerate the extent of radical republican activity. As a result, the regime felt greater pressure to act, since it sought to mitigate social divisions. One purpose of government, Guizot believed, was to maintain the unity and coherence of society. Government, he claimed, was 'a means of union; it is the central node to which isolated individuals attach themselves and from which emanate the strings that hold them together'.[39] The ensuing willingness to reform spurred the development of the concept of 'public utility' which encouraged greater investment in public works.[40] Despite placing additional burdens on the budget, ministers had little doubt that public works were necessary. In 1840, the

---

[37] *Proposition de loi ... 1839; Projet de loi ... 1847.*
[38] Procès-verbaux, commission du budget, 23 March 1842, AN, C 825.
[39] 'Note sur les rapports du roi et des chambres dans le régime représentatif', by Guizot, 1816, Guizot MSS, AN, 42AP/28.
[40] Graber, 'Enquêtes publiques'.

minister of public works noted that he, 'in the time in which we live, is the dispenser of grace'.[41] Public works, wrote Jean Lacave-Laplagne, who succeeded Humann as finance minister in 1842, provided 'the working class' with three benefits: 'an increase in the amount of work, a rise of salaries, a fall in the prices of consumer goods'.[42] Public works were therefore essential to stimulate and manage economic modernisation and industrialisation. In this way, they would address the 'social question', particularly since glory abroad and the forcible repression of revolutionary activity were themselves inadequate to the task, as the uprisings of the early 1830s suggested. Moreover, like the conquest of Algeria, public works offered a way of recouping some of the legitimacy that the regime had lost in its handling of the 1840 Eastern crisis, not least in facilitating economic prosperity and displaying the progress of French civilisation. As with the overhaul of the fiscal-military system after 1815, the growth of public works spending was partly intended to buttress political and social stability.

The Orleanist government made its first major investment in public works in 1833, when Thiers, as minister of commerce and public works, pushed through the Chambers the *loi de cent millions*, which allocated 44 million francs for canals, 29 million for roads and 24 million for monuments and public buildings in Paris.[43] In part, these expenditures were intended to reinforce the regime's legitimacy after the 1830 Revolution. Thus, in Paris, the completion of monuments such as the Arc de Triomphe in 1836 and the Colonne de Juillet in 1840 were intended, recalled one Orleanist minister of public works, to 'reunite all the traditions' of France under the new regime.[44] The state also buttressed its legitimacy in the wake of the 1832 cholera epidemic by asserting its responsibility for public hygiene; whereas the city of Paris constructed only 15,000 metres of sewers between 1814 and 1830, it acquired 62,682 metres from 1832 to 1840.[45] The sharp growth of the Parisian population, from 861,436 in 1831 to 1,226,980 in 1846, increased the pressure to improve sanitation and to remodel the cityscape. Meanwhile, the availability of goods improved as the municipality built new amenities such as roads, markets and train stations, particularly in the 1840s.[46] Republican

---

[41] Jaubert to Thiers, 19 August 1840, Thiers MSS, BNF, NAF 20611, fol. 12.
[42] Lacave-Laplagne, *Observations sur l'administration des finances*, 64.
[43] Marion, *Histoire financière*, V, 153–4.   [44] Dumon, 'De l'équilibre des budgets', 899.
[45] Greenfield, 'Interventionist State', 393.
[46] Chevalier, *Formation de la population parisienne*, 40; Marchand, *Paris*, 48–61; Papayanis, *Planning Paris*, 82–95.

pressure encouraged these improvements. Partly to appease the agitation of the early 1830s, the government extended the franchise for municipal elections in 1834, inducing republicans to discard revolutionary activity in favour of electoral politics. They gained sufficient traction with voters, forcing the Parisian municipality to engage with their agenda of improving the lives of the poor, for instance by abolishing *l'octroi* and ensuring a supply of clean water.[47] Notwithstanding the republicans' desire, *l'octroi* survived; the growth of its revenues was essential to funding the growth of municipal expenditure, which the city augmented in 1837 with a loan of 25 million francs.[48] Consequently, the July Monarchy contributed significantly to the nineteenth-century rebuilding of Paris, despite historians' emphasis on the role of the Second Empire.

Railways only received 500,000 francs in the 1833 law, but they quickly came to absorb most public works expenditure under the July Monarchy. The money allocated in 1833 was for 'studies' to facilitate the creation of a railway network without heavy cost to the government. In the process, though, Thiers asserted the state's responsibility for railway construction, which was reinforced in 1837 when the government established a commission to consider the construction of several trunk lines. In addition to being highly attractive politically, railways had an obvious military value, though commercial and political concerns were often more important in determining the construction of the French railway network than strategic needs. The line built to connect Paris with Strasbourg, for instance, ran along the Franco-German border to incorporate nearby towns; while it therefore delineated a highly contentious borderland, defining these towns as French, it was overly exposed to potential enemy action.[49] Still, by integrating the national territory, railways facilitated administrative centralisation, and increased the army's capacity to fulfil its role of suppressing disorder by potentially hastening the movement of troops; in this respect, as with the fortification of Paris, railways could mitigate the threat of the 'social question'. Like Becquey in 1820, the government also sought an integrated national market to facilitate the movement of grain in times of dearth. In response to food riots in 1838 and 1839, the interior ministry emphasised the need for the free circulation of grain. Railways, though, would transport more than just grain. The Paris–Le Havre line, for instance, would expedite the movement of raw cotton and colonial goods to Paris. In facilitating trade, railways could improve access to commodities

[47] Sawyer, 'Définir un intérêt particulier parisien'.   [48] Massa-Gille, *Histoire des emprunts*, 177.
[49] Cox, *Halt in the Mud*, 152.

and cause prices to fall, thus alleviating socio-economic malaise. Attaining these perceived civilising effects of railway construction became a matter of national pride. In 1842, the minister of public works emphasised that Britain and the United States already had thousands of kilometres of track. European countries such as Prussia, he noted, were also building railways, as were even 'the smallest German states'. France could not allow itself to fall behind the lesser powers; it had to keep up.[50]

Given these advantages, railway construction attracted widespread political support, even if the costs were problematic. Presenting the 1836 budget, Humann announced that:

> The sums that we assign to productive public works . . . should be increased if only for the benefit of the Treasury itself, which profits the most from the good condition of roads, from the improvement of navigation, from the construction of railways: these are, in effect, the conditions in which people benefit, and social income does not flow from another source. The best system to follow in the administration of the finances of a great Empire is to hasten the progress of prosperity, to increase the taxpaying capacity, and not to offer tax cuts at the expense of services which enrich. Is this to say that the burden of expenditure will never be eased? Far from it, sirs; real economies can be obtained . . . a great financial amelioration is available to us: I want to speak of the reduction of interest on the debt.[51]

For Humann, the apostle of fiscal rectitude, a debt conversion would mitigate the borrowing required to finance public works, benefiting from the expiry of Villèle's ten-year guarantee against the redemption of 5 per cent *rentes*. Humann saw conversion in primarily financial, rather than political, terms. Consequently, he failed to inform his colleagues of his plan before announcing it in the Chamber of Deputies and the government collapsed. A new government formed under Thiers who, despite his support for Villèle's 1824 proposal and his backing unsuccessful plans for conversion in 1840, shelved the plan.[52] Small rentiers, he claimed, would suffer and, as in 1824, this argument was fatal.[53] Still, a debt conversion had considerable appeal among the French elite and thus the idea did not die with Humann's resignation, as Thiers's willingness to consider a conversion in 1840 suggests. Many *conseils généraux*, for instance, favoured the principle; as the *conseil général* of the Gard put it, a conversion 'will produce generally good results for agriculture and commerce' by lowering

[50] Greenfield, 'Interventionist State', 393–6.
[51] Humann, 14 January 1836, AP, 2nd series, XCIX, 551.
[52] Thiers to Guizot, 2 April 1840, Thiers MSS, BNF, NAF 20613–14, fols. 50–1.
[53] Thiers, 4 February 1836, AP, 2nd series, C, 185–93; Riviale, *La Presse et le pouvoir*, 103–13.

interest rates and thereby easing credit.[54] By late 1837, one deputy observed, 'the rentiers themselves' were 'expecting' the conversion. The main issue was whether 5 per cent *rentes* should be converted to 4 per cent or to 3 per cent *rentes*, the same question that confronted Chabrol in 1830. While 4 per cent *rentes* would minimise the damage to small rentiers, the deputy noted, it would 'compromise the success of the operation'.[55] Meanwhile, considerable opposition to any conversion remained.[56] Unable to reach a consensus, the government in 1838 'postponed' a conversion, Anselm de Rothschild claimed, 'because the Finance Minister is still unwell & there are so many plans they do not know what to do'.[57] The timing of the illness was sublime, debt conversions being rejected by the Chamber of Peers in 1838, 1840, 1845 and 1846, despite passing the Chamber of Deputies.[58]

Debt conversion stalled, but public works did not. In 1837, Duchâtel, then finance minister, proposed a *budget extraordinaire* to finance public works, which was approved by the Chambers and ultimately set at 193 million francs.[59] The rise of public works spending, without the corresponding debt conversion or cuts elsewhere, meant increasing government expenditure. As with the growth of military and naval expenditure, this attracted fierce criticism. In 1839, Villèle emerged from hibernation in the Garonne to condemn 'this incredible consumption of public wealth'. The 'gouvernement à bon marché', he charged, had given way to higher direct and indirect taxes since 1830, while the budgets of the ministries of the interior, public instruction and public works had increased.[60] The Marquis d'Audiffret, a legitimist peer and a president of the Cour des comptes,[61] was also critical in his two-volume *Système financier de la France* published in 1840. Perhaps seeking to influence the new Soult–Guizot ministry, his remarks were more restrained than Villèle's. He outlined the development of the 'happy financial situation [which] was still so bright at the start of 1840, though it was already threatened by . . . the conquest of Algeria and by the initial undertakings of public works' and by 'political worries and embarrassments which have

[54] Note, *conseil général du Gard*, n.d. [1837–8], Molé MSS, AN, 726Mi/14.
[55] Legendre to Molé, 30 November 1837, Molé MSS, AN, 726Mi/14.
[56] Roussin to Thiers, 20 April 1840, Thiers MSS, BNF, NAF 20612, fol. 144; procès-verbaux, commission du remboursement des rentes inscrites au grand-livre de la dette publique, 1840, AN, C 808.
[57] Anselm de Rothschild to his cousins, 28 April 1838, RAL, XI/101/1.
[58] Vaslin, 'Le Siècle d'or de la rente', 188–90.   [59] Marion, *Histoire financière*, V, 174–7.
[60] Villèle, *Lettres d'un contribuable*, 5–7, 10, 14.
[61] Established in 1807, the Cour des comptes oversaw the public accounts.

lumbered the Treasury with several hundred million in unforeseen engage-
ments contracted in the absence of the Chambers' – presumably a reference to Thiers's war credits of 1840.[62] Their criticisms were perhaps
slightly premature; the budget was in surplus from 1834 to 1839, with
ordinary revenues averaging 105.84 per cent of expenditure.[63] Still, concerned about potential criticism of the growth of the *budget extraordinaire*,
the government integrated it into the main budget when presenting it to
the Chambers for ratification in 1840. The left, too, criticised the rise of
public spending, though on different grounds. In 1843, Léon Faucher, a
deputy of the dynastic opposition, complained that 'Our administration is
like our agriculture. We employ too many men for the results that we
obtain.'[64] Most public works, he believed, alleviated social malaise and
facilitated economic development. Instead of criticising them,
therefore, Faucher resorted to the long-standing opposition discourse
about a bloated state.

Given the pressure to mitigate the costs of public works, the private
sector assumed greater importance. As with canals, railways were financed
by bankers, who formed companies to bid for concessions to construct and
operate particular lines. Less cautious than their Restoration predecessors
about joint-stock finance, Orleanist governments showed greater willingness to countenance the large-scale issuing of shares, which would increase
the private sector's capacity to undertake public works. Thus, joint-stock
companies were created to serve the purposes of the state, much as in
Victorian Britain and elsewhere.[65] Meanwhile, as ministers' interest in a
debt conversion suggests, the regime sought to boost the availability of
credit. In 1837, the Conseil d'état approved Laffitte's proposal for a Caisse
générale du commerce et de l'industrie, a limited partnership capitalised
through shares and, like his proposed finance companies of the 1820s,
intended to provide commercial credit and to invest in industry. The
success of joint-stock financial companies elsewhere, not least the Société
générale de Belgique which was established in 1822 and revamped after
1830, offered a model for such operations and probably assuaged any
doubts about the viability of Laffitte's scheme. His *caisse* reshaped
Parisian banking during the July Monarchy and spawned several imitators
across France, which eased credit in both Paris and the provinces and
furthered the extension of share-ownership.[66] Given the influx of new

[62] Audiffret, *Système financier*, 1st ed., I, 199–200.   [63] Fontvieille, *État*, 1937.
[64] Faucher, 'Situation financière de la France', 1041.   [65] Alborn, *Conceiving Companies*.
[66] Lévy-Leboyer, *Banques européennes*, 503–7.

securities, the Paris Bourse expanded significantly. While the total government debt rose by roughly 20 per cent during the Orleanist period, the
amount held in provincial France increased from around 10 per cent in
1830 to approximately a third of the total by 1848, as Parisian investors
diversified their portfolios.[67] The financial development of provincial
France was also apparent in the growth in credit offered by notaries, which
comprised the principal source of long-term loans and had attained a debt
stock of 3.7 billion francs by 1840, 27 per cent of national income, 3.1
billion francs of which lay outside Paris.[68] The ascent of joint-stock and
provincial finance would prove crucial as a means of mobilising money in
subsequent years, particularly during the Second Empire.

The boom of the late 1830s that permitted the foundation of Laffitte's
caisse ended in 1839, pushing several railway companies towards insolvency and necessitating a government rescue which further extended the
state's involvement in the railway business. In 1840, the state guaranteed
dividends on the Paris–Orléans line and extended credit to other companies. The crisis spurred the growth of the interventionist state by demonstrating the limited ability of the private sector to undertake railway
construction. In 1842, therefore, the government proposed the construction of a series of trunk lines to be undertaken by public and private
finance. Central and local government would purchase the land and
complete the necessary earthworks, while private railway companies would
build and operate the lines. However, only a few lines were constructed on
this model, not least because of the limits to local government resources.
Indeed, the shortcomings in the Orleanist inclination to delegate expenditure to local government where possible were already apparent in education policy. Guizot's 1833 law extending primary education relied on
local taxes to pay teachers a stipend of at least 200 francs. While public
spending on education grew markedly under the July Monarchy, many
local authorities were reluctant or unable to provide the resources necessary
and, in poorer *départements* such as the Ille-et-Vilaine, the law could
impose a heavy financial burden.[69] Still, communal resources increased
during the early Orleanist period, no doubt partly because economic
growth stimulated *octroi* revenues. For example, the budget of Niort, a
town with a population of 18,000, rose from 208,659 francs in 1828 to
352,836 francs in 1835; the revenues of other, smaller communes grew by

[67] Freedman, 'French Securities Market', 76–7.   [68] Hoffman et al., *Dark Matter Credit*, 96–7.
[69] Gildea, *Education in Provincial France*, 74, 93–5; Fontvieille, 'Croissance de la dépense
publique d'éducation'.

even greater proportions.[70] Local government finances remained tight, though, and consequently the costs of public works fell more heavily on the central government and the private sector, which eroded the independence of local government and *notables* and thus facilitated centralisation.

The correspondingly greater burden on the central government did nothing to allay discontent in the Chambers about rising government expenditure, particularly given the strong presence of relatively conservative deputies. Though the 1830 Revolution may have given greater political prominence to financial luminaries such as Laffitte and Perier, more conservative landed elites retained considerable electoral strength. Considering the outcome of the 1842 elections, the liberal banker Adolphe d'Eichthal worried that 'businessmen' had succumbed to a conservative 'invasion' of the Chamber.[71] Partly to appease conservatives, state assistance for private finance came with conditions, beyond those already imposed when the concessions were granted. The growth of state railway expenditure stimulated a wave of new regulation, concerning everything from fares to routes to the taxation of the movement of goods and ticket prices. The growth of the state was not merely a case of rising expenditure but of a new interventionist legal framework. Liberal they may have been, but the Orleanists were not adherents of laissez-faire.[72]

As a result, the state spent significant sums on the railways in the 1840s, rising from 2.4 million francs in 1835 to 282 million in 1847, allowing the 1842 law to fulfil its aim of stimulating private investment. While state subsidies comprised 28.7 per cent of railway spending from 1831 to 1847, the remaining 71.3 per cent was private capital.[73] The *haute banque* dominated railway construction, easing financial centralisation to Paris just as the railways themselves furthered administrative centralisation – though this trend was tempered by the reliance of many regional branch lines on provincial capital, which drew a wide range of people into the financial system as shareholders. Public and private railway expenditure rose in tandem, reaching a peak in the railway boom of 1844–6 before the financial crisis of 1847 necessitated another railway bailout on a greater scale than that of 1840, as we shall see, requiring the largest government loan of the July Monarchy.

[70] Guionnet, *Apprentissage de la politique*, 246.
[71] A. d'Eichthal to G. d'Eichthal, 16 July 1842, Saint-Simonian MSS, Arsenal, Ms 13750, fol. 119.
[72] Greenfield, 'Interventionist State', 396–8.   [73] Leclercq, 'Transferts financiers', 899, 903.

The Limits of Orleanist Fiscal Reform

Though the government raised taxes, the surge in public expenditure still produced deficits averaging 7.76 per cent per year from 1840 to 1847.[74] The ensuing borrowing presented a challenge to fiscal orthodoxy. Humann, noted James de Rothschild in April 1841 as the Chamber considered the 1842 budget, seemed 'discouraged once again by the ease with which the king, the ministers and the Chamber of Deputies vote millions ... He told me: "the more I engage in this debate, the more I worry for our financial future."'[75] Humann's defeat over the 1842 budget reflected the limits to the power of the fiscal elite that had emerged since Napoleon. Despite his authoritative understanding of public finance and his strong personality, Humann was impotent. Politically, he was outgunned by Guizot and Louis-Philippe, both of whom supported boosting military expenditure. In practice, they were supported by the Rothschilds, who contracted 150 million francs of *rentes* to cover the deficits created by rising expenditure; their financial support, however unenthusiastic they and other investors were about rising military expenditure and the fortification of Paris, reinforced the government as the best bulwark against Thiers and foreign policy adventurism.[76] The loan followed the established pattern. Humann outlined his intentions for it to James de Rothschild on 18 May 1841, and the latter arranged subscriptions in Paris and London.[77] On 18 October, the loan, France's first in 3 per cent *rentes*, was awarded at 78.525 to a syndicate of French firms dominated by the Rothschilds.

The divergence in the positions of the bankers and other members of the fiscal elite was crucial to the latter's defeat. Previously, the bankers and fiscal elite had championed the same doctrines. Baring, Laffitte and Corvetto, for example, agreed over policy in 1816–18, as did Rothschild, Louis and Humann in 1831–2. In both these instances, however, borrowing seemed unavoidable – in contrast to the situation in 1841, when borrowing appeared less necessary. Still, the *rente* remained firm in the early to mid-1840s, giving Guizot and Louis-Philippe the latitude to maintain relatively high military expenditure. The latter was a major factor in pushing the government to seek another loan in 1844, despite the deputies' budget commission having forced Soult to accept cuts to the

---

[74] Fontvieille, *État*, 1937.
[75] [James de Rothschild to N.M. Rothschild and Sons], 20 April 1841, RAL, XI/101/4.
[76] Hottinguer et Cie to Baring Brothers, 9 and 28 January 1841, BA, HC 7.1.179–80.
[77] [James de Rothschild to N.M. Rothschild and Sons], 18 and 29 May 1841, RAL, XI/101/5.

army in both France and Algeria.[78] The loan was simultaneously to expedite railway construction, as per the 1842 law. Indeed, for this purpose, Laffitte proposed in February 1844 to arrange a loan of 500 million francs to be issued over ten years, replicating something of his schemes to expedite canal construction in 1821 and 1825.[79] While Guizot, Duchâtel and the minister of public works were apparently interested, Laplagne was unenthusiastic and the idea was dropped.[80] Still, perhaps influenced by the successes of new joint-stock companies, the government in 1844 contemplated using a public subscription, as in 1818 and in 1831. Following a successful public subscription in Belgium for a loan of 84,656,000 francs in March, in July Laplagne wrote to the French ambassador in Brussels seeking 'confidential information' on the subject.[81] Ultimately, the government rejected this option, instead adjudicating the loan of 200 million francs in 3 per cent *rentes* to the Rothschilds and associated receivers general at 84.75 in December. This was a good deal for the government, 3 per cent *rentes* having remained just above 84 over the previous days.[82] A week before the adjudication, Hottinguer, who presented the rival bid for the loan, noted that 'Most unfortunately the Rente is still gaining upon us, having opened today at 84f. Roth[schil]d is evidently more and more annoyed (as well we may all be) at this, and more anxious to effect a junction [between the two groups of bankers].'[83] Ultimately unable to bring their rivals into a single bid for the loan, the Rothschilds had to raise their offer.[84]

Despite declining to issue the 1844 loan by public subscription, the government sought to increase the number of small investors in *rentes* through the *caisses d'épargne*. As we have seen, in encouraging the lower classes to save, they relieved potential pressure on private charity and government assistance and pushed savings into *rentes*, sustaining public credit while turning the poor into rentiers and thus easing the 'social question'. The Orleanists hastened the extension of the *caisses d'épargne* across France, integrating more of the lower classes into the financial

[78] Marion, *Histoire financière*, V, 207–8.
[79] Note, by Laffitte, to Laplagne, 23 February [1844], BA, HC 7.12.
[80] Caisse générale du commerce et de l'industrie, J. Laffitte et Cie to Baring Brothers, 16 March 1844, BA, HC 7.12.
[81] Guizot to Rumigny, 24 July 1844, Guizot MSS, AN, 42AP/9; Richald, *Histoire des finances*, 440.
[82] *Le Moniteur universel*, 3–8 December 1844.
[83] Hottinguer et Cie to Baring Brothers, 2 December 1844, BA, HC 7.1.243.
[84] 'Procès verbal de l'adjudication de l'emprunt de 200 millions', 9 December 1844, and 'soumission pour l'emprunt de 200 millions contre des rentes 3 p%', from de Rothschild frères and the *syndicat des receveurs généraux*, 9 December 1844, Rothschild MSS, ANMT, 132AQ/32.

system. Whereas only 14 *caisses* existed in 1830, that number rose to 364 by 1848, with the sharpest increase in the mid- to late 1830s. While many were established in the south, the largest increase in depositors was across the north and the Île-de-France, the most economically developed part of France and the region most affected by industrialisation.[85] To tap these resources more effectively for the state, a law in 1845 capped total deposits per account at 1,500 francs, causing the Paris *caisse d'épargne* to lose 32 million, a third of its deposits, 14.5 million of which were then channelled into *rentes* through the Caisse des dépôts et consignations as the law prescribed.[86] The *caisses d'épargne* thereby contributed to deepening the capital market in Paris and the provinces, alongside the railway companies which turned some Frenchmen into first-time shareholders, furthering the vision underlying Laffitte's *caisse* and its imitators. Thus, the July Monarchy did much to lay the foundation for the democratisation of finance that developed so dramatically after 1848.

Despite the growth of public expenditure, no new taxes were created under Louis-Philippe. The conservatism that emerged in reaction to Laffitte's 1831 reform was entrenched by the 1840s, though ministers retained greater willingness than their Restoration and Napoleonic predecessors to seek revenue increases from direct taxation, partly because public spending rose substantially under Louis-Philippe and ministers sought to distribute this greater fiscal burden equitably, without overstretching consent to taxation. In 1841, Humann and Laplagne, then president of the deputies' budget commission, determined to finance the surge of military spending through the stricter application of existing taxes, alongside the loan contracted with the Rothschilds.[87] The pursuit of this aim relied largely on improving the collection of direct taxes, though the government enacted some reform of indirect taxes. In the 1830s, the government had begun to abolish exemptions to the salt tax enjoyed by communes such as Salies-de-Béarn, and made the level of duty uniform across France in June 1840.[88] Regarding direct taxation, in June 1840, the finance ministry published an *Instruction générale*, which over 870 pages listed 2,011 regulations concerning the collection of direct taxes, most of which had never before appeared in a single volume. Circulated to every *département*, it reflected 'a long-felt necessity' to standardise

[85] Lepetit, *Les Villes*, 349–54, 356.
[86] Rapport, by F. Delessert, 23 August 1849, in *Rapports et comptes rendus*, 4; Calmon, *Monarchie de Juillet*, IV, 53–61.
[87] Marion, *Histoire financière*, V, 192.   [88] Hissung-Convert, 'Impôt sur le sel', 376–9.

fiscal administration.[89] This may have had some impact; several prefects requested a second copy of the *Instruction générale* 'for their personal use.'[90]

The desire for greater uniformity in the administration of direct taxes was also apparent in renewed pressure to finish and update the cadastre.[91] Perhaps influenced by the failure of Laffitte's attempt to secure more proportional direct taxation in 1831–2, the government pursued a more incremental approach, wary of provoking discontent. To increase revenue, the 1835 budget stipulated that newly built real estate would be taxed at the same rate as other land in its commune. In effect, therefore, the government bypassed the cadastre for urban direct taxation, since the pace of urban development ensured the survey was always outdated, while assessing urban real estate values could raise complicated questions about how to classify various properties. Consequently, the urban *contribution foncière* became more proportional, fulfilling something of the aim of Laffitte's 1831 reform but without abolishing repartition.[92] In rural areas, though, the cadastre remained the basis of direct taxation. As part of the drive to improve tax collection and centralisation, it was extended to Corsica from 1840. The only land survey – *terrier* – of the island dated from the *ancien régime*, and the process of completing the cadastre there was expected to take twenty years.[93] In part, perhaps, this exclusion arose from the sense that Corsica was different, as reflected in the *arrêtés Miot*. 'Corsica is a French *département*,' wrote Alexandre Dumas in 1844, 'but Corsica is still very far from being France.'[94] In this, the Corsicans were not wholly unique; Bretons, for example, were also regarded as uncivilised. Still, the supposed savagery of Corsicans probably left the government wary of imposing the cadastre on Corsica, for fear of stimulating unrest. Despite Miot's efforts, direct taxes in Corsica had continued to elicit resistance into the Restoration, producing 'an irregular situation in the administration of revenue'.[95] Moreover, financing the completion of the cadastre, as in mainland France, depended on the *conseil général*; in Corsica before 1843, the finance ministry noted, 'the *conseil général* has undertaken

---

[89] *Instruction générale sur le service et la comptabilité des receveurs généraux et particuliers des finances, des percepteurs des contributions directes et des receveurs de communes et d'établissements de bienfaisance* (Paris, June 1840), AD, Mayenne, P/41, xxxix.

[90] Circular to the prefects, by Pelet de la Lozère, 5 September 1840, AD, Mayenne, P/59.

[91] Vivier, 'Débats sur la finalité du cadastre', 203–6.   [92] Bourillon, 'Mesurer pour l'impôt'.

[93] Notes, 1844 and 13 April 1846, AN, C 848, dossier 25, C 874, dossier 22; Graziani, 'Du plan terrier au cadastre de la Corse', 309–12, 320–1.

[94] Dumas, *Les Frères Corses*, 36.

[95] Roy to Eymard, 24 June 1820, Eymard MSS, AN, 124AP/1, dossier 1.

no vote of funds.'[96] Indeed, while the central government made financial contributions, the first *départements* with a completed cadastre were those with *conseils généraux* most willing to fund it. For these *départements*, completing and updating the cadastre offered a means of appeasing their residents' complaints about the weight of taxation and ensuring that taxes were repartitioned relatively fairly within the *département*. A completed cadastre could also reinforce claims that the *département* itself was over-taxed, offering a means to pressure the central government to lower the *département*'s allocation of direct taxes. In potentially easing the iniquities of repartition, the cadastre facilitated the preservation of the system of direct taxes, deflecting pressure to change the manner of assessing direct taxes in a way that would ensure more proportional taxation.

Beyond raising the prospect of a more equitable repartition, completing and updating the cadastre benefited the interventionist state. In offering more precise valuations of land and confirmation of its ownership, the cadastre could facilitate land purchases for public works such as railways, and improve the accuracy of the financial planning necessary for the latter.[97] More exact valuations also raised the prospect of enhancing rural credit, the paucity of which drew increasing public attention in the 1840s. In 1845, for example, the *conseil général* of the Vienne sought to use the cadastre to give mortgage lending a 'solid foundation' that would expedite 'the circulation of capital and lending in rural areas'.[98] Investment in the cadastre, therefore, provided a manifestation of the interventionist state on a local level.

In pursuit of revenue through a more equitable repartition, in February 1841 Humann ordered reassessments of the *contributions personnelle et mobilière* and *des portes et fenêtres*.[99] Humann, Guizot later suggested, saw this *recensement* as a first step towards 'a notable increase of public revenue by the transformation of the *contribution mobilière* and that *des portes et fenêtres* ... into proportional taxes susceptible to indefinite increases'.[100] While Humann had opposed Laffitte's attempt to make these taxes proportional in 1831–2, the government needed more revenue by the 1840s. As he put it, 'if I succeed in bringing it [the *recensement*] to a good end, I will have avoided ... financial difficulties that threaten our future.'[101]

---

[96] Note, 1847, AN, C 894, dossier 18.
[97] Circular to the Prefects, by Laplagne, 7 July 1846, *Le Moniteur universel*, 14 July 1846.
[98] *Le Journal des débats*, 10 October 1845.   [99] Ponteil, 'Humann et les émeutes', 317–19.
[100] Guizot, *Mémoires*, VI, 378.
[101] Humann to Louis-Philippe, 8 August 1841, Maison de France MSS, AN, 300AP(III)/44, dossier 2, fol. 2.

Most likely, he saw seeking a fairer repartition as unproblematic; every five years, *conseils généraux*, mayors and *conseils municipaux* were required to reassess direct taxes. While officials such as presidents of *conseils généraux* and mayors were appointed from Paris, mayors in particular often exercised considerable autonomy in adapting to their locality and seeking to preserve its interests vis-à-vis the central government – not least in repartitioning taxes and reassuring taxpayers that they did so fairly.[102] In 1841, however, Humann decided that the *recensement* would be undertaken directly by the finance ministry instead. Vilified in the Chambers, 'this frightful invasion of the commune by the fiscal administration' was denounced as unnecessarily intrusive, infringing liberties to raise taxes on the middle and lower classes.[103]

Seeking to defuse rising discontent over the *recensement*, in June Humann declared his support for eventual proportionality: better to have proportionality than a repartition that taxpayers considered uneven or unjust.[104] Despite this pronouncement, from July to October 1841, the *recensement* faced intensive resistance in northern, south-western and central France, concentrated in and around Toulouse, Bordeaux, Lille and Clermont-Ferrand. While resistance was limited or non-existent in areas such as Brittany, the Île-de-France and Alsace, elsewhere people used the *recensement* as an opening to air pre-existing grievances.[105] In Puy-de-Dôme, for example, resistance arose alongside agitation for electoral reform. In winegrowing regions such as the Auvergne, anger was unleashed against *l'octroi*, reflecting the unpopularity of alcohol duties in these areas. Legitimists and, more consequentially, republicans exploited the opportunity to spread subversive ideas and aggravate discontent. In the south-west, the intrusiveness of the *recensement* provoked rumours that its purpose was to lay the foundation for new taxes on clothing and furniture, which exacerbated resistance. Likewise, in central France, stories of new or higher taxes fuelled unrest.[106] Tax increases in previous years gave these rumours plausibility; the *directeur des contributions directes* in the Drôme noted that a rise in the *patente* in 1840 encouraged resistance from those engaged in commerce.[107] The press, too, played an important role in disseminating information that provoked agitation. From late July, for instance, resistance in Lille was inspired by knowledge of the insurrection in Toulouse, gleaned

[102] Guionnet, *Apprentissage de la politique*, 243–78.
[103] Ponteil, 'Humann et les émeutes', 319–24.   [104] Caron, *Été rouge*, 58–9.
[105] Ponteil, 'Humann et les émeutes', 322, 324–47, 350; Caron, *Été rouge*, 315, 318.
[106] Ploux, 'Politique, rumeurs et solidarités territoriales', 242–52.
[107] Rapport général, *recensement*, Drôme, 30 March 1842, SAEF, B/67459/1.

from Parisian and local newspapers.[108] In this respect, the Orleanist regime's drive for a more integrated national space, not least through the development of railways and telegraph lines, facilitated the development of the unrest.

Several organs of local government, particularly *conseils municipaux*, encouraged resistance to the *recensement* as part of a broader hostility to centralisation. They disliked the encroachment on their power to repartition taxes. The *conseil général* of the Nord, for example, opposed the *recensement* and delayed undertaking it; other *conseils généraux* showed indifference. Their attitude was problematic, since the government sought to legitimate the *recensement* by publicising the support of *conseils généraux*.[109] In August, as the unrest intensified, Humann presented the prefects with four reasons for the *recensement*. First, it would provide the Chambers with a better understanding of how much tax could be levied in future; second, it would allow more revenue to be raised; third, it would ease the government's financial position; finally, it would reduce tax avoidance.[110] The *recensement*, he noted a few days later, 'provokes extreme difficulties; these difficulties may become insurmountable and there is reason to examine whether it is prudent to run the risk'. Given this situation, he offered his resignation, which was refused.[111] Despite Humann's loss of nerve, the government persisted with the *recensement*, determined not to yield 'a victory for the rioters'.[112] Not only did the disorder reflect the difficulties of raising taxes to finance higher expenditure, in weakening Humann politically it further curtailed his ability to resist increases in government borrowing.

As the acquiesence of *conseils généraux* in the unrest suggests, a major obstacle to increasing direct taxation remained the *notables*, the predominantly landed elite that dominated Orleanist politics as they had those of previous regimes. As Audiffret wrote in 1840, 'landed property today supports more than half of public expenditure.'[113] The continued growth of indirect tax revenue thus suited the *notables*, as did the loans floated to finance railway construction and the military expansion of the 1840s. They invested in *rentes* and shares, reaping the (untaxed) dividends, while

[108] Ponteil, 'Humann et les émeutes', 336–7.   [109] Tudesq, *Conseillers généraux*, 34–8.
[110] Ponteil, 'Humann et les émeutes', 331.
[111] Humann to Louis-Philippe, 13 August 1841, and Louis-Philippe to Humann, 14 August 1841, Maison de France MSS, AN, 300AP(III)/44, dossier 2, fols. 3–4.
[112] Duchâtel to Louis-Philippe, 23 August 1841, Maison de France MSS, AN, 300AP(III)/43, dossier 7, fol. 157.
[113] Audiffret, *Système financier*, 1st ed., I, 25.

some of them increased their power through the centralisation that the railways produced.[114]

Alongside the unrest, the electoral ramifications of reforming direct taxes raised further doubts about their potentially adverse effect on political stability. These concerns were most apparent in the debate over the *patente*, which was modified in 1844 following mounting pressure to mitigate perceived iniquities in the tax. While it had changed little since the Restoration, the tax's incidence altered as the French economy developed, particularly since it was not repartitioned. In Paris, for example, the number of *patentés* nearly doubled between 1817 and 1847.[115] Such changes generated pressure for reform. Moreover, the tax was particularly injurious to rural small businesses, which operated on relatively tight margins.[116] Thus, the finance ministry began preparing plans to modify the tax in 1834 and Humann may have considered amending or augmenting the *patente* in line with the finance ministry's inclination to increase revenue through existing taxes. Such an idea, wrote Duchâtel, the interior minister from 1840 to 1848, was 'deplorable ... It would be the most horrible of all electoral reforms', presumably because it risked rebalancing the electorate towards the urban middle and lower middle classes.[117] Preparing for the 1842 elections, the outcome of which was less favourable than the government wished, Duchâtel successfully insisted that 'there will be no increase' of the *patente*.[118] When reform was finally enacted in 1844, the main aim seems to have been to reduce the supposed inequalities in the tax. Opposition deputies and newspapers attacked the reform as designed to disenfranchise middle-class businessmen. Yet, while the Parisian electorate fell by 2,085, the reformed tax increased the size of the overall national electorate by 7,224, around 3 per cent. The reform may not have had adverse electoral consequences for the government, but it also did nothing to ease the state of the public finances. As the *rapporteur* for the bill and officials such as the *directeur des contributions directes* for the Ariège anticipated, revenue from the *patente* fell, from 44,287,220 francs in 1844 to 39,509,150 in 1845.[119]

---

[114] On the assets of the *notables*, see Tudesq, *Grands notables*, I, 429–35; Daumard, 'Problèmes généraux et synthèse des résultats', 104–11, 158–77.

[115] Daumard, *Bourgeoisie parisienne*, 20.   [116] Gaillard, 'Intentions d'une politique fiscale', 18–19.

[117] Duchâtel to Louis-Philippe, 16 August 1841, Maison de France MSS, AN, 300AP(III)/43, dossier 7, fol. 151.

[118] Duchâtel to Louis-Philippe, 21 August 1841, Maison de France MSS, AN, 300AP(III)/43, dossier 7, fol. 155.

[119] 'Examen du rapport de M. Vitet sur la loi des patentes de 1843–1844', *directeur des contributions directes*, Foix, 28 December 1843, SAEF, B/67459/1; Koepke, '*Loi des patentes*', 398–408.

Given the difficulties of raising direct taxes, indirect taxes were essential to increasing revenue, as they had been during the Restoration and Empire. In 1841, Humann abolished exemptions from the *droit de circulation* on alcohol dating from 1816 and reintroduced it and the *droit de licence* in those communes that had amalgamated these taxes with the *droit d'entrée* after 1832.[120] The government made further adjustments to boost indirect tax revenue in subsequent years, but given the popular discontent that such taxes aroused and the interest groups that opposed raising particular taxes, ministers were cautious about increasing them. 'The Country is not at all logical in its wishes and its demands,' Humann complained in 1841; 'it aspires to be powerful everywhere in all things, externally and internally. It wants large armies, a formidable navy, roads, canals, railways and all this on the condition that we do not ask it for money.'[121] As Sylvain Dumon, finance minister in 1847–8, recalled in 1854, 'There was nothing that I envied so much when I was Minister of Finance as the imposability of England.'[122] Indeed, the British income tax, established in 1842, presented an enviable achievement. As a proportional tax, it could be raised by simply adjusting the rate, without having to enter a quagmire comparable to the politics of repartition that dominated any attempt to increase – or decrease – France's direct taxes.

As with direct taxation, the government sought higher revenue by amending existing indirect taxes. In 1843, problems of tax evasion induced the government to contemplate banning domestic sugar production, though the Chamber adopted higher duties for beet sugar instead.[123] As deputies debated the bill in May 1843, Guizot noted the government's position as being one of 'New expenses and useful public works; No new taxes.'[124] The principle that no new taxes were to be created to finance the expansion of the state was still more apparent in the government's response to a proposed tax on dogs in 1845.[125] The bill was sponsored by several deputies and *conseils généraux*, the latter favouring the extension of indirect taxation much as they had under Napoleon. Given the mounting pressure on their finances, many *conseils généraux* sought to minimise the central government's use of the *centimes additionnels* on which they depended. These could only be raised so far and, in pushing the central government

[120] Ponteil, 'Humann et les émeutes', 317.
[121] Humann to Louis-Philippe, 13 August 1841, Maison de France MSS, AN, 300AP(III)/44, dossier 2, fol. 3.
[122] 19 April 1854, Senior, *Conversations*, I, 345–6.   [123] Todd, *Free Trade*, 171–83.
[124] Informal private note by Guizot, May 1843, Guizot MSS, AN, 42AP/36.
[125] AN, C 888, dossier 53, C 902, dossier 48.

away from *centimes additionnels*, *conseils généraux* hoped to secure their own finances while simultaneously gaining new income from a dog tax. Though sceptical that such a tax could be introduced without fomenting unrest, the finance ministry was at least ostensibly open to the idea, and polled the *conseils généraux* on how the tax should be collected. Laplagne outlined two ways in which a dog tax could be assessed: 'the declaration of the owner [or] the mandatory use of a collar with a stamp provided by the administration'.[126] The finance ministry, though, was uncomfortable with such intrusiveness. As we have seen, the main attraction of repartition was that taxpayers did not have to declare their incomes. The unrest produced by the attempted reforms of 1831 and, more importantly, 1841 left the government especially cautious. Unable to '*resolve the very real drawbacks*' that a dog tax would entail, it rejected the bill.[127] Though ostensibly open to new sources of revenue, the ministry could conceive of none that were acceptable. Thus, churning existing indirect taxes to increase revenue assumed a greater importance. This did not just entail raising taxes; in 1843, for instance, duties on surrogate alcohol were reduced.[128] As Laplagne observed, 'there is a compensation between increasing and reducing taxes.'[129] Lowering certain taxes could ease consent to the increase of others, and could also raise revenue by reducing evasion and boosting consumption, particularly given economic growth, which averaged 2.34 per cent per year from 1840 to 1847.

The government's increased reliance on indirect taxation (Figure 7.3) was particularly inopportune for Guizot's policy of strengthening France's position in Europe after the 1840 crisis through commercial agreements. The idea of using customs to extend French influence was not new in the 1840s. The *ancien régime* had pursued such policies and Restoration governments considered doing likewise. The restored Bourbons, however, generally seem to have had limited interest, and less success, in establishing commercial agreements. The impetus grew under Louis-Philippe, given the Prussians' use of customs to extend their influence in Germany from the late 1820s. Like the Austrians, the French followed these developments warily, which in 1834 culminated in the creation of the Zollverein, a customs union of northern and central German states. The Zollverein was an instrument of Prussian power and allegedly stimulated the German

[126] Circular to the prefects, by Laplagne, 13 August 1845, AN, C 902, dossier 48.
[127] Laplagne to Duchâtel, 23 July 1845, AN, C 902, dossier 48. Emphasis in the original.
[128] Calmon, *Monarchie de Juillet*, III, 326–8.
[129] Lacave-Laplagne, *Observations sur l'administration des finances*, 13.

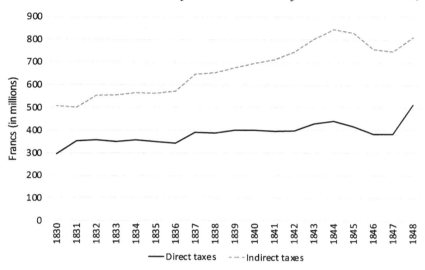

Figure 7.3   Central government revenue from direct and indirect taxes, 1830–48 (in 1815 francs).
(Sources: *Proposition de loi …[1830–1841]; Projet de loi … [1842–1848]*. Nominal prices were adjusted to those of 1815 using the index of agricultural and industrial prices provided in Toutain, 'Imbroglio des indices de prix', 175–6.)

economy; for both of these reasons, it acquired admirers abroad, not least in France.[130] Not only was economic development perceived as a solution to the 'social question', as we have seen, but it also would enhance France's capacity as a great power. Moreover, the French were sensitive to the influence that other powers might wield in the Low Countries, particularly Belgium, and had no desire to see it join the Zollverein. As the Belgian economy boomed in the 1830s with the onset of industrialisation, the Belgian government sought better access to foreign markets to facilitate exports. Looking partly to capitalise on the French customs reforms of the early 1830s, in 1833 the Belgians sought a reduction in French tariffs, which in 1836 culminated in a proposal to have both the French and Belgian legislatures approve lower duties.[131] The Belgian overtures probably reinforced the prevailing view in Paris that the Belgians needed an agreement. Duchâtel, then minister of commerce, considered that the Belgians' domestic market for textiles was too small and that in declaring

---

[130] Todd, *Free Trade*, 145–7.
[131] Le Hon to Broglie, 1833, and Thiers to Passy, 9 March 1836, AN, F¹² 2660.

independence they had lost access to the Dutch colonial market, while Belgian trade was dispensable for France.[132] Moreover, the French underestimated the risk of a Belgian agreement with the Zollverein. Consequently, though some French politicians were sympathetic to further customs reform, the Chambers and successive French governments took a hard line, demanding concessions that undermined the negotiations.[133] In late 1836, the French proposed a customs union, which the Belgians rejected as tantamount to annexation.[134] Soult revived negotiations in 1840, and the potential political advantages of a customs agreement induced Thiers to pursue them, as he had when last in government in 1836. Though he secured a commercial agreement with the Netherlands, negotiations with Belgium were hindered by the crisis over the Near East.

In 1841, Guizot floated the idea of establishing a commercial association of France, Belgium, the Netherlands and Switzerland as an equivalent to the Zollverein.[135] His first move was to secure a Franco-Belgian customs agreement over linens, concluded in July 1842. However, its value was quickly compromised; to French fury, the Belgians granted the same terms to the Zollverein in August. Moreover, the value of the 1842 agreement was limited by its scope, since the government sought to appease disquiet from industrial interests that had no desire to find their business undercut by cheap Belgian imports. Indeed, economic downturn in the late 1830s had stimulated protectionist sentiment, which affected groups such as Mulhouse textile manufacturers that had previously favoured trade liberalisation.[136] Duchâtel, whose support for the 1836 proposal had been lukewarm, joined Humann and Laurent Cunin-Gridaine, the minister of agriculture and commerce, in echoing the doubts of industrialists and worried about the adverse effects of a customs agreement on tax revenue.[137] Cunin-Gridaine argued that 'we must guarantee our industries against the invasion of prohibited goods coming from England or Prussia which cross through Belgium' and such imports, moreover, would reduce customs revenue.[138] Customs and duties on salt and tobacco

---

[132] Duchâtel to Broglie, 30 September 1835, Duchâtel MSS, AN, 2AP/27, dossier 1.
[133] Duchâtel to Broglie, 15 February 1836, AN F[12] 6241; Leopold I to Thiers, 26 April 1836, Thiers MSS, BNF, NAF 20604, fols. 111–13.
[134] Ridder, *Projets d'union douanière*, 9.   [135] Mastellone, *Politica estera del Guizot*, 67.
[136] Todd, *Free Trade*, 156–8, 164–5.
[137] Deschamps, *La Belgique devant la France de Juillet*, 117–27, 142–52, 158–81.
[138] Cunin-Gridaine to Louis-Philippe, 12 August 1841, Maison de France MSS, AN, 300AP(III)/43, dossier 6, fol. 123.

provided around a fifth of tax revenue, Humann noted, and 'it is an imperative obligation to ensure that customs and the taxes on salt and tobacco are not thus exposed to see their revenues diminish.'[139] The rise of indirect taxation and protectionism were mutually reinforcing, since free trade risked exposing French industries to competition for which they were ill-adapted because their costs were affected by indirect taxes and tariffs. Partisans of free trade sought to counter these arguments. Thus, the economist Michel Chevalier claimed in 1843 that 'from the fiscal point of view, the commercial [i.e. customs] union of France and Belgium would be a very advantageous operation' because the costs of both collecting customs duties and tax evasion would fall.[140] Such arguments may have had some effect, contributing to the French decision to seek a new Franco-Belgian commercial agreement covering a wider range of goods, which was concluded in 1845. Perhaps a more important determinant of this decision, however, was the impact of the continuing Belgian rapprochement with the Zollverein and the erection of new tariffs against French exports, which brought the French government close to abrogating the 1842 convention.[141] Given these tensions and enduring opposition in France to trade liberalisation, the agreement of 1845 was little less controversial than that of 1842.

Beyond their implications for tax revenues, commercial agreements could potentially alleviate pressure on the fiscal-military system that arose from higher expenditure by improving relations with France's neighbours. Alongside seeking commercial accords with Belgium, the Netherlands and Piedmont, Guizot repaired the Franco-British relationship after 1841, forging the first *entente cordiale*. Meanwhile, from the mid-1840s, he attempted to develop dynastic ties with Naples and Spain to form a '*ligue des Bourbons*'. The main aim of these initiatives was to strengthen France's position vis-à-vis Britain and Austria. Overall, they had limited success, not least because the needs of domestic and international politics did not always coincide – as the discontent over the Franco-Belgian customs agreements suggests. In the Pacific, Guizot's decision to compensate a British missionary, Pritchard, arrested by a French vice-admiral in Tahiti caused outrage, inducing the opposition to pillory 'Lord Guizot' and his associates as 'pritchardistes'. Though good relations with Britain eased France's international position, the policy produced domestic tensions. It

---

[139] Note by Humann, to Guizot, 30 July 1841, Guizot MSS, AN, 42AP/11.
[140] Chevalier, *Comparaison des budgets de 1830 et de 1843*, 21.
[141] Guizot to Deffaudis, 13 February 1845, MAE, 11MD/8, fol. 318.

is no coincidence that navalism grew in France as the *entente cordiale* deteriorated. Seeking to satisfy French public opinion while furthering his policy of developing dynastic relationships with other countries, Guizot instigated the Spanish marriages of 1846, marrying one of Louis-Philippe's sons to the Spanish queen's sister. British opposition to the marriages destroyed the *entente cordiale*, a loss which Guizot sought to offset by improving relations with Austria. While Guizot saw cooperation with Austria as necessary to quell revolutionary activity in Italy and instability arising from the risk of civil war in Switzerland, his shift to a more counter-revolutionary policy angered the left, as did his acquiescence in the Austrian annexation of Cracow in November 1846. In one crucial respect, though, the needs of domestic and international stability converged. As the 1840 crisis suggests, the great powers were wary of a possible resurgence of French strength. However, many Frenchmen had no desire for the levels of taxation and conscription this would require. In seeking to limit the burden of the fiscal-military system and so maintain stability in France, Guizot was content to incur what he regarded as toothless opprobrium from the left. Indeed, the government increased its majority in the 1846 elections, despite the opposition campaign against the 'pritchardistes'.

The Apogee of the Orleanist Interventionist State, 1846–8

The state's economic interventionism reached new heights following the 1846 elections. Though victorious at the polls, ministers were not complacent. The results were 'a real miracle', wrote Duchâtel, but the government had to continue to strengthen its position, remaining alert to possible future reversals.[142] Following the elections, Guizot proclaimed that once the government had secured 'order and peace', it must 'apply itself to nurturing in society all the seeds of prosperity, of improvement, of grandeur ... All politics promise you progress; only conservative politics will deliver it.'[143] Historians have generally seen Guizot as failing to deliver this 'progress'. Paul Thureau-Dangin suggests that the complications which followed the Spanish marriages diverted Guizot's attention from domestic politics; like other historians, he emphasises Guizot's rejection of proposals for electoral and parliamentary reform in 1847.[144] However, the

---

[142] Duchâtel to Nemours, 4 August 1846, Vendôme-Nemours MSS, AGR, 1586/509.
[143] *Le Journal des débats*, 5 August 1846.
[144] Thureau-Dangin, *Monarchie de Juillet*, VII, 14–15, 78–83, 377–93; Rosanvallon, *Moment Guizot*, 305–12.

government's refusal to accept such reform does not mean that it opposed all change. Indeed, Guizot's speech made no mention of electoral reform. As we can see, he emphasised the government's role in facilitating prosperity. He pledged to maintain the more interventionist state that had emerged over the previous decade, and may have interpreted the election results as an endorsement of this programme.

Harvest failure in late 1846, which provoked a financial crisis the following year, provided a spur for greater economic interventionism. Given their tendency to view the Orleanists as favouring laissez-faire, historians have often understated the extent to which the regime sought to mitigate the effects of these economic crises. Certainly, central government spending on poor relief was limited; by the beginning of 1847, this amounted to 8 million francs, followed by a further 4 million in March.[145] While this money was used to subsidise *ateliers de charité*, established by *conseils municipaux* to provide work for the unemployed, the subsidies were inadequate and many communes that requested assistance were denied. Writing to Duchâtel, the prefect of the Vienne noted that 'the number of subsidies claimed greatly surpasses the fund that you have at your present disposal. You find yourself in the necessity of restricting allocations and of choosing, between the requests submitted, those that are driven by the most urgent of needs.'[146] As with railway finance, central government expenditure was intended to stimulate action by local government and the private sector. Beyond meagre subsidies, the government also sought to incentivise the private sector to import grain. As Louis-Philippe observed, 'I do not doubt that it is a very advantageous speculation for businessmen who undertake it, who buy wheat and even flour on a large scale & import them into France. The advantage for the government is … so great … that I would be … disposed to vote premiums of encouragement.'[147] In addition to reducing duties to stimulate grain imports, the government encouraged *conseils municipaux* to reduce *octrois* on grain – a further burden on already strained local government finances – for the sake of easing the free trade of grain.[148] The government, in short, was not indifferent to the subsistence crisis, and did what it felt it could to alleviate the consequences.

---

[145] Price, 'Poor Relief and Social Crisis'; McPhee, *Politics of Rural Life*, 59, 61.
[146] Prefect of the Vienne to Duchâtel, 22 May 1847, AN, F^{15} 3841.
[147] Louis-Philippe to Duchâtel, 2 October 1846, Duchâtel MSS, AN, 2AP/7.
[148] Thureau-Dangin, *Monarchie de Juillet*, VII, 27.

The crisis complicated the process of fiscal reform, both by increasing the pressure on the public finances and by heightening the government's sensitivity to the risk of unrest. The idea of a dog tax resurfaced, but was rejected more quickly than before.[149] Instead, the tax debate in 1847 was dominated by two proposals, one to reduce the salt tax and another to institute a uniform postal duty for letters, instead of the existing duty that varied depending on the distance a letter had to travel.[150] The more substantial proposal concerned the salt duty. Already the previous year, the deputies had approved a cut to the tax, but the peers had not voted on the measure before the end of the session.[151] The proposal, claimed its sponsor, was a 'necessity for agriculture' – suiting the landed interests that dominated the Chambers – and 'an act of justice and humanity for the poor'.[152] The government regarded this proposition as inadmissible, given the strain on the budget; as Laplagne responded immediately, there was 'no scope to cut taxes'.[153] The desire for revenue probably encouraged the government to pursue tariff reform. The British move towards free trade in 1846, with the abolition of the Corn Laws, provided further impetus. In October that year, Cunin-Gridaine wrote that 'the time has come to overhaul our customs regime.'[154] Meanwhile, Théodore Gréterin, the *directeur général des douanes* and a former protectionist hardliner, had come to regard free traders' criticism of the customs system as meriting 'serious attention' – though he remained committed to 'a just measure of protection' for French industry.[155] In 1847, the government therefore presented a bill to rationalise import duties and their administration, abolishing a range of prohibitionist tariffs. Whereas the latter raised no meaningful revenue, the government expected lower, but still protective, duties to be perhaps more fruitful.[156] The protectionists, though, were too strong and the economic crisis made any proposal that could be attacked as reducing protection particularly sensitive, inducing the government to withdraw the bill. Still, the regime was becoming increasingly open to moderate customs reform.

[149] Remilly, 27 February 1847, *Le Moniteur universel*, 28 February 1847.
[150] Glais-Bizoin, 22 February 1847, *Le Moniteur universel*, 23 February 1847.
[151] AN, C 887, dossier 45.
[152] Demesnay, 27 February 1847, *Le Moniteur universel*, 28 February 1847.
[153] Laplagne, 27 February 1847, *Le Moniteur universel*, 28 February 1847.
[154] Cunin-Gridaine to Laplagne, 16 October 1846, AN, F^{12} 2482.
[155] Rapport au ministre, by Gréterin, 5 October 1846, AN, F^{12} 2482.
[156] Cunin-Gridaine, 31 March 1847, *Le Moniteur universel*, 14 April 1847; AN, F^{12} 6156.

The fiscal constraints facing the government arose partly from the contraction of commerce, which ended the growth of indirect tax revenues that had eased increases in government spending in the 1840s. Whereas economic expansion and adjustments to various duties allowed revenue from indirect taxes and state monopolies to rise from 687,448,840.58 francs in 1840 to a peak of 828,268,573.50 francs in 1845, an average of 28,163,946.53 francs per year at an inflation-adjusted annual growth rate of almost 4 per cent, revenue fell to 824,782,400.06 francs in 1847.[157] This was only a nominal decrease of 0.003 per cent, but if we correct for severe inflation in 1846–7 the decrease was almost 10 per cent, a substantial contraction. Alongside problems of inflation and tax revenue, the inadequacy of government relief efforts partly reflected deputies' concerns over excessive public spending – opposition, in other words, to the interventionist state. Perhaps more importantly, though, for many of the *notables* who dominated the Chambers, donations were a more attractive means of funding poor relief than the *centimes additionnels* on direct taxes which were often used to fund the *ateliers de charité*; consequently, charitable subscriptions to buy grain were widespread.[158] In Laval, for example, with a population of nearly 18,000, a private subscription to purchase flour raised over 100,000 francs, which the municipality supplemented by raising a loan.[159] Private charity further augmented the state's efforts to mitigate the effects of the harvest failure by providing a conduit for state action. Thus, in Brest, a major naval base, local dignitaries sought to enlist the navy to assist them in transporting grain from the United States.[160] The preference for private charity among elites corroborates something of the 'retrenchment hypothesis', the notion that limited suffrage consolidated power among the wealthy, who had little interest in paying extra tax to fund local civic amenities.[161] The ensuing reliance on the *notables* to organise charity reflected the limitations of the mid-nineteenth-century state's centralisation, which were also apparent in the discontent over direct taxes in 1831 and 1841. Local elites retained substantial influence, and they were not necessarily favourable to the regime. In Toulouse, for example, Villèle was a major donor of grain for the city's poor in 1847.[162] Through such acts, local *notables* bolstered their

[157] *Proposition de loi … 1840*; *Projet de loi … 1845*; *Projet de loi … 1847.*
[158] Bourguinat, *Grains du désordre*, 299.
[159] Rapport, by Loynes, 24 March 1847, *Le Moniteur universel*, 25 March 1847; *Le Moniteur universel*, 27 March 1847.
[160] Guilhem to de Rothschild frères, 12 March 1847, Rothschild MSS, ANMT, 132AQ/1P 160.
[161] Aidt et al., 'Retrenchment Hypothesis'.   [162] Godechot, 'Crise de 1846–1847', 104.

influence and thus their independence vis-à-vis Paris. While Tocqueville and others lamented the French state's centralisation, the reality was more nuanced.

Charity was usually better organised in the towns and cities, which partly explains the concentration of government poor relief in urban France. Moreover, the larger and more industrialised of them, such as Lille and Paris, were more prone to republican and socialist agitation. Paris, seen as the harbinger of revolutionary activity, was particularly important. There the municipality raised expenditure on hospitals and orphans from 5,965,000 francs in 1846 to 15,166,000 in 1847.[163] As elsewhere, this expenditure was supplemented by charity; in March 1847, James de Rothschild donated 5 million francs for grain provisions in Paris, at least partly motivated by the fear of unrest.[164] The distribution of government relief efforts may help to explain why there was so little unrest in urban France in the months preceding the 1848 Revolution, though hardship in towns and cities nevertheless increased the engagement of ordinary people in politics, strengthening republicanism.[165] Conversely, the focus on urban relief may also explain why there were more disturbances in rural areas, particularly in western and central France, where assistance was less effective. In the Vendée, for example, a convoy of grain was attacked by a group of women in January 1847, exacerbating the subsistence problem in Nantes, the convoy's destination.[166] Indeed, the urban food supply depended heavily on rural areas. While the urban poor were potentially more politically threatening, providing them with the relief necessary to keep them quiescent was contingent, at least to an extent, on maintaining order in the countryside. As in urban areas, republicanism grew, since the failure to provide greater relief in the countryside weakened the regime's legitimacy in such areas – though the gravity of this problem should not be overstated.[167] The July Monarchy was not destroyed by rural discontent but by revolution in Paris. Moreover, the unrest over the *recensement* in 1841, for instance, indicated both the limitations of the regime's support in some rural areas and its capacity to survive such unpopularity.

Historians have often treated the government's handling of the subsistence crisis separately from the financial crisis, but these two issues were

---

[163] Chevalier, *Classes laborieuses et classes dangereuses*, 245 n. 1.   [164] Ferguson, *World's Banker*, 468.
[165] Aminzade, *Ballots and Barricades*, 113–16, 180.
[166] Prefect of the Loire-Inférieure to the Prefect of the Vendée, 31 January 1847, AD, Vendée, 4M/458.
[167] McPhee, *Politics of Rural Life*, 72–3.

inextricable. Rescuing the railways could provide private finance with greater means for charity and importing grain. Equally, easing the subsistence crisis would improve the availability of credit for railway companies by reducing the amount of money diverted into grain imports. The latter having produced an exodus of specie, in January 1847 the Banque de France raised its discount rate from 4 per cent to 5 per cent, while simultaneously seeking a loan through Barings in London. The tightening of credit compounded the Bourse's existing uncertainties over the international situation. The collapse of the *entente cordiale*, wrote Hottinguer in late 1846, ended 'one of our strongest elements of confidence in the stability of European affairs'.[168] Soon afterwards, the Austrian annexation of Cracow caused 'panic' on the Bourse by arousing fears of war, while investors were uneasy over tensions in Switzerland.[169] The Banque repaid its loan to Barings after the government approved its selling *rentes* worth 50 million francs to the Russians, the latter being motivated by the desire to encourage French purchases of their grain, but the discount rate did not return to 4 per cent until December.[170] Given the severity of the crisis for the railway companies, it was clear that their future depended on the government – much like the construction of the railways in the first place. Indeed, Rothschild's donation for grain in Paris may have been partly intended to ease ministers' goodwill over the railways. Either the government had to modify the terms of the concessions to make them more attractive to investors or it had to provide a bailout to ensure the railway companies' solvency by short-term advances or by purchasing shares. Revising the terms of concessions, however, could loosen the railway regulation that had emerged over the previous years, exposing the government to the charge that it was endorsing unbridled capitalism. The latter was deemed threatening to the social order; in spreading the burden of risk, limited liability joint-stock companies raised a problem of moral hazard, allowing those who acted on shareholders' behalf to potentially avoid accountability for their actions and thus encouraging irresponsible behaviour which increased the likelihood of economic crises.[171] Instead, therefore, the government opted for a series of measures to inject the companies with liquidity. Most importantly, in August, the Chambers approved a 350 million franc loan to reduce the *dette flottante*, allowing the

[168] Hottinguer et Cie to Baring Brothers, 26 September 1846, BA, HC 7.1.279.
[169] Hottinguer et Cie to Baring Brothers, 15 October and 19 November 1846, BA, HC 7.1.286, 302.
[170] Guizot to Rayneval, 19 March 1847, Guizot MSS, AN, 42AP/9; Greenfield, 'Interventionist State', 404.
[171] Lefebvre-Teillard, *Société anonyme au XIXe siècle*, 21–4.

government greater scope to invest in public works. Being landowners, though, many deputies resisted the pressure to act, not wishing to rescue allegedly irresponsible financiers and speculators and attacking the government for having mismanaged the public finances. The criticism and the parsimony of the deputies may have deterred the government from seeking further funds to support the *ateliers de charité*. Already in May, given the chorus of discontent, Dumon had replaced Laplagne, while as late as July there were fears that the budget would fail in the Chamber – though Guizot was confident of success.[172] Faced with continuing disquiet over public borrowing, Dumon opted in concert with Guizot and Duchâtel to borrow only 250 million francs in November, deferring the remaining 100 million until 1848.

The difficulty of securing assistance for the railways reflected a fissure between commercial and landed interests. The two groups could unite in their preference for indirect over direct taxation, since doing so eased the fiscal burden on both. By contrast, rescuing the railways seemed more of a one-way transfer from land to the Bourse. Nevertheless, despite the delays, the economic crisis was met with a substantial response. The loan of 250 million francs, issued by the Rothschilds in 3 per cent *rentes* at 75.25, reflected the apogee of the Orleanist interventionist state. While the government's caution may have prolonged the suffering of ordinary people, and thus contributed to the overthrow of the regime in 1848, it was hard to see how the government could have done more. The charge of fiscal irresponsibility was serious and, as we shall see, became more pronounced during 1848. Without electoral victory in 1846, the ministry would have struggled even more to pass in the Chambers the measures it thought necessary to rescue the economy. Still, the substantial government spending in response to the financial crisis contrasted unfavourably with the limitations of poor relief, particularly given the economic losses that railways inflicted on those areas that had previously prospered as relay posts. Saving the railways, in other words, reinforced a perception of the regime as serving the interests of the rich which, alongside a succession of political scandals, fed the increasingly popular notion that the July Monarchy was morally corrupt.[173] The loan was contracted at an excessive rate, complained the *Constitutionnel*; this, alongside recurrent government deficits, demonstrated 'the necessity of reforming a political and financial

[172] Guizot to Louis-Philippe, 17 July 1847, Vendôme-Nemours MSS, AGR, I586/79.
[173] Fortescue, 'Morality and Monarchy'.

system that prepares for us a still gloomier future'.[174] Though intended to improve political stability, the state's economic interventionism fuelled a destabilising political discourse. Indeed, the regime's corruption had been a prominent theme of the campaign for electoral reform, conducted through a series of banquets in 1847–8.[175] Still, while a limited extension of the franchise would have weakened the opposition, probably assuring the July Monarchy's survival, the reformist banquet that precipitated the Revolution of February 1848 was not intended or expected to overthrow the regime. Dumon's verdict on the revolution, however self-interested, was essentially accurate: the July Monarchy was destroyed 'by the force of events . . . more than by its fault'.[176]

Conclusion

France was transformed under the July Monarchy, as the rise of public works spending made the state a force for economic development and spurred the growth of regulation. The regime's conservatism did not prevent it from implementing a highly innovative economic policy, which emerged by degrees from the 1830s onwards and reached its zenith in the mid-1840s. Alongside the growth of public works, military and naval spending also increased. Despite the regime's reputation for dovishness in foreign affairs, it offered as striking a demonstration as its Restoration predecessor of the advantages of the post-Napoleonic fiscal-military system; taking inflation into account, the July Monarchy had six years in which its combined military and naval spending were higher than they had been at any time during the Restoration (Figure 7.1). The loans that underwrote the rise of public expenditure in the 1840s reflected the state's evolving priorities. The loan of 1841 was primarily for military purposes, that of 1844 was devoted to both the military and public works and that of 1847 was principally to discharge the expenses incurred for public works. As the recourse to credit suggests, however, the government and French elites regarded expansion of government spending as a temporary phenomenon. Deputies had no intention of authorising endless loans, which would then divert their taxes into the pockets of rentiers – even if many of them purchased *rentes* during the 1840s.

Alongside loans, rising tax revenues faciliated the growth of public spending. These revenue increases depended not just on adjusting rates

---

[174] *Le Constitutionnel*, 11 November 1847.   [175] Fortescue, 'Morality and Monarchy', 89–90.
[176] Dumon to Thiers, 20 May 1848, Thiers MSS, BNF, NAF 20617, fol. 314.

of tax but on economic development. In this respect, the ascent of the interventionist state presented a virtuous circle: state expenditure stimulated economic development and thus higher tax revenues that, in turn, provided new resources with which to sustain the interventionist state. The crisis of 1847 broke the circle, since the growth in tax revenues stagnated while the need for government borrowing increased. This is not to say that the Orleanist regime mismanaged the public finances; the loan of 1847 was contracted at a respectable interest rate of 3.99 per cent. Nevertheless, while the increase of government spending in the 1840s foreshadowed the more dramatic expansion of the state under Napoleon III, the continuation of economic interventionism on a more sustainable basis required new means of finance. This, as we shall see, was the achievement of the Second Empire.

CHAPTER 8

The Rise and Fall of Austerity, 1848–1856

Historians have tended to present the two constitutional monarchies of 1814–48 as conservative, despite the differences in their conservatism, in contrast to the more radical Bonapartist regime that emerged following the advent of universal male suffrage in 1848.[1] In this view, the 1848 Revolution marked a major caesura in French history. Scholars have applied a similar chronology to French economic history, arguing that the Bonapartists inaugurated a new economic policy – 'l'économie politique du Deux Décembre' in Louis Girard's phrase – of state interventionism and public works.[2] Only during the Second Empire, contends one recent account, did the French state begin to promote the growth of capitalism.[3] Yet, as we have seen, the July Monarchy was economically interventionist and committed to public works, much as was the Bonapartist regime. Indeed, in terms of political economy, the July Monarchy and the Second Empire had much more in common with each other than either did with the Restoration, which was considerably more parsimonious in its public works spending.

Despite the continuities between the Orleanist and Bonapartist economic policy, there was a modest shift after 1848. The advent of universal suffrage, justified partly as a means of promoting social cohesion, raised the possibility of disrupting the ascendancy that landed and commercial elites had established over fiscal politics since the early 1800s and thus of rebalancing the tax system to the benefit of the poor. Though the republicans in 1848 failed in their attempt to recast the state, and the fiscal system ultimately survived with little change, the memory of the revolution had a lasting impact, while taxation still had to adapt to the new politics. The Crimean War produced a more striking change in public finance. As the fiscal-military system's most impressive performance

---

[1] E.g. Rosanvallon, *Moment Guizot*.   [2] Girard, *Politique des travaux publics*.
[3] Lafrance, *Making of Capitalism in France*.

between 1815 and 1870, the war entailed the rapid mobilisation of resources on a much greater scale, with the government floating loans through public subscription, as in 1818 and 1831. Historians have lauded this 'universal suffrage of capital'; as with 'l'économie politique du Deux-Décembre', they have seen it as evidence of a more ambitious regime than its predecessors.[4] As we shall see, though, the loans, as with the government's economic policies more generally, demonstrated a greater conservatism than historians have suggested. Still, with victory in the Crimea and the general success of its economic policies, the authoritarian Second Empire of the 1850s seemed to have reached its zenith.

The Triumph of Fiscal Conservatism

The republicans who formed the provisional government in February 1848 sought to create a new, more caring state, but this aspiration was undermined by stringent opposition and a severe financial crisis. Ripe for a crash, the Bourse was already fragile before Louis-Philippe's overthrow. As in late 1846, events abroad, particularly the Sicilian Revolution of January 1848, troubled investors.[5] While the worst of the subsistence crisis was over by 1848, grain prices having peaked in early 1847, the Republic still inherited extensive social problems.[6] Thus, the provisional government established *ateliers nationaux* in Paris on 26 February, giving work to the unemployed. These developed a model previously implemented under Louis-Philippe, for instance in Paris in 1830–1 and in towns and cities across France in 1847. The *ateliers* were essentially Orleanist social spending on a larger scale, but with greater central government involvement and a different ideological thrust: work, the radicals believed, was an entitlement to be guaranteed by the state. Partly to finance the *ateliers*, the provisional government embarked on fiscal reform. Already in February, Michel Goudchaux, the new finance minister, had promised an end to the supposed fiscal excesses of Orleanism, pledging retrenchment and tax cuts.[7] In general, the republicans sought to alleviate the burden on the poor by rebalancing the fiscal constitution away from regressive indirect taxation.[8] As in 1830, the revolution stimulated refusals to pay taxes and

---

[4] Dansette, *Naissance*, 126–9.
[5] Hottinguer et Cie to Baring Brothers, 24 January 1848, BA, HC 7.1.474.
[6] Labrousse, 'Panoramas de la crise', viii–ix.
[7] Declaration, by the provisional government [29 February 1848], *Le Moniteur universel*, 1 March 1848.
[8] Schnerb, 'Hommes de 1848', 123–5.

rumours of abolition. *Octroi* barriers, for example in Paris, were destroyed, crowds attacked receivers' offices and tax remittances fell into arrears.[9] The government exacerbated its financial difficulties by yielding to pressure to abolish the *timbre* on newspapers on 4 March, which prompted Goudchaux's resignation.[10] More consequentially, as after the 1830 Revolution, military spending rose: adjusted for inflation, the war ministry's budget was 48.6 per cent higher in 1848 than in 1847.[11] While Lamartine, the foreign minister, had announced the Republic's commitment to peace and the European order in a published circular to French diplomats, he nevertheless sought higher military spending to ensure the security of France's borders.[12]

Goudchaux was a banker, moderate republican and former deputy of the dynastic opposition under the July Monarchy; his views on finance were not especially radical. More so were those of his successor, Louis-Antoine Garnier-Pagès, another former deputy of the Orleanist dynastic opposition turned republican, who was willing to go further in recasting the fiscal system. Faced with a growing deficit, he had three means of raising the funds necessary: borrowing, raising taxes or issuing paper money as governments had in the 1790s. The difficulties inherent in each option have prompted some historians to defend Garnier-Pagès's actions as the best available in the situation, largely because he avoided emulating the disaster of the *assignats*.[13] Still, as we shall see, his policies were not particularly well thought through and their execution left a lot to be desired.

Hoping to minimise the recourse to taxation, Garnier-Pagès attempted to meet the government's needs through the sale of state-owned forests and by issuing the remaining 100 million francs of the 1847 loan through a public subscription of 5 per cent *rentes* at par. The financial crisis having stalled the issuance of the 250 million franc loan of November 1847, only 82 million francs of which had been subscribed, Garnier-Pagès argued that the lack of other investment opportunities combined with investors' patriotism would facilitate the public subscription.[14] Investors, though, proved wary as the Bourse descended into panic and banking firms and businesses failed, increasing unemployment, while those firms that survived struggled to obtain liquidity.[15] Given the situation, the *emprunt*

[9] Antony, *Politique financière*, 34–5.   [10] La Gorce, *Seconde République*, I, 153.
[11] *Projet de loi … 1847*; *Projet de loi … 1848*.   [12] Garnier-Pagès, *Révolution de 1848*, VI, 268.
[13] Heywood and Heywood, 'Rethinking the 1848 Revolution', 398–400.
[14] Rapport, by Garnier-Pagès, 9 March 1848, *Le Moniteur universel*, 10 March 1848.
[15] J. Delahante to Enfantin, 2 and 3 April 1848, Enfantin MSS, Arsenal, Ms 7712, fols. 10–11.

Figure 8.1   Weekly closing prices of *rentes*, as quoted in Paris, January 1846–March 1852.
(Source: *Le Moniteur universel*)

national raised only 20 million francs; for much the same reason as in 1831, credit by public subscription had little success (Figure 8.1).[16] Uncertainty arising from both political instability and concerns about the revolutionary government's agenda deterred investors, particularly the larger financiers with the means necessary to drive up the *rente*.

Struggling to issue long-term debt, the government resorted to short-term expedients, securing a three-month loan of 50 million francs from the Banque de France.[17] Meanwhile, ministers did little to restore confidence. Having potentially a lot to lose from the collapse of the Bourse, not least because his firm held most of the remaining unsold *rentes* of the 1847 loan, James de Rothschild asked his British nephews at the beginning of March about the possibility of issuing *rentes* in London in order to resuscitate French public credit.[18] However, as his son Gustave wrote at the end of the month, 'the provisional government takes no measures to improve credit', pursuing instead a 'war on capital'.[19] Unlike previous governments, Garnier-Pagès was therefore unable to borrow to avoid raising taxes.

---

[16] Marion, *Histoire financière*, V, 261.   [17] Ramon, *Banque de France*, 232–3.
[18] James de Rothschild to his nephews, 2 March 1848, RAL, XI/85/26B/1.
[19] Gustave de Rothschild to his sister and cousins, 31 March 1848, RAL, XI/109/65B/1.

Instead, on 16 March, he decreed *45 centimes additionnels* – a 45 per cent one-off increase – to the *contributions foncière, personnelle et mobilière, des portes et fenêtres* and the *patente*. The tax increases provoked major discontent, particularly since falling grain prices produced shortages of specie in rural areas that made paying the surtaxes more difficult.[20] Simultaneously, the *45 centimes* provided an outlet to express dissatisfaction with the sociopolitical order and to settle local grievances.[21] The surtaxes compounded existing discontent over wine duties, provoking especially intense resistance in the south-west, which reached its peak in the spring and summer when collection of the surtaxes began, following the election of a new Constituent Assembly in April.[22] Since the Assembly took until 23 May to sanction the *45 centimes*, recalcitrant taxpayers claimed that 'the tax was not definitively established, that it needed the approval of the Constituent [Assembly].'[23] The press propagated such ideas and, as in 1841, stimulated unrest. In the Hautes-Pyrénées, resistance not only entailed 'isolated acts of rebellion but a veritable sedition ... Some communes ... have united to oppose by armed force the execution of all measures which would compel them to pay this tax.'[24] As in 1841, too, local government could not always be relied on to counter unrest and sometimes even encouraged it. The *conseil général* of the Basses-Alpes, for example, complained that the repartition placed an excessive burden on the *département*.[25]

Hoping to defuse and pre-empt unrest, Garnier-Pagès sought to ease the burden of the *45 centimes* on the poor by granting reductions and exemptions.[26] This, however, raised new disputes over repartition and the size of reductions.[27] In Oraison, in the Basses-Alpes, for instance, the reductions were so little that they produced fresh unrest.[28] The attempt to ease the burden on the poor reflected Garnier-Pagès's hope of turning the *45 centimes* into a de facto progressive income tax.[29] He saw the latter as more equitable, but it would take too long to establish formally in time to

---

[20] Vigier, *Seconde République dans la région alpine*, I, 226–7; Lévêque, *Une société en crise*, 79–81.
[21] Corbin, *Archaisme et modernité*, I, 500–12.
[22] Gossez, 'Résistance à l'impôt', 90–1, 114–24, 132.
[23] *Commissaire du Gouvernement*, Maine-et-Loire, to Crémieux, 10 May 1848, AN, BB[18] 1462. The Assembly's approval did not stop complaints that the surtaxes had not been sanctioned by the nation's elected representatives (e.g. *procureur général*, Caen, to Marie, 14 August 1848, AN, BB[18] 1462).
[24] *Procureur général*, Agen, to Bethmont, 10 June 1848, AN, BB[18] 1462.
[25] *Procureur*, Digne, to the *procureur général*, Aix-en-Provence, 28 October 1848, AN, BB[18] 1462.
[26] Decree of 5 April 1848, *Lois*, XLVIII, 133.   [27] Gossez, 'Résistance à l'impôt', 93.
[28] *Procureur*, Digne, to the *procureur général*, Aix-en-Provence, 28 October 1848, AN, BB[18] 1462.
[29] Garnier-Pagès, *Révolution de 1848*, VIII, 341.

meet the government's needs in 1848. Garnier-Pagès, therefore, regarded the *45 centimes* as the least bad option.[30] His desire for the 'right' form of direct taxation was also apparent in his aspiration to abolish the *contribution des portes et fenêtres*. Though partly intended as a tax on the wealthy, it 'deprives the farmer of the air he breathes in his pitiful cottage and takes away his share of light'. In the meantime, the government prepared to introduce a progressive income tax for 1849, while simultaneously further reforming the fiscal constitution to render it more progressive.[31] From 15 April, eight days before the general election, the *droit de circulation* and the *droit de détail*, both on the sale of alcohol, were replaced with a tax on alcohol consumption, which rapidly became as unpopular as the duties it replaced.[32] Likewise, on 15 April the government decreed that the salt tax would cease to be collected from 1849; on 19 April, Garnier-Pagès introduced a temporary 1 per cent duty on mortgages for 1848, intended as a tax on capitalists. Meanwhile, the government replaced *l'octroi* on meat in Paris with sumptuary and property taxes, and reduced the city's *octroi* on alcohol.[33] Since *l'octroi* raised almost two-thirds of the municipality's total revenue from 1831 to 1847, rising from just over half of revenue during the Restoration, outright abolition was effectively impossible: the tax was essential to funding civic amenities such as hospitals.[34] Still, both nationally and locally, the fiscal system was to be rebalanced towards progressive taxation.

The unrest over the *45 centimes* gave Garnier-Pagès's fiscal programme a more radical appearance than it deserved. His ideas were much milder than, for example, the anarchist Pierre-Joseph Proudhon's proposal for an 'impôt du tiers', a one-third tax on income which would be redistributed to the needy while expediting the abolition of property.[35] The radicalism of Proudhon's proposal arose more from its objective and the rate of taxation than from the principle of an income tax, which was not especially novel in 1848; Britain had established such a tax in 1842 and Austria and Prussia did likewise following the 1848 revolutions. Moreover, the salt tax, alcohol duties and *contribution des portes et fenêtres* were all unpopular and susceptible to reform. The *contribution des portes et fenêtres*, wrote the *directeur général des contributions directes* in 1855, was among those taxes that aroused 'the greatest hostility from the population'. The tax was

[30] Garnier-Pagès, *Un épisode de la Révolution*, 119–58.
[31] Garnier-Pagès, *Révolution de 1848*, VIII, 348–9, 352.   [32] Marion, *Histoire financière*, V, 255–6.
[33] Decrees of 15, 18 and 19 April 1848, *Lois*, XLVIII, 142, 144–5, 147–8.
[34] Faure, 'L'Industriel et le politique', 37 n. 30; Bédard, 'Finances de Paris', 24.
[35] Proudhon, 31 July 1848, *Le Moniteur universel*, 1 August 1848.

particularly problematic in urban areas – the republicans' electoral base – where property values varied more widely and were less contingent on size than in rural areas. Offering a poor indication of the value of a property, the tax was 'perhaps the one of our four direct taxes that is most contrary to the principle of equality'. The government's attempt in 1832 to alleviate the burden the tax imposed on the poor had little success, and it remained on the agenda for fiscal reform into the Second Empire.[36] Just as Garnier-Pagès's resort to the *45 centimes* sought to operate within the structure of the existing fiscal system, if not within its spirit, his reforms in 1848 were largely incremental and intended as pragmatic.

Fiscal reform was part of a broader project of reorienting the state towards what republicans believed was the wider public interest. Aside from financing tax cuts by streamlining the supposedly bloated Orleanist bureacracy, the republicans proposed to expand the state, as their solution to the ongoing railway question suggests. The financial crisis that followed the revolution had aggravated the problems affecting railway companies, further reducing bankers' willingness to invest. In May, Eugène Duclerc, a moderate republican who succeeded Garnier-Pagès as finance minister, proposed to nationalise the railways, which would cull the 'new aristocracy' of financiers and businessmen whose ownership of a public service contravened the values of the Republic. The cost of this plan, however, produced strong opposition in the newly elected Assembly, moderates and conservatives having triumphed in the April elections. The government therefore withdrew its proposal on 3 July.[37] Meanwhile, the new Assembly opted to dissolve the *ateliers nationaux*. Many deputies agreed with the royalist, Catholic Comte de Falloux when he denounced the scheme as being 'from an industrial point of view, a permanent strike organised at 170,000 fr. per day, that is 45 million per year; from a political point of view, it is an active hotbed of menacing fermentation; from the financial point of view, a blatant daily dilapidation; from the moral point of view, the most evident alteration of the worker's charac-ter'.[38] Never keen on the notion that the state should guarantee employ-ment, much of the right and the centre feared that radical republicans aspired to an open-ended entitlement to poor relief. Consequently, the *ateliers* were suddenly closed in June, prompting the June Days uprising from Parisian workers, which was bloodily suppressed by the army,

---

[36] *Directeur général des contributions directes* to Magne, 26 November 1855, Billault MSS, AD, Loire-Atlantique, 20J/20, dossier 11.
[37] Leclercq, *Réseau impossible*, 201–6.   [38] La Gorce, *Seconde République*, I, 313.

National and Mobile Guards, the latter being a militia recruited from the young Parisian poor. With the defeat of the insurgents, moderates reasserted their ascendancy and General Cavaignac, who had quelled the uprising, became leader of the government.

The *ateliers* were the high-water mark of government intervention to counter the slump and alleviate social malaise. Still, the 1848 Revolution gave the 'social question' renewed prominence. Goudchaux, who returned as finance minister after the uprising, claimed that 'The February revolution did not just overthrow a throne, it acknowledged that there was a social malaise that shook [the throne] profoundly; the February revolution has promised to solve this problem.'[39] The moderate republican government formed after the insurrection remained committed to social reform. In the last six months of 1848, central and local government combined spent 13 million francs on poor relief in Paris, only slightly less than the 13.5 million francs spent on the *ateliers nationaux* between February and the June Days.[40] As under the July Monarchy in 1847, and in countries such as Prussia that were affected by revolution in 1848, moderates embraced spending on relief to mitigate working-class discontent and thus forestall disorder.[41]

The *rente* rose after the uprising ended, easing public credit in the latter half of 1848. Furthermore, following a request from Duclerc at the beginning of the month, on 30 June the Banque de France granted the government a loan of 150 million francs.[42] Then, in July, Goudchaux rescued the 1847 loan. To attract investors, he opted to issue 5 per cent *rentes* at 75.25 to cover what remained of the 250 million francs, allowing those who had already subscribed to exchange their 3 per cent *rentes* for the new 5 per cents.[43] Despite the increase in public borrowing, Goudchaux retained the *45 centimes* to finance some of the increase in government expenditure. Local officials were 'as active as they are firm' in ending the continuing resistance which was, wrote the justice minister, 'in fact necessary for public order as much as the interests of the treasury'.[44] Ultimately, the surtaxes raised 191,260,000 francs.[45] Meanwhile, Goudchaux continued to pursue the fiscal reform that he had espoused in February, seeking to create a more progressive fiscal system. He proposed to modify Garnier-Pagès's mortgage tax, shifting the incidence from the capital to the interest earned by the creditor, but this plan was

[39] Goudchaux, 15 June 1848, *Le Moniteur universel*, 16 June 1848.   [40] Luna, *Cavaignac*, 272.
[41] Eddie, '1848 Revolution in Prussia', 118–19.   [42] Ramon, *Banque de France*, 233–5.
[43] Marion, *Histoire financière*, V, 276–8.
[44] Circular to the *procureurs généraux*, by Marie, 4 August 1848, AN, BB[18] 1462.
[45] *Projet de loi . . . 1848.*

scuppered by the Assembly. His proposal for progressive inheritance taxes also faced criticism, particularly for seeking graduated duties, and the Assembly did not pass the bill during Goudchaux's tenure.[46]

Goudchaux's most controversial proposal was for an *impôt sur les revenus mobiliers*, essentially an income tax. Though proportional, with a 2 per cent tax rate, the threshold was high enough to exclude 90 per cent of the working class.[47] Simultaneously, Goudchaux sought to allay fears that the tax would entail a more intrusive state which, as we have seen, had been a major impediment to Orleanist fiscal reform. Thus, despite the 2 per cent proportion, he proposed to assess the tax according to the principles of repartition. Mayors and *conseils municipaux* would prepare lists of those eligible for the tax, and *conseils généraux* would set a minimum threshold – those whose incomes fell below this would be exempt. Goudchaux's proposal, therefore, inevitably entailed reopening the endless discontent over the iniquities of repartition. The bill, though, made little progress in the Assembly and was not debated before Goudchaux left office. Given the opposition to his new direct taxes, Goudchaux resorted to seeking revenue from existing taxes. Though the Assembly rejected his proposal to reinstate the salt tax, he secured the postal reform that the Orleanist government had rejected in 1847, instituting a uniform duty for letters.[48] Meanwhile, *l'octroi* on meat in Paris, the abolition of which seemed to have done little to reduce prices, was revived without much opposition.[49]

The fiscal reforms that followed the Revolution of 1848 were therefore largely abortive, arguably to a greater degree than they had been after that of 1830. Once the plans for progressive taxation foundered, little remained beyond the abolition of the salt tax, which was partially reversed at the end of 1848, as we shall see. For many of the moderates and conservatives who dominated politics after the June Days, new taxes risked exacerbating political instability.[50] Like Garnier-Pagès, therefore, Goudchaux was pushed into relying on old expedients; both men accepted *centimes additionnels* over progressive taxation and, contrary to their wishes, found themselves unable to dispense with indirect taxes. The upcoming election for the president of the Republic offered a way around the impasse. Campaigning for the presidency in 1848, Cavaignac revived the slogan 'no more *droits réunis*'.[51] Indeed, universal suffrage, in making the poor

[46] Schnerb, 'Hommes de 1848', 131–40.   [47] Luna, *Cavaignac*, 308–9.
[48] Marion, *Histoire financière*, V, 281–5.
[49] 'Note sur les résultats de la suppression des droits d'octroi sur la viande à Paris en 1848', 15 February 1860, AN, F¹² 2483.
[50] La Gorce, *Seconde République*, I, 412.   [51] Tudesq, *Élection présidentielle*, 115.

potential voters, increased the attractiveness of promising the abolition of alcohol duties. He also pledged to end the *45 centimes*, in line with many candidates who proposed to abolish or reimburse these taxes in the election campaigns of 1848–9. The Republic, though, was indissolubly tainted by the *45 centimes*, which greatly undermined its legitimacy and damaged the standing of republicanism until at least the 1870s.[52]

Constructing the Bonapartist State

The 1850s were the heyday of the 'delegating-market' state in France, as the rapid growth of public expenditure that began under the July Monarchy was, fleetingly, curbed. In December 1848, Louis-Napoleon Bonaparte, the principal beneficiary of the republicans' discredit and the extended franchise, was elected president on a promise of retrenchment in reaction against the republicans' tax reforms and social spending. He was backed by the *parti de l'ordre*, a loose alliance of conservatives, Orleanists and Bonapartists that aimed to moderate the effects of the 1848 Revolution and assure stability, for which Louis-Napoleon seemed an ideal tool. Once elected, however, Louis-Napoleon declined to be the puppet his conservative supporters had intended, using military intervention in Italy to assert his independence. Effectively continuing the Orleanist policy of extending French influence in Italy, he sent troops to Rome in 1849 to restore the pope, who had been overthrown by revolution in 1848. In strengthening his support among Catholics, he gained the latitude to dismiss the conservative ministry he had appointed following his election. He entrenched his political supremacy with a *coup d'état* in December 1851, legitimating it with a plebiscite. A year later, with the endorsement of another plebiscite, he proclaimed himself Emperor Napoleon III.

The new government faced rising pressure to streamline the state, in the aftermath of Orleanist and then republican public expenditure. The deficit rose from 14.51 per cent of expenditure in 1847 to 16.18 per cent in 1848 and peaked at 21.89 per cent the following year, pushing policy-making elites to unite in favour of fiscal rectitude.[53] In a pamphlet published in 1848, Audiffret pilloried Orleanist fiscal irresponsibility, writing that 'the administration, the Chambers, the *départements*, the communes, finally the whole of France were enticed, from [1842 onwards], by the benefits and by the hopes of a new era of abundance

---

[52] Corbin, *Village des cannibales*, 31–46.   [53] Fontvieille, *État*, 1937.

and of credit, into excessive spending.'[54] A new edition of his *Système financier de la France*, published in 1854, reiterated these attacks on the July Monarchy for increasingly reckless borrowing after 1841.[55] As finance minister, Garnier-Pagès had been similarly critical, exaggerating the gravity of the situation the Republic inherited. Presenting the budget for 1848, he claimed that 'when the nation proclaimed the Republic, a catastrophe was inevitable ... For several years, the budget regularly showed a large deficit.'[56] Mortgaged to the bankers, the July Monarchy, Karl Marx wrote in 1850, had been a regime of the 'finance aristocracy'.[57] Attacking Orleanist finance suited agendas on both the left and the right. For the former, the Republic's inheritance excused the failure to create a utopia; for the latter, the July Monarchy's faults helped to explain its collapse and thus justified retrenchment.

The Orleanists defended themselves by emphasising the failings of the provisional government. While the Orleanist stewardship of the public finances was not 'unassailable', wrote the banker Benjamin Delessert, the provisional government had presided over the deterioration by spending irresponsibly, mismanaging public credit and bungling taxation.[58] In 1848, Laplagne published a lengthy defence of Orleanist public finance and, a year later, Dumon did likewise.[59] The July Monarchy, wrote the latter, was not 'irrevocably committed on the path of deficits, when it clearly only used credit for extraordinary and productive expenses'. Good governments, Dumon argued, had to borrow for 'supreme and passing necessities, or for fruitful expenses'.[60] In making their arguments, neither the Orleanists nor their critics denied the dire state of the public finances. Rather, the debate turned on who was responsible for causing the deterioration. Consequently, the pressure for retrenchment became overwhelming.

Pledging to 'restore the finances' during his 1848 election campaign, Louis-Napoleon committed 'to undertake all possible economies that, without disrupting public services, permit the reduction of the taxes most onerous to the people'.[61] As a result, corrected for inflation, the army budget was reduced by 42.5 per cent and that of the navy by 40.3 per cent between 1848 and 1853; meanwhile that of public works fell 53 per cent

---

[54] Audiffret, *Crise financière*, 23.   [55] Audiffret, *Système financier*, 2nd ed., I, 497–8.
[56] Rapport, by Garnier-Pagès, 8 May 1848, *Le Moniteur universel*, 9 May 1848.
[57] Marx, 'Class Struggles in France', 48–51.   [58] Delessert, 'De la situation financière', 502.
[59] Lacave-Laplagne, *Observations sur l'administration des finances*; Dumon, 'De l'équilibre des budgets'.
[60] Dumon, 'De l'équilibre des budgets', 890–1.
[61] [Anon.], *Élection de Louis-Napoléon Bonaparte*, 32.

from 1848 to 1852 and in 1853 the ministry was amalgamated with that of agriculture and commerce.[62] In 1852, the budget registered a surplus for the first time since 1839, with ordinary revenues at 102.46 per cent of expenditure.[63] The Bonapartist commitment to fiscal probity was reflected in the invitation to Audiffret to become finance minister in 1852.[64] The spending reductions shaped the government's solution to the railway companies' ongoing difficulties. To keep the companies afloat, the government initially found itself compelled to follow the Orleanist policy of subsidies; public expenditure on railways reached new heights in 1849 before falling 52.63 per cent in 1850, adjusted for inflation.[65] Seeking to reduce the risk of future crises and ensure that companies would have the means to undertake more extensive railway construction, the government encouraged a series of mergers in the early 1850s, facilitating these through guarantees of railway bonds while increasing the duration of concessions. Thus, on one level, the government mitigated its expenditure by doing what the Orleanists had tried to avoid in 1847, amending the terms of railway concessions to make them more attractive to investors. Nevertheless, the bond guarantees raised the prospect of higher railway expenditure in future. Indeed, just as the Orleanists had gradually curbed whatever commitment they had to a *gouvernement à bon marché* after 1830, the Bonapartists too presided over the renewed growth of public expenditure from 1853 onwards, which accelerated with the outbreak of the Crimean War.

Despite the cuts, the government remained sensitive to the 'social question'. Benefiting from preparatory work undertaken by the governments of 1848, the Bonapartists enacted measures intended to promote economic well-being. In 1850–1, for example, the Assembly passed new laws to curtail the exploitation of apprentices, to protect orphans and improve hospice provision for the infirm, and further such measures were enacted under the Second Empire. Meanwhile, in 1848 and 1849, the government capitalised on good harvests to ensure that major cities were well supplied with bread and, following another harvest failure in 1853, established a Caisse de service de la boulangerie in Paris to mediate between bakers and their suppliers to ensure that bread remained affordable.[66] Though spending cuts curbed elements of the Orleanist interventionist state, the government remained active in the economy.

---

[62] *Projet de loi ... 1848; Projet de loi ... 1852; Projet de loi ... 1853.*   [63] Fontvieille, *État,* 1937.
[64] Audiffret, *Souvenirs,* 387–8.   [65] Fontvieille, *État,* 1907.
[66] Miller, *Mastering the Market,* 285–90.

Spending reductions were complemented by tax increases, as the regime gradually abandoned many of the fiscal reforms of 1848 and reasserted the state's dependence on indirect taxation. Indeed, despite Garnier-Pagès's intentions, the disorder that accompanied the *45 centimes* hindered the chances of reforming direct taxation, pushing the Bonapartists away from the July Monarchy's relative openness to raising direct taxes. Thus, between 1849 and 1869, direct tax revenues rose merely 4.6 per cent, corrected for inflation.[67] The conservative reaction shaped the tax policy of Louis-Napoleon's first finance minister, Hippolyte Passy, who had previously held the post under Louis-Philippe. Upon taking office, Passy denounced Goudchaux's graduated inheritance duty, ensuring that the Assembly rejected it. Then, in January, he withdrew Goudchaux's income tax proposal, probably because of its unpopularity among the deputies. Instead, in December 1848, Passy secured a slim majority for the reinstitution of the salt tax for 1849, though with a two-thirds reduction, as the Chamber of Deputies had proposed in 1847; the legislature, like its predecessors, was dominated by landowners who largely despised the tax. Indeed, some of the reforms of 1848 retained considerable appeal, which precluded any attempt to re-establish fiscal equilibrium through the complete restoration of the pre-1848 tax system. Given the emphasis on fiscal responsibility, the result was greater pressure to cut spending. Presented with the 1849 budget, the Assembly abolished alcohol duties, despite Passy's opposition. Unable to find an alternative to these taxes, however, Passy and his successor Achille Fould secured their reinstatement following the triumph of moderate conservatives and the *parti de l'ordre* in the legislative elections of May 1849. Despite gains by the left, the conservative majority, representing mainly rural areas, saw alcohol duties as preferable to higher taxes on land.

A member of the Fould banking dynasty who withdrew from the family firm in 1848, Fould had been a critic of Orleanist public spending.[68] His appointment following the dismissal of the conservative ministers marked, perhaps paradoxically, a new stage in the return to conservative fiscal policy. In addition to ensuring the retention of alcohol duties, he withdrew an unpopular proposal of Passy's for a 1 per cent income tax to be repartitioned on the basis of the *contribution mobilière*.[69] For Faucher, now the interior minister, Passy's proposed income tax would strip

[67] *Projet de loi ... 1849*; *Projet de loi ... 1869*.
[68] Fould, 22 June 1847, *Le Moniteur universel*, 23 June 1847.
[69] Marion, *Histoire financière*, V, 296–300, 302–4.

taxpayers of their assets and was therefore 'disagreeable for our social order'.[70] Still, an income tax remained attractive in influential quarters. As president of the Assembly's budget commission in 1851, Passy declared that 'the income tax will necessarily be the first tax that one would think to establish in France.'[71] Similarly, a commission established that year to consider reforms to alcohol duties received several petitions seeking their replacement with some form of income tax, though others sought to substitute them with various indirect taxes.[72] Fould therefore remained cautious, opting to raise the postal duty, the *timbre* and *l'enregistrement* in 1849 and 1850, instead of seeking higher revenue from the more contentious duties on alcohol and salt. The government went further in resurrecting the old politics in 1851 with a minor reduction in the *centimes additionnels* on the *contribution foncière*, rationalised, as on previous occasions, by the need to alleviate the excessive burden on land.[73] Indeed, cosseting land retained considerable political appeal, given Bonapartism's dependence on rural voters; meanwhile, the regime remained wary of attempting to wholly revive the pre-1848 system of indirect taxes. The government, wrote Jules Baroche, one of Faucher's predecessors as interior minister and a staunch Bonapartist, sought 'new resources, either by establishing greater proportionality of taxation between landed property, *la fortune mobilière* [i.e. liquid assets] and industry, or by imposing the *patente* or another duty on certain professions which, to this day, have remained free of charges'.[74] As part of this programme, the government sought to reassess the *contribution des portes et fenêtres*. Meanwhile, ministers contemplated reducing the *patente* for small businesses, entrenching the regime's support in the new mass electorate by reducing taxes on the middle and lower classes, particularly in rural areas where the *patente* remained a heavy burden. Indeed, of the four main direct taxes – the *quatre vieilles* – the *patente* perhaps aroused the most discontent in the early 1850s.[75] Thus, partly because of universal suffrage, the Orleanist logic of raising direct taxes to reinforce the legitimacy of the fiscal system by distributing its burden more equitably did not disappear completely, despite the legacy of the *45 centimes*.

[70] Faucher, 'De l'impôt sur le revenu', 94.
[71] Procès-verbaux, commission du budget, 1 April 1851, AN, C 985.
[72] AN, C 1013, dossier 1327.   [73] Marion, *Histoire financière*, V, 304, 308–12.
[74] Circular to the prefects, by Baroche, 12 April 1850, AD, Vendée, La Roche-sur-Yon, 1M/429.
[75] 'Inspection générale des départements – 1853', Persigny MSS, AN, 44AP/13; Prefect of the Calvados to Maupas, 28 February 1852, AN, F7 12163.

The desire to cultivate popular support through fiscal reform was apparent in 1852 when the government considered restoring the pre-1848 salt tax. In 1849, revenue from the tax was 52.2 per cent lower than in 1848, adjusted for inflation, despite benefiting from a fall in smuggling and an increase in consumption following the reduction in the duty.[76] Consumers having deferred salt purchases in anticipation of the tax cut, officials anticipated a further revenue decrease in 1850.[77] Ministers sought to reverse this decline, but worried about the possibility of resistance from the lower classes. Thus, in 1852 they polled local officials on whether the abolition of the *contribution des portes et fenêtres* would be 'received with favour by the same classes and accepted as compensation for the re-establishment of the salt tax' and if the salt tax could be revived without abolishing the *contribution des portes et fenêtres*.[78] For the regime, the issue was highly sensitive: 'the measures proposed affect essentially and almost uniquely the interests of the working class in towns and certainly in the countryside, and it is there that the Napoleonic power resides in all its force.'[79] The government pursued a delicate balancing act. Taxing the rich, as the republicans had sought to do in 1848, risked the ire of the political elite, while taxing the masses could weaken the vital popular appeal of Bonapartism. Officials were divided on the wisdom of restoring the salt tax. The prefect of the Côtes-du-Nord, for example, wrote that reintroducing the tax 'offers serious dangers', a view which perhaps reflected the legacy of Brittany's exemption from the *ancien régime* gabelle; meanwhile, his counterpart of the Ain claimed that the unpopularity of the salt tax 'certainly comes much more from the claims of the press and the tribune'.[80] Presented with conflicting advice, the government remained cautious, introducing only a light duty on salt used in soda manufacture.[81]

Officials were generally more favourable towards retaining the *contribution des portes et fenêtres*. Though unpopular, wrote the commander of the gendarmerie in Chartres, the tax 'does not seem to weigh so heavily on the rural population and on the working class to arouse discontent'.[82] As we have seen, though, it was more of a problem in urban areas. Given its

[76] *Projet de loi . . .1848*; *Projet de loi . . . 1852*.
[77] Circular to the *receveurs des douanes*, by Gréterin, 15 January 1850, AD, Vendée, 5P/26.
[78] Maupas to the *directeur général*, Lyon, 14 February 1852, AN, F⁷ 12163.
[79] Note, [1852], AN, F⁷ 12163.
[80] Prefect of the Côtes-du-Nord to Maupas, 29 February 1852, and prefect of the Ain to Maupas, 5 March 1852, AN, F⁷ 12163.
[81] Marion, *Histoire financière*, V, 325.
[82] Lt. Colonel *commandant la 2ᵉ légion de gendarmerie* to Maupas, 2 March 1852, AN, F⁷ 12163.

unpopularity, wrote the *inspecteur général* of police in Lille, abolishing the *contribution des portes et fenêtres* could benefit the regime. 'The reduction ... to the *contribution foncière* in 1851', he observed, was so small that it 'has been almost unnoticed by all property owners'. The reduction, he suggested, should be rescinded to finance the abolition of the *contribution des portes et fenêtres*, which would leave the government free to re-establish the salt tax for other purposes.[83] Such a move was probably too bold for the government, which contented itself with inaction over the *contribution des portes et fenêtres*. Like its Orleanist predecessor, the Bonapartist regime sought to avoid drawing attention to changes to the fiscal system, since these risked arousing discontent. Instead, reforms were to be undertaken as quietly as possible.

The reversion to indirect taxation was evident in the triumph of protectionism. While customs had received relatively little attention in 1848, many of those most committed to free trade supported an income tax – much as in Britain, where the creation of income tax had facilitated the repeal of the Corn Laws.[84] Others saw the 1848 Revolution as an opportunity for less drastic tariff reform. The customs system, wrote one liberal economist, presented 'a frightening complication'; to simplify it by eliminating export duties and reducing or abolishing import duties, he argued, would boost trade and thus increase revenue.[85] Such a proposal did not necessarily entail free trade. The provisional government had considered pursuing the abortive Orleanist reforms of 1847 to import duties and had contemplated similar modifications to export duties. In 1852, Fould proposed enacting these reforms, simultaneously emphasising his commitment to protectionism.[86] The idea made little progress, but that year the government renewed the 1845 commercial treaty with Belgium and, in 1854, ratified an arrangement to replace import duties on Belgian cottons and trouser fabrics with *ad valorem* taxes of up 25 per cent.[87] Seeking to 'profit' from ongoing customs negotiations with Belgium to achieve further tariff reform, observed the British ambassador, the government in 1852 sought a similarly limited agreement with Britain

[83] *Inspecteur général*, Lille, to Maupas, 18 March 1852, AN, F⁷ 12163.

[84] Todd, *Identité économique*, 395–401. Income tax and free trade were not necessarily regarded as complementary in the mid-nineteenth century. British radicals regarded the income tax as linked to the preservation of the Corn Laws, since the latter suited landowners by raising food prices and rents. The income tax, they argued, simply diverted this rent to the Treasury, so that landowners were essentially untaxed (Daunton, *Trusting Leviathan*, 82–3).

[85] Coquelin, 'Les Douanes et les finances publiques', 371.

[86] Fould to Lefebvre-Duruflé, 14 January 1852, AN, F¹² 2482.

[87] Treaty of 13 April 1854, *Le Moniteur universel*, 24 April 1854; AN, F¹² 6156.

over customs duties on coal and alcohol.[88] While, as we have seen, British agents such as Bowring had sought a Franco-British commercial agreement in the 1830s, they had had little success. In 1843, Guizot had rejected a commercial accord, since when negotiations had stalled, not least because as the British unilaterally adopted free trade after 1846, their interest in commercial agreements with other states receded. In 1852, therefore, they responded to the French proposal by demanding a wide-ranging overhaul of French tariffs, which the French refused.[89] Like their Orleanist predecessors, the Bonapartists in the 1850s preferred limited commercial agreements which could reduce the risk of serious displeasure from major economic interests. Moreover, protectionism offered a means of appealing to the peasantry by reducing competition in the grain trade while also satisfying the working class by preserving employment, albeit at the cost of higher food prices. Thus, in 1851 the government was content to see Thiers rebut, in a widely reported speech, a proposal made in the Assembly for trade liberalisation. Not until later in the decade did the government begin to favour more extensive tariff reform.

As part of the programme of retrenchment, the government wanted to reduce the costs of the public debt, which had increased with the new issues of 5 per cent *rentes* and the growth in short-term borrowing in 1848. Fould, therefore, assiduously pursued amortisation to reassure investors of French creditworthiness.[90] After the 5 per cent *rente* reached par in December 1851 (Figure 8.1), Fould's successor, Jean-Martial Bineau, arranged a conversion to 4½ per cent and 3 per cent *rentes*. Partly to gain concessions from the government in the ongoing process of railway company 'fusion', influential members of the *haute banque* supported the proposed conversion, especially since the 3 per cent *rentes* they took were likely to rise.[91] Circumventing the legislature, the graveyard of previous proposals, the government simply decreed the conversion on 14 March 1852, two weeks before the Corps législatif convened.[92]

While the government did what it could to mitigate opposition, for instance guaranteeing 4½ per cent *rentes* against conversion for ten years just as Villèle did with 5 per cent *rentes* in 1825, the passage of time had not made conversion any more palatable to its habitual opponents. The conversion, declared the *Journal des débats*, 'is the most serious

[88] Cowley to Malmesbury, 12 September 1852, National Archives, Kew, FO 146/454.
[89] Persigny to Drouyn de Lhuys, 17 November 1852, AN, F¹² 2482.
[90] Barbier, *Finance et politique*, 151–2.
[91] Marion, *Histoire financière*, V, 324; Greenfield, 'Crédit mobilier', 51–2.
[92] Plessis, *Politique de la Banque*, 99.

infringement which has been brought against public credit for half a century ... it is primarily the small rentiers who will be affected by the measure of the conversion. It is the working class, whose fate seems to be the exclusive preoccupation of those presently in power, that will see their revenue fall by a tenth.'[93] In this respect, the conversion perhaps entailed some political risk but elections were not imminent, having just happened, and it offered clear advantages. First, it suited the politics of fiscal rectitude inaugurated after 1848 by reducing the servicing costs of the public debt and by distinguishing the Bonapartist regime from its Orleanist predecessor, the latter having failed to achieve a conversion. Second, though projected to save only 18 million francs annually, the conversion mitigated pressure on the tax system.[94] This was no small concern – as we have seen, the government was wary of raising taxes. Third, the conversion eased the curtailment of the legislature's power, since the government could present itself as prioritising the needs of the public finances ahead of the sectional interest of rentiers. Asserting itself as custodian of the national interest, the government revised budgetary politics in its favour. Whereas under Louis-Philippe the Chambers had voted on individual chapters of the budget, after 1852 the Corps législatif was only permitted to vote on the budgets of ministries. The chapters into which these were divided, previously the preserve of the legislature, were now left to the government's discretion, and this power was only slightly eroded in the 1860s with the liberalisation of the Empire.[95] Thus, exploiting the mandate accorded by plebiscite, Louis-Napoleon reduced the legislature's power over finance to secure both the debt conversion and new budgetary politics.

Partly to facilitate the conversion by easing credit, the Banque de France lowered its discount rate from 4 per cent to 3 per cent, benefiting from the gold rush that followed discoveries in Australia and California. Though beneficial in the short term, the influx of gold prompted outflows of silver from France, reversing a trend of previous decades in which the stock of silver in the economy had increased and placing pressure on the rate of convertibility between gold and silver – gold being, officially, the more valuable.[96] As we shall see, by the 1860s, shortages of silver were becoming problematic. Still, for the moment, the conversion together with the rate cut produced a 'general relaunch of economic activity' after the financial

---

[93] *Le Journal des débats*, 15 March 1852.
[94] Rapport au prince-président, by Bineau, *Le Moniteur universel*, 14 March 1852.
[95] The Chambers' power to approve the budget of each ministry had been first established in 1817; in 1831, they had obtained the power to consent to individual chapters.
[96] Flandreau, *Glitter of Gold*, 35–9, 93–5.

crisis of 1848.[97] Lower interest rates eased the railway companies' difficulties by stimulating investment, which presaged the continuing economic and administrative integration of France, in turn facilitating the ongoing mobilisation of small capital that kept interest rates low. In boosting private finance, the loosening of credit complemented budget cuts to public works. While military and naval expenditure rose in the mid-1850s, government spending on public works remained lower than it had been under the July Monarchy until the 1860s.

To hasten the recovery from the crisis of 1848 and strengthen the private sector's capacity for the policy of railway company 'fusion', the regime also acquiesced in the creation of new financial institutions. In 1852, Comte Victor de Persigny, one of Louis-Napoleon's close associates who was then minister of the interior, agriculture and commerce, promoted the creation of the Crédit mobilier, a joint-stock enterprise to invest in public debt, railways and other such projects. Founded by Benoît Fould, brother of Achille and head of the eminent bank B.L. Fould et Fould-Oppenheim, and the railway entrepreneurs Émile and Isaac Pereire, the Crédit mobilier was dominated by bankers seeking to recoup their losses after the crisis of 1848.[98] While historians have seen the Crédit mobilier as representing a departure in economic policy, they have exaggerated its novelty. In many respects, it was an Orleanist *caisse* writ large. Like Laffitte's *caisse* and its imitators, the Crédit mobilier was capitalised through shares, albeit as a joint-stock company rather than as a limited partnership. The government's approval for the project reflected its relative unoriginality. Joint-stock finance was hardly a novelty by the 1850s and the 60 million francs capital of the Crédit mobilier was only 5 million francs greater than the nominal capital approved for Laffitte's *caisse* in 1837. That the Crédit mobilier actually raised its nominal capital – in contrast to Laffitte's *caisse* – in part reflected the experience of 1848, when undercapitalisation had left the Orleanist *caisses* without the means to survive the financial crisis. Though those such as the Rothschilds feared the consequences of a large competitor, the size of the Crédit mobilier was generally reassuring, as was the presence of distinguished bankers such as Mallet and Eichthal on its *conseil d'administration*. Approved three days before the plebiscite on the establishment of the Empire, for which ministers wanted a rising *rente*, the creation of the Crédit mobilier reflected the government's confidence that the creation of the new institution would

---

[97] Plessis, *Politique de la Banque*, 92–9.
[98] The rest of this paragraph draws on Greenfield, 'Crédit mobilier'.

not risk a market panic and undermine the Bonapartist regime's efforts to build a reputation for financial competence.

Once established, the Crédit mobilier did not restrict itself to expediting railway construction in France, but embarked on a pan-European competition for railway concessions with the Rothschilds. The private sector – and thus the government's programme of retrenchment – benefited from the growing internationalisation of finance in the mid-nineteenth century, which was facilitated by the proliferation of shares that accompanied the growth of joint-stock finance. British investment had been essential to the French railway boom of the 1840s, and remained indispensable in the 1850s. German capital, too, played a major role. As Eichthal observed in 1856, 'the German markets continue to absorb many French securities and particularly railway bonds.'[99] Indeed, the Crédit mobilier counted among its initial investors the distinguished banks Oppenheim of Cologne, Heine of Hamburg and Torlonia of Rome.

The mobilisation of the private sector to expedite commercial development and public works was similarly apparent in the foundation of the Crédit foncier, established in Paris in March 1852 with the support of many of the *haute banque* and the political elite. Drawing on old ideas that had gained prominence under the July Monarchy to provide 'territorial property' with 'expanded credit', the Crédit foncier reflected the government's desire to 'hasten the moment when owners of soil would see the interest rate at which they borrow gradually lowered and made increasingly proportional to the typical revenue from the land'.[100] As with the reduction to the *contribution foncière*, therefore, the creation of the Crédit foncier reflected the ongoing pressure to cosset land, smaller farmers being both a bedrock of Bonapartist support and among those expected to benefit from the Crédit foncier. Though initially restricted in its remit to Paris and the surrounding *départements*, in December 1852 the institution was revamped to serve the whole country as the Crédit foncier de France, with a capital equal to that of the Crédit mobilier.

The regime approved the foundation of both the Crédit foncier and the Crédit mobilier partly with the aim of increasing the resources available to local government, which was also enlisted to undertake public works. Whereas local government resources had proved too limited to contribute extensively to the expansion of the state in the 1840s, the Bonapartists

[99] Eichthal to Baring, 27 May 1856, BA, HC 7.27.
[100] Circular to the prefects, by Persigny, 23 February 1853, AD, Mayenne, P/16; Wolowski, *Réforme hypothécaire*, 3; Yates, 'Double Life of Property', 259–73.

sought to increase the means available to local government and so relieve the fiscal pressure on the central government. From its foundation, the Crédit foncier received requests for loans from communes and *départements*.[101] Likewise, the Crédit mobilier found itself entering loan negotiations with local authorities, with ministers' approval.[102] Another important creditor to communes and *départements*, the Caisse des dépôts et consignations, eased their borrowing by reducing the interest rate it charged to 4.5 per cent in 1852 and then to 4 per cent in January 1853.[103] In June that year, the regime approved the conversion of local government debts, for *départements* and communes with revenues greater than 100,000 francs, aimed at facilitating lower local taxes.[104] Meanwhile, the central government also expanded the tax base of communes and *départements*, and thus their creditworthiness, by relaxing the restrictions on the ability of *conseils généraux* and *municipaux* to impose *centimes additionnels*.[105] Moreover, while communes had been permitted since 1823 to withhold giving the central government 10 per cent of any temporary *centimes additionnels* levied on *l'octroi* if they wished to devote the money to debt repayment or public works, in 1852 the central government forfeited all its claims to *l'octroi*, offsetting the loss through other indirect taxes.[106] Furthermore, though rejected by the government in 1845, 1847 and 1849, the dog tax (*taxe sur les chiens*) was established in 1856 for communal finances, partly influenced by a similar tax in Britain.[107] Benefiting from these resources, many municipalities and *départements* became willing borrowers in the 1850s, and their access to credit greatly increased after 1860, when they were empowered to borrow at lower rates from the Crédit foncier.[108]

Much of this local government borrowing was intended to finance improvements to public hygiene and civic amenities, since municipalities sought to manage urbanisation and forestall its potentially adverse consequences of squalor and unrest. The growth of urban populations raised the prospect of higher future tax revenues, giving municipalities greater confidence to borrow. Thus, in the 1850s Paris floated two loans, in 1852 and

[101] Note to Magne, by Wolowski, 17 August 1853, AN, F¹² 6775.
[102] Frémy to Magne, 3 August 1853, AN F¹² 6791; Persigny to Magne, 23 August 1853, AN, F¹² 6791.
[103] Circular to the prefects, by Persigny, 8 February 1853, AD, Pyrénées-Atlantiques, Pau, 1M/1.
[104] Law of 10 June 1853, *Lois*, LIII, 224; circular to the prefects, by Persigny, 20 June 1853, AD, Pyrénées-Atlantiques, 1M/2.
[105] Conrad, *Conseil général du Haut-Rhin*, 517–8.   [106] Marion, *Histoire financière*, V, 326.
[107] AN, C 988, dossiers 268–9; Montherot to La Hitte, 18 December 1849, MAE, 5ADP/9; decree of 4 August 1855, *Lois*, LV, 262–3.
[108] Law of 12 July 1860, *Lois*, LX, 254–5.

1855, to finance the construction of sewers, parks and public buildings, accelerating the rebuilding undertaken by the July Monarchy. Spurred by the memory of unrest in 1848, the government sought to reduce former centres of insurrection while boosting sanitation in the wake of another cholera epidemic in 1849, increasing employment and providing monuments to glorify the regime. As with other municipalities, the renovation of Paris quickened in the 1860s, given the growth of local government credit. Rather than necessarily easing the 'social question', however, the rebuilding displaced destitution from the city centre to the suburbs, where it was exacerbated by continuing immigration.[109] The result was increasing pressure on the government, particularly from the relatively well-off such as prosperous farmers and owners of country houses, to impose order in suburban areas. Partly owing to this pressure, in 1860 the city of Paris annexed several suburban communes, extending the power of its police forces into the suburbs, while in Paris and other cities police forces became more professionalised as they adapted to this desire for public order.[110] The annexation also allowed the municipality to impose order by integrating the suburban populations into the city through amenities such as sewers and more substantial poor relief.[111] Such expenditures, as with public works more generally, could enhance the legitimacy of the regime. Indeed, across France, the emperor and empress frequently presided over the opening of new railways and hospitals, celebrating, and associating themselves with, social amelioration and the progress of French civilisation. The regime, in short, retained responsibility for public works, mainly railways and urban improvements, but delegated them to local government and private finance, thus furthering the central government's aim of restraining its own expenditures.

Financing the Crimean War

Like the Restoration and the July Monarchy, the Second Empire demonstrated the strengths of the post-1815 fiscal-military system, which allowed it to adopt an aggressive foreign policy. As they had Louis-Philippe, the other powers regarded Louis-Napoleon with suspicion. Persigny, then ambassador to Prussia, observed in 1850 that the 'great monarchies have at root the same prejudices which in the time of Louis-Philippe caused them ceaselessly to ask the upstart king for small services that were

[109] Gaillard, *Paris, la ville*, 204–14, 222–9.   [110] Merriman, *Margins of City Life*, 201–2.
[111] Faure, 'Paris, 1860'.

humiliating to the national character'.[112] The Bonapartists' desire to avoid incurring fresh humiliations perhaps pushed them to be more assertive in the Near East. Domestic political considerations were also important in shaping French policy in the region. Continuing the cultivation of Catholic support that had encouraged him to restore the pope in 1849, Louis-Napoleon asserted France's role as the protector of Catholics in the Ottoman Empire. The Russians, though, claimed responsibility for safeguarding Christians in the Ottoman Empire and had no desire to see France increase its influence at Constantinople. Ultimately, the Russians resorted to force, provoking the sultan to declare war in October 1853.

The Crimean War placed unprecedented demands on the post-Napoleonic fiscal-military system. Though the French fought in a coalition alongside the British, the Ottomans and later the Sardinians, the Crimean campaign was principally a terrestrial operation, dominated by the French on the allied side. After the battle of Inkerman in November 1854 ended Russian hopes of victory in the field, the French took over several British positions, an indication of the superiority of the French army over the British. Accustomed to the rigours of warfare in Algeria, French troops adapted relatively well to the harshness of life in the Crimea. For much of the war, their organisation and leadership were superior to those of the British, as was their medical care and equipment.[113] While British military organisation and provisions improved – by August 1855, for example, Palmerston, again foreign secretary, was complaining that unsanitary conditions in the French camp were spreading disease to British troops – the French army generally outperformed its counterparts during the war.[114] Still, the effectiveness of the French army should not be overstated. Most notably, scholars have criticised the conduct of the allied siege of Sevastopol, which dominated the Crimean campaign from October 1854 to September 1855.

As with previous interventions abroad, war finance relied heavily on public credit. Before France entered the war on 27 March 1854, the government announced its intention on 6 March to contract a loan of 250 million francs in *rentes*, reducing the *dette flottante* in preparation for large-scale wartime borrowing. Already at the beginning of 1852, the *dette flottante* was 886 million francs, to which the debt conversion added a further 78 million given the need to repurchase 5 per cent *rentes* from

---

[112] Persigny to Falloux, 24 February 1850, Persigny MSS, AN, 44AP/10, dossier 1.
[113] Baumgart, *Crimean War*, 73–8.
[114] Palmerston to Clarendon, 16 August 1855, Palmerston MSS, BL, Add MSS 48579, fol. 42.

investors unwilling to accept 4½ per cent or 3 per cent *rentes*.[115] The size of the *dette flottante* was a recurring cause of concern throughout the war. Nevertheless, Bineau declared, 'tax increases … are not a resource applicable to large and prompt supplementary expenditures, such as those necessitated by the transition from the state of peace to the state of war.'[116] By contrast, on that same 6 March, Gladstone, the chancellor of the exchequer, condemned any recourse to borrowing to finance Britain's war effort – though six weeks later he approved the issue of £6 million in bonds.[117] Thus, the disparity between British and French war finance should not be exaggerated. As Hottinguer observed, it was only after much agonising that Bineau decided to contract a loan.[118] Moreover, despite Gladstone's alleged aversion to financing the war through credit, Lewis, his successor as chancellor in February 1855, borrowed more readily, allowing Gladstone to burnish his reputation as a deficit hawk in opposition. Indeed, when, in the spring of 1855, several of his ministers advocated seeking a joint Franco-British loan, Napoleon rejected the idea on the grounds that the British were 'spending more than us', and that such a loan would therefore depress the *rente*.[119]

While the loan was decided by the beginning of March 1854, how it would be contracted was not. As talk of an imminent loan flourished, both the Rothschilds and the Crédit mobilier lobbied Bineau, each hoping to secure it before the adjudication. Firms such as Hottinguer paid court to both parties to be sure of a share from whichever ultimately triumphed.[120] Unable to bring the two together and perhaps fearful that neither had the means to issue the loan alone, the government responded by reviving the old idea of a public subscription.[121] This was effectively a victory for the Crédit mobilier, breaking the Rothschilds' monopoly on French government loans established since the 1820s. Though the idea of a subscription was not new, it involved some risk. While that of 1818 had succeeded, those of 1831 and 1848 had failed to meet expectations, albeit in times of economic crisis. Furthermore, as Thiers observed following the March loan's initial success, small investors purchased *rentes* expecting them to rise. Should they have to sell some of their holdings to make the remaining

[115] Rapport à l'Empereur, by Magne, 29 October 1857, *Le Moniteur universel*, 30 October 1857.
[116] Rapport à l'Empereur, by Bineau, 6 March 1854, *Le Moniteur universel*, 7 March 1854.
[117] Anderson, *Liberal State at War*, 195.
[118] Jean-Henri Hottinguer to Baring, 26 January 1854, BA, HC 7.1.953.
[119] 14 April 1855, Fortoul, *Journal*, I, 151.
[120] Jean-Henri Hottinguer to Baring, 24 February 1854, HC 7.1.955.
[121] Mirès, *A mes juges*, 23–4; Jean-Henri Hottinguer to Baring, 2 March 1854, BA, HC 7.1.957.

payments – *rentes* being purchased in instalments – or should the war go badly, the *rente* would probably fall, devastating these investors, French public credit and thus the regime.[122] Presumably given these risks, Pierre Magne, the minister of agriculture, commerce and public works who had served under Fould at the finance ministry in 1849–51, recalled that he, Bineau and Fould had all favoured adjudicating the loan.[123] The *rente*, though, was strong and the Bourse was little averse to a subscription. Moreover, as we have seen, under Louis-Philippe railway construction had mobilised resources beyond Paris, new *caisses d'épargne* had been formed in provincial France and the use of the telegraph to transmit financial news had become more widespread, reflecting the emergence of a more national capital market, the development of which accelerated in the early 1850s.[124] While in 1847 there were 207,000 rentiers, three-quarters of whom were in Paris, by 1854 there were 664,000, half of whom lived in other *départements* and 94,000 of whom had less than 20 francs of *rentes*.[125] Already following the 1848 financial crisis, Nathaniel Rothschild had observed a tendency for small investors to put their money into *rentes*, bankers commanding little confidence and offering low rates of return.[126] Meanwhile, a run on the *caisses d'épargne* in 1848 had brought many of them close to insolvency, forcing them to suspend withdrawals; in July that year, Goudchaux had orchestrated a rescue, reimbursing depositors in 5 per cent *rentes* and thus greatly increasing the number of rentiers in provincial France. Though the extension of the *caisses* across France continued after 1848, they performed sluggishly through the 1850s. One former employee of the Paris *caisse d'épargne* noted in 1853 that it offered investors too low a rate of return, which hardly served to attract depositors – and those deposits the *caisses* took were, from 1852, to be invested wholly in government securities.[127] Not only had the number of provincial rentiers increased since 1848, but the means for undertaking a nationwide public subscription had already been employed by the Rothschilds when they had floated the loans of the 1840s, the network of receivers general and particular being used to issue *rentes* across France.[128] Rather than representing a revolution in public credit, the loans of 1854–5 developed

---

[122] 14 March 1854, Senior, *Conversations*, I, 306.   [123] Durieux, *Magne*, I, 347.

[124] Flichy, *Une histoire de la communication moderne*, 63–72.

[125] Rapport à l'Empereur, by Bineau, 11 March 1854, *Le Moniteur universel*, 11 March 1854.

[126] Nathaniel Rothschild to his brothers, 10 May 1848, RAL, XI/109/66/2.

[127] Christen-Lécuyer, *Caisses d'épargne*, 576–600, 603; Prat to Persigny, 12 January 1853, SAEF, B/56971/1.

[128] Montanier to de Rothschild frères, 8 January 1848, Rothschild MSS, ANMT, 132AQ/1P1.

the practices of the 1840s to increase more rapidly the number of rentiers in provincial France. As Laffitte and others had realised years earlier, small investors represented a potential bonanza of underutilised capital, which proved essential to the French wartime economy.

To mobilise small investors, Bineau instructed prefects to appeal to their patriotism and give the subscription 'the greatest and most rapid publicity possible'.[129] Consequently, the loan received offers worth a total of 467 million francs in 3 per cent and 4½ per cent *rentes* at 65.25 and 92.5 respectively from 98,000 subscribers. Of the latter, 26,000 were from Paris – which included most foreign firms – and provided 214 million francs; 72,000 were from the *départements*, offering 253 million. The figures from the *départements* included most of the 60,000 small investors who purchased less than 50 francs of *rente* and raised a total of 49 million francs.[130] To stimulate subscriptions, the Banque de France advanced credit to those seeking to invest, easing the purchase of *rentes* on margin.[131] Unsurprisingly, urban areas seem to have provided most of the subscriptions. In Bordeaux, noted the prefect of the Gironde, 'they go in crowds to the Receiver General.'[132] By contrast in Bazas, a rural arrondissement a few miles away, the sub-prefect found himself having to explain a 'paltry' result; the area was 'almost exclusively agricultural', which perhaps reduced the amount of liquidity available to invest, and the population retained an ingrained suspicion of paper wealth.[133] In general, though, the prefects reported an enthusiastic reception for the subscription.

Following the outcome of the 1854 loan, the government used the same method to issue two more loans in 1855 to finance the war. The first, of 500 million francs raised through 3 per cent *rentes* at 65.25 and 4½ per cent *rentes* at 92, was floated in January and received subscriptions for 2,175 million francs from 177,000 subscribers. Of the latter, 126,000 were from the *départements* offering 777 million francs, while 51,000 subscribers from Paris provided the rest.[134] Indeed, the *haute banque* invested readily and reprised its role in issuing *rentes* in the City. The London Rothschilds opened their usual subscription, while Eichthal, as vice-

[129] Circular to the prefects, by Bineau, 12 March 1854, AN, F$^{\text{1cl}}$ 34.
[130] Rapports à l'Empereur, by Bineau, 11 and 28 March 1854, *Le Moniteur universel*, 11 and 29 March 1854.
[131] Plessis, *Politique de la Banque*, 140.
[132] Prefect of the Gironde to Persigny, 17 March 1854, AN, F$^{\text{1cl}}$ 34.
[133] Sub-prefect of Bazas to the Prefect of the Gironde, 18 March 1854, AN, F$^{\text{1cl}}$ 34.
[134] Rapports à l'Empereur, by Baroche, 31 December 1854 and 17 January 1855, *Le Moniteur universel*, 31 December 1854 and 18 January 1855.

president of the Crédit mobilier, arranged a list with Barings.[135] Though other Paris bankers, Bartholony for example, also approached London firms, the most significant lists were those of the Rothschilds and the Crédit mobilier and Barings.[136] The amount subscribed raised a question of whether the government should retain more than 500 million francs. Magne, who became finance minister in February, was the only minister in favour; increasing the loan to 700 million, he argued, would reduce the pressure to raise taxes.[137] The government rejected the idea, but it sought to avoid major changes to taxation to finance the war, preferring instead the old expedient of churning indirect taxes. When Napoleon approved a plan to raise the *centimes additionnels* on the *contribution foncière* so as to avoid restoring the pre-1848 salt duty, Magne vetoed it, opposing both the *centimes additionnels* and the higher salt tax.[138] Instead, he preferred to raise *l'enregistrement*, reintroducing duties that had been abolished in 1850.[139] Meanwhile, the government opted to raise 15 million through the sale of state forests, provoking fierce criticism from deputies in the process.[140] Still sensitive to the fragility of the tax system after the turmoil of the Second Republic, the government was wary of raising taxes.

The loan of 500 million was the largest contracted by any French government since the creation of the franc. Yet within two months the war ministry had spent half of it. Such a rate of expenditure, Magne worried, was unsustainable.[141] Already in April he envisaged the need for a further 400 million francs to be procured from 'various sources' to finance the government until the end of the year – potentially requiring the enormous sum of 140 million francs from the Banque de France in short-term credit.[142] By July, as victory at Sevastopol remained elusive, Magne decided to borrow a further 750 million francs through public subscription, intended to allow the government to continue the war until the end of the year without greatly increasing the *dette flottante*. The 3 per cent and 4½ per cent *rentes* were issued at 65.25 and 92.25 respectively,

[135] Gille, *Rothschild*, II, 130–1, 276; Eichthal to Baring, 4 January 1855, BA, HC 7.27; circular, by Baring Brothers, 3 January 1855, BA, HC 7.28.
[136] Note to Baroche, by Bartholony, 31 December 1854, Baroche MSS, BT, MsT 985, fol. 92.
[137] 13 January 1855, Fortoul, *Journal*, I, 62.
[138] 31 January and 10 February 1855, Fortoul, *Journal*, I, 83, 94.
[139] Marion, *Histoire financière*, V, 373.
[140] 31 March 1855, Fortoul, *Journal*, I, 139; procès-verbaux, commission du budget, 18, 19, 25, 26 and 29 March 1855, AN, C 1041.
[141] 17 March 1855, Fortoul, *Journal*, I, 126.
[142] 'Conférences avec M. Magne, Ministre des finances, les mercredi 25, jeudi 26 et vendredi 27 avril 1855', by d'Argout, ABF, 1069199608/3.

with the usual commitment to 'popularising the rente' and thereby 'enlarging the foundations of the state's credit'.[143] As before, prefects were required to publicise the loan as widely as possible, while Barings and Rothschilds opened lists in London.[144] Thus, 310,000 subscribers yielded 3,600 million francs. 230–235 million came from those purchasing 50 francs of *rente* or less, a 369–380 per cent increase from the loan of 1854, while those subscribing for 60 francs of *rente* or more provided the rest. There were 230,000 subscribers from the *départements*, producing more than 1,000 million francs in capital, while foreign investors provided 600 million.[145] These figures represented a marked increase both in the amount of capital raised and in the number of investors in French public credit. Though the greatest increases in subscription size came from the wealthy, the *rente* was nevertheless democratised on an unprecedented scale in 1854–5 (Table 8.1). This mobilisation of money was all the more impressive given the loans floated by, most notably, Britain, Sardinia, Russia, Austria and Turkey, which placed further demands on capital markets. The democratisation of government borrowing strengthened the state's creditworthiness, cementing the *rente*'s recovery after 1848; no government could risk the widespread dissatisfaction that default would provoke, particularly since all French investors could vote. To cover the interest payments, Magne raised taxes, placing a *décime de guerre* on existing indirect taxes while introducing new taxes on train travel and *eaux de vie*.[146] While Magne saw these duties as offering the only way of taxing '*la fortune mobilière*' they received considerable criticism from deputies.[147] In one minister's words, 'each rejects the tax that he would pay and discards the burden onto his neighbour.'[148] Despite these difficulties, as Marion observes, war finance marked a triumph for indirect taxation.[149]

Given the role of the City, the loans of 1854–5 produced successful Franco-British financial cooperation, but they also contributed to tensions that arose between the two governments over monetary policy. While the French government pressured the Banque to maintain a low discount rate to stimulate the price of *rentes*, the Banque risked straining its reserves as a result. In the early months of the war, this was no problem. The continuing gold rush kept the Banque and the Bank of England well supplied,

[143] Rapport à l'Empereur, by Magne, *Le Moniteur universel*, 15 July 1856.
[144] Circular to the prefects, by Magne, 14 July 1855, AD, Mayenne, P/22; Eichthal to Baring Brothers, 16 July 1855, BA, HC 7.27.
[145] Rapport à l'Empereur, by Magne, 30 July 1855, *Le Moniteur universel*, 31 July 1855.
[146] Marion, *Histoire financière*, V, 374.   [147] 27 June 1855, Fortoul, *Journal*, I, 213.
[148] 7 July 1855, Fortoul, *Journal*, II, 23.   [149] Marion, *Histoire financière*, V, 375.

Table 8.1. *The loans of 1854–5*

	250 million, March 1854	500 million, January 1855	750 million, July 1855	Percentage increase, March 1854–July 1855
Total amount subscribed	467 million	2,175 million	3,600 million	671%
From Paris and abroad, with percentage of the total	214 million (46%)	1,398 million (64%)	2,600 million (72%)	1,115%
From other *départements*, with percentage of the total	253 million (54%)	777 million (36%)	1,000 million (28%)	295%
Total number of subscribers	98,000	177,000	310,000	216%
From Paris and abroad, with percentage of the total	26,000 (27%)	51,000 (29%)	80,000 (26%)	208%
From other *départements*, with percentage of the total	72,000 (73%)	126,000 (71%)	230,000 (74%)	219%

Source: *Le Moniteur universel*

allowing both to maintain low interest rates. Following the success of the 500 million franc loan, Hottinguer expressed surprise 'at the ease with which they [investors] have found so great a mass of money to make the payments', most of which came from French investors; 'we do not think the English have sent much capital here with the purpose of placing it in the loan ... The Treasury has received 366 million in a fortnight & on this sum the Banque has not advanced more than 50 million, the rest was floating capital or money imported from abroad.'[150] From July 1855, however, the Banque's reserves began to fall sharply. The 750 million loan provoked renewed speculation in *rentes* while the war, an Ottoman loan of August 1855 and the grain imports necessitated by a poor harvest also consumed specie.[151] Indeed, the cost of assistance to communes and *départements* to counter food shortages added to the government's financial

[150] Jean-Henri Hottinguer to Baring, 22 January 1855, BA, HC 7.1.974.
[151] 3 October 1855, Fortoul, *Journal*, II, 100; 'Note sur la visite faite par moi et M. Gautier à M. Rouher, Intérimaire des finances, vendredi 7 7ᵇʳᵉ 1855', by d'Argout, ABF, 1069199608/4.

burdens, albeit only marginally because, as before, relief depended heavily on local government and private charity; the same was true for assistance following floods in 1855 and 1856.[152] While the government continued to pressure the Banque not to increase rates, a raise proved unavoidable particularly since the Bank of England – also losing reserves – opted for a higher discount rate.[153] The Crédit mobilier exacerbated the monetary crisis, seeking to double its capital to 120 million francs and prompting criticism from British observers.[154] To maintain the *rente*, the government opposed the plan and subsequently vetoed a bond issue that the firm proposed instead. Likewise, the government prohibited the shares of a planned Austrian *crédit mobilier* from being listed on the Paris Bourse, effectively scuppering the new company.[155] The war had done little to divert the Crédit mobilier from its pan-European ambitions. Precisely when Eichthal was in London arranging Barings' list for the loan of 500 million francs, Isaac Pereire, who succeeded Benoît Fould as president of the Crédit mobilier in 1853, was in Vienna finalising a railway concession.[156] Meanwhile, the Pereires pursued business in Spain in 1855, culminating in the creation of the Credito mobiliario español the following year, and sought to establish a branch in Piedmont. Turin, though, resisted the Pereires' advances, delaying the foundation of the Credito mobiliare italiano until 1863.[157] The Crédit mobilier was not alone in issuing securities during the war. In June 1855, the municipality of Paris borrowed 60 million francs by public subscription to finance the city's ongoing renovation, placing a further demand on the Bourse a month before the government floated its loan of 750 million.[158] Meanwhile, the Banque, under government pressure, continued to provide advances on railway securities during the war, albeit on ever tighter terms. While the mobilisation of provincial capital drew specie into the financial system and thus mitigated these pressures – Hottinguer noted in November that 'there continues to arrive a lot of money from the provinces to make purchases in cash' – they ultimately proved too much.[159]

---

[152] Rapport à l'Empereur, by Billault, 1856, Billault MSS, AD, Loire-Atlantique, 20J/21, dossier 1.
[153] 'Conférence avec M. Rouher, samedi, 22 sept[bre] [1855] à 4 heures de l'après-midi', by d'Argout, ABF, 1069199608/4.
[154] Anderson, *Liberal State at War*, 234–5.
[155] Cameron, *France and the Economic Development of Europe*, 154–5.
[156] Eichthal to Baring, 2 January 1855, BA, HC 7.27.
[157] La Rüe to Hambro, 7 September and 5 October 1855, Hambro MSS, London Metropolitan Archives, Ms 19054.
[158] Massa-Gille, *Histoire des emprunts*, 219–20.
[159] Jean-Henri Hottinguer to Baring, 28 November 1855, BA, HC 7.1.991.

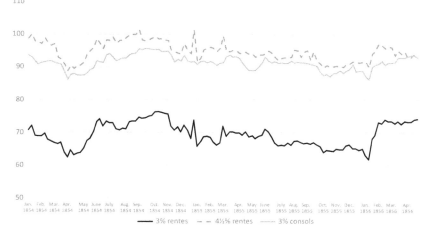

Figure 8.2   Weekly closing prices of French *rentes*, as quoted in Paris, and of British consols, as quoted in London, during the Crimean War.
(Sources: *Le Moniteur universel; The Economist*)

The Banque responded to the crisis with large purchases of gold and silver.[160] In October, James de Rothschild sought for the Banque an advance of £2 million in bullion from the Bank of England. Considering the Banque's reserves, however, Lewis did not regard its position as 'urgent'.[161] Palmerston, meanwhile, dismissed Rothschild's request as 'consummate imprudence'.[162] Moreover, the drain of specie from the Bank of England placed pressure on the Bank Charter Act, which specified the ratio of reserves to notes in circulation. The British government, though, had no desire to risk financial turbulence by suspending the law. Instead, it preferred higher discount rates and gold purchases, leaving no latitude for a loan to the Banque. From the British perspective, the French worried too much and too openly about the financial situation, a relatively easy position for them to adopt since they borrowed more cheaply than the French (Figure 8.2). In November, Lewis noted that Magne had said 'quite openly that France could not continue the war much longer on the present scale, & at the present rate of expenditure. I cannot help fearing that the French ministers talk in this manner with very little

---

[160] Plessis, *Politique de la Banque*, 167.
[161] Lewis to Palmerston, 17 October 1855, Palmerston MSS, HL, PP/GC/LE/43.
[162] Palmerston to Lewis, 18 October 1855, Palmerston MSS, BL, Add. MSS 48579, fol. 81.

reserve, & that declarations of this sort have by this time been telegraphed to Petersburg.'[163] Indeed, as peace negotiations began in the winter of 1855, the Russians temporised – despite their own financial problems – in the hope that mounting financial pressures would push the French towards more favourable terms.[164]

The war ended following the Congress of Paris in February–March 1856, a public relations triumph for Napoleon, but the French government's financial travails continued. In February, Magne exploited the imminence of peace to tighten his control over other ministries' expenditures, since spending continued to exceed government revenue.[165] Partly as a result, the ministries of finance and commerce proposed to replace prohibitive tariffs with more revenue-raising duties, along the lines Fould had advocated in 1851–2.[166] Presented to the Corps législatif, though, the proposal aroused fierce opposition. The prefect of the Nord noted that 'anxiety spreads among workers,' while industrialists lobbied deputies, inducing the government to withdraw the bill.[167] Meanwhile, Magne, in line with his preference for indirect taxation, suggested reducing the *contribution personelle et mobilière* on less affluent taxpayers 'as soon as circumstances permit' – which Napoleon decided was not then.[168] Pressure on the capital market created a further potential difficulty. At the start of January, the government was still to receive from subscribers 450 million francs of the loan of 750 million, while the Parisian municipality was still to emit 50 million francs of its 60 million loan. Meanwhile, railway companies claimed that they needed to raise 517 million francs in 1856 to sustain the rate of construction.[169] At the same time, Hottinguer observed, much of the new business on the Bourse was foreign: the Credito mobiliario español, the Austrian Kreditanstalt and railways in Piedmont and elsewhere.[170] Seeking to restrain the demands on the Bourse and thus to maintain the *rente*, on 9 March the government prohibited the issue of new securities, though this proved difficult to

[163] Lewis to Palmerston, 24 November [1855], Palmerston MSS, HL, PP/GC/LE/48.
[164] Figes, *Crimea*, 406. By 1856, Russia faced mounting war debt and rising inflation, which greatly concerned the tsar's ministers (Baumgart, *Friede von Paris*, 116–23).
[165] Procès-verbaux, conseil des ministres, 9 February 1856, Fould MSS, AN, 247AP/1.
[166] Procès-verbaux, conseil des ministres, 13 February 1856, Fould MSS, AN, 247AP/1.
[167] Prefect of the Nord to Billault, 20 and 29 June 1856, Billault MSS, AD, Loire-Atlantique, 20J/21, dossier 7.
[168] Procès verbaux, conseil des ministres, 27 February 1856, Fould MSS, AN, 247AP/1.
[169] Procès verbaux, conseil des ministres, 8 March 1856, Fould MSS, AN, 247AP/1.
[170] Jean-Henri Hottinguer to Baring, 3 March 1856, BA, HC 7.1.1013.

enforce.[171] 'Speculation continues to be very lively here,' wrote Hottinguer a month later, though without the prohibition 'we would be inundated.'[172] In June, he noted that 'new companies are created daily.'[173] As the Duc de Morny observed, 'it is impossible to stop this financial movement of Europe. Capital goes where it is drawn and despite all the measures that seek to restrain it.'[174] For industrialists such as Morny, Napoleon's half-brother and president of the Corps législatif, one attraction of peace was the economic opportunity it offered. Sent as ambassador to Russia after the war, he pursued a Franco-Russian rapprochement and a commercial treaty, signed in June 1857. With his assistance, in October 1856 a group of bankers consisting mainly of the Crédit mobilier and several of the *haute banque*, in addition to several prominent foreign firms, secured a major but ill-fated railway concession in Russia.[175] Thus, with the return of peace, the Bourse strengthened its position at the centre of European finance.

In mobilising provincial capital for the loans of 1854–5, the Second Empire mitigated the reliance on Parisian resources that had facilitated the centralisation of public and private finance under the July Monarchy. Though facilitated by the infrastructural improvements – railways and the telegraph – that permitted greater centralisation, the new-found importance of provincial capital militated in favour of decentralisation, as did the new licence accorded to municipalities to raise loans and retain all revenues from *l'octroi*. With the delegation of public works to local government and the private sector and the mobilisation of provincial capital, financial decentralisation allowed the government to fund an aggressive foreign policy and simultaneously address socio-economic problems through public works while restraining its expenditure as much as possible. While greater powers were given to local government, the latter was kept under strict control. As under Louis-Philippe, mayors and presidents of *conseils généraux* were appointed from Paris. Though the power of prefects was increased in 1852 and 1855, the information they provided to the interior ministry facilitated political centralisation, most notably in easing the government's management of elections. Such centralisation provoked criticism, but not until the late 1850s did the government initiate a process of political decentralisation which contributed to the liberalisation of the

[171] *Le Moniteur universel*, 9 March 1856.
[172] Jean-Henri Hottinguer to Baring, 12 April 1856, BA, HC 7.1.1017.
[173] Jean-Henri Hottinguer to Baring, 10 June 1856, BA, HC 7.1.1021.
[174] Morny to Walewski, 25 October [1856], Walewski MSS, MAE, 177PAAP/21, fol. 197.
[175] Rieber, 'Grande Société des Chemins de Fer Russes'.

Empire in the 1860s.[176] Still, financial decentralisation was already apparent by the mid-1850s, with the deepening of the capital market. The latter facilitated the growth of the state which, as we shall see, accelerated in the 1860s.

Conclusion

The development of the 'delegating-market' state in the 1850s rested on a foundation established by the Orleanist regime, as the Bonapartists realised the state envisioned by the Orleanists and some of their critics. In this respect, the notion of a new departure in economic policy in 1852 is largely myth. Rejecting economic liberals' conception of a small state, both Orleanists and Bonapartists regarded the state as an agent of prosperity, even if they differed, for instance, over how to address the railway crisis that began in 1847. In enhancing the private sector's capacity, the 'great boom' of the 1850s facilitated the creation of a 'delegating-market' state more than any revolution in government economic policy. With the issuing of new shares and *rentes*, the state and the private sector were mutually reinforcing, both drawing investors into the financial system. The delegation of public works probably eased the success of the fiscal-military system in 1854–6 by reducing the pressure on the public finances, which may have reassured rentiers even if the Crimean War interrupted the pursuit of retrenchment. With the ascent of the 'delegating-market' state and the triumph of the fiscal-military system during the Crimean War, the mid-1850s were a high-water mark for the post-1815 French state.

The 1850s were also important in evincing a shift in the politics of taxation. While the fiscal system survived the 1848 Revolution with little alteration, universal suffrage rendered tax politics more sensitive to the needs of the poor, even if the Bonapartist commitment to the rural poor suited the long-standing tendency to favour land. In encouraging the growing popularisation of tax politics and in providing a legitimate outlet for the expression of grievances over taxation and other issues, universal suffrage perhaps eased another change in popular politics. Whereas tax revolts were common enough in the 1840s, with the unrest of 1841 and 1848, the difficulties over the *45 centimes* marked the last spontaneous tax revolt on a national scale in French history. From the 1850s, the frequency of spontaneous unrest declined as protest became increasingly

---

[176] Hazareesingh, *Subject to Citizen*, 41–2, 45–7, 51–95.

sophisticated, as the growing politicisation of the French population evident under the July Monarchy continued.[177] Spurred by railway construction, industrialisation and urbanisation changed the way that people lived and interacted with the world around them. The mobilisation of small capital likely furthered this politicisation. Though it may not have converted many 'peasants into Frenchmen', increasing numbers of people across France invested in the national project through purchases of *rentes* which probably reinforced a French identity. Not only did this suit the regime's desire for popular legitimacy; the financial transformation wrought under the Second Empire may also have expedited the creation of a republican national identity during the Third Republic.

---

[177] Tilly, 'How Protest Modernized in France'.

CHAPTER 9

Reaching the Limits of the Fiscal-Military System, 1856–1871

The Crimean War had profound consequences for the Second Empire, and certainly for the expansion of the state over which the regime presided. The war produced reasonably good Franco-British relations, and preserving these after the war was a priority for the Empire, not least in offering a way to avoid the isolation that risked reconstituting the dreaded 'coalition of 1840'.[1] Moreover, the 'union of the two governments and the two countries', in Napoleon's mind, was the only way to assure, 'without upheaval in Europe, the progress of civilisation'.[2] The latter entailed economic development, which in the case of France drew heavily on British capital to finance public works and thus benefited from good Franco-British relations. The quest for development and closeness to Britain also pushed the government towards trade liberalisation, which could extend French influence in Europe much as Guizot had tried to do with commercial treaties after 1840. The tariff reforms that the government proposed in 1856 were, Fould wrote, 'no less important for our good relations with England than for the development of our prosperity and power'.[3] The desire for freer trade and the maintenance of the British relationship culminated in the Franco-British commercial treaty of 1860, which presaged a period of fiscal reform in France.

The fiscal reforms of the Second Empire in the late 1850s and 1860s had a more direct connection to the war. As we have seen, the government introduced new taxes to pay for it and, consequently, the impact of universal suffrage on the tax system, apparent in the tax politics of the early 1850s, became more pronounced. More significantly, following the success of the loans of 1854–5, the government generally resorted to public

---

[1] Persigny to Napoleon III, 18 and 28 January 1859, Persigny MSS, BNF, NAF 23066, fols. 64–5, 67–70.
[2] Napoleon III to Baroche, 27 July 1856, Baroche MSS, BT, MsT 1468A, fol. 44.
[3] Fould to Persigny, 19 June 1856, Persigny MSS, AN, 44AP/11.

subscription when issuing *rentes* – though not, as we shall see, because ministers thought this method inherently preferable to adjudication. The success of public credit in 1854–5 prompted Persigny to suggest using it to stimulate French agriculture by bolstering the Crédit foncier.[4] Yet the latter, though partly established to ease rural credit, issued most of its loans in cities such as Paris, where the state's more extensive registration of real-estate transactions allowed the Crédit foncier to assess better the credit-worthiness of potential borrowers; meanwhile, notaries, who tended to be well informed about their clients, remained the principal creditors in rural areas.[5] Persigny's suggestion reflected broader pressure for the regime to ensure greater economic prosperity as a peace dividend, and similar demands emerged in 1860 following the Wars of Italian Unification.[6] The Crimean War's encouragement of economic interventionism was apparent, too, in the rebuilding of Paris. 'The simplest and the best' way to finance the renovation of the city, Georges Haussmann wrote in November 1855, would be 'to negotiate with a company'; however, 'no eminence of the Bourse wanted, given the situation of Europe, to engage in sponsoring an operation that will last five years.'[7] The government, therefore, had to finance public works itself, hence the loan the city contracted in 1855. Municipal taxes were also raised. More generally, wars contributed to the volatility of the Bourse in the 1860s and to economic malaise, both of which stimulated greater economic interventionism as the regime sought to preserve the stability of the post-revolutionary order. These were not just wars that France fought; the American Civil War, for instance, provoked the 'cotton famine' that so troubled the textile industry in the 1860s.

Historians, though, have generally overlooked war in explaining the economic interventionism of the Second Empire despite, for instance, the obvious military justifications for railway construction. Instead, they have focused on domestic political considerations and ideology, not least Saint-Simonianism and 'l'économie politique du Deux-Décembre'.[8] Historians have also emphasised the importance of electoral considerations, character-ising the Bonapartist regime – based on universal suffrage – as marking a vital stage in the emergence of mass politics in France.[9] Though partial, these explanations have some merit. The rationale for renovating Paris, for

[4] Persigny to Napoleon III, 30 July 1855, Persigny MSS, AN, 44AP/5.
[5] Hoffman et al., *Priceless Markets*, 257–72.   [6] Glikman, *Monarchie impériale*, 188–90.
[7] Haussmann to Billault, 18 February 1855, Billault MSS, AD, Loire-Atlantique, 20J/20, dossier 11.
[8] Girard, *Politique des travaux publics*; Dansette, *Naissance*.
[9] Hazareesingh, *Subject to Citizen*; Glikman, *Monarchie impériale*; Nord, *Republican Moment*; Price, *Second Empire*; Price, *People and Politics*; Anceau, *Empire libéral*.

instance, did not result from the Crimean War. Following the 'deplorable' results in the 1857 legislative elections in Paris, Haussmann, the prefect of the Seine, sought to accelerate the rebuilding of the city to disrupt the political and social organisation of the government's opponents and to ease the movement of troops through the city, should they be needed to quell unrest.[10] Meanwhile, in Paris and elsewhere, economic malaise from the late 1850s encouraged the revival of the interventionist state after the austerity of the Second Republic, which did not necessarily align with the commitment to economic liberalisation and a smaller state implicit in the Franco-British commercial treaty.

The diplomatic revolution wrought by the Crimean War provided another stimulant for the state's expansion during the Second Empire by giving Napoleon greater freedom than Louis-Philippe to seek prestige abroad. Defeated, the Russians ceased to be a conservative power buttressing the post-1815 international order. Gorchakov, appointed foreign minister in 1856, reciprocated Morny's desire for a Franco-Russian rapprochement, aimed at revising the peace terms. The Russians, therefore, sanctioned international upheaval in Europe in the hope of securing recompense for their defeat, inaugurating a period of international instability. As in the 1820s, Russian support provided the French with the latitude for an active policy in Europe, leading directly to the Wars of Italian Unification in 1859–60 as Napoleon pursued the 'principle of nationalities'. Emulating previous governments, the Bonapartists commemorated their military successes to glorify the dynasty and reinforce the regime.[11] The continuing pressures to accrue prestige abroad and maintain the buoyancy of the economy encouraged Napoleon's interventionist foreign policy from the late 1850s. Though historians have recently given greater attention to the economic dimensions of mid-nineteenth-century French imperialism, they have not yet fully analysed these in the context of domestic fiscal politics; conversely, accounts of nineteenth-century French public finance, such as Marion's, have underplayed the significance of extra-European imperialism.[12] Consequently, historians have not always appreciated how much the financial and political costs of interventionism abroad weakened the legitimacy of the regime in the late 1860s. In considering the ensuing crisis of the fiscal-military system, we can understand better the emergence of

[10] Haussmann to Napoleon III, 8 July 1857, Billault MSS, AD, Loire-Atlantique, 20J/23, dossier 4.
[11] Hazareesingh, *Saint-Napoleon*, 63–9.
[12] On the economics of French imperialism, see, most recently, Todd, *Velvet Empire*. On colonial finance in the mid- and late century, see Bobrie, 'Finances publiques et conquête coloniale'.

the reformed 'Liberal Empire' in the 1860s and why the state proved unable to mobilise the resources necessary to prosecute the Franco-Prussian War more successfully in 1870. Thus, war both made and unmade the Bonapartist state of Napoleon III, as it had that of his uncle.

Bonapartism in Economic Crisis

The return of peace in 1856 presaged a boom in economic activity as we have seen, but by the late 1850s the outlook was bleaker. Whereas GDP, corrected for inflation, had grown at an average rate of 2.28 per cent annually during the years 1851–8, this fell to 1.08 per cent for 1859–69.[13] The falling rate of economic growth coincided with rising public expenditure. Having borrowed 29.3 per cent of expenditure from 1854 to 1856, the government briefly re-established a budget surplus in 1858, as ordinary revenues totalled 103.03 per cent of spending; the deficit reappeared in 1859, averaging 6.74 per cent of annual expenditure until 1869.[14] Still, the immediate post-war period was marked by retrenchment. With the return of peace, Magne claimed in 1857, 'the *grand-livre* [which recorded all *rentes* issued] would be closed and only reopened for the most urgent needs.' In the meantime, he sought to reduce gradually the *dette flottante*. As we have seen, its size was a major concern during the Crimean War and, in 1857, Magne described it as 'excessive'. Without greatly raising taxes, he asserted, France could emulate either the policy of Law in the 1710s, of issuing securities, or that of Turgot in the 1770s, of imposing economies; while both had pursued the same aim of reducing public debt and taxation, Law's ideas had produced disaster in 1720 and again when they were resurrected through the *assignats*.[15] Moreover, government deleveraging would liberate funds for privately financed public works, while government borrowing would crowd them out. Indeed, when the state floated a loan in 1859, Magne proved as reluctant as he had been in 1856 to condone the issuing of railway securities, for fear of diverting investment from *rentes*.[16] Economy was therefore preferable, which Magne and his successors, like Turgot, saw as a means of economic liberalisation. The limitations of other resources increased the pressure on the government's finances. As Magne noted, the *caisses d'épargne* had little to offer;

---

[13] Toutain, 'Produit intérieur brut'.   [14] Fontvieille, *État*, 1937–8.
[15] Magne, *Notes sur l'administration des finances*, 7, 15–19, 21.
[16] Proces-verbaux, conseil des ministres, 9 June 1859, Fould MSS, AN, 247AP/1; Durieux, *Magne*, I, 363–5.

only in 1859 did the amount invested in them reach the level it had been in 1847.[17] The loans of 1854–5 probably hindered their recovery from the crisis of 1848 by pushing potential deposits directly into *rentes*, while new institutions such as the Crédit mobilier and the Crédit foncier drew capital into their own securities and those of other companies. Magne had more success with the Banque de France. In 1857, in exchange for renewing its privilege until 1899, the government doubled the Banque's capital, stipulating that it should invest 100 million francs more in 3 per cent *rentes* to relieve the Caisse d'amortissement. At the same time, the government obtained a 'permanent advance' of 80 million francs, which would fall to 60 million in 1862.[18] As Charles Mallet, a regent of the Banque, complained, 'I don't see any other advantage in that plan but the renewal of the charter. I am at a loss to understand what profits the Bank will derive from the proposed arrangements.'[19]

With the post-war boom, the competition between the Rothschilds, the Pereires and their respective allies intensified. Following the Pereires' advances into Austria at the beginning of 1855, the Rothschilds reinforced their position in Vienna, already weakened there following the 1848 financial crisis, by establishing the Kreditanstalt. Meanwhile, the two groups competed for concessions in the Low Countries, Spain, Russia, Switzerland and the German and Italian states. To sustain this contest, in January 1856 James de Rothschild and his allies in the *haute banque* formed a financial syndicate, known from April as the Réunion financière. The purpose of the Réunion was 'the study and organisation of great commercial and industrial enterprises (banking and loan operations excepted)': in other words, to challenge the Crédit mobilier.[20] In March, with peace imminent, the syndicate proposed to further this objective by forming a *comptoir impérial des travaux publics, du commerce et de l'industrie*, a joint-stock company to finance railways. Probably seeking to minimise the pressure on the Bourse and thus on the *rente*, and perhaps affected by pressure from the Pereires and others, Magne pushed the Réunion to join with the Crédit mobilier in this operation – which Vernes, deputy governor of the Banque de France, observed 'would amount to the destruction of the Réunion'.[21] Ultimately, the Conseil

[17] Rapport à l'empereur, by Magne, *Le Moniteur universel*, 12 December 1858; Christen-Lécuyer, *Caisses d'épargne*, 604.
[18] Plessis, *Politique de la Banque*, 203–4.
[19] Mallet to Dobrée [17 April 1857], Dobrée MSS, BoE, 14A185/2.
[20] 12 January and 26 April 1856, Gille, 'Procès-verbaux de la Réunion', 12, 28.
[21] 29 November 1856, Gille, 'Procès-verbaux de la Réunion', 55.

d'état, having already approved a capital increase for the Comptoir d'escompte and concerned about overburdening the Bourse, vetoed the formation of the new company.[22]

The *comptoir impérial* had been intended to provide credit for railway companies, which came under increasing financial pressure after the war and found themselves heavily reliant on advances from the Banque de France.[23] Seeking to ensure the affordability of bread given the subsistence problems of the mid-1850s, the government imposed reductions on the prices of transporting grain by train, reducing railway companies' income. In the second half of 1857, the companies' profits fell, while the liquidation of the Grand Central company that year prompted a reorganisation of railway concessions.[24] The companies' difficulties contributed to a sluggishness on the Bourse in 1857, but there was little sign of alarm from investors, perhaps partly because of the strong position of the Banque de France which, following the difficulties of 1855, continued large-scale purchases of gold and silver into 1857.[25] While a financial crisis convulsed London in November, at its centre was George Peabody, whose business concerned chiefly Anglo-American finance. Hottinguer noted that 'We feel the crisis much less here' in Paris than in London.[26] As Mallet explained, 'foreign business is carried on here on a very limited scale' while 'the branches of trade' affected by the crisis had been so profitable over the last two years that 'they could very well afford to part with a portion of their gains.'[27] Still, the crisis compounded a series of scandals affecting the Bourse in 1857, while political considerations also left investors cautious. In January 1858, Hottinguer noted that 'the Bourse worries about the interior politics of France, & the arbitrary laws that they seem to want to propose against the press.'[28] While historians have often depicted a cosy relationship between government and business during the Second Empire, this was not without its frictions.

Business found a further cause for complaint in fiscal policy, as Magne sought to raise revenue. Given the continuing pressure to ease the burden on land and a widespread sense that existing taxes could not be raised

[22] Gille, *Rothschild*, II, 205–10.
[23] Procès-verbaux, Réunion financière, 4 December 1856, Rothschild MSS, ANMT, 132AQ/124, fols. 42–7.
[24] Émile Pereire to Mocquard, 4 September 1856, Rouher MSS, AN, 45AP/3; Caron, *Chemins de fer*, I, 234–5.
[25] Plessis, *Politique de la Banque*, 167.
[26] Jean-Henri Hottinguer to Baring, 23 November 1857, BA, HC 7.1.1126.
[27] Mallet to Dobrée, 10 February 1858, Dobrée MSS, BoE, 14A185/12.
[28] Jean-Henri Hottinguer to Baring, 31 January 1858, BA, HC 7.1.1141.

much more, the question of income tax re-emerged as an obvious means of tapping the increasing amount of untaxed industrial wealth, evident in the sharp proliferation in the number of shares issued since the 1840s. While the Crédit foncier had done little to improve the condition of agriculture, observers noted, industry and commerce were flourishing.[29] Hence, as we have seen, Magne's tax increases during the Crimean War had targeted '*la fortune mobilière*'. An income tax, though, remained too radical, partly because it would hit *rentes*, potentially impairing public credit through a 'disguised reduction of interest', and partly because of expected difficulties in collection. The success of Britain's income tax relied on taxpayers declaring their assets which, as one member of the legislature's budget commission put it, was 'not possible' in France where defrauding the government was 'not considered dishonesty'. Instead, therefore, Magne began preparing a tax on securities in 1855, which at least some exponents of income tax regarded as a precursor to the latter.[30] Moreover, taxing securities suited those in government and the legislature who wished to curb speculation at the Bourse. Collected from 1858 onwards, the *impôt sur les valeurs mobilières* was levied on the transaction of securities.[31] Anticipating the revenue from the new tax, the government repealed the 1855 increase to *l'enregistrement*, which would ease the burden on land and thus allow the regime to tout a shift of some of the fiscal burden towards industry in time for the 1857 elections.[32]

Though the *impôt sur les valeurs mobilières* suited the regime's rural supporters, it elicited immediate protests. In April, several luminaries of the Bourse, including James de Rothschild and Émile Pereire, produced a memorandum criticising the tax for 'the profound perturbation it has caused in business' while it had yielded little for the treasury.[33] The Corps législatif, too, raised objections, though several deputies had, for instance, backed introducing a securities transaction tax in 1855.[34] Magne defended the tax as not contravening any 'fundamental principle of our financial law; it is not retroactive and does not constitute an income tax'.[35] Still, the sharp increase in foreign – especially railway – securities on the

---

[29] Procès-verbaux, commission du budget, 1 April 1857, AN, C 1051.
[30] 23 April 1855, Fortoul, *Journal*, I, 160; procès-verbaux, commission du budget, 27 March and 3 April 1856, AN, C 1045.
[31] Decree of 17 July 1857, *Lois*, LVII, 251–2.
[32] Law of 23 June 1857, §2 art. 13, *Lois*, LVII, 169; *Le Moniteur universel*, 12 June 1857.
[33] 'Note sur la nécessité de rapporter l'impôt sur la circulation des valeurs mobilières', by the Duc de Noailles et al., April 1858, Baroche MSS, BT, MsT 1069, fol. 2.
[34] Procès-verbaux, commission des impôts, 7 and 9 July 1855, AN, C 1044, dossier 8.
[35] Magne to Baroche, n.d. [1858?], Baroche MSS, BT, MsT 1069, fol. 14.

Bourse after 1855 presented a problem, since foreign firms found it easier than their French counterparts to issue unauthorised securities and thus evade the tax. At the same time, the increase in the number of foreign securities rendered a tax more attractive as a means not only of taxing foreigners but of controlling the influx, which risked diverting funds away from French companies and *rentes*. In 1858, the government prohibited the advertisement of unauthorised foreign securities, though to little effect. Many foreign securities simply switched from being listed by the official Parquet to trading through the unofficial brokers of the coulisse. Committed to the tax, though, the government reiterated the eligibility of securities in new rules promulgated in 1862 and 1863; ministers also encouraged the Parquet's unsuccessful attempt to take over the coulisse in 1859 and thus capture the latter's business.[36]

The *impôt sur les valeurs mobilières* did nothing to ease the financial problems facing the railway companies, which continued to grow – as did their military and economic importance, hence the government's desire to expedite railway construction. Already in 1851, the state had guaranteed 150 million francs of railway bonds.[37] As the economic downturn prompted railway magnates to request further improvements to the terms of concessions, the government responded by guaranteeing 4.65 per cent interest on railway bonds for fifty years for all recently established companies, beginning in January 1864 for the Compagnie de l'Est and a year later for the rest. Approved by the Corps législatif in July 1859, the railway conventions attracted considerable criticism. The size of the companies and concessions arising from the process of 'fusion' earlier in the decade raised concerns that these companies would enjoy a monopoly. They had become so large and their obligations to the state so great, that a railway crisis risked destroying the government's investments and impairing public credit. Indeed, the government saw the ensuing expenditures 'less as an expense and more as an investment' which would provide a return once the companies reimbursed the state for any advances that it made on their behalf.[38] The commitment of potentially more public money to the railways also encouraged the old opposition discourse of the need to streamline the state, particularly since the increased regulation that the companies accepted in exchange aroused fears that the convention marked

---

[36] 'Note concernant les valeurs étrangères', *direction du mouvement général des fonds*, 8 June 1864, SAEF, B/65767; decree of 11 January 1862 and law of 13 May 1863, §2 arts. 6 and 7, *Lois*, LXII, 2, LXIII, 249; Hautcoeur and Riva, 'Paris Financial Market', 1336–7, 1338–1441; Hissung-Convert, *Spéculation boursière*, 380–98.
[37] Caron, *Chemins de fer*, I, 207.   [38] Note, n.d. [1860s], Rouher MSS, AN, 45AP/20.

Figure 9.1   Public works spending, 1840–70 (in 1815 francs).
(Source: Fontvieille, *État*, 2110–16. Nominal prices were adjusted to those of 1815 using the index of agricultural and industrial prices provided in Toutain, 'Imbroglio des indices de prix', 175–6.)

a stage en route to a state-owned railway system. Most notably, company accounts were to be subjected to government scrutiny, developing the system of oversight instituted by the July Monarchy in the 1840s.[39]

The railway conventions of 1859 presaged a considerable increase in public works spending in the 1860s, which reverted to the levels of the Orleanist state in the 1840s (Figure 9.1). Alone, however, they proved insufficient to assure railway finance, prompting a series of further conventions in 1863. The latter provided substantial state subsidies and thus provoked renewed criticism of fiscal irresponsibility, but the state simultaneously divested itself of obligations to construct several lines, which were transferred to the companies.[40] The growth in public works spending from the end of the decade compounded a surge in military and naval spending. In 1859–60, France and Sardinia fought Austria in two short but expensive wars to unify Italy. Meanwhile, in 1860, French troops intervened in Syria and joined a British expedition to China. French action in the Far East also entailed military and naval action in Cochinchina

[39] Caron, *Chemins de fer*, I, 207, 235–7; Picard, *Chemins de fer*, II, 169–203.
[40] Girard, *Politique des travaux publics*, 285–93.

beginning in 1858, while from 1862 to 1867 France intervened militarily in Mexico.

The costs of these actions abroad complicated the government's efforts to boost the economy, which relied not just on spending but on lowering taxes. The centrepiece in the latter policy was the Franco-British commercial treaty of January 1860, the so-called Cobden–Chevalier Treaty. It owed less to either Richard Cobden, a British Liberal MP and free-trader, or Chevalier than such a name implies. Historians have seen Chevalier, who gained political prominence under the Second Empire as a member of the Conseil d'état and then as a senator, as orchestrating the treaty, but they have exaggerated his importance.[41] Rather than being simply the work of a couple of supposed pioneers, the idea of a commercial treaty had a long existence, as we have seen. It was not because of Cobden or Chevalier that the French were willing to undertake in 1859 the wide-ranging commercial negotiations that they had refused in 1852. Instead, the treaty arose following a convergence of different interests in the Bonapartist elite, which reflected the international situation in 1859 and the growing influence of several of the more dynamic sectors of the French economy. Moreover, the failure of previous efforts at tariff reform, not least in 1856, imbued the government with greater willingness to contemplate more drastic action.

Persigny, then ambassador in London, seems to have been the one who took the initiative. He frequently offered Napoleon advice, not least on economic policy, though Cobden and Chevalier very likely encouraged him. While Persigny had been cautious about trade liberalisation in 1852, Chevalier's commendation of him to Cobden as having been 'the most energetic supporter of free trade' since his days as a minister reflected his long-standing acquaintance with Chevalier.[42] Favouring good Franco-British relations, in July 1859 Persigny proposed to reinforce these through a commercial treaty which would simultaneously stimulate trade and so invigorate the French economy after its recent travails. French participation in the War of Italian Unification in 1859 had strained relations with the British, who were suspicious of French designs in Italy. The

[41] Dunham, *Anglo-French Treaty*. There is some circularity to Dunham's argument that Chevalier was the principal architect of the treaty. Since his book relies heavily on the correspondence of Cobden and Chevalier, he inevitably emphasises their importance. His account of the negotiations, for example, begins with Cobden's visit to Paris in October 1859, overlooking the actions of Persigny and Rouher during the summer.
[42] Chevalier to Cobden, 17 May 1859, Cobden MSS, BL, Add. MSS 43647, fol. 96; Dunham, *Anglo-French Treaty*, 21.

construction of the Suez Canal, then being undertaken by the French entrepreneur Ferdinand de Lesseps with French and Egyptian money, created further tension, given British interests in the Mediterranean and their commitment to preserving the Ottoman Empire. With a commercial treaty, Persigny wrote, 'the prosperity of the two peoples will calm passions.'[43] In encouraging economic activity, moreover, trade liberalisation would ultimately increase revenue from customs and other taxes, thereby offering the government greater scope for economic interventionism to assure future prosperity. To stimulate the economy and ease the adjustment to free trade, he argued, the government should invest 2 billion francs in agriculture, industry, reforestation, flood defences and irrigation; these expenses would then be recouped from the growth of tax revenue.[44] Persigny's proposition thus reflected the long-standing inclination to economic interventionism that had been similarly apparent in his 1855 proposal to use public credit to bolster the Crédit foncier.

Persigny's scheme would probably have made little progress without backing in Paris from several of his long-time rivals: Eugène Rouher, minister of agriculture, commerce and public works, Baroche, president of the Conseil d'état, and Fould, then *ministre d'état*. Not only had Rouher been the principal architect of the 1856 tariff reform bill, but in spring 1859 he seems to have been contemplating a new attempt to overhaul prohibitive duties – knowledge of which encouraged Chevalier and probably Persigny in their machinations.[45] Thus, just over a month after Persigny's initial suggestion, Rouher wrote to him offering advice on dealing with Napoleon's hesitations, which arose from 'the fear of facing a certain unpopularity' due to a commercial accord.[46] As the letter implies, Rouher and Fould directed Cobden, Chevalier and others in the task of persuading Napoleon to accept a treaty. Yet, for Rouher and Fould in particular, trade liberalisation was less about facilitating prosperity through state interventionism à la Persigny than about retrenchment, reducing the size of the state and so stimulating enterprise. As Baroche and Rouher wrote upon the ratification of the treaty, 'tariffs high enough to become prohibitive constitute a charge or a tax that burdens most consumers, not to the profit of the state, but to the profit of industry. They are only justified as a temporary measure that impose on all exceptional sacrifices,

[43] Persigny to Napoleon III, 21 November 1859, Persigny MSS, AN, 44AP/4.
[44] Wright, 'Origins of Napoleon III's Free Trade'.
[45] AN F[12] 2479; Chevalier to Cobden, 21 July 1859, Cobden MSS, BL, Add. MSS 43647, fols. 99–101; Schnerb, *Rouher*, 96–8, 102–5.
[46] Rouher to Persigny, 31 August 1859, Persigny MSS, AN, 44AP/12.

in exchange for a legitimate and certain hope of a gradual fall in consumer prices.'[47]

As Rouher's concerns about Napoleon's hesitations suggested, reducing tariffs required sufficient acquiescence from economic interests, deputies and the finance ministry. Indeed, the dangers of opposition meant that the negotiations on the French side were conducted in secret by Chevalier, Fould, Baroche and Rouher. Still, the treaty secured considerable support. Émile Pereire, for instance, sent Napoleon a lengthy memorandum advocating lower tariffs in October 1859. Reductions in duties on coal and iron would benefit the Pereires' railway empire; at the same time, the Crédit mobilier could profit from the government borrowing that Pereire observed would be necessary to cover the short-term deficit that would arise from lowering duties. Moreover, the Pereires disliked indirect taxes as regressive and injurious to enterprise, and thus supported the treaty as a means of reducing them, as did several other industrial interests.[48] Many wine producers favoured trade liberalisation, as they had since the 1820s, in the hope of reducing the duties borne by their exports; silk manufacturers and other luxury goods industries were similarly supportive.[49]

The government sought to mitigate opposition by stressing that it was not endorsing free trade but was replacing 'prohibition' with 'protection', in line with proposed customs reforms since the 1840s. British imports were to face *ad valorem* taxes of up to 30 per cent, which fell to 25 per cent in 1864, in a fashion similar to the 1854 Franco-Belgian treaty.[50] Aside from serving as generally valuable experiments in the politics and economics of tariff reform, in test-driving *ad valorem* taxation the Franco-Belgian agreements were instrumental in validating the government's proposed 'protection'. Though a long-standing part of customs duties, *ad valorem* taxes had previously been condemned with respect to Belgium as providing 'only nominal protection' since their value would fluctuate with prices, unlike that of a fixed duty; by 1860, however, *ad valorem* taxes were essential to the notion that French industry would retain 'protection'.[51] Thus, for example, the Metz Chamber of Commerce, representing an important industrial town, supported the substitution 'of customs prohibitions with duties that are equally protective, for the sake of easing our

[47] Rapport à l'Empereur, by Baroche and Rouher, 24 January 1860, *Le Moniteur universel*, 11 March 1860.
[48] Ratcliffe, 'Napoleon III and the Anglo-French Commercial Treaty', 596–604.
[49] Nye, 'Changing French Trade Conditions', 464, 467, 469.
[50] Marion, *Histoire financière*, V, 419–22.
[51] Note pour le ministre, 14 April 1860, AN, F[12] 2482; *Le Journal des débats*, 14 October 1852.

trade abroad'. Simultaneously, though, the Chamber expressed reservations about the possible consequences of tariff reductions for industries
such as metallurgy, pottery and glass, which would need better transport
links in order to compete with foreign imports.[52] Anticipating such
objections, days before the treaty was signed the government had reaffirmed its commitment to extending railways, other public works and
lowering taxes to stimulate the economy, utilising leftover money from
the loan floated, as we shall see, to finance the 1859 Italian war.[53] Still, the
government's caution did not deter opponents of the treaty from attacking
it by claiming that 'the protective system' would 'degenerate into free
trade'.[54]

At the finance ministry, Gréterin, who had added the Direction générale
des contributions indirectes to his remit in 1851 when it merged with
customs, was replaced in March by Adolphe de Forcade La Roquette, a
free-trader described by one of Persigny's informants as 'Rouher's right
hand'.[55] In November, Forcade succeeded Magne – the latter, like
Gréterin, having been excluded from the treaty negotiations. The expected
costs of trade liberalisation undoubtedly reduced its appeal in the finance
ministry. Besides extending *ad valorem* taxes, the government sharply
reduced import duties on tea, coffee, cacao and sugar, seeking to bolster
support for the regime by lowering the prices of these commodities.
Despite hopes that lower duties would stimulate consumption and thus
mitigate losses, revenue from import duties fell from 189,489,283.11
francs in 1859 to 131,164,647.81 in 1860, a 34.7 per cent decrease when
accounting for inflation.[56] The greatest loss arose from the cut to sugar
duties, which drew criticism for fiscal irresponsibility and in subsequent
years prompted proposals to raise import taxes, particularly those on tea,
coffee and cacao, as government borrowing increased in the 1860s.[57]
Instead, the government compensated by raising other indirect taxes.
Adjusting for inflation, between 1859 and 1869, customs revenue fell
46.88 per cent, while overall indirect tax revenue including that from

[52] Metz Chamber of Commerce to Napoleon III, 2 March 1860, Baroche MSS, BT, MsT 1185, fol. 212.
[53] Napoleon III to Fould, 5 January 1860, *Le Moniteur universel*, 15 January 1860; Magne to Napoleon III, September 1861, Baroche MSS, BT, MsT 1070, fol. 21.
[54] Cézard, *Traité de commerce*, 46.
[55] Richemont to Persigny, n.d. [1860], Persigny MSS, AN, 44AP/2; Bordas, *Directeurs généraux des douanes*, 175, 195, 201.
[56] *Projet de loi … 1859*; *Projet de loi … 1860*.
[57] E.g. procès-verbaux, commission du budget, 20 and 23 April 1860, 3 April 1862, and 6 April 1868, AN, C 1065, 1080, 1121; Marion, *Histoire financière*, V, 423–5.

customs rose by 7.3 per cent.[58] While the loss of customs revenue was undesirable, the finance ministry did not uniformly oppose tariff reform. In 1859, Chevalier had noted the growing support for trade liberalisation among customs officials, who evinced mounting frustration at the difficulties of implementing an ever-growing battery of protectionist measures.[59] By May 1860, following the reduction of opposition within government and the charm offensive without, Fould was declaring victory: 'The more I see the more I am convinced that we are right & that the Country is with us; the *départements* that inform me are particularly favourable to our new commercial policy and like the Emperor's government all the more.'[60]

For both the British and the French, the treaty offered a means of alliance management through fiscal reform. Concerned though the British were about French ambitions in Italy and the Mediterranean, at least as troubling was the growth of French naval power. Renovating their fleet after the experience of the Crimean War, in 1859 the French launched *La Gloire*, a new class of ironclad battleship. The British responded the following year with HMS *Warrior*, but the cost of a naval arms race risked upsetting Gladstonian finance.[61] For Gladstone, back in office as chancellor, the treaty offered a means of further reducing indirect taxes and tariffs in Britain by inducing the French to follow a similar policy that would preclude excessive naval spending on their part. As Gladstone put it in 1863, 'the finance and expenditure of the two countries have inevitable and important relations one to the other. The upward and downward movement in either is pretty sure, subject to various limitations of time and degree[,] to find its echo, and a pretty solid echo[,] in the other.'[62]

Fortunately for Gladstone, economically liberal Bonapartists saw the treaty as a means of reforming the French state on the British model, thereby curbing government expenditure. Like the July Monarchy in the 1840s, the Bonapartist regime in the mid- to late 1850s faced substantial criticism for fiscal irresponsibility not least from so-called *budgétaires*, which increased in tandem with spending on French military interventionism abroad and public works, giving new vitality to the long-standing opposition discourse about the need to streamline the state. The censure was largely unjustified; in 1864, Magne published an account of his tenure

[58] *Projet de loi ... 1859*; *Projet de loi ... 1869*.
[59] Chevalier to Cobden, 21 July 1859, Cobden MSS, BL, Add. MSS 43647, fols. 99–101.
[60] Fould to Baroche, 26 May 1860, Baroche MSS, BT, MsT 979, fol. 150.
[61] Hamilton, *Anglo-French Naval Rivalry*; Battesti, *Marine*; Iliasu, 'The Cobden–Chevalier Treaty'.
[62] Gladstone to Fould, 4 April 1863, Gladstone MSS, BL, Add. MSS 44400, fol. 156.

from 1855 to 1860 to prove 'that the Government never ceased to be economical with state funds'.[63] Still, Fould, echoing criticisms of rising supplementary and extraordinary expenditures, presented Napoleon with an agenda for reform and earned himself the finance ministry in November 1861 as the emperor sought to conciliate the *budgétaires*.[64] One of Fould's first moves was to establish a *budget extraordinaire*, intended to tighten control over expenditures. At the same time, he proposed a series of tax increases to restrain government borrowing.[65] In office until January 1867, Fould ultimately aimed to curb public spending, implementing something of a Gladstonian vision of lower taxes and a smaller state. He had 'much esteem and affection' for Gladstone, and was grateful for his 'appreciation of the operation of our finances and the impulsion that I have sought to give them'.[66] In invoking Gladstone, the doyen of responsible government finance, Fould sought to burnish his own credentials as a paragon of fiscal virtue, honed since his days as a critic of Orleanist finance in the 1840s.

Gladstone's authority was such that Fould's opponents likewise sought his imprimatur. In 1865, Persigny, still pressing the economic interventionism that had driven his commitment to the 1860 treaty, wrote to Napoleon that

> you know what M. Gladstone, the alleged model of M. Fould, said, he said firmly and added that he was ready to sign with both hands that I was a hundred times right, that far from harming credit, a loan for major productive works either by inscription on the *grand-livre* or by thirty- or fifty-year bonds would only relieve it, that if your Majesty undertook the great loan of peace, if you asked for a billion [francs], the *rente* would rise by 5 francs merely at the news of the plan and that there would result for France and England a trend of prosperity without example in the history of the world.[67]

Despite Persigny's fall from favour in the 1860s, Napoleon remained receptive to such ideas, himself favouring a loan of 600 million francs for public works coupled with a 30 million franc cut to *l'enregistrement*, a proposal that Fould rejected as unfeasible.[68] Resistance to curbing the interventionist state also arose in the ministry of agriculture, commerce

[63] Magne to Baroche, 2 May 1864, Baroche MSS, BT, MsT 998, fol. 25.
[64] Mémoire à l'empereur, by Fould, 29 September 1861, *Le Moniteur universel*, 14 November 1861; Darimon, *Histoire de douze ans*, 124–5.
[65] Rapport à l'empereur, by Fould, 20 January 1862, *Le Moniteur universel*, 22 January 1862.
[66] Fould to Panizzi, 1 February 1864, Panizzi MSS, BL, Add. MSS 36722, fol. 297; Fould to Gladstone, 10 February 1865, Gladstone MSS, BL, Add. MSS 44405, fol. 98.
[67] Persigny to Napoleon III, 19 February 1865, Persigny MSS, AN, 44AP/4.
[68] Napoleon III to Rouher 17 October 1868, Napoleon MSS, AN, 400AP/44.

and public works. Armand Béhic, the minister from 1863 to 1867, noted that Fould's 'ideas were in almost all things the opposite of mine'.[69] Such opposition, alongside mounting commitments to public works in addition to military and naval spending, mitigated Fould's pursuit of retrenchment.

The 1860 treaty was a product of the authoritarian empire of the 1850s; it was not intended to foreshadow the liberalisation of the Empire in the 1860s. For Persigny, the treaty was to entail greater state economic interventionism and so only limited economic liberalisation. Fould's economic liberalism, meanwhile, did not extend to politics, where he inclined to authoritarianism, as did Baroche and Rouher. Though some such as Morny supported both political and economic liberalisation, the commercial treaty was supposed to unleash prosperity that would buttress the existing political system, not to initiate its reform; meanwhile, good relations with Britain were meant to give France the latitude to seek glory abroad and thus improve the regime's standing, further reinforcing the political status quo.[70] Reducing taxes as Rouher, Fould and other economic liberals proposed could also enhance the state's legitimacy. The trope of an overbearing fiscal system remained pervasive in the 1860s and was probably strengthened by tax increases under the Second Empire, as the publication in 1864 of *L'Ami Fritz*, a novel by Erckmann-Chatrian, suggests. Depicting Alsatian life during the July Monarchy, the novel's 'fat tax-collector Hâan' – avaricious, parasitical and venal – presented a caricature that reflected the unpopularity of the tax system.[71]

The Italian wars made it more imperative that the treaty reinforce support for the regime. Though Napoleon remained committed to papal independence, the anticlerical undertones of unifying Italy under Sardinia aroused Catholic anger, particularly in 1860 when most of the Papal States were incorporated into Italy. Meanwhile, the treaty itself undercut support from protectionists. The regime's limited moves towards political liberalisation in November that year, allowing the legislature to respond to the annual speech from the throne and appointing ministers to defend government policy there, marked the beginning of an attempt to develop new bases of support. Indeed, many of the liberals whose electoral progress in 1863 and 1869 encouraged the liberalisation of the Empire were not free-traders; the unveiling of the 'Liberal Empire' with the appointment of Émile Ollivier's ministry in 1870 raised expectations of greater protectionism, particularly since the economic downturn and increased popular

[69] Béhic to Rouher, 10 October 1867, Rouher MSS, AN, 45AP/4.
[70] Price, *Second Empire*, 58, 61, 231.   [71] Erckmann-Chatrian, *L'Ami Fritz*.

political activity of the late 1860s intensified agitation over tariffs.[72] Other opposition liberals such as Thiers had long-standing protectionist credentials. Moreover, the 1860 treaty, being a product of the authoritarian Empire, may have reinforced their protectionist tendencies. The treaty, in short, was not necessarily intended to precipitate political liberalisation and, for some, was meant to pre-empt it.

The most striking impact of the 1860 treaty was on customs duties, since it was relatively easy to extend the reductions accorded to Britain to other countries. From 1862 to 1866 the government concluded a series of commercial agreements with Belgium, the Zollverein, Italy, Switzerland, the Hanseatic cities, Spain and Austria, driving a process of trade liberalisation across Europe.[73] The enhanced economic interdependence that ensued from these lower tariffs encouraged greater monetary integration, stimulating the formation of the Latin Monetary Union (LMU) in 1865 by France, Belgium, Italy and Switzerland. Designed to stabilise the monetary system, the LMU marked an attempt to reduce the minting of inferior-quality silver coins. The export of these coins, encouraged by the inflow of gold since the 1850s, had contributed to a scarcity of silver in the early 1860s.[74] Furthermore, in facilitating international exchange, foreign investment and extending the use of the franc, the LMU offered, Fould wrote, a 'great advantage to international relations and to the political influence of France in the world'.[75] Like the commercial treaties of the 1860s, the LMU was intended partly to enhance stability in Europe, reducing the pressure on the fiscal-military system and thus providing greater scope for retrenchment.

Despite some of the aspirations underlying the 1860 treaty, the continued growth of expenditure and the regime's desire to minimise borrowing hindered tax cuts. As part of the financial programme he developed on resuming office, Fould in 1863 raised duties on salt and sugar in addition to the *timbre* and *l'enregistrement*.[76] Though intended as temporary, pending reductions in public expenditure, these tax increases aroused discontent. The prefect of the Meurthe, for example, stressed the unpopularity of the increase to the salt tax, particularly among the 'working classes' who were already displeased by a rise in tobacco prices; in this context, news of cuts to the army, which raised the prospect of reductions to public

---

[72] Smith, *Tariff Reform*, 35–6.   [73] Marsh, *Bargaining on Europe*, 28–61.
[74] Einaudi, *Money and Politics*, 37–46; Flandreau, 'The Economics and Politics of Monetary Unions'.
[75] Fould to Drouyn de Lhuys, 27 January 1866, MAE, 1ADC/603, dossier 2, fol. 10.
[76] Law of 2 July 1862, *Lois*, LXII, 176–99.

spending and thus to taxes, received 'unanimous approbation'.[77] This public pressure for retrenchment and lower taxes continued through the 1860s, pushing the government towards reform.[78] While revenue from *l'enregistrement* rose by 15.9 per cent between 1860 and 1869, accounting for inflation, the government contemplated reform for much of the 1860s to reduce the tax.[79] In 1867, an inquiry into agriculture noted continued pressure 'to alleviate the charges' that *l'enregistrement* imposed on land.[80] Indeed, in 1866, Napoleon instructed Fould to consider reforms to *l'enregistrement*, the *contribution foncière* and the *patente*.[81] Revenues from the latter grew substantially during the Second Empire, partly because of the development of industry and commerce. In 1852, the *patente* provided 12.64 per cent of direct tax revenue, which grew to 19.11 per cent in 1869, as revenue from the tax rose by 80.5 per cent, adjusted for inflation.[82] As with *l'enregistrement*, this growth in revenue – reflecting rising numbers of *patentés* – increased the pressure to cut the tax. Already during the 1860s, Fould sought to reduce the tax, and the *contribution personnelle et mobilière*, for 'less affluent' taxpayers; as in the 1850s, the Bonapartists sought to use fiscal policy to cultivate lower-class support, especially in the countryside.[83] The extension of free primary education in the 1860s, targeted at rural France in particular, was justified along similar lines. Framed as 'the reduction of a heavy tax', it was meant to be as noticeable as possible to the lower classes, the intended beneficiaries.[84] The economic crisis caused by the collapse of American cotton exports during the civil war stimulated further attempts to alleviate working-class hardship, as Napoleon demanded exemption from direct taxes for those paying a monthly rent of 250 francs, while seeking to minimise food prices and duties on necessities.[85] Nevertheless, many indirect taxes, not least on alcohol, remained high as the government continued to prioritise rural over urban interests (Figure 9.2).

---

[77] Prefect of the Meurthe to the Marshal commanding the 3rd army corps, 4 April and 9 May 1862, SHD, 8G 181.
[78] Price, *Second Empire*, 305–7.
[79] Procès-verbaux, commission de l'enregistrement, Rouher MSS, AN, 45AP/10; *Projet de loi … 1860*; *Projet de loi … 1869*.
[80] Note, Ministère de l'agriculture, du commerce et des travaux publics, 18 October 1867, Rouher MSS, AN, 45AP/23.
[81] Procès-verbaux, conseil des ministres, 28 March 1866, Rouher MSS, AN, 45AP/1.
[82] *Projet de loi … 1852*; *Projet de loi … 1869*.
[83] Rapport à l'empereur, by Fould, 20 January 1862, *Le Moniteur universel*, 22 January 1862.
[84] Duruy to Persigny, 6 January 1865, Persigny MSS, AN, 44AP/2.
[85] Ollivier, *Empire libéral*, V, 282–3.

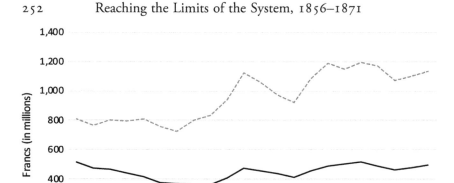

Figure 9.2   Central government revenue from direct and indirect taxes, 1848–69 (in 1815 francs. Nominal prices were adjusted to those of 1815 using the index of agricultural and industrial prices provided in Toutain, 'Imbroglio des indices de prix', 175–6.).
(Source: *Projet de loi... [1848–1869]*)

Besides churning existing taxes, the government imposed new ones. In 1856, the Parisian municipality was permitted to tax horses and carriages, as part of a process that mirrored something of the reintroduction of *l'octroi* after 1798, in which the city was used to trial a tax that was then applied nationally. In 1863, the tax (*contribution sur les chevaux et les voitures*) was extended across the country, with 10 per cent of its revenue going to the commune in which the tax was collected and the rest to the central government as part of Fould's package of tax increases. The tax, though, quickly became controversial. In 1865, the government proposed that from 1866 all revenues from the tax would go to the *départements*, with the communes retaining their 10 per cent.[86] Instead, the Corps législatif's budget commission suggested abolishing it, a proposal Magne – then out of office but still an influential voice on financial questions – was willing to accept. Though justified as a tax on the rich, the navy minister noted, in reality it posed an electoral problem since the tax 'is far from applying only to the rich, [and] in the south it certainly hits a group of farmers who have

---

[86] 'Projet de loi portant fixation du budget général des dépenses et des recettes de l'exercice 1866' (titre I, §2, art. 8), *Le Moniteur universel*, 24 February 1865.

a small horse and a cart' – a core Bonapartist constituency. Indeed, the government had attempted to pre-empt this problem by granting exemptions to horses used exclusively for agriculture or for the work of professions liable for the *patente*.[87] Despite their unease over the tax, ministers deferred a decision on abolition, perhaps unwilling to reduce local government resources and feeling that they had sufficiently offloaded responsibility for the tax to avoid unwelcome repercussions.[88]

As with the *impôt sur les valeurs mobilières* which was also intended to target the rich, the *contribution sur les chevaux et les voitures* reflected a revival of what was effectively sumptuary taxation, in part for the sake of justifying increases to regressive indirect taxes on commodities such as salt, sugar and alcohol. These new taxes were to offer a means of preserving the legitimacy of the tax system without more radical fiscal reforms, not least the income tax, which some republicans and liberals demanded. When, in 1865, Garnier-Pagès advocated replacing the salt tax, surtaxes on indirect taxes and the *timbre* on newspapers with an income tax, Thiers denounced the latter, probably to the government's satisfaction.[89] Several liberal economists were similarly critical of such proposals, arguing that the incidence of indirect taxation could be equitably distributed.[90] The regime also avoided other means of taxing the wealthy. Death duties, used in Britain to tax the rich and thus legitimise a proportional income tax, were barely considered. The rise in inheritance tax imposed in 1850 as part of the increase to *l'enregistrement*, complained one deputy in 1859, amounted to 'encumber[ing] real estate that in certain cases is already so overburdened with taxes and debt'.[91] The recourse to sumptuary taxation offered a way of circumventing the tension in Bonapartist fiscal policy that arose from seeking to raise the burden on the rich while simultaneously cosseting land, a major asset of most wealthy people.

The *contribution sur les chevaux et les voitures* was part of the ongoing augmentation of local governments' resources so that they could become more effective instruments of the interventionist state. Faced with rising costs for urban renovation, the Parisian municipality introduced a *droit d'entrée* to the Bourse in 1856, a means of taxing financiers that preceded the *impôt sur les valeurs mobilières*, though the tax raised little revenue and

---

[87] Law of 2 July 1862, §2, arts. 6 and 8, *Lois*, LXII, 185–6, 188.
[88] Procès-verbaux, conseil des ministres, 6 May 1865, Rouher MSS, MAE, 232PAAP/13.
[89] Garnier-Pagès, 1 June 1865, Thiers, 2 June 1865, *Le Moniteur universel*, 2 and 3 June 1865.
[90] Silvant, 'Fiscalité et calcul économique'.
[91] Procès-verbaux, commission du budget, 25 February 1859, AN, C 1059.

was scrapped in 1861.[92] The annexation of the suburban communes in 1860 added substantially to the costs of rebuilding the city, given the need to integrate several relatively squalid areas.[93] Moreover, to forestall unrest, these acquisitions were initially exempt from the heavier Parisian *octroi*, further increasing the bill for the annexation. When the taxes were finally imposed in 1867, fierce discontent among manufacturers and workers forced Haussmann to lower *l'octroi* on coal; indeed, the end of exemptions was partly intended to deindustrialise the city by taxing raw materials such as coal, downsizing the potentially combustible Parisian working class, and thus continuing to address the alleged threat to public order that was one of the principal reasons for rebuilding the city.[94] Moreover, the extension of the boundary of *l'octroi* raised not only the municipality's revenue, but also that of the *droit d'entrée* collected for the central government.[95] Meanwhile, the city, like other municipalities, continued to enhance its resources through credit. The *département* of the Seine borrowed in 1857, while the municipality opened public subscriptions in 1860, 1865 and 1869, in addition to borrowing from the Crédit foncier.[96]

The recourse to debt and new taxes reflected new pressures to reduce *l'octroi*, partly arising from the trade liberalisation of the 1860s and which intensified later in the decade.[97] Cuts to *l'octroi*, wrote the *procureur général* in Agen, were 'the natural and necessary consequence of commercial liberty' given the internal barriers the tax imposed on trade and the costs to industry and urban residents.[98] Reducing *l'octroi*, however, was complicated by the expense of urban renovation. As the *procureur général* in Angers noted in 1870, people 'consider it fair that the inhabitants of towns sustain the expenditures from which they benefit' instead of relying on central government money.[99] *L'octroi*, therefore, remained indispensable; Paris aside, 1,529 communes raised a net revenue of 84,666,122 francs from the tax in 1866.[100] Indeed, revenue from the tax generally increased over the nineteenth century, in line with the growth of economic activity.[101] These pressures over the tax perhaps encouraged the central government, as part of an ongoing process of decentralisation, to renounce its

[92] Marion, *Histoire financière*, V, 379.   [93] Faure, 'Paris, 1860', 128–9, 136–47.
[94] Faure, 'L'Industriel et le politique', 54–62.
[95] Haussmann to Rouher, 15 September 1867, Rouher MSS, AN, 45AP/20.
[96] Massa-Gille, *Histoire des emprunts*.   [97] Cohen, *Urban Government*, 50–2.
[98] *Procureur général*, Agen, to Ollivier, 8 January 1870, AN, BB[30] 390.
[99] *Procureur général*, Angers, to Ollivier, 8 April 1870, AN, BB[30] 390.
[100] 'Produit des octrois en 1866', Thiers MSS, BT, MsT 555, fol. 23.
[101] Laurent, *Octroi de Dijon*.

control over *l'octroi* in 1867, a decision that was reinforced after 1871.[102] Given the difficulties with *l'octroi* and despite new indirect taxes, much local government finance continued to depend on direct taxation, not least because of the limitations of indirect taxation in some remoter areas. Even the relatively well-developed rural commune of Osthouse in the Bas-Rhin, for example, relied heavily on the *patente* for the growth of its revenues from the late 1850s.[103] The importance of direct taxes to local government probably encouraged government's focus on *l'enregistrement* as a means of easing the burden on land, since the *contribution foncière*, the principal direct tax, was essential to funding the growth of local government expenditure. With their new resources, not just in taxes but in the greater borrowing capacity provided by the Crédit foncier, local authorities could make a more significant contribution to public works than hitherto, easing the administrative decentralisation of the 1860s.[104]

Beyond stimulating attempts to improve the elasticity of local government finances, the pressure on taxation encouraged Fould's drive for economies. Thus, he sought to streamline the fiscal administration, continuing efforts made by Magne in the 1850s to reorganise the 'major finance services' of the ministry.[105] Most notably, in 1865, the receivers general were abolished and their functions merged with those of the *trésoriers payeurs généraux*, who were charged with overseeing government expenditure in each *département*.[106] The following year, Fould undertook a minor reorganisation of what one official described as the 'pretentious administration' of customs, continuing a gradual rationalisation initiated with the 1860 commercial treaty.[107] Indeed, the customs service had to be adapted to trade liberalisation and the ensuing decline in smuggling – though the latter experienced a resurgence in the late 1860s as the economic outlook deteriorated.[108]

The quest for economies placed particular pressure on the armed services. As Rouher, *ministre d'état* from 1863 to 1869 and briefly finance minister in 1867, observed:

> our financial position is tight. The balance of our budgets is difficult and contested ... To assure their balance, we did not resort to either borrowing or taxes. The sale of forests is condemned by an insurmountable prejudice.

[102] David, 'Les Octrois', 566–7.   [103] Igersheim, *Politique et administration*, 309.
[104] On the political decentralisation of the 1860s, see Hazareesingh, *Subject to Citizen*; Anceau, *Empire libéral*, I, 154–72.
[105] Magne to Baroche, 21 November 1860, Baroche MSS, BT, MsT 998, fol. 34.
[106] Pinaud, *Receveurs généraux*, 66–9.   [107] Trollard, *Mémoires*, 31–4.
[108] Clinquart, *Administration ... de 1848 à la Commune*, 356–8.

The only narrow and difficult path that remains to us is that of economies and the principal ones can only be done through a reduction of the armed forces on land and sea.[109]

Indeed, both Fould and Gladstone pressed lower military and naval expenditure on the other, each hoping to ease the politics of retrenchment in his own country. As Gladstone put it, 'There is evidently a little question between us – *who* is entitled to expect, & *who* is bound to make, a downward step in that huge hanch of expenditure which is connected with fleets and armies.'[110] However, not only did the war ministry resist cuts, but French foreign policy made lower military expenditure difficult, impeding economic liberalisation and hindering public works spending.[111] While one war – in Italy – pushed the government towards the commercial treaty, others – in Mexico and elsewhere – undermined the attendant programme of retrenchment. As Fould informed Gladstone in 1863, 'you are very happy to be able to relieve taxpayers so considerably; without the Mexican war I might have been able to do something similar and it would have been for the Emperor's government, certainly for the elections being prepared, a very favourable circumstance.'[112] The problem that the French intervention in Mexico presented for tax politics was apparent in Bordeaux, for example. Trade liberalisation being popular there, 'the Mexican expedition is judged severely... and the increase in the sugar duty has produced many malcontents.'[113] While French military action abroad during the 1860s was, as before, partly intended to glorify the regime, in hindering tax cuts it impeded the realisation of the benefits expected from trade liberalisation and contributed to discontent with the regime. Moreover, if military spending could not be reduced to lighten the fiscal burden, wrote the *procureur général* in Aix-en-Provence in 1868, then other expenditures should be, not least those concerning the 'incessant transformation of the big cities against which public opinion becomes more pronounced each day'.[114] Military spending thus threatened public works, a problem rendered more acute because the economic crises of the 1860s, given their effects on private finance, diluted the policy of delegation pursued in the 1850s.

[109] Note à l'empereur, by Rouher, n.d. [between 1863 and 1869], Rouher MSS, AN, 45AP/1.
[110] Gladstone to Fould, 29 December 1863, Gladstone MSS, BL, Add. MSS 44401, fol. 287. Emphases in the original.
[111] Randon, *Mémoires*, II, 107–18.
[112] Fould to Gladstone, 28 April 1863, Gladstone MSS, BL, Add. MSS 44400, fol. 214.
[113] Forcade to Persigny, 21 September 1862, Persigny MSS, AN, 44AP/11.
[114] *Procureur général*, Aix-en-Provence, to Baroche, 4 October 1868, AN, BB[30] 389.

The Political Economy of Global Military Interventionism

Though the French sought to minimise the costs of an aggressive foreign policy, they had limited success. The Italian wars of 1859–60 were expensive enough to force the government to suspend temporarily the amortisation of debt. The cost of interventionism abroad not only impeded tax cuts; it also required substantial borrowing. Given his incessant concern for the *dette flottante*, Magne was quick to issue *rentes* to cover the costs of the 1859 Italian war. In May, the government opened a public subscription for a loan of 500 million francs in 3 per cent and 4½ per cent *rentes* at 60.50 and 90 respectively.[115] While the subscription produced 2,307 million francs, it went less smoothly than previous ones.[116] Before it began, Hottinguer noted that 'we must not expect the same enthusiasm' as the loans of 1854–5 elicited, since 'the Bourse is badly shaken, and all securities continue to fall.'[117] Indeed, four days before the loan closed, Fould observed that 'until now the subscriptions arrive slowly.'[118] Alone, small investors were inadequate to fulfil the government's needs and 'the big ones wait for the end', a habit they developed 'to avoid causing a loss of interest' among investors.[119] While Fould still expected the subscription to raise twice the amount required, the difficulties on the Bourse pushed the real issuing rate of the 3 per cent *rente* from 4.34 per cent in 1855 to 4.95 per cent in 1859.[120] The minor anxieties that attended the 1859 subscription perhaps reinforced ministers' consciousness that this was not the only means of issuing *rentes*. Such doubts were probably increased by the Parisian municipality's difficulties with public subscription in 1860: having set the issuing rate too high, the municipality turned to the Rothschilds to rescue its loan.[121] Despite the successes of public subscription in the 1850s, when Fould undertook the next major *rente* issue in 1864 he considered both an adjudication and 'the American system where everybody fixes his price and the amount that he wishes to take in the loan. The minister having set his minimum in a sealed envelope, adjudicates all those that are above it, giving preference to those subscriptions that have offered the highest price.'[122] While Fould ultimately issued the 1864 loan by

[115] *Le Moniteur universel*, 4 May 1859.
[116] Rapport à l'empereur, by Magne, 16 May 1859, *Le Moniteur universel*, 17 May 1859.
[117] Jean-Henri Hottinguer to Baring, 3 May 1859, BA, HC 7.1.1188.
[118] Fould to Napoleon III, 11 May 1859, Fould MSS, AN, 247AP/1.
[119] Alphonse de Rothschild to his cousins, 28 January 1870, RAL, XI/109/101.
[120] Gille, *Rothschild*, II, 347.   [121] Massa-Gille, *Histoire des emprunts*, 261–4.
[122] Fould to Gladstone, 13 December 1863, Gladstone MSS, BL, Add. MSS 44401, fol. 256.

public subscription, raising 300 million in 3 per cent *rentes* at 66.30, he was to some degree pushed into this by the reluctance of bankers to resurrect the system of adjudication.[123] 'The *rente* is really at a very low price. . .' wrote Salomon de Rothschild in October 1863. 'The loan will be very difficult to do if it is to happen by adjudication, and I hope that the government will renounce this method, which has no advantage but to make the *rente* more expensive, and to put us in competition with a load of groups who are as capable as we are of doing the business.'[124] Rather than competing with other firms and thus paying more for *rentes* – unattractive since the latter were so low – speculation after a successful public subscription seemed more profitable. The difficulties on the Bourse left the government more desirous to offload some of the risk of a loan by adjudicating it to bankers, while leaving the latter less willing to bear this risk.

The time that elapsed between the loans of 1859 and 1864 caused some surprise, given the scale of government expenditure in that period. 'I cannot get it into my head that M. Fould does not need a loan,' wrote James de Rothschild in 1862, 'and that he will want to leave a *dette volante* [i.e. *flottante*] so long.'[125] Eventually, the growth of the *dette flottante* determined the need for the 1864 loan – which Fould labelled the 'Mexican loan', given the costs of the Mexican expedition.[126] While he appreciated the need 'to consolidate part of the *dette flottante*', his waiting until 1864 perhaps reflected his desire to avoid provoking renewed criticism of government borrowing.[127] Thus, instead of arranging a loan, soon after resuming office Fould sought economies by converting 4½ per cent and 4 per cent *rentes* and thirty-year bonds into 3 per cent *rentes*, as the ten-year guarantee of 4½ per cent *rentes* that had eased Bineau's conversion expired. Seeking to counter discontent and so facilitate the operation, the government used the Crédit foncier to provide communes and public institutions with annuities through which to finance the conversion.[128] Still, the dissatisfaction provoked by the conversion, which was treated to the usual criticism in the legislature, risked provoking a reduction in the numbers of small rentiers and thus mitigating the democratisation of public credit. Fould observed that some notaries, who often served as

[123] *Le Moniteur universel*, 14 January 1864.
[124] Salomon de Rothschild to his cousins, 17 October 1863, RAL, XI/109/85/3.
[125] James de Rothschild to his children, 11 January 1862, Rothschild MSS, ANMT, 132AQ/5902.
[126] Fould to Baroche, 27 September 1863, Baroche MSS, BT, MsT 980, fol. 82.
[127] Fould to Gladstone, 4 December 1863, Gladstone MSS, BL, Add. MSS 44401, fol. 229.
[128] Circular to the prefects, by Persigny, 12 February 1862, SAEF, B/57073.

brokers for small investors, were offering to relieve their clients of 4½ per cent *rentes* in exchange for other opportunities in shares; he demanded that they stop.[129] For the same reason, receivers general, another conduit for small investors, had already been temporarily banned from trading in shares.[130] The price of *rentes* probably increased Fould's anxiety over potential dumping. Both the 4½ per cent and 3 per cent *rentes* had been generally stable over the previous years, the former oscillating around the mid- to high 90s and the latter generally remaining in the mid- to high 60s, with only a slight fall during the 1859 Italian campaign. Still, the 4½ per cent *rente* touched par just before the conversion, and the government procured 157 million francs from the operation which, alongside Fould's tax increases, allowed it to defer a major loan.[131]

Despite this seeming stability, foreign policy imbued the *rente* with an underlying fragility, providing another reason to delay a loan until 1864. Bond prices in general were highly sensitive to war in the mid-nineteenth century, and the new Italian state imposed a further burden.[132] Like the French, the Sardinian government financed the Wars of Unification through credit, borrowing in London and Paris. As James de Rothschild noted, the large influx of Italian bonds on the Bourse left French investors 'too interested'; French *rentes* would only rise if Italian bonds did likewise.[133] Coming between the Italian wars, the Franco-British commercial treaty posed another complication. 'This treaty', wrote Hottinguer, '& Italian politics stop financial affairs as they do commercial affairs,' given the political and fiscal uncertainties they created.[134]

The Sardinians bought French assistance with 60 million francs and the surrender of Nice and Savoy. These territories were taken in the hope of surmounting popular discontent with the peace terms Napoleon had agreed with Austria in 1859 at Villafranca, in which he had obtained Lombardy for Sardinia. While the annexations produced the favourable public reaction that Napoleon desired, the territories had to be integrated into France, a process complicated by Sardinian resistance.[135] The officer sent to arrange the incorporation of Savoyard and Niçois troops into the French army was received with 'little good grace' in Turin, for

[129] Fould to Delangle, February 1862, AN, BB³⁰ 458. [130] Gille, *Rothschild*, II, 390.
[131] Marion, *Histoire financière*, V, 442–5.
[132] Ferguson, 'Political Risk and the International Bond Market', 79–83.
[133] James de Rothschild to his children, 25 December 1861, Rothschild MSS, ANMT, 132AQ/5902.
[134] Jean-Henri Hottinguer to Baring, 27 February 1860, BA, HC 7.1.1210.
[135] Case, *French Opinion on War and Diplomacy*, 118–23.

instance.[136] Still, the commander of the gendarmerie in the Savoie noted that population accepted the transition from Sardinian to French law 'without any opposition' and was 'very satisfied' that the French military conscripted fewer men than its Sardinian counterpart.[137] Fiscal integration, however, was more difficult. Like the legal system, taxation in Piedmont had been heavily shaped by Napoleon I, but it had never been identical to that of France and, moreover, the two had diverged since 1815. The litany of minor differences sufficed to produce discontent. While the *contribution foncière* was repartitioned in both states, for example, the French applied it to all land whereas the Piedmontese granted greater exceptions to rural farms.[138] Meanwhile, those artisans and small businesspeople who found themselves subjected to a heavier *patente* – the Piedmontese schedules differed from the French – and more indirect taxes were inevitably displeased.[139] Customs presented another problem. After 1815, the Swiss had obtained from France and Sardinia the creation of a 'neutral' customs area around Geneva, furthering the economic integration of the city and northern Savoy. To deflect the ensuing agitation of some in northern Savoy to join Switzerland, the plebiscite endorsing the annexation backed a '*grande zone*', incorporating the territory into France while allowing the Genevans to retain their privileged customs arrangement with Savoy.[140] Likewise, the prospective reduction of trade barriers stimulated Niçois support for annexation. Still, incorporation into the larger French market, with its increasing openness to international trade, imposed costs. One Savoyard leather business, for example, complained of the influx of foreign competition, while access to its former Italian market was more complicated than before.[141] As the customs issue suggests, annexation raised potentially expensive expectations of greater prosperity. Thus, the mayor of Chambéry, emphasising the penury and indebtedness of his town following Sardinian neglect, sought assistance from the new French prefect to finance urban renovations.[142] Though the government provided impoverished towns with meagre credits for construction projects, the

---

[136] Randon to Saget, 26 June 1860, SHD, 3G 1.
[137] Commin to Randon, 26 May 1865, SHD, 3G 94.   [138] Lovie, *La Savoie*, 80–1, 385.
[139] Commin to Randon, 26 May 1865, SHD, 3G 94.
[140] Clinquart, *Administration ... de 1848 à la Commune*, 131–6.
[141] *Directeur des contributions indirectes*, Chambéry, to the prefect of the Savoie, 12 August 1861, AD, Savoie, Chambéry, 2FS/10.
[142] 'Note de M. le maire de Chambéry sur la situation financière et les besoins de la ville', 24 August 1860, Billault MSS, AD, Loire-Atlantique, 20J/28, dossier 2, fols. 12–14.

abolition of the gabelle, a relic of the *ancien régime* administered alongside *l'octroi*, eroded municipal revenues.[143] The government compensated for tax reductions such as this by raising *centimes additionnels* and, in 1861, authorising loans for the new *départements*.[144] Indeed, with the annexation, Savoyard *départements* and communes probably secured better access to credit, benefiting from the Crédit foncier. Using credit and *centimes additionnels*, local authorities undertook some improvements to roads and railways in the annexed territories, beyond which the central government also had to fund the construction or modification of military installations.[145]

The issuing rights of the Banque de Savoie presented a further complication. Since the 1857 law had renewed the privilege of the Banque de France without explicitly granting it a monopoly, the Banque de Savoie raised the possibility of a system of free banking, much to the Banque de France's displeasure. Not wishing to alienate Savoyard opinion, the government was wary of taking a harsh line on the Banque de Savoie, especially since unification with France had been sold partly on the promise of economic prosperity. As negotiations to merge the two issuing banks foundered in the aftermath of annexation, the Banque de Savoie announced its intention of opening branches elsewhere in France. Losing ground in the ongoing railway competition to the Paris–Lyon–Marseille company, the Pereires concluded an arrangement with the Banque de Savoie in 1862–3 to raise its capital from 4 to 40 million francs, funds which would be used chiefly for railway finance. While Rouher may have given the project lukewarm support, Fould was firmly opposed, committed to defending the position of the Banque de France from which he was then in the process of soliciting 50 million francs. Indeed, the weight of government expenditure in the 1860s and the recourse to the *dette flottante* entailed a considerable reliance on the Banque. The Pereires' contract with the Banque de Savoie was therefore nullified, and the Banque bought its rival's privilege for 4 million francs in 1864.[146] Thus, the integration of Nice and Savoy into the French fiscal-military system was essentially completed.

The Italian wars were about European geopolitics, ultimately intended to strengthen France in Europe even if they did the opposite, producing an Italy disgruntled about the loss of Nice and Savoy and encouraging German unification. The Second Empire's extra-European imperialism is less easily explained. In part, it comprised a series of reactions against a

[143] AD, Savoie, 2FS/20; decree of 8 September 1860, *Lois*, LX, 505.
[144] Decree of 30 December 1860, *Lois*, LXI, 12–13.   [145] Lovie, *La Savoie*, 204–23.
[146] Plessis, *Politique de la Banque*, 261–6; Bouvier, 'Les Pereire et l'affaire de la Banque de Savoie'.

rapidly changing global order, not least the expansion of the British Empire, for the sake of reinforcing French prestige. Extra-European action was also intended to strengthen France in Europe, on which French security depended, not least by extending French commerce, a factor that historians have often underplayed.[147] On one level, therefore, intervention abroad reflected the mid-nineteenth-century state's aim of promoting French economic development, even if this motivation alone was generally insufficient to justify military action. As with the economic interventionism of the Bonapartist state, the push to extend French commercial interests abroad maintained the priorities of Orleanist policy, as did the continuing increases in naval spending necessary to pursue global power. Moreover, the development of French commerce outside Europe dovetailed with the policy of extending it in Europe through the commercial treaties of the 1860s and the formation of the LMU.

The other major rationale offered for extra-European intervention was Catholicism, which was often invoked in tandem with commerce. Thus, while scholars have recently presented the French intervention in Syria in 1860 as driven by humanitarianism following massacres of Christians, economic considerations were also important.[148] Not only did the French want to mitigate Ottoman opposition to the Suez Canal by gaining leverage in Syria, they also wished to pacify a region that offered a potential source of raw silk, silk prices in France having risen following a fall in production. Commerce aside, the intervention offered means of potentially extending French influence in the Mediterranean by developing a pro-French Syrian state, effectively reviving the Near Eastern policy that had provoked the crisis of 1840, with Syria reprising Egypt's role.[149]

Commerce was likewise a motivation for French intervention in the Far East which, as with policy in the Near East, reflected the Orleanist legacy. While in 1843 the value of Sino-French trade did not exceed 2 million francs, Guizot expected this to increase with the British opening of Chinese ports through the 1842 Treaty of Nanjing, not least because of rising French demand for such commodities as tea.[150] Thus, he sent an emissary to China to obtain for the French the same commercial rights as the British – acquired through a Sino-French treaty in 1844 – and to research Chinese commercial law in the hope of boosting French textile

---

[147] On the importance of commerce in the Second Empire's imperialism: Todd, 'Imperial Meridian', 173–85.

[148] Bass, *Freedom's Battle*, 155–232.   [149] Émerit, 'Crise syrienne'.

[150] Rapport au roi, by Guizot, 23 April 1843, MAE, 15MD/4, fols. 121–5.

exports.[151] The Second Empire continued to pursue the extension of French commerce in China; 'the Catholic question', wrote Charles de Chassiron, sent on an extraordinary mission to the Far East, 'must not, at least for the present, preoccupy the French government'. Instead, trade should take priority.[152] Thus, the French concluded commercial treaties with Siam in 1856 and with Japan in 1858, increasing French imports of Japanese raw silk.[153]

As with the Syrian intervention, historians have overstated the importance of Catholicism as a driver of French imperialism in the Far East.[154] Though, in 1857, the regime took the execution of a French missionary in Guangdong as reason to join the British in the Second Opium War against China, the government was delighted to obtain commercial concessions when it concluded a peace treaty with the Chinese in 1860.[155] Indeed, as with the Levant and Japan, China became increasingly important as a source of raw silk for French industry from the late 1850s.[156] Likewise, while the execution of two Catholic missionaries in 1857 prompted France's initial intervention in Cochinchina, the ministry of agriculture, commerce and public works was represented alongside the navy and foreign ministries on the committee formed to consider the matter.[157] The resulting expedition gave the French knowledge of, among other things, 'the nature and the variety of the products to be given to trade' there.[158] Moreover, besides having commercial potential of its own, Indochina's location made it a good staging post from which to extend French economic interests in China.[159]

The aspiration to develop commerce in East Asia probably reinforced the government's commitment to the Suez Canal, but French economic activity in the region never rivalled that of Britain or the United States. As one pessimist observed, 'we have in the Far East only very minimal interests compared to England.'[160] Hence, for some advocates of a global policy, Catholicism seemed a better cause than commerce.[161] As the debate among policymakers over the rationale for interventionism

[151] Guizot to Lagrené, 9 November 1843, MAE, 15MD/4, fols. 130–9.
[152] Chassiron to Baroche, 28 August 1858, Baroche MSS, BT, MsT 1468/D.
[153] Polak, *Soie et lumières*, 27–9.   [154] E.g. Martin, *Empire renaissant*, 233–49.
[155] 'Note sur le traité de 1860 avec la Chine annotée par l'Empereur', n.d.[1860s], Napoleon MSS, AN, 400AP/42 dossier 3.
[156] Todd, *Velvet Empire*, 164–5.
[157] Rouher to Walewski, 15 April 1857, MAE, 8MD/27, fol. 303.
[158] Randon to Montauban, 28 February 1860, SHD, 5G 1.
[159] Kang, *Francophonie en Orient*, 38–44.   [160] Note, 20 March 1857, MAE, 8MD/27, fol. 298.
[161] Bruley, *Quai d'Orsay impérial*, 204.

suggests, no single cause was sufficient to necessitate action in the Far East. Perhaps the principal attraction was the prestige France accrued from simulating global interests to match Britain's. Furthermore, as with the 1860 commercial treaty, Franco-British cooperation in China offered a means of lubricating the British relationship.

Given the weakness of arguments in favour of foreign interventions, these actions abroad had to be cheap, particularly given the pressure for retrenchment in France. Faced with the massacres in Syria, Napoleon wrote, 'my first thought was to collaborate with England ... I really wanted not to go alone into Syria, firstly because this will be a great expense and secondly because I fear that this intervention will affect the Eastern Question.'[162] Partly to push the British into participation, Napoleon sought to turn intervention in Syria into a European action.[163] The British, though, refused to join, leaving the French with the full costs. Indeed, Napoleon's unilateral intervention, alongside the resumption of war in Italy, reinforced the logic that had brought them into the commercial treaty, that France's armed forces should be downsized. At the same time, though, their refusal to join the intervention impeded reductions to French military spending, at least immediately. Principally to fund military action abroad, the government raised extraordinary and supplementary credits totalling 352 million francs in 1860–1, while the decision to leave a garrison in Rome from 1861 to 1870 added further costs.[164] In the Far East, however, the French were more successful than in Syria, not only in securing Franco-British cooperation, but in offloading the costs. In 1860, the French imposed an indemnity of 52 million francs on the Chinese to cover the costs of their intervention, while in 1862 they levied another indemnity of 10.8 million francs on the Cochinchinese.

An indemnity, though, was insufficient in Cochinchina, over which the French established a protectorate in 1863, despite reservations in Paris over the costs. 'I would dread the expenses of a prolonged occupation,' Fould wrote.[165] Cochinchina cost 60 million francs in 1860, an expense inflated by the intervention in China, which fell to 57 million in 1862 and then to 22 million in 1863, before stabilising at around 19–20 million a year thereafter.[166] Still, the 'men on the spot' having established the protectorate, it then had to be governed. For this, the system of the *bureaux arabes*

[162] Napoleon III to Persigny, 25 July 1860, Persigny MSS, AN, 44AP/6.
[163] Echard, *Napoleon III and the Concert of Europe*, 129–40.
[164] Marion, *Histoire financière*, V, 425–8.
[165] Fould to Baroche, 18 September 1864, Baroche MSS, BT, MsT 980, fol. 102.
[166] Silvestre, 'Politique française dans l'Indochine', 313.

used to oversee the Algerian tribes served as the initial model, though the expense of Algeria made it an otherwise unattractive blueprint.[167] Seeking to minimise costs, the French sought to raise revenues. One of Cochinchina's governors noted that its main source of wealth was agriculture, which could be developed. The French also could benefit, he wrote, from European penetration of Cochinchina's internal trade: 'the expenses that will fall to the metropole will be largely compensated by the development of its commerce and its merchant marine in these waters.'[168] Such compensation clearly lay in the future; Cochinchina remained in deficit into the Third Republic. Still, revenue there rose quickly, as the French imposed new taxes. Most notably, in 1861, they established a monopoly on opium that eventually came to provide over half the colony's revenue.[169] Such measures limited losses in Indochina, though the colony was too small to be a major expense in any case.

If Syria, China and Cochinchina were minor financial sinks, Algeria and Mexico were more serious. Algeria continued to expand in the 1850s as Marshal Randon, governor-general from 1852 to 1858, conquered Kabylia, which helped to increase colonial tax revenues under the Second Empire. Indeed, by the mid-1850s, receipts were enough to make the *recette générale* of Algiers, in one observer's eyes, almost as valuable as its small French counterparts.[170] As in Cochinchina, the government pursued the economic development of Algeria, which would make the colony profitable, or at least self-sustaining – which was essential given the financial pressures the government faced. Thus, the Bonapartists maintained the Orleanist commitment to extending credit through the development of financial institutions; in 1860, the minister for Algeria and the colonies sought to stimulate the colonial economies through the creation of a Société de crédit colonial, 'which alone can save our colonies'.[171] For the same purpose, restrictions on colonial trade were also relaxed, following a similar logic to that used to justify the 1860 Franco-British commercial treaty. In 1863, Napoleon proposed to develop Algeria as a *royaume arabe*, with greater autonomy for the Algerians that would enhance economic prosperity and so ease the cost of empire for France.

[167] Chasseloup-Laubat to Charner, 10 January and 26 May 1861, and to Bonard, 25 August 1861, Chasseloup-Laubat MSS, AN, 230Mi/1.

[168] 'Note sur les ressources des trois provinces de la Basse Cochinchine', by La Grandière, n.d. [between 1863 and 1868], Rouher MSS, AN, 45AP/17.

[169] Descours-Gatin, *Quand l'opium finançait la colonisation*, 27–8; Vial, *Cochinchine française*.

[170] Bouqueney to Persigny, 11 September 1857, Persigny MSS, AN, 44AP/11.

[171] Chasseloup-Laubat to Magne, 11 September 1860, Chasseloup-Laubat MSS, AN, 230Mi/1.

He sought to improve Algerians' affluence, strengthening their property rights and thereby boosting their creditworthiness and interest in economic development.[172] Moreover, in exchange for land, he proposed to extract military service from the Algerians, lessening the burden on the French army. The projected *royaume arabe*, though, attracted fierce criticism, not least from European settlers in Algeria. Their generally violent expropriation of Algerian land would have to stop to realise Napoleon's vision of Algerian prosperity. Faced with resistance from colonists and their supporters in metropolitan France, the policy had little impact. Instead, the government resorted to seeking private investment to pursue public works, as it did in metropolitan France. In 1866, ministers facilitated the creation of the Société générale algérienne, a joint-stock company to finance Algerian economic development, which contributed to a boom in public works in the late 1860s.[173] Nevertheless, despite such efforts to stimulate its economy, Algeria continued to drain resources. From 1849 to 1870, the colony cost 1,493,521,651 francs more than it produced in tax receipts, a deficit that was on average 23.3 per cent greater per year than between 1831 and 1848 when adjusted for inflation.[174]

Though less expensive than Algeria, the attempt to install the Habsburg archduke Maximilian as emperor of Mexico also entailed substantial outlays of over 363 million francs.[175] Ostensibly, French, Spanish and British intervention in Mexico at the end of 1861 was justified by the Mexican government's default on foreign debts. As with other overseas ventures during the 1860s, though, commerce was also a factor, as it had been in the restored Bourbons' interest in the Americas; the Orleanists, too, had intervened in Latin America, not least in Mexico, for the sake of extending French commerce.[176] With 'regeneration', wrote Napoleon, Mexico 'would form an impassable barrier to the encroachments of North America, it would offer an important outlet for English, Spanish and French commerce, in exploiting its own wealth; finally, it would render a great service to our factories by extending its cultivation of cotton'.[177] Indeed, with the fall of American cotton exports during the civil war, the

[172] Napoleon III to Malakoff, 6 February 1863, *Le Moniteur universel*, 7 February 1863.
[173] Rey-Goldzeiguer, *Royaume arabe*.   [174] Douël, *Un siècle de finances coloniales*, 202.
[175] *Le Moniteur universel*, 25 June 1867. A further 31,713,000 francs were spent on a range of overseas actions encompassing Mexico, China, Japan, Indochina and Syria, but the navy ministry was unable to disaggregate these expenditures.
[176] Morgan, 'French Policy in Spanish America'. There is a large literature on French involvement in Mexico before 1861; e.g. Shawcross, *France, Mexico and Informal Empire*.
[177] Napoleon III to Flahaut, 12 October 1861, Rouher MSS, MAE, 232PAAP/10.

Europeans sought new sources. The silver shortages of the late 1850s and early 1860s provided another reason for the intervention, given Mexico's renowned deposits of precious metals. Thus, French imports of Mexican silver increased markedly during the 1860s.[178] On one level, the Mexican expedition was supposed to replicate the intervention in China. Undertaken in concert with the British and the Spanish, it was to showcase Franco-British cooperation at little net financial cost – given the expectation of indemnity – while potentially securing commercial and political benefits.

The British, however, did not support Maximilian's installation as emperor, despite French efforts to secure their backing for the enterprise, leaving France as the only great power committed to intervention after 1862. Moreover, though Maximilian agreed to reimburse the costs of the intervention, as in the Far East, his regime never had the means to fulfil this commitment. The French struggled to extract the resources they needed, fuelling the fears in Paris about the costs of establishing a protectorate in Cochinchina.[179] While the French imposed whatever control they could over the Mexican fiscal system, at least ostensibly they continued to seek Maximilian's approval to impose taxes, for example, and he did not always adhere to French demands. Already before the French intervention, the Mexican fiscal system had been inadequate – hence, in part, the default that prompted the initial expedition. The civil war in which the French found themselves embroiled during the intervention, as republicans resisted the imposition of the empire, undermined attempts to impose more effective taxation. Maximilian's government therefore borrowed, floating two loans in 1864 and 1865 at a high risk premium with 6 per cent bonds issued at real rates of 14.43 per cent and 15.6–16.49 per cent respectively. The French reclaimed a portion of these loans to cover Mexico's obligations to them, while some of the money also went to the victims of the 1861 default; of the 534 million francs nominally issued, only 34 million went to Maximilian's government.[180] Using the network of receivers general, the loans relied heavily on French small investors, giving the 'middle class' to whom the liberalisation of the Second Empire in the 1860s was partly meant to appeal a greater stake in Mexico.[181] Faced with the rising unpopularity of the Mexican expedition and the taxes it

[178] Black, *Mexican Silver*.   [179] Brocheux and Hémery, *Indochine*, 34–5.
[180] Fould to Randon, 27 October 1864 and 14 March 1865, MAE, 31MD/8, fols. 122–3, 139; Topik, 'When Mexico Had the Blues', 719; Gille, 'Capitaux français', 207.
[181] SAEF, B/32495.

necessitated in France and growing pressure from the United States following the end of its civil war, Napoleon decided to withdraw in 1866. The last French troops left Mexico in 1867 and Maximilian's regime collapsed shortly afterwards.

The Mexican debacle ended Napoleon's flirtation with military interventionism abroad. Not until the 1880s would France resurrect its aspirations to global power. Presented in 1866 with an American invitation to join an expedition to extract a commercial treaty from Korea, the costs of which would be covered by an indemnity, Napoleon refused, noting 'the disgust of opinion with distant expeditions'.[182] Still, the 'men on the spot' in East Asia, responding to the execution of French missionaries and seeking to check Russian advances towards the Pacific, orchestrated an expedition later that year, but to little effect.[183] While these interventions may appear to mark a striking departure in French foreign policy, they arose from policies the Bonapartists inherited from their Orleanist predecessors; French overseas interventions under the Second Empire largely occurred in places that the French had begun to penetrate under the July Monarchy if not before. As with the foreign policy of previous regimes, the interventionism of the 1860s suited the constraints of the post-1815 fiscal-military system insofar as the latter did not need to be overhauled, but the expense imposed an increasingly unpalatable burden particularly when taken in tandem with the French government's other expenditures. Still, cost was not the only factor shaping public opinion towards action abroad; competence was also an issue. While Algeria was the most expensive overseas commitment of the Second Empire, failure in Mexico had a greater impact on French domestic politics in the late 1860s. Whereas Frenchmen were generally accustomed to the burdens of Algeria, which could be ascribed to the legacy of previous regimes, many associated the Mexican expedition with the Second Empire, and its humiliating outcome reinforced public discontent with Napoleon's foreign policy.[184] As in the 1820s and the 1840s, therefore, interventions abroad stimulated opposition demands to streamline the state while preventing Fould from satisfying these demands. Recounting the growth of public expenditure during the Second Empire and listing the taxes that had been raised or introduced as a result, Thiers told the Corps législatif in 1864 that 'you have a series of taxes that are all taxes of war'; these, he declared, needed to 'disappear',

[182] Proces-verbaux, conseil des ministres, 23 March 1866, Rouher MSS, AN, 45AP/1.
[183] Roux, *La Croix, la baleine et le canon*, 308–27.   [184] Greenfield, 'Mexican Expedition'.

along with the aggressive foreign policy that had necessitated them.[185] The growing dissatisfaction and mounting pressures on the fiscal-military system gradually eroded its legitimacy, and thus that of the regime, hindering French preparedness for the challenge of 1870.

The Crisis of the Fiscal-Military System

The decision to withdraw from Mexico coincided with a deterioration in European international relations, exacerbating the crisis of the French fiscal-military system that arose from the Mexican debacle and further constraining Napoleon's capacity for action abroad.[186] Prussia's defeat of Austria in 1866 transformed the balance of power in Germany and thus in central Europe. Having expected an indecisive Austro-Prussian war, which would then end with French intervention or mediation to preserve a balance of power in Germany, Napoleon found his foreign policy upended. 'Italy, Germany unified, will grip us in their arms,' Thiers fumed; a united Germany 'will be a formidable enemy, too strong perhaps against us; for it will be the struggle of 38 million Frenchmen against 50 million Germans exhilarated by the idea of unity'.[187] Rouher, briefly taking control of foreign policy, contemplated rescuing the situation by annexing Belgium and Luxembourg, overlooking the rupture this would cause with Britain. In exchange for Prussian consent to these acquisitions, Rouher offered 'an offensive and defensive alliance'.[188] But against what might Prussia need French protection? Austria was defeated, Russia was amicable, Britain was quiescent. The only threat came from France. Prussia, therefore, was being asked to make concessions to defuse Franco-Prussian tensions. This may have had some attraction in Berlin, but not for the price that Napoleon and Rouher demanded.

The domestic political outlook also darkened. Already in 1865, Fould worried that commerce was slowing, as loans for Mexico and the Parisian municipality drained the market of money.[189] Indeed, the sharp increase in the number of foreign government securities quoted on the Bourse since

---

[185] Thiers, 6 May 1864, *Le Moniteur universel*, 6 and 7 May 1864.

[186] The decision to withdraw from Mexico was publicised before the Austro-Prussian War, though the government subsequently accelerated its initial withdrawal timetable, probably in part because of the domestic and international crises that arose over Europe in addition to continuing pressure from the United States and Mexican guerrillas.

[187] Thiers to Saint-Hilaire, 31 July 1866, Thiers MSS, BT, MsT 561(2), fol. 30. Thiers's figure for the German population was somewhat exaggerated.

[188] Rouher to Benedetti, 16 August 1866, Rouher MSS, MAE, 232PAAP/1.

[189] Fould to Baroche, 28 August 1865, Baroche MSS, BT, MsT 980, fol. 119.

1860, with Italian, Russian, Ottoman, Tunisian and Austrian in addition to Mexican loans, raised questions about exactly how much control Villèle's 1823 ordonnance allowed the government. From 1852 to mid-1865, the Bourse funded a nominal 8,000 million francs of French railway securities, 5,000 million of French government loans and 4,000 million each of foreign government loans and foreign railway shares and bonds – 19,000 million francs in total, equal to 90.9 per cent of France's GDP in 1865.[190] As the *directeur du mouvement général des fonds* observed, while opening the Bourse to foreign government securities 'procures very productive investments for our nationals' and 'can be a means of political influence by interesting foreign governments in the stability of our institutions', it entails 'exports of specie that impoverish for a long time our metal reserves and thus contributes to raising interest rates'.[191] The LMU exacerbated this problem by encouraging capital exports. The ensuing concerns over specie pushed the Banque to bolster its reserves, which rose substantially from 300 million francs in mid-1864 to 500 million a year later and 1,300 million by September 1868.[192] A financial crisis in 1866, triggered by the failure of Overend, Gurney in London a month before the outbreak of Austro-Prussian hostilities, reinforced the desire for reserves, as did unease over the impending war. While matters were less severe in Paris than in London, financiers remained anxious. Rodolphe Hottinguer, having taken control of the family firm following his father's death in March, wrote that 'the war which seems inevitable will push capitalists to remit their money to a country with the fortune of being outside these terrible political crises.'[193] Growing difficulties at the Crédit mobilier compounded the turmoil in the City and concerns about war, though the bank, finally granted permission in 1866 to double its capital, staved off crisis until September 1867.[194] A few months thereafter, the republican Jules Ferry delivered a cause célèbre with a searing indictment of the municipal Parisian finances.[195] These economic difficulties,

---

[190] Note, 'Des emprunts d'États', *direction du mouvement général des fonds*, 19 May 1865, Rouher MSS, AN 45AP/20; Toutain, 'Produit intérieur brut'. The *direction du mouvement général des fonds* gives 21,000 million francs as the total, a figure that does not appear to correspond with the others provided in the document.

[191] Note pour le ministre, by the *directeur du mouvement général des fonds*, 12 January 1866, SAEF, B/65766.

[192] Plessis, *Politique de la Banque*, 307–14.

[193] Rodolphe Hottinguer to Baring, 6 June 1866, BA, HC 7.1.1436.

[194] *La Presse*, 20 May, 11 and 22 June 1866; Rodolphe Hottinguer to Baring, 23 June 1866, BA, HC 7.1.1438.

[195] Ferry, *Comptes fantastiques d'Haussmann*.

exacerbated by the continuing weight of taxation, undermined the regime's reputation for economic competence. In the meantime, manifestations of popular discontent increased. In 1864, the government repealed the prohibition of workers' unionisation, seeking to buttress its appeal among the working classes in part to compensate for the hostility it faced from industrialists over trade liberalisation.[196] Thus, the regime facilitated the strikes that replaced subsistence riots as the principal form of popular protest during the Second Empire. Though frequently caused by wages and working conditions, the strikes often reflected a myriad of grievances, and became more numerous and increasingly militant in the later 1860s.[197] The sluggishness of certain sectors of the economy and rising discontent over foreign policy contributed to the government's losses in the elections of 1869, which pushed the regime to further liberalisation, with greater power for the legislature enshrined in a new constitution that was ratified by plebiscite in May 1870.

Economic and diplomatic problems aggravated the strains on the legitimacy of the fiscal-military system. Being levied mostly on commodities of mass consumption with relatively inelastic demand, indirect tax revenues were undiminished (Figure 9.2), but economic malaise reduced the capacity of taxpayers and increased discontent with the fiscal system, though this seldom translated into unrest. Still, public pressure for spending cuts, which would translate into lower taxes, seems to have increased, while debate around tariffs and indirect taxes such as *l'octroi* became more animated. One economist, for example, proposed to stimulate commerce by abolishing *l'octroi*, the costs of which could be covered by cutting the military budget.[198] Indeed, liberal reforms such as decentralisation, wrote the *procureur général* in Caen in 1870, mattered less to the 'great mass of voters' than those changes 'destined to favour the prosperity of the countryside through the reduction of several taxes' and 'the revision of railway fares', to which the 'Liberal Empire' was committed.[199] Several other *procureurs généraux* likewise noted this popular desire for economies in public expenditure. Given the costs of public works and interventionism abroad, the more authoritarian Empire of the early and mid-1860s had failed to produce economies, or at least the appearance of them, a problem which the new 'Liberal Empire' was expected to rectify.

[196] Glineur, 'Coalitions ouvrières'. [197] Price, *People and Politics*, 338–56.
[198] Bonnal, *De l'abolition et du remplacement des octrois*.
[199] *Procureur général*, Caen, to Ollivier, 11 July 1870, AN, BB[30] 390.

Faced with the unpopularity of military spending, which war-weariness arising over Mexico intensified, the government's plans for military reform faltered. Already, the army's shortcomings in the Crimea and Italy, apparent in the heavy losses incurred during both campaigns, had spurred moves towards military reform, for instance producing a law to end replacement in 1855 and plans for the reconstitution of the reserve in 1861. The effectiveness of the Prussian army in 1866, which rapidly mobilised 356,000 men, gave new impetus to reform; given the deployment of troops abroad, only 250,000 were ready to defend metropolitan France. Besides the introduction of the new breach-loading *chassepot* rifle, Napoleon backed proposals for broader military service to create an army of 1.2 million men, which would include a reserve alongside a *garde mobile* partly modelled on the Prussian Landwehr. Thus, the army would revert towards Saint-Cyr's vision of 1818, reconstituting something of the reserve that had been abolished in 1824. The ongoing quest for economies guaranteed the plan a frosty reception in the finance ministry. 'We will only evidently attain the objective we propose if we do not compromise the finances which will always be the sinews of war,' Fould wrote.[200] Seeking a means of mitigating public discontent over military reform, in 1866 Napoleon asked him about the possibility of reducing taxes while simultaneously accelerating public works, both of which entailed further spending.[201] Napoleon likewise faced opposition in the war ministry. Preferring to retain a relatively professional army, Randon, now the war minister, resigned in protest. His replacement, Marshal Niel, who presented the reform to the Corps législatif, was also less inclined than Napoleon to overhaul the military system. Consequently, the government ultimately eschewed comprehensive reform. Replacement was to be reinstated for the reserve and, while a *garde mobile* was to be created, it would amount to two weeks of annual service for five years; active service, too, was to fall to five years. Even this timid plan was lambasted in the Corps législatif, eliciting criticism from conservatives who feared the consequences of arming the masses, from opposition liberals who saw the enlargement of the army as threatening state oppression and from republicans who advocated universal conscription. The government therefore withdrew the bill, reintroducing a diluted version that permitted replacement even for the *garde mobile*, which the legislature approved in January 1868. Though the government's initial plan had lauded the *garde mobile* as

---

[200] Fould to Baroche, 20 September 1866, Baroche MSS, BT, MsT 980, fol. 160.
[201] Procès-verbaux, conseil des ministres, 28 September 1866, Rouher MSS, AN, 45AP/1.

inexpensive, a lack of money impeded its creation and General Lebœuf, Niel's successor in 1869, was content to let it decay.[202]

Despite its shortcomings, the reform created the mistaken public impression that the army was ready for war. Perhaps more seriously, the army law debate exacerbated the legitimacy problems facing the regime following the global military interventionism of the 1860s. Widely vilified as irresponsible, the Mexican expedition in particular raised fears that a larger army would encourage the regime's aggression abroad. Opposition politicians exploited the debate to seek a more consultative political system as a means of restraining unpopular foreign escapades. Moreover, the army reform also increased the pressure for the liberalisation of the Empire by raising the prospect of higher military spending.[203] The legitimacy crisis of the fiscal-military system hindered its capacity to mobilise the resources necessary to counter the Prussian threat. Not only was universal military service shelved, but the continuing pressure for retrenchment impeded the fortification of the border that would allow a smaller French army to resist more effectively its larger German adversary.[204]

Public credit looked stronger than the tax or military systems in the late 1860s, though it too had shortcomings. In January 1867, Rouher became finance minister, succeeding Fould whose departure, wrote Hottinguer, 'arouses fears of a loan that he had always opposed'.[205] The continued agitation of the Bourse following the 1866 crisis perhaps reinforced some investors' wariness of a loan. Still, in November 1867, Magne resumed the finance ministry and his crusade against the *dette flottante*. The latter having grown over the previous years, Magne regarded its reduction, particularly the government's account with the Crédit foncier, as an 'absolute necessity & urgent'; his zeal was such that he felt the need to compel the *directeur du mouvement général des fonds*.[206] To redeem some of the *dette flottante* and to expedite the modernisation of the army and navy, border fortifications and public works, the government opened a public subscription in August 1868 for 429 million francs, raising a potential capital of 15,000 million francs in 3 per cent *rentes* at 69.25.[207] This success benefited from the sluggishness of the Bourse in the late 1860s. The financial crises of 1866–7 and rising international tensions created a

---

[202] *Le Moniteur universel*, 12 December 1866; Crépin, *Défendre la France*, 275–314; Casevitz, *Une loi manquée*.

[203] Greenfield, 'Mexican Expedition', 678–80.   [204] Holmes, *Road to Sedan*, 154–6.

[205] Rodolphe Hottinguer to Baring, 24 January 1867, BA, HC 7.1.1445.

[206] Magne to Baroche, 8 and 17 September 1868, Baroche MSS, BT, MsT 1063, fols. 65–6, 69–70.

[207] *Le Moniteur universel*, 3 and 15 August 1868.

climate of uncertainty, leaving investors cautious. Given the improbability of a government default, the *rente* became a safe haven, allowing the loan to be issued at a relatively high price.

The triumph of public credit in 1868, the limitations of military reform and the continuing pressure for tax cuts underscore the strengths and weaknesses of the French fiscal-military system at the outbreak of the Franco-Prussian War. The appointment in January 1870 of Ollivier as justice minister and de facto leader of the government, with a programme 'for liberty and against licentiousness', was fiscally inconsequential.[208] The unveiling of the 'Liberal Empire' merely reaffirmed the regime's existing commitment to retrenchment. Though Napoleon hoped to retain Magne, his successors changed little.[209] The new finance minister, the centre-left deputy Louis Buffet, resigned in April over the plebiscite and was replaced by Alexis Segris, a regular on the Corps législatif's budget commissions. For 1871, Segris presented a budget of further economies that Magne had prepared at the end of 1868, inter alia reducing the war ministry's budget by 13 million francs.[210] The quest for retrenchment was likewise apparent in French proposals for Franco-Prussian disarmament in early 1870, though these were also intended to help improve relations with Britain, which had deteriorated as tensions over Belgium and Luxembourg had intensified after 1866.[211]

Despite the problems the fiscal system faced in the late 1860s, it performed admirably until the collapse of the Second Empire. After the outbreak of Franco-Prussian hostilities on 19 July 1870, Segris reassured Ollivier: 'Do not worry about the financial side. Our measures are taken, in general I am not unhappy.'[212] Not wanting to depress the *rente*, and thus precipitate a fall in other securities, Segris sought to finance the war through short-term treasury bills.[213] Yet, as Alphonse de Rothschild observed, these were woefully insufficient to raise the funds the government needed, particularly since the outbreak of war increased investors' caution.[214] When Magne reluctantly resumed the finance ministry in August after Ollivier's government collapsed following early military defeats, he faced a deteriorating financial situation. As Rothschild's attitude suggests, investors were unenthusiastic about Segris's treasury bills, while

[208] Duruy to Ollivier, 17 January 1870, Ollivier MSS, AN, 542AP/12.
[209] Durieux, *Magne*, II, 156, 170–1.   [210] *Le Moniteur universel*, 5 July 1870.
[211] Daru to La Valette, 13 February 1870, in *Origines diplomatiques*, XXVI, no. 7931.
[212] Segris to Ollivier, 1 August 1870, Ollivier MSS, MAE, 127PAAP/1, fol. 73.
[213] Segris to Ollivier, 30 May 1871, Ollivier MSS, AN, 542AP/17.
[214] Alphonse de Rothschild to his cousins, 4 August 1870, RAL, XI/109/102B.

depositors were pulling their savings from the *caisses d'épargne*, curtailing another source of credit.[215] Magne, therefore, unveiled a public subscription for 750 million francs in 3 per cent *rentes* at 60.60, permitting investors in Segris's bills to convert.[216] Meanwhile, minor reductions to *l'enregistrement* and customs duties in the budget were revoked.

The outcome of the subscription was 'marvellous', given that the Prussians occupied 'part of our provinces'.[217] By contrast, an early Prussian public subscription proved unsuccessful, the outbreak of war having brought the Berlin financial market to near-panic; only in the wake of victories in early August did Prussian credit improve.[218] Indeed, given these victories, the French loan's success was fleeting. France lacked sufficient troops and its military leadership was ineffectual, which contributed to a fatally chaotic mobilisation and thereafter demoralised the army. This ineptitude exacerbated the regime's legitimacy crisis, which was then compounded by the defeats of early August. Concerns over the regime's survival pushed Napoleon and his troops into their disastrous march to Sedan in late August, the more militarily sensible option of withdrawal towards Paris being deemed politically suicidal.

Napoleon's surrender at Sedan on 2 September precipitated the proclamation of the Third Republic two days later. Lacking reserves to replace their losses, French forces retreated, disintegrating, while the Prussians besieged Paris. Nevertheless, the Republic determined to continue the war, for which more money was essential. Investors, though, were understandably wary. From 72.62½ on 1 July, the 3 per cent *rente* fell to 54 following the proclamation of the Republic and remained in the low 50s thereafter (Figure 9.3).[219] The Bourse, wrote Alphonse de Rothschild, was 'nominal' since investors felt unable to sell *rentes* at such a loss.[220] The ensuing financial crisis acquired mythic status. Indeed, it became a point of reference in July 1914, as the markets faced the possibility of the First World War, with 'old traders' complaining that the financial crisis of that month represented something unseen since 1870.[221] Already, the outbreak of war had pushed investors to pull their money from the market. Deposits in the Crédit lyonnais, for example, fell from 60 million francs on 30 June 1870 to 23 million by 31 August, not rising above 24 million for the rest of

---

[215] Durieux, *Magne*, II, 196–204; *Le Moniteur universel*, 19 August 1870.
[216] *Le Moniteur universel*, 22 August 1870.
[217] Alphonse de Rothschild to his cousins, 24 August 1870, RAL, XI/109/102B.
[218] Stern, *Gold and Iron*, 130–1.   [219] *Le Moniteur universel*, 2 July and 6 September 1870.
[220] Alphonse de Rothschild to his cousins, 5 and 12 September 1870, RAL, XI/109/102B.
[221] Robert de Rothschild to his cousins, 25 July [1914], RAL, XI/101/103/69.

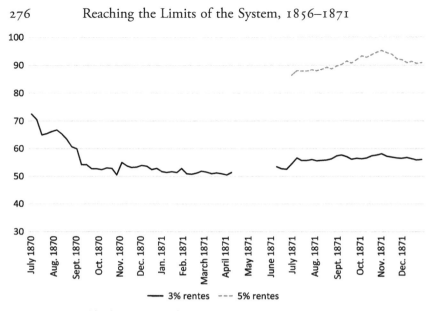

Figure 9.3   Weekly closing prices of *rentes*, as quoted in Paris, July 1870–December 1871.
(Source: *Le Moniteur universel*)

the year.[222] Sedan and the ensuing siege of Paris exacerbated the situation. The Paris Bourse, integral to European finance only days earlier, imploded, leaving London as 'the only' market where operations such as government loans could be undertaken 'with some success'.[223] Needing credit, and facing resistance to further advances from the Banque, the government therefore despatched an emissary to London in October. The City, however, proved reluctant. The Rothschilds refused to engage, while Barings had already underwritten a Prussian loan. Instead, Laurier, the interior minister, and Germiny, a former finance minister and regent and ex-governor of the Banque de France, negotiated 250 million francs in November from the Anglo-American firm of J.S. Morgan, which saw in the operation an opportunity to broaden their business. Given the seizure in the market for *rentes*, and since borrowing in these would risk further depressing the 3 per cent, the loan was contracted in fifteen-year 6 per cent bonds issued at 85.[224] The collapse of the Paris Bourse was so severe that

[222] Bouvier, *Crédit lyonnais*, I, 192.
[223] Crédit lyonnais to N.M. Rothschild and Sons, 10 January 1871, RAL, XI/38/68A.
[224] Boreau-Lajanadie, *Rapport fait au nom de la commission*; Carosso, *The Morgans*, 131–3.

the Crédit lyonnais established an agency in London to facilitate its participation in the loan.[225]

The government contracted the Morgan loan with the intention of conversion as soon as the price of *rentes* allowed. A rise in the latter, though, was effectively contingent on peace; the Morgan loan, in other words, was short-term war finance. Still, a preliminary peace in February 1871 did not produce an immediate boon for French finances, since the terms entailed an indemnity, ultimately of 5,000 million francs, in addition to the costs of a German army of occupation and the loss of Alsace-Lorraine. The size of the indemnity provoked doubts that French government credit was sufficient to borrow on the scale required, prompting a short-lived suggestion in London that the British government should underwrite part of the necessary loans.[226] Moreover, the Paris Commune, lasting from March to May, alongside unrest in cities such as Lyon, did nothing to raise the *rente* and deeply worried many of the French elite. Still, some financiers, at least, were not unduly concerned. As one wrote in late March, 'I do not doubt that before the 30 June the political situation of France will be stable again and will present complete security to capital invested in business.'[227] Benefiting from such sentiments, the government sought to arrange a loan as quickly as possible. Besides the desire for a quick end to the German occupation, noted the governor of the Banque de France, if the loan were not arranged before the budget were presented to the legislature, the government risked having to negotiate it alongside the deputies' 'too eloquent exposition of our poverty and our [financial] embarrassments', which could unsettle investors. Moreover, during the last three years, he wrote, capital had generally been underemployed, yielding only a low rate of return; investors thus had an appetite for a potentially profitable loan.[228]

Unwilling to issue 3 per cent *rentes*, then still in the low 50s, and thus incur a nominal debt of nearly 10,000 million francs to finance the reparations, in June the French government unveiled a loan of 2,000 million francs in 5 per cent *rentes*.[229] These were issued at 82.5 by public subscription, with the second 1,000 million francs guaranteed by the Rothschilds and their associates who also floated the *rentes* abroad.[230] The terms of the loan were sufficiently generous that it received

[225] Bouvier, *Crédit lyonnais*, I, 197–200.
[226] Broglie to Thiers, 2 and 11 March 1871, Thiers MSS, BNF, NAF 20621, fols. 70–80.
[227] Schall to André, 28 March 1871, Neuflize MSS, ANMT, 44AQ/4.
[228] Rouland to Thiers, 13 March 1871, Thiers MSS, BNF, NAF 20623, fol. 38.
[229] Alphonse de Rothschild to his cousins, 18 February 1871, RAL, XI/109/104.
[230] Gille, 'Emprunts de libération'.

subscriptions worth nearly nearly 5,000 million francs on the day that it opened, with 2,500 million francs coming from investors in Paris, 1,300 million from those in provincial France and 1,100 million from those abroad.[231] Reintroduced after its withdrawal from circulation in the 1852 debt conversion, the 5 per cent *rente* proved attractive to speculators seeking a profit. Though the 3 per cent *rente* rose in tandem with the 5 per cent following the success of the loan (Figure 9.3), the 3 per cent was less attractive to speculators. By September, its price having exceeded 90, the 5 per cent *rente* yielded 'a margin of around 10 francs . . . There is, it seems,' wrote an agent of the Crédit lyonnais, 'a campaign to raise the loan [i.e. the 5 per cent] at the expense of its 3 per cent counterpart.'[232] A similar speculative dynamic facilitated the success of a further subscription for 3,000 million francs in 1872, for which the government also offered generous terms. As before, the third 1,000 million was guaranteed by the bankers, while the loan was issued at 84.5, a rate which some contemporaries judged as too low.[233] Hottinguer worried that it risked an 'artificial success', with the loan being covered by speculators who would seek to sell.[234] Despite such fears, the speculation that followed the flotation did not produce much downward pressure on the *rente*. In total, the subscriptions were worth 43,000 million francs, a sum no doubt inflated by investors exaggerating their bids as they sought to secure a share in the loan, which reflected sufficient demand to sustain the *rente*.[235] While the issuing rate and the recourse to 5 per cent *rentes* reflected ongoing caution about French creditworthiness, that France could borrow on such a scale so soon after the devastating defeat of 1870 and the trauma of *l'année terrible* was a striking achievement. The success of the loans of 1871–2 demonstrated brilliantly the potential of the financial system that France had developed since the Restoration.

Conclusion

While the fiscal-military system ultimately changed little during the Second Empire, the advent of universal suffrage continued to reshape tax politics. Though the difficulties over repartition that had hitherto impeded major reform to direct taxation remained in any case, the regime's reliance on rural voters reinforced the preference of landed interests for higher

---

[231] *Le Moniteur universel*, 2 July 1871.
[232] Crédit lyonnais to N.M. Rothschild and Sons, 11 September 1871, RAL, XI/38/68A.
[233] Gille, 'Emprunts de libération'.
[234] Rodolphe Hottinguer to Baring, 26 July 1872, BA, HC 7.1.1548.
[235] Marion, *Histoire financière*, V, 571.

taxation on commerce and industry. While the regime's most fiscally consequential tax reform was the liberalisation of trade, which benefited some industries, the government compensated for the fall in customs duties with sharp increases in revenue from other indirect taxes in the 1860s. Likewise, rising revenues from the *patente*, too, reflected a shift of the fiscal burden towards industry and commerce. Beyond taxing industry, the regime's fiscal reforms reflected a departure from the consensus that had emerged since the First Empire. Sumptuary taxation, a feature of the fiscal politics of the 1790s until its abolition under the Consulate, effectively reappeared, though, as before, it made little impact on tax receipts. Still, both in the 1790s and in the 1850s and 1860s, sumptuary taxation was a response to doubts about the legitimacy of the fiscal system, fears that consent was at risk. For those such as Fould, this problem should be addressed by streamlining the state; by contrast, others, such as Persigny, preferred greater economic interventionism that would legitimise the state by making it the agent of prosperity.

Growing economic problems in the 1860s, though, impeded Fould's ambitions for retrenchment, contributing not only to the resurgence of government spending on public works but to the regime's willingness to intervene abroad militarily. The costs of an aggressive foreign policy, particularly in Algeria and Mexico, and the failure in the latter exacerbated the legitimacy problems of the fiscal-military system that Fould's proposals for retrenchment had aimed to resolve. While these difficulties stimulated the liberalisation of the Empire as the regime sought to reconstitute its political capital, the legitimacy issue was only resolved by the Republic in the 1870s, when the legislature asserted its primacy over the executive, imposing the kind of oversight that opposition politicians demanded in the 1860s. Executive power under the Empire, one deputy observed in 1871, meant that 'parliament could not discharge its mission to control' spending, facilitating profligacy.[236] Consequently, Thiers, who became president of the Republic in 1871, reinforced the legislature's control over finance. The growth of public expenditure in the 1860s was therefore one factor, among others, that expedited the creation of parliamentary democracy in France. Moreover, though the politics of public finance remained contentious, the gradual renewal of the state's legitimacy under the Third Republic eased the accelerated growth of public expenditure in the late nineteenth century.[237]

[236] Riant, 14 September 1871, *Le Journal officiel de la République française*, 15 September 1871.
[237] Sawyer, 'Fiscal Revolution', 1161–3.

CHAPTER 10

The Triumph of the Notables

Despite the upheavals of the nineteenth century, the French fiscal system evolved gradually, in a process of incremental change. The most dramatic transformation came with the 1789 Revolution, given the abolition of privilege on 4 August. The ensuing overhaul of taxation, argued the liberal republican Léon Say in 1887, marked 'the apotheosis of Turgot' as the Constituent Assembly decided that 'taxes should be impersonal, and consequently applied only on visible wealth and give no opening to any arbitrary act in their collection.'[1] This is not to say that he saw no difference either side of 1789. The new taxes, in contrast to those of the *ancien régime*, were to be uniformly and universally applied. Unable to fulfil this vision, the governments of the 1790s failed to create a stable system of direct taxation, stimulating the resurgence of indirect taxation under the Directory and Napoleon, which drew on the legacy of the *ancien régime*. René Stourm, a friend of Say who served as an *inspecteur des finances* and then became Magne's *chef de cabinet* in 1868, wrote in 1885 that 'the origin of our financial institutions dates to the *ancien régime*. Numerous regulations still in force are modelled on the code of the *fermes générales*.'[2] After the Consulate, according to this narrative, the 'immobilism' of the fiscal system became entrenched, leaving it essentially unchanged for the rest of the nineteenth century.

As we have seen, such an interpretation has its limits. The fiscal system was in a state of flux between 1789 and 1815; only during the Restoration was it entrenched. Nevertheless, the Revolutionary and Napoleonic eras were decisive in establishing most of the taxes and institutions of the nineteenth-century fiscal constitution and in shaping the conception of the fiscal system that largely determined subsequent reform. Thus, in rationalising the Franco-British commercial treaty of 1860, for example,

---

[1] Say, *Turgot*, 190.
[2] Stourm, *Finances de l'ancien régime*, II, 501; Cardoni et al., *Dictionnaire historique*, 427, 937–8.

Rouher and Baroche cited Turgot and Mollien as authorities.[3] Say, a serial finance minister during the Third Republic, sought retrenchment, freer trade and lower taxes to stimulate enterprise, hence his interest in Turgot.[4] From the Consulate onwards, fiscal policy was distinguished by gradual reform, as successive governments sought to implement what they regarded as the ideals inaugurated by the quarter-century after 1789 in a manner conducive to the stability of the sociopolitical order. Despite historians' tendency to dismiss the years 1815–70 as a parenthesis, an 'age of revolution' comprising a succession of unstable reactionary governments, the fiscal policy of the period was generally consistent, though it shifted slightly under different regimes. The Orleanists in the 1830s proved more willing than the restored Bourbons after 1815 to raise direct taxes. Despite these variations, the politics of public finance to an extent reflected Tocqueville's famous claim that the Revolution of 1789 facilitated continuity, marking a stage in a process of administrative centralisation that began with Louis XIV and lasted long into the nineteenth century.[5] Simultaneously, the history of public finance demonstrates some of the limits to Tocqueville's depiction of an excessively centralised French state. Most notably, local governments were crucial to financing public works and poor relief and their autonomy in these respects grew during the mid-century as their resources increased. Local government, and thus a degree of decentralisation, was essential to the nineteenth-century state's economic interventionism, which paradoxically encouraged the notion of an overbearing central state.

In regarding the regimes of 1815–70 as inherently flawed, historians have explained the longevity of the Third Republic by deeming its politics to have been fundamentally different, overlooking the continuities between the Republic and previous regimes. Daniel Halévy influentially characterised the 1870s as heralding 'the end of the *notables*', as the *République des ducs* gave way to a republican consensus, genuinely making the Republic into 'the government that divides us the least', as Thiers famously put it in 1850.[6] The *seize mai* crisis of 1877, when the royalist president of the Republic, Patrice de MacMahon, dismissed the republican *président du conseil* Jules Simon only to have the voters return a reduced but still republican majority in the National Assembly, marked the

---

[3] Rapport à l'Empereur, by Baroche and Rouher, 24 January 1860, *Le Moniteur universel*, 11 March 1860.
[4] Garrigues, 'Léon Say et le centre gauche.'   [5] Tocqueville, *L'Ancien régime et la Révolution*.
[6] Halévy, *Fin des notables*.

triumph both of the legislature over the executive and of the Republic over monarchy. The republican victory settled the question of the balance of power between the legislature and the executive that had encouraged the liberalisation of the Empire in the 1860s. In this respect, 1870–1 marked less a caesura than the continuation of a process of political reconstruction that culminated in a parliamentary regime. Just as historians such as Sudhir Hazareesingh and Philip Nord have shown that the Republic's political culture arose from that of the Second Empire, the republican state emerged from the legitimacy crisis that beset the Bonapartist regime in its final years.[7] Likewise, the reform of the fiscal-military system after 1871 showed notable continuities between the Second Empire and the Third Republic.

The new republican elites sanctioned the continuing growth of government expenditure and in so doing buttressed the politics of public finance that the *notables* had championed since the Napoleonic era. As with previous regime changes, the survival of finance ministry personnel eased continuity in fiscal policy and, in 1873–4, Magne returned as minister. With the support of such men, the architects of a conservative republic discarded the republican programme of fiscal reform honed since the 1840s, rebuffing the income tax that had been its centrepiece. While many of the Republic's founders were former Orleanists, the Opportunist Republicans who dominated politics in the 1880s proved similarly committed to the established fiscal system. The economist Paul Leroy-Beaulieu was indicative of this shift against income tax, having supported it in the 1870s as a route to fairer taxation, before reversing his position.[8] In 1881, he argued that income tax in states such as Britain and Prussia had demonstrated how few great fortunes existed, and did little to redistribute wealth; echoing old arguments, he claimed that taxation was about raising money, not redressing 'social inequality'.[9] Instead, to finance the sharp increase of public spending in the 1870s, the growth of which accelerated in subsequent decades, the Republic used indirect taxes. As previous regimes had done, the republicans appealed to rural voters, avoiding higher land taxes. The Third Republic thus fulfilled the Second's reputation for high taxes, just with indirect taxation instead of the *45 centimes*, and the fiscal system sustained over the previous decades by the *notables* to serve their interests as a landed elite survived. Given the accusations of profligacy

---

[7] Hazareesingh, *Subject to Citizen*; Nord, *Republican Moment*.
[8] Delalande, *Batailles de l'impôt*, 63.
[9] Leroy-Beaulieu, *Essai sur la répartition des richesses*, 527–45, 555–6, 564.

levelled against the Second Empire, the Republic was established, like the Restoration, July Monarchy and Second Republic, amid pressure to streamline the state, and republicans subsequently lauded themselves as having done so.[10] The tax increases of the 1870s were less about financing a permanent expansion of the state but, rather, were largely intended to expedite the amortisation of the debt contracted in 1871–2; in 1871, the finance minister even suggested that this could be repaid in fifteen years.[11]

The recovery of public credit, apparent in the loans of 1871–2, eased the stabilisation of the fiscal system. As in 1817–18, borrowing mitigated pressure on the tax system, allowing the government to forgo fundamental reforms while maintaining a sufficient degree of consent to taxation. The republicans' programme of raising indirect taxes entailed a reaction against the trade liberalisation of the 1860s; Thiers and Augustin Pouyer-Quertier, a former Rouen textile magnate who served as finance minister from 1871 to 1872, were both committed protectionists and sought to raise revenue through higher customs duties, though with limited success.[12] Meanwhile, hoping that their reputations as protectionists would reassure industrialists that higher indirect taxes would not benefit foreign competition, they sought to raise duties on textiles, which Pouyer-Quertier considered to be the most equitable tax since the rich used many more clothes than the poor.[13] Yet, their plan failed, since their means for taxing textiles, a new *impôt sur les matières premières*, provoked fierce opposition from industrialists and only passed in the Assembly with a much lower duty than Thiers and Pouyer-Quertier wanted.[14] While the government nevertheless pursued customs negotiations with the British, only in the 1880s was there a marked resurgence of protectionism. In 1882, the 1860 trade treaty lapsed and the liberalisation of European trade it had inaugurated began to recede.

With the failure to introduce supposedly less regressive indirect taxation, the Republic resorted to the expedients of the Second Empire. Thus, most of the supposedly temporary tax increases of the 1850s and 1860s were retained or raised. Moreover, as in the 1850s and 1860s, many tax increases in the 1870s were directed at commerce and industry, not least

[10] E.g. *Le Siècle*, 31 August 1877.
[11] Pouyer-Quertier to Thiers, 17 June 1871, Thiers MSS, BNF, NAF 20622, fols. 263–4.
[12] Smith, *Tariff Reform*, 34–9. While Thiers sought to raise tariffs, he needed British consent for this since he had no wish to repudiate the 1860 Franco-British commercial treaty, and thus risk souring relations with Britain. The treaty revisions were finalised in 1872.
[13] Pouyer-Quertier to Thiers, 17 June 1871, Thiers MSS, BNF, NAF 20622, fols. 263–4.
[14] Marion, *Histoire financière*, V, 555–8.

through a new 3 per cent tax on revenue from securities, the *impôt sur le revenu des valeurs mobilières*, established in 1872.[15] New taxes also targeted luxury. In 1871, for example, the government introduced a tax on billiards, which were used by many people of all social groups, and consequently had the potential to raise substantial sums. At the same time, billiards could be labelled a luxury and the tax would therefore be 'voluntary', in a manner reminiscent of the debates on indirect taxation of the Revolution or the Consulate.[16] The indirect taxes of the Republic, like those of the Second Empire, reflected the growing democratisation of politics in the mid-nineteenth century. Pushed to cultivate a wider electorate, a major part of tax politics lay in mitigating the discontent that could arise from an increasingly regressive fiscal system – hence the re-emergence of sumptuary taxation under the Second Empire. As after the Crimean War, therefore, the alternative to income tax after 1871 was to tax industry and luxury. Despite the alleged 'immobilism' of the fiscal system, it evolved considerably over the course of the century, the rise of sumptuary taxation being one of the more notable shifts.

To facilitate the entrenchment of the existing fiscal system, the Republic established its conservative credentials. Likewise, the reform of the army, which had proved ill-designed for the *guerre à outrance* that the Republic proclaimed after Sedan, reinforced the new regime – as after 1815. Between 1872 and 1875, a series of compromises produced a new system of more universal conscription, which overcame the long-standing aversion to military service and refashioned the army as an object of French national pride.[17] The Republic thus ensured its survival by remaking the fiscal-military system in line with conservative nationalism. Moreover, just as the army was remade into the school of the nation, the expansion of the interventionist state, and the emergence of the early welfare state – apparent, for instance, in education provision – encouraged the transformation of 'peasants into Frenchmen'. As the growth of nationalism accelerated under the Republic, the concept of the 'nation' acquired greater prominence in the politics of taxation, offering the state new means to justify the burdens of the fiscal-military system.[18] In increasing the resources available to the government, the higher taxation that ensued eased the state's continued economic interventionism, allowing the Third Republic to build on the foundations laid by the Orleanist and Bonapartist regimes. The reparations of 1871–2 drained the French economy of investment, a

[15] Hissung-Convert, *Spéculation boursière*, 454–8.   [16] Burgaud, 'Taxation du plaisir'.
[17] Chanet, *Vers l'armée nouvelle*.   [18] Delalande, *Batailles de l'impôt*, especially 55–62, 98–104.

problem compounded by an international financial crisis in 1873 which produced protracted economic stagnation, stimulating state interventionism to mitigate the consequences.[19]

The continuities in fiscal politics allow us to reconsider the way in which historians have tended to present each of the regimes of 1815–70 as ideologically distinct, largely following René Rémond's tripartite conception of the French right.[20] In this reading of the nineteenth century, the ultras offered the most authentic representation of the Restoration, with their commitment to decentralisation, paternalistic hierarchy and a romantic attachment to the absolutist past. The July Monarchy was the regime of political liberty, parliamentarianism, and social conservatism sustained by a 'gouvernement à bon marché'. Finally, the more nationalistic Second Empire was the rule of populist authoritarianism, with a more interventionist economic policy determined by Saint-Simonian technocrats. However, this schema is too clear-cut. As Rémond himself noted, for instance, the liberal Empire of the late 1860s was fairly 'Orleanist' in favouring greater political liberties and parliamentarianism. With regard to political economy, the differences between successive regimes should not be overstated. In public works, for example, the differences materialised gradually. While government spending on public works increased in the 1830s, only after 1839 did it really surge. Moreover, the paternalism of many ultras was not necessarily averse to economic interventionism. The similarities in the political economy of the July Monarchy and the Second Empire were more pronounced, with both regimes committed to interventionism. The Saint-Simonians may have promoted notions of public investment, but they did not have a monopoly on these ideas, and there is no reason to think they had an outsize influence on Bonapartist economic policy. While historians have seen proof of the regime's Saint-Simonianism in the Crédit mobilier, for example, the company was founded by bankers to make money: it was not a primarily ideological project.[21] In short, the economic policies of these three regimes are not indicative of three divergent traditions. There were differences but, certainly between the July Monarchy and the Second Empire, these were relatively small.

As the state's economic interventionism suggests, the case of nineteenth-century France is not merely one in which 'war made the state,' to use

---

[19] Lévy-Leboyer and Bourguignon, *Économie française au XIXe siècle*, 236–9; Breton et al., *Longue stagnation*.
[20] Rémond, *Droite en France*.   [21] Dansette, *Naissance*, 98–108; Greenfield, 'Crédit mobilier'.

Charles Tilly's famous phrase.[22] While war, not least the Revolutionary, Napoleonic, Crimean and Franco-Prussian wars, stimulated state formation, too narrow a focus on war tends to overemphasise the importance of central at the expense of local government and overlooks socio-economic developments such as the emergence of a national market and the extension of communications, which expedited the democratisation that further reshaped the state as French elites sought to contain the risk of revolution. This counter-revolutionary tendency was crucial to reforming the state. Indeed, despite historians' emphasis on revolution, neither that of 1830 nor that of 1848, though they unleashed pressure for reform, produced a lasting overhaul of the state. The advent of universal suffrage in 1848 was momentous, but its importance should not be overstated. Though a regime of limited suffrage, the July Monarchy was highly sensitive to public opinion, not least because of the unrest it faced in the 1830s. Moreover, many of the newly enfranchised only gradually grew accustomed to voting, while governments either side of 1848 remained committed to controlling the electoral process. Meanwhile, the fiscal-military system and the structure of the state remained largely unaltered. Still, as government spending increased and as the French population became increasingly politicised, complaints about the post-revolutionary consensus that underlay the fiscal system amplified. While the fiscal system survived the 1870s, under the Third Republic its legitimacy was increasingly challenged, producing protracted debates that culminated in the passage of an income tax in 1914, which was collected from 1916 onwards. Given the development of an embryonic welfare state by the end of the century and the growth of military spending in the years preceding the First World War, the solution to discontent pursued by those such as Fould in the 1860s, of seeking to streamline the state and reduce taxes, became untenable. In this respect, the growth of the state eased the demise of the post-revolutionary fiscal system that had made higher public spending possible in the first place.

---

[22] Tilly, 'History of European State-Making', 42.

References

Archives

Archives de la Banque de France, Paris

1069199608   Papiers des gouverneurs de la Banque
1069199609   Relations Banque de France/Trésor
1069200401   Correspondance, organisation etc. de la Banque

Archives départementales de la Savoie, Chambéry

2FS   Fonds dit de l'annexion de 1860

Archives départementales de la Loire-Atlantique, Nantes

20J   Billault MSS
P   Finances, impôts, cadastre

Archives départementales de la Mayenne, Laval

P   Finances, impôts, cadastre

Archives départementales de la Vendée, La Roche-sur-Yon

M   Administration générale
P   Finances, impôts, cadastre

Archives départementales des Pyrénées-Atlantiques, Pau

M   Administration générale

Archives départementales du Nord, Lille

M   Administration générale

Archives du Ministère des Affaires étrangères, La Courneuve

60PAAP	Desages MSS
413PAAP	Miot de Mélito MSS
127PAAP	Ollivier MSS
232PAAP	Rouher MSS
177PAAP	Walewski MSS
1ADC	Affaires diverses commerciales
5ADP	Affaires diverses politiques, Angleterre
27ADP	Affaires diverses politiques, Espagne
7MD	Mémoires et documents, Angleterre
8MD	Mémoires et documents, Asie
11MD	Mémoires et documents, Belgique
15MD	Mémoires et documents, Chine
22MD	Mémoires et documents, Grèce
31MD	Mémoires et documents, Mexique
53MD	Mémoires et documents, France

Archives générales du Royaume, Brussels

I586   Vendôme-Nemours MSS

Archives nationales, Pierrefitte-sur-Seine

40AP	Beugnot MSS
230Mi	Chasseloup-Laubat MSS
226AP	Clauzel MSS
359AP	Clermont-Tonnerre MSS
2AP	Duchâtel MSS
124AP	Eymard MSS
247AP	Fould MSS
61AQ	Greffulhe MSS
42AP	Guizot MSS
232AP	Lainé MSS
300AP(III)	Maison de France MSS
726Mi	Molé MSS

542AP	Ollivier MSS
44AP	Persigny MSS
29AP	Rœderer MSS
45AP	Rouher MSS
558AP	Siméon MSS
400AP	Napoléon MSS
AF/III	Directoire exécutif
AF/IV	Secrétairerie d'État impériale et cabinet de Napoléon Ier
AF/V	Secrétairerie d'État royale provisoire et Secrétairerie des conseils
BB^{18}	Ministère de la justice: correspondance générale de la division criminelle
BB^{30}	Ministère de la justice: versements divers
C	Assemblées nationales
F^{1cl}	Esprit public
$F^3(II)$	Ministère de l'intérieur: administration communale. Série départementale
F^7	Ministère de l'intérieur: police générale
F^{12}	Commerce et industrie
F^{15}	Hospices et secours

Archives nationales du monde du travail, Roubaix

44AQ	Neuflize MSS
132AQ	Rothschild MSS
68AQ	Thuret MSS

Baring Archive, London

HC 7	House Correspondence, France

Bank of England Archive, London

14A185	Dobrée MSS

Bibliothèque de l'Arsenal, Paris

Ms 7601–7861	Enfantin MSS
Ms 13728–17359	Saint-Simonian MSS

Bibliothèque interuniversitaire de la Sorbonne, Paris

MSRIC   Richelieu MSS

Bibliothèque nationale de France, Paris

NAF 23064–6   Persigny MSS
NAF 20280   Richelieu MSS
NAF 24605–14   Saint-Simonian MSS
NAF 20601–84   Thiers MSS

Bibliothèque Thiers, Paris

Ms T 1339–86 ter   Barante MSS
Ms T 960–1243   Baroche MSS
Ms T 1–661   Thiers MSS

British Library, London

Add. MSS 43647–78   Cobden MSS
Add. MSS 44086–835   Gladstone MSS
Add. MSS 48417–589   Palmerston MSS
Add. MSS 36714–29   Panizzi MSS

Hartley Library, University of Southampton

PP   Palmerston MSS

London Metropolitan Archives

CLC/B/110 (Ms 19031–223)   Hambro MSS

National Archives, Kew

FO 146   France: General correspondence

Rothschild Archive, London

'T files'   Transcripts of Rothschild correspondence
XI/38/68A   Crédit lyonnais, 1870–4
XI/82/6   Correspondence from Lionel and Nathaniel de
             Rothschild, 1831–2

XI/85   Business Correspondence from de Rothschild frères,
         1810–1935
XI/101   Correspondence from de Rothschild frères, 1837–1918
XI/109   Private Correspondence Sundry, 1814–1913

Service des archives économiques et financières, Savigny-le-Temple

B/14935, 56971   Dossiers des caisses d'épargne
B/65766   Valeurs mobilières et produits d'épargne
B/65767   Fiscalité des valeurs mobilières
B/67458, 67459   Inspection générale des finances
B/57073   Mouvement général des fonds
B/32495   Direction des finances extérieures

Service historique de la Défense, Vincennes
Service historique de l'armée de terre

1K 598   Martimprey MSS
1H   Algérie, 1830–1964
1M   Mémoires et reconnaissances
3D   Correspondance générale, 1815–30
3G   Armée d'Italie, 1859–60
5G   Expédition de Chine, 1858–64
8G   Correspondance générale, 1852–70

Service historique de la marine

BB^1 Décisions, rapports au roi, 1789–1870

Stadsarchief, Amsterdam

735   Hope & Co. MSS

Newspapers and Periodicals

Le Constitutionnel
The Economist
La Gazette de France
Le Globe
Le Journal des débats
Le Journal du commerce

Le Journal du commerce de la ville de Lyon et du département du Rhône
Le Journal officiel de la République française
Le Moniteur universel
Le National
La Presse
La Revue des deux mondes
Le Siècle
The Times

Official Publications

Les Origines diplomatiques de la guerre de 1870–1871, 29 vols. (Paris, 1910–32).
Présentation des comptes de finances et règlement du budget définitif du budget de [1818–1821], 4 vols. (Paris, 1819–23).
Présentation des comptes de finances; règlement définitif du budget de [1822–1827]; ouverture de crédits supplémentaires sur l'exercice [1823–1828]; fixation des dépenses et des recettes de [1826–1830], 5 vols. (Paris, 1824–9).
Projet de loi portant règlement définitif du budget de l'exercice de [1842–1938], 97 vols. (Paris, 1844–1939).
Proposition de loi pour le règlement définitif du budget de l'exercice de [1828–1841], 16 vols. (Paris, 1830–43).
Proposition de loi pour le règlement des budgets de 1815, 1816, 1817 et la rectification provisoire de celui de 1818 (Paris, 1819).

Printed Primary Sources

Albarèdes, P.-B. d', *Mémoires du baron Portal (Pierre-Barthélemy d'Albarèdes): contenant ses plans d'organisation de la puissance navale de la France* (Paris, 1846).
[Anon.], *Élection de Louis-Napoléon Bonaparte, président de la République française élu par le peuple et proclamé par l'Assemblée nationale, le 20 décembre 1848* (Paris, 1849).
[Anon.], *Réflexions sur les 280 millions de francs qui restent à payer aux puissances étrangères (4 juin)* (Paris, [1818]).
Audiffret, C.L.G. d', *La Crise financière de 1848* (Paris, 1848).
Souvenirs de l'administration financière de M. le comte de Villèle (Paris, 1855).
Souvenirs de ma famille et de ma carrière dédiés à mes enfants, 1787–1878, ed. M. Bruguière and V. Goutal-Arnal (Paris, 2002).
Système financier de la France, 1st edition, 2 vols. (Paris, 1840).
Système financier de la France, 2nd edition, 5 vols. (Paris, 1854).
Ayliés and Martin [*sic*], *Observations pour M. Julliard, marchand brasseur, appelant; contre l'administration de l'octroi de la ville de Paris, intimée* (Paris, 1828).
[Barthélemy, H.-C.-F. de], *Souvenirs d'un ancien préfet, 1787–1848* (Paris, 1885).
Becquey, L., *Rapport au roi sur la navigation intérieure de la France* (Paris, 1820).

Bonaparte, N., *Correspondance générale*, ed. T. Lentz et al., 15 vols. (Paris, 2004–18).

Bonnal, E., *De l'abolition et du remplacement des octrois* (Paris, 1869).

Boreau-Lajanadie, C.-J.-F., *Rapport fait au nom de la commission d'enquête sur les actes du gouvernement de la Défense nationale, emprunt Morgan* (Paris, 1873).

Broglie, V. de, *Souvenirs, 1815–1870*, 4 vols. (Paris, 1886).

Caritat, M.-J.-A.-N. de, *Œuvres complètes de Condorcet*, 21 vols. (Paris, 1804).

Cézard, A., *Le Traité de commerce et la législation douanière* (Paris, 1860).

Chabrol de Crousol, C.A.J., *Rapport au roi sur l'administration des finances* (Paris, 1830).

Charléty, S. (ed.), *Lettres du duc de Richelieu au marquis d'Osmond, 1816–1818* (Paris, 1939).

Chevalier, M., *Comparaison des budgets de 1830 et de 1843: budget des recettes* (Paris, 1843).

Coquelin, C., 'Les Douanes et les finances publiques: augmentation possible des recettes de la douane – révision des tarifs', *Revue des deux mondes*, période initiale, nouvelle série, 22 (1848), 356–87, 557–89, 861–93.

Corbière, J.-J.-G.-P. de, *Rapport au roi sur la situation, au 31 mars 1825, des canaux* (Paris, April 1825).

Corcelle, F. de, 'Économie politique: de l'impôt progressif', *Revue des deux mondes, période initiale*, 2e série, 2 (1833), 63–87.

Delessert, B., 'De la situation financière: le Ministre et le Comité des Finances', *Revue des deux mondes, période initiale, nouvelle série*, 23 (1848), 500–22.

Dumas, A., *Les Frères Corses*, ed. C. Schopp (Paris, 2007).

Dumon, S., 'De l'équilibre des budgets sous la monarchie de 1830', *Revue des deux mondes, nouvelle période*, 3 (1849), 885–926.

Duvergier, J.B., *Collection complète des lois, décrets, ordonnances, règlements et avis du Conseil d'État*, 149 vols. (Paris, 1834–1949).

Un électeur de Seine-et-Marne, *Le Ministère peut-il, sans violer la charte, réduire les listes électorales en vertu des dégrèvemens sur la contribution foncière?* (Paris, May 1821).

Erckmann-Chatrian, *L'Ami Fritz* (Paris, 1864).

Faucher, L., 'De l'impôt sur le revenu', *Revue des deux mondes, nouvelle période*, 4 (1849), 62–95.

   'Situation financière de la France, 1843', *Revue des deux mondes, période initiale, nouvelle série*, 1 (1843), 1017–53.

Ferry, J., *Comptes fantastiques d'Haussmann, lettre adressée à MM. les membres de la commission du Corps législatif chargés d'examiner le nouveau projet d'emprunt de la Ville de Paris* (Paris, 1868).

Fortoul, H., *Journal d'Hippolyte Fortoul, ministre de l'instruction publique et des cultes (1811–1856)*, ed. G. Massa-Gille, 2 vols. (Geneva, 1979–89).

Garnier-Pagès, L.-A., *Un épisode de la Révolution de 1848: l'impôt des 45 centimes* (Paris, 1850).

   Histoire de la Révolution de 1848, 10 vols. (Paris, 1861–72).

Gaudin, M.-C.-C., *Mémoires, souvenirs, opinions et écrits du duc de Gaëte*, 2 vols. (Paris, 1826).

Notice historique sur les finances de France (de l'an 8 – 1800 – au 1ᵉʳ avril 1814) (Paris, 1818).

Gille, B., 'Procès-verbaux de la Réunion financière (1858–1860)', *Histoire des entreprises*, 9 (1962): 5–111.

Gotteri, N. (ed.), *La Police secrète du Premier Empire: bulletins quotidiens adressés par Savary à l'Empereur*, 7 vols. (Paris, 1997–2004).

Guernon-Ranville, M.C.A.P.M., *Journal d'un ministre, œuvre posthume du cte du Guernon-Ranville, ancien membre de l'académie des sciences, arts et belles-lettres de Caen* (Caen, 1873).

Guizot, F., *Mémoires pour servir à l'histoire de mon temps*, 8 vols. (Paris, 1858–67).

Hock, K. von, 'Le Ministère des finances vu par un autrichien en 1855', ed. G. Thuillier, *Histoire économique et financière de la France: études & documents*, 6 (1994), 631–9.

Jourdan, [A.J.G.,] 'Les Receveurs généraux en 1819', ed. G. Thuillier, *Histoire économique et financière de la France: études & documents*, 7 (1995), 571–80.

Lacave-Laplagne, P.-J.-J., *Observations sur l'administration des finances pendant le Gouvernement de Juillet et sur ses résultats, en réponse aux rapports de M. le Ministre des finances des 9 mars et 8 mai 1848* (Paris, 1848).

Laffitte, J., *Réflexions sur la réduction de la rente, et sur l'état du crédit* (Paris, 1824).

Lainé, J.H.J., *Rapport au roi, secours et travaux de charité* (Paris, 1817).

Leroy-Beaulieu, P., *Essai sur la répartition des richesses et sur la tendance à une moindre inégalité des conditions* (Paris, 1881).

'Les Ressources de la France et de la Prusse dans la guerre', *Revue des deux mondes*, 2ᵉ période, 89 (1870), 135–55.

Magne, P., *Notes sur l'administration des finances du commencement de 1855 à la fin de 1860* (Paris, 1864).

Marx, K., 'The Class Struggles in France, 1848 to 1850', in K. Marx and F. Engels, *Collected Works*, 50 vols. (London, 1975–2004), X, 45–145.

Mavidal, J. et al. (eds.), *Archives parlementaires de 1787 à 1860: recueil complet des débats législatifs et politiques des Chambres françaises*, 222 vols. (Paris, 1862–present).

Metternich, C. von, *Aus Metternich's nachgelassenen Papieren*, ed. R. Metternich-Winneburg, 8 vols. (Vienna, 1880–4).

Mirabeau, V.R., *Théorie de l'impôt* (Paris, 1760).

Mirès, J., *A mes juges: ma vie et mes affaires* (Paris, 1861).

Mollien, F.-N., *Mémoires d'un Ministre du Trésor public, 1780–1815*, 4 vols. (Paris, 1845).

Mʳ M. J. B. B., *Observations contre le système d'emprunter pour l'état en vendant des rentes; et Projet d'emprunt, en remplacement du crédit de seize millions demandé par le budget de 1818* (Paris, 1818).

Noailles, H.G.H., *Le Comte Molé, 1781–1855*, 6 vols. (Paris, 1922–30).

Ollivier, É., *L'Empire libéral: études, récits, souvenirs*, 18 vols. (Paris, 1895–1918).

Pasquier, É.-D., *Mémoires du chancelier Pasquier: histoire de mon temps,* 6 vols. (Paris, 1893–5).

Perier, C., *Réflexions sur le projet d'emprunt* (Paris, 1817).

Reflexions sur l'emprunt de 16 millions (Paris, 1818).

Pozzo di Borgo, C. (ed.), *Correspondance diplomatique du comte Pozzo di Borgo, ambassadeur de Russie en France, et du comte de Nesselrode, depuis la Restauration des Bourbons jusqu'au Congrès d'Aix-la-Chapelle,* 2 vols. (Paris, 1890–7).

Quesnay, F., *Essai sur l'administration des terres* (Paris, 1759).

Randon, J.-L.-C.-A.P., *Mémoires du maréchal Randon,* 2 vols. (Paris, 1875–7).

Rapports et comptes rendus des opérations de la Caisse d'épargne de Paris pendant l'année 1848 (Paris, 1849).

Rémusat, C. de, *Mémoires de ma vie,* ed. C. Pouthas, 5 vols. (Paris, 1958–67).

Rœderer, P.-L., *Mémoires sur quelques points d'économie publique, lus au lycée en 1800 et 1801* (Paris, 1840).

Say, J.-B., *Cours complet d'économie politique pratique,* 6 vols. (Paris, 1828–9).

Traité d'économie politique, ou Simple exposition de la manière dont se forment, se distribuent et se concomment les richesses, 2nd edition, 2 vols. (Paris, 1814).

Say, L., *Turgot* (Paris, 1887).

Senior, N.W., *Conversations with M. Thiers, M. Guizot and Other Distinguished Persons during the Second Empire,* ed. M.C.M. Simpson, 2 vols. (London, 1878).

Thiers, A., *Histoire de la Révolution française,* 10 vols., 9th edition (Paris, 1839).

'Law', in *Encyclopédie progressive, ou Collection de traités sur l'histoire, l'état actuel et le progrès des connaissances humaines* (Paris, 1826), 49–128.

Thomas, L. (ed.), *Correspondance générale de Chateaubriand: publiée avec introduction, indication des sources, notes et tables doubles,* 5 vols. (Paris, 1912–24).

Trollard, E., *Mémoires d'un inspecteur des Finances au XIXe siècle* (Paris, 1998).

Turgot, A.-J.-R., *Œuvres de Turgot et documents le concernant, avec biographie et notes,* ed. G. Schelle, 5 vols. (Paris, 1913–23).

Vial, P.A., *Cochinchine française: rapport sur la situation de la colonie, ses institutions et ses finances* (Saigon, May 1867).

Villèle, J. de, *Lettres d'un contribuable adressés à la Gazette du Languedoc* (Montpellier, 1839).

Mémoires et correspondance du comte de Villèle, 5 vols. (Paris, 1888–90).

Wellington, Duke of (ed.), *Supplementary Despatches, Correspondence and Memoranda of Field Marshal Arthur Duke of Wellington,* 15 vols. (London, 1858–72).

Wolowski, L., *Réforme hypothécaire: organisation du crédit foncier* (Paris, 1844).

Secondary Sources

Aaslestad, K., 'Paying for War: Experiences of Napoleonic Rule in the Hanseatic Cities', *Central European History,* 39.4 (2006), 641–75.

Agulhon, M., *La République au village: les populations du Var de la Révolution à la Seconde République* (Paris, 1970).

Aidt, T.S., et al., 'The Retrenchment Hypothesis and the Extension of the Franchise in England and Wales', *Economic Journal*, 120 (2010), 990–1020.

Alborn, T.L., *Conceiving Companies: Joint-Stock Politics in Victorian England* (London, 1998).

Alexander, R.S., *Re-writing the French Revolutionary Tradition* (Cambridge, 2003).

Alimento, A., 'Le Rêve de l'uniformité face à l'impôt: le projet du premier cadastre général en France', *Histoire & mesure*, 8.3 (1993), 387–416.

Aminzade, R., *Ballots and Barricades: Class Formation and Republican Politics in France, 1830–1871* (Princeton, 1993).

Anceau, É., *L'Empire libéral*, 2 vols. (Paris, 2017).

'La Réforme du régime douanier devant le parlement (1830–1837)', in P. Harismendy (ed.), *La France des années 1830 et l'esprit de réforme* (Rennes, 2006), 137–48.

Anderson, O., *A Liberal State at War: English Politics and Economics during the Crimean War* (London, 1967).

Antonetti, G., *Louis-Philippe* (Paris, 1994).

Antony, A., *La Politique financière du Gouvernement provisoire, février–mai 1848* (Paris, 1910).

Ardant, G., *Histoire de l'impôt*, 2 vols. (Paris, 1971–2).

Armitage, D. and S. Subrahmanyam (eds.), *The Age of Revolutions in Global Context, c.1760–1840* (Basingstoke, 2010).

Baccouche, M., 'Les Déterminants sociaux et politiques du système fiscal français (1789–1918)', *Revue historique*, 271.2 (1984), 339–67.

Balland, F.-J., 'La Vie et l'œuvre de Dominique Vincent Ramel, ministre des Finances du Directoire', Ph.D. dissertation, 6 vols. (University of Paris IV, 2002).

Barbier, F., *Finance et politique: la dynastie des Fould, XVIII*e*–XX*e* siècle* (Paris, 1991).

Barker, R.J., 'The Perier Bank during the Restoration (1815–1830)', *Journal of European Economic History*, 2.3 (1973), 641–56.

Barreyre, N. and C. Lemercier, 'The Unexceptional State: Rethinking the State in the Nineteenth Century (France, United States)', *American Historical Review*, 126.2 (2021), 481–503.

Bass, G.J., *Freedom's Battle: The Origins of Humanitarian Intervention* (New York, 2008).

Battesti, M., *La Marine de Napoléon III: une politique navale*, 2 vols. (Vincennes, 1997).

Baumgart, W., *The Crimean War, 1853–1856*, 2nd edition (London, 2020).

Der Friede von Paris 1856: Studien zum Verhältnis von Kriegführung, Politik und Friedensbewahrung (Munich, Vienna, 1972).

Bayly, C.A., *The Birth of the Modern World, 1780–1914: Global Connections and Comparisons* (Oxford, 2004).

Beauvais, F., 'Monnayer l'incalculable? L'indemnité de Saint-Domingue entre approximations et bricolage', *Revue historique*, 655.3 (2010), 609–36.

Bédard, R., 'Les Finances de Paris sous la Restauration: une analyse quantitative', MA dissertation (Université Laval, 1994).

Beer, A., *Die Finanzen Oesterreichs im XIX. Jahrhundert nach archivalischen Quellen* (Vienna, 1973).

Belhoste, J.-F., 'Le Financement de la guerre de 1792 à l'an IV', in *État, finances et économie pendant la Révolution française* (Paris, 1989), 317–45.

Bell, D.A., *The First Total War: Napoleon's Europe and the Birth of Modern Warfare* (London, 2007).

Bergeron, L., *Banquiers, négociants et manufacturiers parisiens du Directoire à l'Empire* (Paris, 1978).

'Problèmes économiques de la France napoléonienne', *Revue d'histoire moderne et contemporaine*, 17.3 (1970), 469–505.

Bernot, J., *Le Comte Roy (1764–1847): de la fortune privée au service de l'État* (Paris, 2017).

Bertier de Sauvigny, G., *Metternich et la France après le congrès de Vienne*, 3 vols. (Paris, 1968–71).

Black, S.J., *Napoleon III and Mexican Silver* (Silverton, CO, 2000).

Blaufarb, R., *The Politics of Fiscal Privilege in Provence, 1530s–1830s* (Washington, DC, 2012).

'The Western Question: The Geopolitics of Latin American Independence', *American Historical Review*, 112.3 (2007), 742–63.

Bobrie, F., 'Finances publiques et conquête coloniale: Le coût de l'expansion française entre 1850 et 1913', Annales. *Histoire, sciences sociales*, 31.6 (1976), 1225–44.

Bogani, L., '"À bas les rats! À bas les contributions!" Les résistances à l'impôt des boissons dans le département du Puy-de-Dôme au cours du premier XIXe siècle (1811–1851)', *Revue d'histoire du XIXe siècle*, 48 (2014), 125–43.

Bolt, J. et al., 'Rebasing "Maddison": New Income Comparisons and the Shape of Long-Run Economic Development', Maddison Project Working Paper, no. 10. Maddison Project Database, version 2018.

Bonney, R., 'The Apogee and Fall of the French Rentier Regime, 1801–1914', in J.L. Cardoso and P. Lains (eds.), *Paying for the Liberal State: The Rise of Public Finance in Nineteenth-Century Europe* (Cambridge, 2010), 81–102.

Bordas, J., *Les Directeurs généraux des douanes: l'administration et la politique douanière, 1801–1939* (Paris, 2004).

Borscheid, P., 'L'Influence du modèle fiscal français sur la fiscalité allemande au XIXe siècle', in M. Lévy-Leboyer et al. (eds.), *L'Impôt en France aux XIXe et XXe siècles* (Paris, 2006), 375–84.

Bosher, J.F., *French Finances, 1770–1795: From Business to Bureaucracy* (Cambridge, 1970).

Bossenga, G., *The Politics of Privilege: Old Regime and Revolution in Lille* (Cambridge, 1991).

Boudon, J.-O., *Ordre et désordre dans la France napoléonienne* (Paris, 2008).

Bourdieu, P., *Sur l'État: cours au Collège de France (1989–1992)*, ed. P. Champagne (Paris, 2012).

Bourguinat, N., *Les Grains du désordre: l'État face aux violences frumentaires dans la première moitié du XIXᵉ siècle* (Paris, 2002).

Bourillon, F., 'Mesurer pour l'impôt: l'évaluation de la richesse foncière urbaine', in P. Harismendy (ed.), *La France des années 1830 et l'esprit de réforme* (Rennes, 2006), 149–59.

Bouvier, J., *Le Crédit lyonnais de 1863 à 1882: les années de formation d'une banque de dépôts*, 2 vols. (Paris, 1961).

'Les Pereire et l'affaire de la Banque de Savoie', *Cahiers d'histoire*, 5.4 (1960), 383–410.

'Le Système fiscal français du XIXᵉ siècle: étude critique d'un immobilisme', in J. Bouvier and J. Wolff (eds.), *Deux siècles de fiscalité française, XIXᵉ–XXᵉ siècle* (Paris, 1973), 226–62.

Bouvier, J. and J. Wolff (eds.), *Deux siècles de fiscalité française, XIXᵉ–XXᵉ siècle* (Paris, 1973).

Branda, P., 'La Guerre a-t-elle payé la guerre?', in T. Lentz (ed.), *Napoléon et l'Europe: regards sur une politique* (Paris, 2005), 258–73.

Le Prix de la gloire: Napoléon et l'argent (Paris, 2007).

Brandt, H.-H., *Der österreichische Neoabsolutismus: Staatsfinanzen und Politik, 1848–1860*, 2 vols. (Göttingen, 1978).

Braudel, F. and E. Labrousse (eds.), *Histoire économique et sociale de la France*, 4 vols. (Paris, 1970–82).

Breton, Y. et al. (eds.), *La Longue Stagnation en France: l'autre grande dépression, 1873–1897* (Paris, 1997).

Brewer, J., *The Sinews of Power: War, Money and the English State, 1688–1783* (London, 1989).

Brière, J.-F., *Haïti et la France, 1804–1848: le rêve brisé* (Paris, 2008).

Brocheux, P. and D. Hémery, *Indochine: la colonisation ambiguë, 1858–1954* (Paris, 2001).

Broers, M., 'Napoleon, Charlemagne and Lotharingia: Acculturation and the Boundaries of Napoleonic Europe', *Historical Journal*, 44.1 (2001), 135–54.

The Napoleonic Empire in Italy, 1796–1814: Cultural Imperialism in a European Context? (Basingstoke, 2005).

Napoleon's Other War: Bandits, Rebels and Their Pursuers in the Age of Revolutions (Oxford, 2010).

Brophy, J.M., *Capitalism, Politics and Railroads in Prussia, 1830–1870* (Columbus, 1998).

Brown, H.G., *Ending the Revolution: Violence, Justice and Repression from the Terror to Napoleon* (Charlottesville, 2006).

War, Revolution and the Bureaucratic State: Politics and Army Administration in France, 1791–1799 (Oxford, 1995).

Bruguière, M., *Gestionnaires et profiteurs de la Révolution: l'administration des finances françaises de Louis XVI à Bonaparte* (Paris, 1986).

La Première Restauration et son budget (Geneva, 1969).

'Les Techniques d'intervention de la Caisse d'Amortissement dans le cour de la rente (1816–1824)', *Revue historique*, 258.1 (1977), 93–104.

Bruley, Y., *Le Quai d'Orsay impérial: histoire du Ministère des Affaires étrangères sous Napoléon III* (Paris, 2012).

Burgaud, E., 'La Taxation du plaisir comme impôt d'après guerre: la taxation sur les billards', *Revue historique de droit français et étranger*, 84.1 (2006), 87–102.

Butrón Prida, G., *La Ocupación francesa de España, 1823–1828* (Cadiz, 1996).

Calmon, A., *Histoire parlementaire des finances de la monarchie de Juillet*, 4 vols. (Paris, 1895–9).

Histoire parlementaire des finances de la Restauration, 2 vols. (Paris, 1868–70).

Cameron, R.E., *France and the Economic Development of Europe, 1800–1914: Conquests of Peace and Seeds of War* (Princeton, 1961).

Cardoni, F. et al. (eds.), *Dictionnaire historique des inspecteurs des finances, 1801–2009: dictionnaire thématique et biographique* (Paris, 2012).

Cardoso, J.L. and P. Lains (eds.), *Paying for the Liberal State: The Rise of Public Finance in Nineteenth-Century Europe* (Cambridge, 2010).

Caron, F., *Histoire des chemins de fer en France*, 3 vols. (Paris, 1997–2017).

Caron, J.-C., *L'Été rouge: chronique de la révolte populaire en France (1841)*, (Paris, 2002).

Carosso, V.P., *The Morgans: Private International Bankers, 1854–1913* (Cambridge, MA, 1987).

Carrier, R., 'Répartition ou quotité? Les enjeux autour de la contribution personnelle mobilière et de l'impôt sur les portes et fenêtres au début de la monarchie de Juillet', in M. Lévy-Leboyer et al. (eds.), *L'Impôt en France aux XIXᵉ et XXᵉ siècles* (Paris, 2006), 141–68.

Case, L.M., *French Opinion on War and Diplomacy during the Second Empire* (Philadelphia, 1954).

Casevitz, J., *Une loi manquée: la loi Niel, 1866–1868, l'armée française à la veille de la guerre de 1870* (Rennes, 1960).

Centeno, M.A., 'Blood and Debt: War and Taxation in Nineteenth-Century Latin America', *American Journal of Sociology*, 102.6 (1997), 1565–1605.

Chabal, E., *A Divided Republic: Nation, State and Citizenship in Contemporary France* (Cambridge, 2015).

Chanet, J.-F., *Vers l'armée nouvelle: République conservatrice et réforme militaire, 1871–1879* (Rennes, 2006).

Chevalier, L., *Classes laborieuses et classes dangereuses à Paris pendant la première moitié du XIXᵉ siècle* (Paris, 1958).

La Formation de la population parisienne (Paris, 1950).

Christen-Lécuyer, C., *Histoire sociale et culturelle des caisses d'épargne en France, 1818–1881* (Paris, 2004).

Church, C.H., *Revolution and Red Tape: The French Ministerial Bureaucracy, 1770–1850* (Oxford, 1981).

Clark, C., 'After 1848: The European Revolution in Government', *Transactions of the Royal Historical Society*, 6th series, 22 (2012), 171–97.

Clinquart, J., *L'Administration des douanes en France de la Révolution de 1848 à la Commune (1848–1871)* (Neuilly, 1983).

L'Administration des douanes en France sous le Consulat et l'Empire (1800–1815) (Neuilly, 1979).

L'Administration des douanes en France sous la Restauration et la Monarchie de Juillet (1815–1848) (Neuilly, 1981).

Cobb, R.C., *The Police and the People: French Popular Protest, 1789–1820* (Oxford, 1970).

Cohen, W.B., *Urban Government and the Rise of the French City: Five Municipalities in the Nineteenth Century* (Basingstoke, 1998).

Collins, J.B., *The State in Early-Modern France* (Cambridge, 2009).

Connelly, O., *Napoleon's Satellite Kingdoms* (New York, 1965).

Conrad, O., *Le Conseil général du Haut-Rhin au XIXe siècle: les débuts d'une collectivité territoriale et l'influence des notables dans l'administration départementale (1800–1870)* (Strasbourg, 1998).

Coq, P., 'De la conversion des rentes projetée en 1824; le 3 pour cent de M. de Villèle', *Journal des économistes*, 6 (1879), 57–84.

Corbin, A., *Archaisme et modernité en Limousin au XIXᵉ siècle, 1845–1880*, 2 vols. (Paris, 1975).

Le Village des cannibales (Paris, 1990).

Corti, E.C., *Das Haus Rothschild in der Zeit seiner Blüte, 1830–1871, mit einem Ausblick in die neueste Zeit* (Leipzig, 1928).

Coste, C., 'Penser l'impôt au XIXᵉ siècle: controverses fiscales et contributions saint-simoniennes dans la France des années 1830', *Cahiers d'histoire. Revue d'histoire critique*, 124 (2014), 45–62.

Cottez, A., *Un Fermier général sous le Consulat et l'Empire* (Paris, 1938).

Cottrell, P.L., 'Anglo-French Financial Cooperation, 1850–1880', *Journal of European Economic History*, 3.1 (1974), 54–86.

Cox, G.P., *The Halt in the Mud: French Strategic Planning from Waterloo to Sedan* (Boulder, 1994).

Craiutu, A., *Liberalism under Siege: The Political Thought of the French Doctrinaires* (Lanham, 2003).

Crépin, A., *La Conscription en débat, ou Le triple apprentissage de la nation, de la citoyennete, de la République (1798–1889)* (Arras, 1998).

Défendre la France: Les Français, la guerre et le service militaire, de la guerre de Sept Ans à Verdun (Paris, 2005).

'Une France plurielle devant la conscription', in J.-O. Boudon (ed.), *Armée, guerre et société à l'époque napoléonienne* (Paris, 2004), 13–30.

Crouy Chanel, E. de, 'La Définition de l'impôt idéal sous le Directoire: la question de l'établissement d'un impôt sur le sel', in M. Lévy-Leboyer et al. (eds.), *L'Impôt en France aux XIXᵉ et XXᵉ siècles* (Paris, 2006), 119–39.

Crouzet, F., *La Grande inflation: la monnaie en France de Louis XVI à Napoléon* (Paris, 1993).

'The Historiography of French Economic Growth in the Nineteenth Century', *Economic History Review*, 56.2 (2003), 215–42.

Dakin, D., *The Greek Struggle for Independence, 1821–1833* (London, 1973).

Dansette, A., *Naissance de la France moderne: le Second Empire* (Paris, 1976).

Darimon, A., *Histoire de douze ans (1857–1869)* (Paris, 1883).

Darriulat, P., *La Muse du peuple: chansons politiques et sociales en France, 1815–1871* (Rennes, 2010).

Daudet, E., *Louis XVIII et le duc Decazes* (Paris, 1899).

Daumard, A., *La Bourgeoisie parisienne de 1815 à 1848* (Paris, 1963).

'L'État libéral et le libéralisme économique', in F. Braudel and E. Labrousse (eds.), *Histoire économique et sociale de la France*, 4 vols. (Paris, 1970–82), III.i, 137–59.

'Problèmes généraux et synthèse des résultats', in A. Daumard (ed.), *Les Fortunes françaises au XIXᵉ siècle: enquête sur la repartition et la composition des capitaux privés à Paris, Lyon, Lille, Bordeaux et Toulouse d'après l'enregistrement des déclarations de succession* (Paris, 1973), 3–177.

Daunton, M., 'Tax Transfers: Britain and Its Empire, 1848–1914', in J. Tiley (ed.), *Studies in the History of Tax Law*, III(Oxford, 2009), 91–112.

Trusting Leviathan: The Politics of Taxation in Britain, 1799–1914 (Cambridge, 2001).

David, J., 'Les Octrois et leur suppression', *Revue historique de droit français et étranger*, 66.4 (1988), 561–85.

Decroix, A., *Question fiscale et réforme financière en France (1749–1789): logique de la transparence et recherche de la confiance publique* (Aix-en-Provence, 2000).

Delalande, N., *Les Batailles de l'impôt: consentement et résistances de 1789 à nos jours* (Paris, 2011).

'L'Économie politique des réformes fiscales: une analyse historique', *Revue de l'OFCE*, 122 (2012), 35–59.

Démier, F., *La France de la Restauration (1814–1830): l'impossible retour du passé* (Paris, 2012).

Desan, S. et al. (eds.), *The French Revolution in Global Perspective* (Ithaca, 2013).

Deschamps, H.-T., *La Belgique devant la France de Juillet: l'opinion et l'attitude françaises de 1839 à 1848* (Paris, 1956).

Descours-Gatin, C., *Quand l'opium finançait la colonisation en Indochine: l'élaboration de la régie générale de l'opium (1860 à 1914)* (Paris, 1992).

Dickson, P.G.M., *The Financial Revolution in England: A Study in the Development of Public Credit, 1688–1756* (London, 1967).

Dincecco, M., 'Fiscal Centralization, Limited Government, and Public Revenues in Europe, 1650–1913', *Journal of Economic History*, 69.1 (2009), 48–103.

et al., 'Warfare, Taxation and Political Change: Evidence from the Italian Risorgimento', *Journal of Economic History*, 71.4 (2011), 887–914.

Douël, M., *Un siècle de finances coloniales* (Paris, 1930).

Dubois, L., *Avengers of the New World: The Story of the Haitian Revolution* (Cambridge, MA, 2004).

Dunham, A.L., *The Anglo-French Treaty of Commerce of 1860 and the Progress of the Industrial Revolution in France* (Ann Arbor, 1930).

Dunlavy, C.A., *Politics and Industrialization: Early Railroads in the United States and Prussia* (Princeton, 1994).

Durand, Y., *Les Fermiers généraux au XVIIIe siècle* (Paris, 1996).

Durieux, P., *Le Ministre Pierre Magne, 1806–1879, d'après ses lettres et ses souvenirs*, 2 vols. (Paris, 1929).

Echard, W.E., *Napoleon III and the Concert of Europe* (Baton Rouge, 1983).

Eddie, S., 'The 1848 Revolution in Prussia: A Financial Interpretation', in J. Hoppit et al. (eds.), *Money and Markets: Essays in Honour of Martin Daunton* (Woodbridge, 2019), 109–25.

Freedom's Price: Serfdom, Subjection, and Reform in Prussia, 1648–1848 (Oxford, 2013).

Edling, M.M., *A Hercules in the Cradle: War, Money and the American State, 1783–1867* (London, 2014).

Einaudi, L., *Money and Politics: European Monetary Unification and the International Gold Standard, 1865–1873* (Oxford, 2001).

Einhorn, R.L., *American Taxation, American Slavery* (Chicago, 2006).

Émerit, M., 'La Crise syrienne et l'expansion économique française en 1860', *Revue historique*, 207.2 (1952), 211–32.

Engberg-Pedersen, A., *Empire of Chance: The Napoleonic Wars and the Disorder of Things* (Cambridge MA, 2015).

Evans, R.J.W., *Austria, Hungary and the Habsburgs: Essays on Central Europe, c. 1683–1867* (Oxford, 2006).

Faure, A., 'L'Industriel et le politique: qui a peur de l'industrie à Paris au XIXe siècle?', *Revue d'histoire moderne et contemporaine*, 65.1 (2018), 29–69.

'Retour sur une annexion: Paris, 1860', *Revue historique*, 695.3 (2020), 93–157.

Ferguson, N., 'Political Risk and the International Bond Market between the 1848 Revolution and the Outbreak of the First World War', *Economic History Review*, 59.1 (2006), 70–112.

The World's Banker: The History of the House of Rothschild (London, 1998).

Figes, O., *Crimea: The Last Crusade* (London, 2011).

Flandreau, M., 'The Economics and Politics of Monetary Unions: A Reassessment of the Latin Monetary Union, 1865–1871', *Financial History Review*, 7 (2000), 25–43.

The Glitter of Gold: France, Bimetallism and the Emergence of the International Gold Standard, 1848–1873 (Oxford, 2004).

Flandreau, M. and J.H. Flores, 'Bonds and Brands: Foundations of Sovereign Debt Markets, 1820–1830', *Journal of Economic History*, 69.3 (2009), 646–84.

Flichy, P., *Une histoire de la communication moderne: espace public et vie privée* (Paris, 1997).

Fontana Lázaro, J., *Hacienda y estado en la crisis final del antiguo regimen español, 1823–1833* (Madrid, 1973).

La quiebra de la monarquia absoluta, 1814–1820 (Barcelona, 1974).

Fontvieille, L., 'La Croissance de la dépense publique d'éducation en France, 1815–1987', *Formation emploi*, 31 (1990), 61–71.

Évolution et croissance de l'administration départementale française, 1815–1974 (Paris, 1981).

Évolution et croissance de l'État français: 1815–1969 (Paris, 1976).

Fortescue, W., 'Morality and Monarchy: Corruption and the Fall of the Regime of Louis-Philippe in 1848', *French History*, 16.1 (2002), 83–100.

Franke-Postberg, A., *Le Milliard des émigrés: die Entschädigung der Emigranten im Frankreich der Restauration (1814–1830)* (Bochum, 1999).

Freedman, C.E., 'The Growth of the French Securities Market, 1815–1870', in C.K. Warner (ed.), *From the Ancien Régime to the Popular Front: Essays in the History of Modern France in Honor of Shepard B. Clough* (New York, 1969), 75–92.

Fritschy, W., 'Staatsvorming en financieel beleid onder Willem I', in C.A. Tamse and E. Witte (eds.), *Staats- en Natievorming in Willem I's Koninkrijk (1815–1830)* (Brussels, 1992), 215–36.

Fureix, E. and F. Jarrige, *La Modernité désenchantée: relire l'histoire du XIXᵉ siècle français* (Paris, 2015).

Furet, F., *Penser la Révolution française* (Paris, 1978).

La Révolution: de Turgot à Jules Ferry, 1770–1880 (Paris, 1988).

Gabillard, J., 'Le Financement des guerres napoléoniennes et la conjoncture du Premier Empire', *Revue économique*, 4.4 (1953), 548–72.

Gaillard, J., 'Les Intentions d'une politique fiscale: la patente en France au XIXᵉ siècle', *Bulletin du Centre d'histoire de la France contemporaine*, 7 (1986), 15–38.

Paris, la ville (1852–1870) (Paris, 1976).

Gain, A., *La Restauration et les Biens des émigrés: la législation concernant les Biens nationaux de seconde origine et son application dans l'Est de la France (1814–1832)*, 2 vols. (Nancy, 1929).

Garrigues, J., '*Léon Say et le centre gauche, 1871–1896: la grande bourgeoisie libérale dans les débuts de la Troisième République*', Ph.D. dissertation, 3 vols. (University of Paris X, 1993).

Gaudin, A., *Le Régime fiscal de la Corse: les arrêtés Miot* (Bastia, 1876 [Nîmes, 2006]).

Gebhart, M. and C. Mercadier, *L'Octroi de Toulouse à la veille de la Révolution* (Paris, 1967).

Gerstle, G., *Liberty and Coercion: The Paradox of American Government from the Founding to the Present* (Princeton, 2015).

Gildea, R., *Education in Provincial France, 1800–1914: A Study of Three Departments* (Oxford, 1983).

Gille, G., 'Les Capitaux français et l'expédition du Mexique', *Revue d'histoire diplomatique*, 79 (1965), 191–250.

Gille, B., *La Banque et le crédit en France de 1815 à 1848* (Paris, 1959).

'Les Emprunts de libération en 1871–1872', in *La France au XIX siècle: études historiques: mélanges offerts à Charles-Hippolyte Pouthas* (Paris, 1973), 166–98.

Histoire de la maison Rothschild, 2 vols. (Geneva, 1965–7).

Girard, L., *Les Libéraux français, 1814–1875* (Paris, 1985).

La Politique des travaux publics du Second Empire (Paris, 1952).

Glikman, J., *La Monarchie impériale: l'imaginaire politique sous Napoléon III* (Paris, 2013).

Glineur, C., 'Les Coalitions ouvrières dans le département du Nord sous le second Empire', *Revue historique de droit français et étranger*, 90.1 (2012), 85–113.

Goblot, J.-J., *La Jeune France libérale: le Globe et son groupe littéraire, 1824–1830* (Paris, 1995).

Godechot, J., 'La Crise de 1846–1847 dans le sud-ouest de la France', *Bibliothèque de la Révolution de 1848*, 16 (1954), 88–108.

Gonnet, P., 'Esquisse de la crise économique en France de 1827 à 1832', *Revue d'histoire économique et sociale*, 33.3 (1955), 249–92.

Gontard, M., *La Bourse de Paris (1800–1830)* (Aix-en-Provence, 2000).

Gossez, R., 'La Résistance à l'impôt: les quarante-cinq centimes', *Bibliothèque de la Révolution de 1848*, 15 (1953), 89–132.

Gouette, P.H. and G. Klotz, 'Turgot: A Critic of Physiocracy? An Analysis of the Debates in *Éphémérides du Citoyen* and Correspondence with Dupont', *European Journal of the History of Economic Thought*, 22.3 (2015), 500–33.

Graaf, B. de, *Fighting Terror after Napoleon: How Europe Became Secure after 1815* (Cambridge, 2020).

Grab, A., 'The Politics of Finance in Napoleonic Italy (1802–1814)', *Journal of Modern Italian Studies*, 3.2 (1998), 127–43.

'State Power, Brigandage and Rural Resistance in Napoleonic Italy', *European History Quarterly*, 25.1 (1995), 39–70.

Graber, F., 'Enquêtes publiques, 1820–1830: définir l'utilité publique pour justifier le sacrifice dans un monde de projets', *Revue d'histoire moderne et contemporaine*, 63.3 (2016), 31–63.

Grafe, R. and M.A. Irigoin, 'The Spanish Empire and Its Legacy: Fiscal Redistribution and Political Conflict in Colonial and Post-colonial Spanish America', *Journal of Global History*, 1.2 (2006), 241–67.

Graumann, S., *Französische Verwaltung am Niederrhein: das Roerdepartement, 1798–1814* (Essen, 1990).

Graziani, A.-M., 'Du plan terrier au cadastre de la Corse: ruptures et continuités (1770–1880)', in M. Touzery (ed.), *De l'estime au cadastre en Europe: l'époque moderne* (Paris, 2007), 309–21.

Greenfield, J., '"As Solid As and More Precious Than Gold": Gabriel-Julien Ouvrard, John Law and the Legacy of the Assignats in Nineteenth-Century France', *French History*, 34.2 (2020), 191–212.

'Le Crédit mobilier avant la suprématie des Pereire', *Histoire, économie et société*, 2 (2020), 46–63.

'Financing a New Order: The Payment of Reparations by Restoration France, 1817–18', *French History*, 30.3 (2016), 376–400.

'The Mexican Expedition of 1862–1867 and the End of the French Second Empire', *Historical Journal*, 63.3 (2020), 660–85.

'The Origins of the Interventionist State in France, 1830–1870', *English Historical Review*, 135.573 (2020), 386–416.

'The Price of Violence: Money, the French State and "Civilization" during the Conquest of Algeria, 1830–1850s', *French Historical Studies*, 43.4 (2020), 537–69.

Griffith, P., *Military Thought in the French Army, 1815–1851* (Manchester, 1989).

Gross, J.-P., 'Progressive Taxation and Social Justice in Eighteenth-Century France', *Past & Present*, 140 (1993), 79–126.

Guéna, Y., *Le Baron Louis, 1755–1837* (Paris, 1999).

Guerrin, Y., *La France après Napoléon: invasions et occupations, 1814–1818* (Paris, 2014).

Gueslin, A., *L'État, l'économie et la société française, XIXᵉ–XXᵉ siècle* (Paris, 1992).

'L'Invention des Caisses d'épargne en France: une grande utopie libérale', *Revue historique*, 282.2(572) (1989), 391–409.

Guionnet, C., *L'Apprentissage de la politique moderne: les élections municipales sous la monarchie de Juillet* (Paris, 1997).

Gunn, J.A.W., *When the French Tried to Be British: Party, Opposition and the Quest for Civil Disagreement, 1814–1848* (Montréal, 2009).

Halévy, D., *La Fin des notables*, 2 vols. (Paris, 1930–7).

Hamilton, C.I., *Anglo-French Naval Rivalry, 1840–1870* (Oxford, 1993).

'The Diplomatic and Naval Effects of the Prince de Joinville's *Note sur L'état des forces navales de la France* of 1844', *Historical Journal*, 32.3 (1989), 675–87.

Hammond, B., *Banks and Politics in America from the Revolution to the Civil War* (Princeton, 1957).

Hantraye, J., *Les Cosaques aux Champs Élysées: l'occupation de la France après la chute de Napoléon* (Paris, 2005).

Hardman, J., *Overture to Revolution: The 1787 Assembly of Notables and the Crisis of France's Old Regime* (Oxford, 2010).

Harismendy, P. (ed.), *La France des années 1830 et l'esprit de réforme* (Rennes, 2006).

Harling, P. and P. Mandler, 'From "Fiscal-Military" to Laissez-Faire State', *Journal of British Studies*, 32.1 (1993), 44–70.

Harris, R.D., 'French Finances and the American War, 1777–1783', *Journal of Modern History*, 48.2 (1971), 233–58.

Hautcoeur, P.-C. and G. Gallais-Hamonno (eds.), *Le Marché financier français au XIXᵉ siècle*, 2 vols. (Paris, 2007).

Hautcoeur, P.-C. and A. Riva, 'The Paris Financial Market in the Nineteenth Century: Complementarities and Competition in Microstructures', *Economic History Review*, 65.4 (2012), 1326–53.

Haynes, C., *Our Friends the Enemies: The Occupation of France after Napoleon* (Cambridge MA, 2018).

Hazareesingh, S., *From Subject to Citizen: The Second Empire and the Emergence of Modern French Democracy* (Princeton, 1998).

The Saint-Napoleon: Celebrations of Sovereignty in Nineteenth-Century France (Cambridge MA, 2004).

Hérody-Pierre, C., *Robert Schnerb, un historien dans le siècle, 1900–1962: une vie autour d'une thèse* (Paris, 2011).

Herrmann-Mascard, N., *L'Emprunt forcé de l'an II: un impôt sur la fortune* (Paris, 1990).

Heywood, O.E. and C.M. Heywood, 'Rethinking the 1848 Revolution in France: The Provisional Government and Its Enemies', *History*, 79.257 (1994), 394–411.

Hincker, F., *Les Français devant l'impôt sous l'ancien régime* (Paris, 1971).

Hippler, T., 'Conscription in the French Restoration: The 1818 Debate on Military Service', *War in History*, 13.3 (2006), 281–98.

Hirsch, J.-P., *La Nuit du 4 août* (Paris, 1978 [2013]).

Hissung-Convert, N., 'L'Impôt sur le sel à Salies-de-Béarn, la fin d'un privilège ancien sous la Monarchie de Juillet', *Annales du Midi*, 121.267 (2009), 365–84.

La Spéculation boursière face au droit, 1799–1914 (Paris, 2009).

Hobsbawm, E.J., *The Age of Capital, 1848–1875* (London, 1975).

Hoffman, P.T. et al., *Dark Matter Credit: The Development of Peer-to-Peer Lending and Banking in France* (Princeton, 2019).

et al., *Priceless Markets: The Political Economy of Credit in Paris, 1660–1870* (Chicago, 2000).

Holmes, R., *The Road to Sedan: The French Army, 1866–70* (London, 1984).

Hoppit, J., *Britain's Political Economies: Parliament and Economic Life, 1660–1800* (Cambridge, 2017).

'Compulsion, Compensation and Property Rights in Britain, 1688–1833', *Past & Present*, 210 (2011), 93–128.

Horn, J., *The Path Not Taken: French Industrialization in the Age of Revolution, 1750–1830* (Cambridge MA, 2006).

Igersheim, F., *Politique et administration dans le Bas-Rhin (1848–1870)* (Strasbourg, 1993).

Iliasu, A.A., 'The Cobden–Chevalier Treaty of 1860', *Historical Journal*, 14.1 (1971), 67–98.

Jacoud, G., *Le Billet de banque en France (1796–1803): de la diversité au monopole* (Paris, 1996).

Jainchill, A., *Reimagining Politics after the Terror: The Republican Origins of French Liberalism* (Ithaca, 2008).

Jardin, A., *Histoire du libéralisme politique: de la crise de l'absolutisme à la constitution de 1875* (Paris, 1985).

Jarvis, K., *Politics in the Marketplace: Work, Gender, and Citizenship in Revolutionary France* (Oxford, 2019).

Jaume, L., *L'Individu effacé ou Le paradoxe du libéralisme français* (Paris, 1997).

Joachim, B., 'L'Indemnité coloniale de Saint-Domingue et la question des rapatriés', *Revue historique*, 246.2(500) (1971), 359–76.

Jones, C. and R. Spang, 'Sans Culottes, *Sans Café, Sans Tabac*: Shifting Realms of Necessity and Luxury in Eighteenth-Century France', in M. Berg and H. Clifford (eds.), *Consumers and Luxury: Consumer Culture in Europe, 1650–1850* (Manchester, 1999), 37–62.

Jones, P., *Liberty and Locality in Revolutionary France: Six Villages Compared, 1760–1820* (Cambridge, 2003).

The Peasantry in the French Revolution (Cambridge, 1988).

Judson, P.M., *The Habsburg Empire: A New History* (Cambridge MA, 2016).

Kang, M., *Francophonie en Orient: aux croisements France-Asie, 1840–1940* (Amsterdam, 2018).

Kang, Z., 'L'État constructeur du marché financier', in P.-C. Hautcoeur and G. Gallais-Hamonno (eds.), *Le Marché financier français au XIXᵉ siècle* (Paris, 2007),I, 159–94.

Karila-Cohen, P., *L'État des esprits: l'invention de l'enquête politique en France (1814–1848)* (Rennes, 2008).

Kemp, T., *Economic Forces in French History* (London, 1971).

Kent, S., *The Election of 1827 in France* (Cambridge, MA, 1975).

Kieswetter, J.K., 'The Imperial Restoration: Continuity in Personnel and Policy under Napoleon I and Louis XVIII', *Historian*, 45.1 (1982), 31–46.

Kindleberger, C.P., *A Financial History of Western Europe* (New York, 1993).

Koepke, R.L., 'The *Loi des patentes* of 1844', *French Historical Studies*, 11.3 (1980), 398–430.

Kott, S., 'Restaurer la monarchie et restaurer les finances en France: le financement de l'expédition d'Espagne', in A. Dubet and J.-P. Luis (eds.), *Les Financiers et la construction de l'État: France, Espagne (XVIIᵉ–XIXᵉ siècle)* (Rennes, 2011), 217–35.

Kroen, S., *Politics and Theater: The Crisis of Legitimacy in Restoration France, 1815–1830* (Berkeley, 2000).

Kwass, M., *Contraband: Louis Mandrin and the Making of a Global Underground* (Cambridge MA, 2014).

Privilege and the Politics of Taxation in Eighteenth-Century France: Liberté, Égalité, Fiscalité (Cambridge, 2000).

Labrousse, E., 'Panoramas de la crise', *Bibliothèque de la Révolution de 1848, 19* (1956), iii–xxiv.

Lafrance, X., *The Making of Capitalism in France: Class Structures, Economic Development, the State and the Formation of the French Working Class, 1750–1914* (Leiden, 2019).

La Gorce, P. de, *Histoire de la Seconde République française*, 2 vols. (Paris, 1887).

Larrère, M., *L'Urne et le fusil: la garde nationale parisienne de 1830 à 1848* (Paris, 2016).

Larroche, E., *L'Expédition d'Espagne, 1823: de la guerre selon la Charte* (Rennes, 2013).

Latour, F., *Le Grand argentier de Napoléon* (Paris, 1962).

Laurent, R., *L'Octroi de Dijon au XIXe siècle* (Paris, 1960).

Le Bihan, J., 'La Réintégration des percepteurs des Contributions directes au cours du premier XIXe siècle en Ille-et-Vilaine', *Histoire & mesure*, 29.2 (2014), 47–64.

Leclercq, Y., *Le Réseau impossible: la résistance au système des grandes compagnies ferroviaires et la politique économique en France, 1820–1852* (Geneva, 1987).

'Les Transferts financiers: état-compagnies privées de chemin de fer d'intérêt général', *Revue économique*, 33.5 (1982), 896–924.

Lefebvre-Teillard, A., *La Société anonyme au XIXe siècle: du code de commerce à la loi de 1867, histoire d'un instrument juridique du développement capitaliste* (Paris, 1985).

Legay, M.-L., 'Capitalisme, crises de trésorerie et donneurs d'avis: une relecture des années 1783–1789', *Revue historique*, 312.3(655) (2010), 577–608.

Le Goff, T.J.A. and D.M.G. Sutherland, 'La Révolution française et l'économie rurale', *Histoire & mesure*, 14.1/2 (1999), 79–120.

Lemercier, C., *Un si discret pouvoir: aux origines de la chambre de commerce de Paris, 1803–1853* (Paris, 2003).

Lentz, T., *Le Grand Consulat* (Paris, 1999).

Nouvelle histoire du Premier Empire, 4 vols. (Paris, 2002–10).

Lepetit, B., *Les Villes dans la France moderne, 1740–1840* (Paris, 1988).

Leuchter, T., 'Finance beyond the Bounds of the Fiscal-Military State: Debt, Speculation and the Renovation of Nineteenth-Century French Financial Capitalism', *French History*, 34.3 (2020): 317–41.

'The Illimitable Right: Debating the Meaning of Property and the *Marché à Terme* in Napoleonic France', *Modern Intellectual History*, 15.1 (2018), 3–32.

Lévêque, P., *Une société en crise: la Bourgogne au milieu du XIXe siècle (1846–1852)* (Paris, 1983).

Levi, M., *Of Rule and Revenue* (Berkeley, 1988).

Lévy-Leboyer, M., *Les Banques européennes et l'industrialisation internationale dans la première moitié du XIXe siècle* (Paris, 1964).

Lévy-Leboyer, M. and F. Bourguignon, *L'Économie française au XIXe siècle: analyse macro-économique* (Paris, 1985).

Lévy-Leboyer, M. et al. (eds.), *L'Impôt en France aux XIXe et XXe siècles* (Paris, 2006).

Lewis, M.D., 'Legacies of French Slave-Ownership, or the Long Decolonization of Saint-Domingue', *History Workshop Journal*, 83 (2017), 151–75.

Lignereux, A., *La France rébellionnaire: les résistances à la gendarmerie (1800–1859)* (Rennes, 2008).

Lindert, P.H., *Growing Public: Social Spending and Economic Growth since the Eighteenth Century*, 2 vols. (Cambridge, 2004).

Livesey, J., *Making Democracy in the French Revolution* (Cambridge MA, 2001).

López Castellano, F., *Liberalismo económico y reforma fiscal: la contribución directa de 1813* (Granada, 1995).

López-Morell, M.Á., *La Casa Rothschild en España (1812–1941)* (Madrid, 2005).

Lovie, J., *La Savoie dans la vie française de 1860 à 1875* (Paris, 1963).

Luis, J.-P., *L'Ivresse de la fortune: A.M. Aguado, un génie des affaires* (Paris, 2009).

Luna, F.A. de, *The French Republic under Cavaignac, 1848* (Princeton, 1969).

Maier, C.S., *Leviathan 2.0: Inventing Modern Statehood* (Cambridge, MA, 2012).

Mandler, P., 'Introduction: State and Society in Victorian Britain', in P. Mandler (ed.), *Liberty and Authority in Victorian Britain* (Oxford, 2006), 1–21.

Mann, M., *The Sources of Social Power*, 4 vols. (Cambridge, 1986–2013).

Marchand, B., *Paris, histoire d'une ville: XIXᵉ–XXᵉ siècle* (Paris, 1993).

Margadant, J.B., 'Gender, Vice and the Political Imaginary in Postrevolutionary France: Reinterpreting the Failure of the July Monarchy, 1830–1848', *American Historical Review*, 104.5 (1999), 1461–96.

Margerison, K., 'P.-L. Rœderer: Political Thought and Practice during the French Revolution', *Transactions of the American Philosophical Society*, 73.1 (1983), 1–166.

Markoff, J., *The Abolition of Feudalism: Peasants, Lords and Legislators in the French Revolution* (University Park, PA, 1996).

Marichal, C., *Bankruptcy of Empire: Mexican Silver and the Wars between Spain, Britain and France, 1760–1810* (Cambridge, 2007).

Marion, M., *Histoire financière de la France depuis 1715*, 6 vols. (Paris, 1914–31). 'Le Recouvrement des impôts en 1790', *Revue historique*, 121.1 (1916), 1–47.

Markovic, M., 'La Révolution aux barrières: l'incendie des barrières de l'octroi à Paris en juillet 1789', *Annales historiques de la Révolution française*, 2 (2013), 27–48.

Marsh, P.T., *Bargaining on Europe: Britain and the First Common Market, 1860–1892* (London, 1999).

Martin, J., *L'Empire renaissant, 1789–1871* (Paris, 1987).

Marzagalli, S., *Les Boulevards de la fraude: le négoce maritime et le Blocus continental, 1806–1813* (Villeneuve d'Ascq, 1999).

Massa-Gille, G., *Histoire des emprunts de la ville de Paris* (Paris, 1973).

Mastellone, S., *La Politica estera del Guizot (1840–1847): l'unione doganale, la lega borbonica* (Florence, 1957).

Mazzucato, M., *The Entrepreneurial State: Debunking Public vs Private Sector Myths* (London, 2018).

McPhee, P., *The Politics of Rural Life: Political Mobilization in the French Countryside, 1846–1852* (Oxford, 1992).

Merriman, J.M., *The Margins of City Life: Explorations on the French Urban Frontier, 1815–1851* (New York, 1991).

Meyssonnier, S., *La Balance et l'horloge: la genèse de la pensée libérale en France au XVIIIᵉ siècle* (Paris, 1989).

Michelat, C.-A., *Les Placements des épargnants français de 1815 à nos jours* (Paris, 1968).

Miller, J.A., *Mastering the Market: The State and the Grain Trade in Northern France, 1700–1860* (Cambridge, 1999).

Miller, S., 'Provincial Assemblies, Fiscal Reform and the Language of Politics in the 1770s and 1780s', *French Historical Studies*, 35.3 (2012), 441–75.

Mitchell, B.R., *British Historical Statistics* (Cambridge, 1988).

Morgan, I., 'French Policy in Spanish America, 1830–1848', *Journal of Latin American Studies*, 10.2 (1978), 309–28.

Morineau, M., 'Budgets de l'État et gestion des finances royales en France au dix-huitième siècle', *Revue historique*, 264.2(536) (1980), 289–336.

Neal, L., 'Conclusion: The Monetary, Fiscal and Political Architecture of Europe, 1815–1914', in J.L. Cardoso and P. Lains (eds.), *Paying for the Liberal State: The Rise of Public Finance in Nineteenth-Century Europe* (Cambridge, 2010), 279–302.

Nervo, J.B.R.G. de, *Le Comte Corvetto, ministre secrétaire d'État des finances sous le roi Louis XVIII* (Paris, 1869).

Newman, E.L., 'The Blouse and the Frock Coat: The Alliance of the Common People of Paris with the Liberal Leadership and the Middle Class during the Last Years of the Bourbon Restoration', *Journal of Modern History*, 46.1 (1974), 26–59.

Nicolas, J., *La Rébellion française: mouvements populaires et conscience sociale, 1661–1789* (Paris, 2002).

Nicoll, A., *Comment la France a payé après Waterloo* (Paris, 1929).

Nieradzik, G., 'La Construction du réseau de canaux français et son financement boursier (1821–1868)', in P.C. Hautcoeur and G. Gallais-Hamonno (eds.), *Le Marché financier français au XIXᵉ siècle* (Paris, 2007), II, 459–506.

Nord, P., *The Republican Moment: Struggles for Democracy in Nineteenth-Century France* (Cambridge MA, 1995).

'The Welfare State in France, 1870–1914', *French Historical Studies*, 18.3 (1994), 821–38.

North, D.C. and B.R. Weingast, 'Constitutions and Commitment: The Evolution of Institutions Governing Public Choice in Seventeenth-Century England', *Journal of Economic History*, 49.4 (1989), 803–32.

Novak, W.J., *The People's Welfare: Law and Regulation in Nineteenth-Century America* (Chapel Hill, 1996).

et al., 'Beyond Stateless Democracy', *The Tocqueville Review/La Revue Tocqueville*, 36.1 (2015), 21–41.

Nye, J.V., 'Changing French Trade Conditions, National Welfare, and the 1860 Anglo-French Treaty of Commerce', *Explorations in Economic History*, 28 (1991), 460–77.

O'Brien, P., 'L'Embastillement de Paris: The Fortification of Paris during the July Monarchy', *French Historical Studies*, 9.1 (1975), 63–82.

O'Brien, P. and C. Keyder, *Economic Growth in Britain and France, 1780–1914: Two Paths to the Twentieth Century* (London, 1978).

Oliveira, M. de, *Les Routes de l'argent: réseaux et flux financiers de Paris à Hambourg (1789–1815)* (Paris, 2011).

Oosterlinck, K. et al., 'Baring, Wellington and the Resurrection of French Public Finances Following Waterloo', *Journal of Economic History*, 74.4 (2014), 1072–1102.

Orsini, L., *Les Arrêtés Miot* (Ajaccio, 1990).

Pagano, E., *Enti locali e stato in Italia sotto Napoleone: Repubblica e Regno d'Italia (1802–1814)* (Rome, 2007).

Pammer, M., 'Public Finance in Austria-Hungary, 1820–1913', in J.L. Cardoso and P. Lains (eds.), *Paying for the Liberal State: The Rise of Public Finance in Nineteenth-Century Europe* (Cambridge, 2010), 132–61.

Papayanis, N. *Planning Paris before Haussmann* (Baltimore, 2004).

Petiteau, N., *Les Français et l'Empire (1799–1815)* (Paris, 2008).

Pfeil, T., *'Tot redding van het vaderland': het primaat van de Nederlandse overheidfinanciën in de Bataafs-Franse tijd, 1795–1810* (Amsterdam, 1998).

Picard, A., *Les Chemins de fer français: étude historique sur la constitution et le régime du réseau*, 6 vols. (Paris, 1884).

Piketty, T., *Le Capital au XXIe siècle* (Paris, 2013).

Pilbeam, P., *The 1830 Revolution in France* (London, 1991).

'Popular Violence in Provincial France after the 1830 Revolution', *English Historical Review*, 91.359 (1976), 278–97.

Pinaud, P.-F., 'Les Ministres des Finances de 1790 à 1832: rupture ou continuité?', *Revue historique*, 293.2(594) (1995), 289–320.

Les Receveurs généraux des finances, 1790–1865: étude historique, repertoires nominative et territorial (Geneva, 1990).

'The Settlement of the Public Debt from the *Ancien Régime*, 1790–1810', *French History*, 5.4 (1991), 414–25.

Pincus, S. and J. Robinson, 'Faire la guerre et faire l'État: nouvelles perspectives sur l'essor de l'État développementaliste', trans. É. Grossi, *Annales. Histoire, sciences sociales*, 71.1 (2016), 5–36.

Pinkney, D.H., 'Les Ateliers de secours à Paris (1830–1831), précurseurs des Ateliers nationaux de 1848', *Revue d'histoire moderne et contemporaine*, 12.1 (1965), 65–70.

Decisive Years in France, 1840–1847 (Princeton, 1986).

The French Revolution of 1830 (Princeton, 1972).

Pisanelli, S., *Condorcet et Adam Smith: réformes économiques et progrès social au siècle des Lumières* (Paris, 2018).

Plack, N., 'Drinking and Rebelling: Wine, Taxes and Popular Agency in Revolutionary Paris, 1789–1791', *French Historical Studies*, 39.3 (2016), 599–621.

Plessis, A., *De la fête impériale au mur des fédérés, 1852–1871* (Paris, 1973).

'L'Impôt des français au XIXe siècle, replacé dans une perspective européenne', in M. Lévy-Leboyer et al. (eds.), *L'Impôt en France aux XIXe et XXe siècles* (Paris, 2006), 13–47.

La Politique de la Banque de France de 1851 à 1870 (Geneva, 1985).

Ploux, F., *De bouche à oreille: naissance et propagation des rumeurs dans la France du XIXe siècle* (Paris, 2003).

'Politique, rumeurs et solidarités territoriales dans les résistances au recensement de 1841', *Cahiers d'histoire*, 44.2 (1999), 237–66.

'Rumeurs et expériences collectives de la discontinuité temporelle (1814–1815)' *Revue d'histoire du XIXe siècle*, 2 (2014), 21–35.

Polak, C., *Soie et lumières: l'age d'or des échanges franco-japonais (des origines aux années 1950)* (Tokyo, 2002).

Ponteil, F., 'Le Ministre des finances Georges Humann et les émeutes antifiscales en 1841', *Revue historique*, 179.2 (1937), 311–54.

Un Type de grand bourgeois sous la monarchie parlementaire: Georges Humann, 1780–1842 (Paris, 1977).

Porch, D., *Army and Revolution: France, 1815–1848* (London, 1974).

Price, M., '"Our Aim Is the Rhine Frontier": The Emergence of a French Forward Policy, 1815–1830', *French History*, 33.1 (2019), 65–87.

The Perilous Crown: France between Revolutions (London, 2007).

Price, R., *The French Second Empire: An Anatomy of Political Power* (Cambridge, 2001).

People and Politics in France, 1848–1870 (Cambridge, 2004).

'Poor Relief and Social Crisis in Mid-Nineteenth-Century France', *European Studies Review*, 13.4 (1983), 423–54.

'Popular Disturbances in the French Provinces after the July Revolution of 1830', *European History Quarterly*, 1.4 (1971), 323–50.

Procacci, G., *Gouverner la misère: la question sociale en France, 1789–1848* (Paris, 1993).

Rabault-Mazières, I., 'Discours et imaginaire du crédit dans la France du premier XIXe siècle', *Histoire, économie et société*, 34.1 (2015), 48–64.

Radtke, W., *Die preussische Seehandlung zwischen Staat und Wirtschaft in Frühphase der Industrialisierung* (Berlin, 1981).

Ramon, G., *Histoire de la Banque de France d'après les sources originales* (Paris, 1929).

Ratcliffe, B.M., 'Napoleon III and the Anglo-French Commercial Treaty of 1860: A Reconsideration', *Journal of European Economic History*, 2.3 (1973), 582–613.

'The Tariff Reform Campaign in France, 1831–1836', *Journal of European Economic History*, 7.1 (1978), 61–138.Rémond, R., *La Droite en France de 1815 à nos jours: continuité et diversité d'une tradition politique* (Paris, 1954).

Reverdy, G., *Les Travaux publics en France, 1817–1847: trente années glorieuses* (Paris, 2003).

Rey-Goldzeiguer, A., *Le Royaume arabe: la politique algérienne de Napoléon III* (Algiers, 1977).

Richard, L., *Histoire des finances publiques de la Belgique depuis 1830* (Brussels, 1884).

Ridder, A. de, *Les Projets d'union douanière franco-belge et les puissances européennes (1836–1843)* (Brussels, 1932).

Rieber, A.J., 'The Formation of La Grande Société des Chemins de Fer Russes', *Jahrbücher für Geschichte Osteuropas*, 21.3 (1973), 375–91.

Rietsch, C., 'Le "Milliard des Émigrés" et la création de la rente 3%', in P.-C. Hautcoeur and G. Gallais-Hamonno (eds.), *Le Marché financier français au XIXᵉ siècle* (Paris, 2007), II, 209–62.

Riviale, P., *La Presse et le pouvoir sous la monarchie de Juillet, 1830–1839* (Paris, 2019).

Robert, V., *Le Temps des banquets: politique et symbolique d'une génération (1818–1848)* (Paris, 2010).

Roberts, A., *America's First Great Depression: Economic Crisis and Political Disorder after the Panic of 1837* (Ithaca, 2012).

Robertson, W.S., *France and Latin American Independence* (Baltimore, 1939).

Romani, R., 'Reluctant Revolutionaries: Moderate Liberalism in the Kingdom of Sardinia, 1849–1859', *Historical Journal*, 55.1 (2012), 45–73.

Rosanvallon, P., *L'État en France de 1789 à nos jours* (Paris, 1990).

Le Modèle politique français: la société civile contre le jacobinisme de 1789 à nos jours (Paris, 2004).

Le Moment Guizot (Paris, 1985).

La Monarchie impossible: les chartes de 1814 et de 1830 (Paris, 1994).

Rose, R. and T. Karran, *Taxation by Political Inertia: Financing the Growth of Government in Britain* (London, 1987).

Rosenthal, J.-L., *The Fruits of Revolution: Property Rights, Litigation and French Agriculture, 1700–1860* (Cambridge, 1992).

Rothschild, E., *Economic Sentiments: Adam Smith, Condorcet and the Enlightenment* (Cambridge MA, 2002).

Roux, P.-E., *La Croix, la baleine et le canon: la France face à la Corée au milieu du XIXᵉ siècle* (Paris, 2012).

Rowe, M., *From Reich to State: The Rhineland in the Revolutionary Age, 1780–1830* (Cambridge, 2003).

Rule, J. and C. Tilly, 'Political Process in Revolutionary France, 1830–1832', in J.M. Merriman (ed.), *1830 in France* (New York, 1975), 41–85.

Sage, E.M., *A Dubious Science: Political Economy and the Social Question in 19th-Century France* (New York, 2009).

Sánchez, R.T. (ed.), *War, State and Development: Fiscal-Military States in the Eighteenth Century* (Pamplona, 2007).

Santana-Acuña, A.A., '*The Making of a National Cadastre (1763–1807): State Uniformization, Nature Valuation and Organizational Change in France*', Ph.D. dissertation (Harvard University, 2014).

Sawyer, S.W., 'Définir un intérêt particulier parisien: les élections municipales et l'administration municipale de Paris au milieu du XIXᵉ siècle', *Annales. Histoire, science sociales*, 64.2 (2009), 407–33.

Demos Assembled: Democracy and the International Origins of the Modern State, 1840–1880 (Chicago, 2018).

'A Fiscal Revolution: Statecraft in France's Early Third Republic', *American Historical Review*, 121.4 (2016), 1141–66.

Schama, S., *Patriots and Liberators: Revolution in the Netherlands, 1780–1813* (London, 1977).

Schisani, M.C., 'How to Make a Defaulting Country Credible: Karl Rothschild, the Neapolitan Debt and Financial Diplomacy (1821–26)', *Rivista di storia economica*, 2 (2010), 233–77.

Schnerb, R., 'De la Constituante à Napoléon: les vicissitudes de l'impôt indirect', *Annales. Économies, sociétés, civilisations*, 2.1 (1947), 17–29.

'La Dépression économique sous le Directoire après la disparition du papier-monnaie (an V–an VIII)', *Annales historiques de la Révolution française*, 11.61 (1934), 27–49.

'Les Hommes de 1848 et l'impôt', in J. Bouvier and J. Wolff (eds.), *Deux siècles de fiscalité française, XIXᵉ–XXᵉ siècle* (Paris, 1973), 105–57.

La Péréquation fiscale de l'Assemblée Constituante (1790–1791) (Clermont-Ferrand, 1936).

'Quelques observations sur l'impôt en France dans la première moitié du XIXᵉ siècle', in J. Bouvier and J. Wolff (eds.), *Deux siècles de fiscalité française, XIXᵉ–XXᵉ siècle* (Paris, 1973), 71–8.

Rouher et le Second Empire (Paris, 1949).

Schöller, P., 'La Transformation économique de la Belgique de 1832 à 1844', *Bulletin de l'Institut des Recherches Économiques et Sociales*, 14.3, 5 (1948), 525–96.

Scholz, N., *Die imaginierte Restauration: Repräsentationen der Monarchie im Frankreich Ludwigs XVIII* (Darmstadt, 2006).

Schönhärl, K., *Finanziers in Sehnsuchtsräumen: europäische Banken in Griechenland im 19. Jahrhundert* (Göttingen, 2017).

Schroeder, P.W., *The Transformation of European Politics, 1763–1848* (Oxford, 1994).

Serna, P., *La République des girouettes (1789–1815… et au delà): une anomalie politique: la France de l'extrême centre* (Seyssel, 2005).

Sessions, J.E., *By Sword and Plow: France and the Conquest of Algeria* (Ithaca, 2011).

Sewell, W.H., 'The Empire of Fashion and the Rise of Capitalism in Eighteenth-Century France', *Past & Present*, 206 (2010), 81–120.

Shapiro, G. and J. Markoff, *Revolutionary Demands: A Content Analysis of the Cahiers de Doléances of 1789* (Stanford, 1998).

Shawcross, E., *France, Mexico and Informal Empire in Latin America, 1820–1867* (Basingstoke, 2018).

Silvant, C., 'Fiscalité et calcul économique au milieu du XIXᵉ siècle français', *Revue d'économie politique*, 120.6 (2010), 1015–34.

Silvestre, J., 'La Politique française dans l'Indochine: Annam', *Annales de l'École libre des sciences politiques*, 11 (1896), 289–320.

Simal, J.L., 'National Credit and the International Financial Market: The Spanish Debt and Its Foreign Bondholders, 1820–1834', *Journal of Iberian and Latin American Studies*, 25.3 (2019), 381–402.

Simms, B., *Europe: The Struggle for Supremacy, 1453 to the Present* (London, 2014).

Skocpol, T., 'Bringing the State Back In: Strategies of Analysis in Current Research', in P.B. Evans et al. (eds.), *Bringing the State Back In* (Cambridge, 1985), 3–37.

States and Social Revolutions: A Comparative Analysis of France, Russia and China (Cambridge, 1993).

Sluga, G., 'Economic Insecurity, "Securities" and a European Security Culture after the Napoleonic Wars', in B. de Graaf et al. (eds.), *Securing Europe after Napoleon: 1815 and the New European Security Culture* (Cambridge, 2019), 288–305.

'"Who Hold the Balance of the World?" Bankers at the Congress of Vienna, and in International History', *American Historical Review*, 122.5 (2017), 1403–30.

Smith, M.S., *Tariff Reform in France, 1860–1900: The Politics of Economic Interest* (Ithaca, 1980).

Sonenscher, M., 'The Nation's Debt and the Birth of the Modern Republic: The French Fiscal Deficit and the Politics of the Revolution of 1789', part 2, *History of Political Thought*, 18.2 (1997), 267–325.

Sans-Culottes: An Eighteenth-Century Emblem in the French Revolution (Princeton, 2008).

Spang, R.L., *Stuff and Money in the Time of the French Revolution* (Cambridge MA, 2015).

Spoerer, M., *Steuerlast, Steuerinzidenz und Steuerwettbewerb: Verteilungswirkungen der Besteuerung in Preußen und Württemberg (1815–1913)* (Berlin, 2004).

Stanziani, A., *Rules of Exchange: French Capitalism in Comparative Perspective, Eighteenth to the Early Twentieth Centuries* (Cambridge, 2012).

Stasavage, D., *Public Debt and the Birth of the Democratic State: France and Great Britain, 1688–1789* (Cambridge, 2003).

Stedman Jones, G., *An End to Poverty? A Historical Debate* (London, 2004).

Stern, F., *Gold and Iron: Bismarck, Bleichröder and the Building of the German Empire* (New York, 1979).

Storrs, C. (ed.), *The Fiscal-Military State in Eighteenth-Century Europe: Essays in Honour of P.G.M. Dickson* (Farnham, 2009).

Stoskopf, N., *Banquiers et financiers parisiens* (Paris, 2002).

Stourm, R., *Les Finances de l'ancien régime et de la Révolution: origines du système financier actuel*, 2 vols. (Paris, 1885).

Les Finances du Consulat (Paris, 1902).

Surleau, G., *Les Réformes financières de M. de Villèle* (Paris, 1901).

Sutherland, D.M.G., 'Peasants, Lords and Leviathan: Winners and Losers from the Abolition of French Feudalism, 1780–1820', *Journal of Economic History*, 61.2 (2002), 1–24.

'Taxation, Representation and Dictatorship, 1789–1830', in W.M. Ormrod et al. (eds.), *Crises, Revolutions and Self-Sustained Growth: Essays in European Fiscal History, 1130–1830* (Stamford, 1999), 414–26.

Sylla, R., 'Experimental Federalism: The Economics of American Government, 1789–1914', in S.L. Engerman and R.E. Gallman (eds.), *The Cambridge*

Economic History of the United States, 3 vols. (Cambridge, 1996–2000), II, 483–542.

Taylor, M., 'The 1848 Revolutions and the British Empire', *Past & Present*, 166 (2000): 146–80.

Thadden, R. von, *Restauration und Napoleonisches Erbe: der Verwaltungszentralismus als politisches Problem in Frankreich (1814–1830)* (Wiesbaden, 1972).

Théret, B., 'Le Système fiscal français au XIXᵉ siècle: bureaucratie ou capitalisme?', *Histoire économique et financière de la France: études & documents*, 3 (1991), 137–224.

Thoral, M.-C., *L'Émergence du pouvoir local: le département de l'Isère face à la centralisation, 1800–1837* (Rennes, Grenoble, 2010).

Thuillier, G., 'En Nivernais au XIXᵉ s.: pour une histoire monétaire régionale', *Annales. Histoire, sciences sociales*, 18.3 (1963), 437–58.

La Monnaie en France au début du XIXᵉ siècle (Paris, 1983).

Thureau-Dangin, P., *Histoire de la monarchie de Juillet*, 7 vols. (Paris, 1884–92).

Tilly, C., 'How Protest Modernized in France, 1845–1855', in W.O. Aydelotte et al. (eds.), *The Dimensions of Quantitative Research in History* (Princeton, 1972), 192–255.

'Reflections on the History of European State-Making', in C. Tilly (ed.), *The Formation of National States in Western Europe* (Princeton, 1975), 3–83.

Tilly, R., 'The Political Economy of Public Finance and the Industrialization of Prussia, 1815–1866', *Journal of Economic History*, 26.4 (1966), 484–97.

Tocqueville, A. de, *L'Ancien régime et la Révolution* (Paris, 1856).

Todd, D., *Free Trade and Its Enemies in France, 1814–1851* (Cambridge, 2015).

'A French Imperial Meridian, 1814–1870', *Past & Present*, 210 (2011), 155–86.

L'Identité économique de la France: libre-échange et protectionnisme, 1814–1851 (Paris, 2008).

'Retour sur l'expédition d'Alger: les faux-semblants d'un tournant colonialiste français', *Monde(s)*, 10 (2016), 205–22.

A Velvet Empire: French Informal Imperialism in the Nineteenth Century (Princeton, 2021).

Tombs, R. and I. Tombs, *That Sweet Enemy: The French and the British from the Sun King to the Present* (London, 2007).

Topik, S.C., 'When Mexico Had the Blues: A Transatlantic Tale of Bonds, Bankers and Nationalists, 1862–1910', *American Historical Review*, 105.3 (2000), 714–38.

Tort, O., *La Droite française: aux origines de ses divisions (1814–1830)* (Paris, 2013).

Toutain, J.-C., 'L'Imbroglio des indices de prix français du XIXe siècle', *Économies et sociétés, Histoire économique quantitative*, 1.11 (1997), 137–87.

'Le Produit intérieur brut de la France, 1789–1990', *Économies et Sociétés, Histoire économique quantitative*, 1.11 (1997), 5–136.

Touzery, M., *L'Invention de l'impôt sur le revenu: la taille tarifée, 1715–1789* (Paris, 1994).

Tudesq, A.-J., *Les Conseillers généraux en France au temps de Guizot, 1840–1848* (Paris, 1967).

L'Élection présidentielle de Louis-Napoléon Bonaparte, 10 décembre 1848 (Paris, 1965).

Les Grands notables en France (1840–1849): étude historique d'une psychologie sociale, 2 vols. (Paris, 1964).

Tulard, J., *Les Thermidoriens* (Paris, 2005).

Vaslin, J.-M., 'Le Siècle d'or de la rente perpétuelle française', in P.-C. Hautcoeur and G. Gallais-Hamonno (eds.), *Le Marché financier français au XIXe siècle* (Paris, 2007), II, 117–208.

Vause, E., *In the Red and in the Black: Debt, Dishonor and the Law in France between Revolutions* (Charlottesville, 2018).

Vidalenc, J., *Les Émigrés français, 1789–1825* (Caen, 1963).

Vigier, P., *La Seconde République dans la région alpine: étude politique et sociale*, 2 vols. (Paris, 1963).

Vivier, N., 'Les Débats sur la finalité du cadastre, 1814–1870', in F. Bourillon et al. (eds.), *De l'estime au cadastre en Europe: les systèmes cadastraux aux XIXe et XXe siècles* (Paris, 2008), 191–215.

Vries, J. de, *The Industrious Revolution: Consumer Behavior and the Household Economy, 1650 to the Present* (Cambridge, 2008).

Walton, C., 'The Fall from Eden: The Free-Trade Origins of the French Revolution', in S. Desan et al. (eds.), *The French Revolution in Global Perspective* (Ithaca, 2013), 44–56.

'Why the Neglect? Social Rights and French Revolutionary Historiography', *French History*, 33.4 (2019), 503–19.

Waresquiel, E. de, *Le Duc de Richelieu (1766–1822): un sentimental en politique* (Paris, 1990).

Un groupe d'hommes considérables: les pairs de France et la Chambre des pairs héréditaire de la Restauration, 1814–1831 (Paris, 2006).

Waresquiel, E. de and B. Yvert, *Histoire de la Restauration (1814–1830): naissance de la France moderne* (Paris, 1996).

Weber, E., *Peasants into Frenchmen: The Modernization of Rural France, 1870–1914* (Stanford, 1976).

Weulerrse, G., *La Physiocratie à l'aube de la Révolution, 1781–1792*, ed. C. Beutler (Paris, 1985).

White, E.N., 'The French Revolution and the Politics of Government Finance, 1770–1815', *Journal of Economic History*, 55.2 (1995), 227–55.

'Making the French Pay: The Costs and Consequences of the Napoleonic Reparations', *European Review of Economic History*, 5.3 (2001), 337–65.

'Was There a Solution to the Ancien Régime's Financial Dilemma?', *Journal of Economic History*, 49.3 (1989), 545–68.

Whiteman, J.J., 'Trade and the Regeneration of France, 1789–91: Liberalism, Protectionism and the Commercial Policy of the National Constituent Assembly', *European History Quarterly*, 31.2 (2001), 171–204.

Wolff, J., *Napoléon et l'économie: l'impuissance du politique* (Paris, 2007).

Woloch, I., *The New Regime: Transformations of the French Civic Order, 1789–1820s* (New York, 1994).

Woolf, S., *Napoleon's Integration of Europe* (London, 1991).

Wright, G., 'The Origins of Napoleon III's Free Trade', *Economic History Review*, 29.1 (1938), 64–7.

Yamada, N., 'George Canning and the Concert of Europe, September 1822–July 1824', Ph.D. dissertation (London School of Economics, 2004).

'George Canning and the Spanish Question, September 1822 to March 1823', *Historical Journal*, 52.2 (2009), 343–62.

Yates, A., 'The Double Life of Property: Mobilising Land and Making Capitalism in Modern France', *Critical Historical Studies*, 6.2 (2019), 247–78.

Yvert, B., *La Restauration: les idées et les hommes* (Paris, 2012).

Zanden, J.L. van and A. van Riel, *Nederland, 1780–1914: staat, instituties en economische ontwikkeling* (Amsterdam, 2000).

Zylberberg, M., *Une si douce domination: les milieux d'affaires français et l'Espagne vers 1780–1808* (Paris, 1993).

Index

319

For EU product safety concerns, contact us at Calle de José Abascal, 56–1°, 28003 Madrid, Spain or eugpsr@cambridge.org.